FORGOTTEN PARTNERSHIP

FORGOTTEN PARTNERSHIP

U.S.-Canada Relations Today

CHARLES F. DORAN

The Johns Hopkins University Press

BALTIMORE AND LONDON

© 1984 by The Johns Hopkins University Press
All rights reserved
Printed in the United States of America

The Johns Hopkins University Press, Baltimore, Maryland 21218
The Johns Hopkins Press Ltd., London

Library of Congress Cataloging in Publication Data

Doran, Charles F.
Forgotten partnership.

Includes bibliographical references and index.
1. United States—Foreign relations—Canada.
2. Canada—Foreign relations—United States. I. Title.
E183.8.C2D67   1984   327.73071   83-48052
ISBN 0-8018-3033-8

CONTENTS

v

PREFACE

A disparity exists between the importance of Canada to the United States and the amount of attention Canada and Canada-U.S. relations receive in the United States. Unchecked, this disparity of information and analysis will deepen at a time when tough questions of policy and outlook face both governments. As an American scholar I have attempted in this book to do something about the disparity by highlighting the sensitiveness and complexity of the relations between these two great democracies.

Members of the decision-making elites in Washington and Ottawa are engrossed with the issues examined in this book. No less involved are the labor leaders and business executives who are affected by the policies that evolve in a relationship in which more jobs and more capital are at stake on both sides of the border than in any other relationship. Whether these issues are changing, and perhaps sometimes straining, the relationship is a consideration that ought to matter to Americans. This book was written in that belief.

Friends and colleagues have contributed generously of their time and commentary to make this book possible. Joel Sokolsky and two anonymous reviewers read the entire manuscript, leaving their mark upon it. Robert Spencer kindly invited me to give a lecture at the University of Toronto, which enabled me to benefit from the spirited discussion of the participants. Although none of the material in this book has been published previously, an article, "Left Hand, Right Hand," in Volume 36 of the *International Journal* and a second article in the Winter 1983 issue, became the springboards for the more extended discussions in Chapters 1 and 3. A lecture to the Vancouver Institute sharpened ideas for Chapters III and IV. A paper that I coauthored with Brian Job and delivered in September of 1982 at a Harvard Conference organized by Alfred Hero was particularly useful in preparing Chapter 5. Similarly, a paper presented at a symposium on minerals economics, sponsored by the American Institute of Mining, Metallurgical, and Petroleum Engineers in Washington, D.C., became the basis of the material in Chapter 7. Appearances on a number of television and radio shows, such as

Good Morning, America, Canada A.M., and *Cross-Country Check-Up*, forced me to stay in touch with public and press opinion regarding issues. Throughout, the wisdom and encouragement of John Holmes has been indispensible.

Appreciation is due a number of members of the Canadian and the American governments, who have been helpful on many occasions. I have learned to respect the courage and patience of those members of the Canadian Department of External Affairs and of the U.S State Department who operate continuously at the interface, where pressure can at times become quite intense.

The Center of Canadian Studies at the Johns Hopkins School of Advanced International Studies is fortunate to have the services of an Advisory Council chaired by the Honorable Donald MacDonald and the Honorable Edmund Muskie. The illustrious members of this council have drawn deeply upon their experience in government and the private sector, even when they disagree among themselves or with the author, to ensure that academic analysis does not remain academic.

As Director of the Center of Canadian Studies, I owe a debt to my students, who were the real teachers. The center's secretary, Elaine Ferat, typed many a manuscript page. But perhaps my deepest gratitude is due my wife and my three young sons, who know best the arduousness involved in writing yet another book.

FORGOTTEN PARTNERSHIP

INTRODUCTION

An introduction is, in a way, an apology both for what an author has not done, for which he tries to claim credit, and for what he has done, for which he tries to escape responsibility. An introduction is both an entry and a retreat. It promises and it retracts. Its utility is properly qualified by the observation of Sir John A. MacDonald, Canada's first prime minister, regarding the election of 1882. "Any election is like a horse-race," said Sir John A., "in that you can tell more about it the next day." So the introduction may have greater meaning for the reader after he or she has sampled the body of the text, rather than before.

This introduction examines the role of an international relations perspective in the study of relations between Canada and the United States, the place of theory, and the nature of the major themes that unite the work. The matter of the intended audience also receives attention.

THE INTERNATIONAL RELATIONS PERSPECTIVE

This book proposes that to understand relations between Canada and the United States one must understand the politics of the international system as a whole. One cannot lift U.S.-Canada relations out of the context of global politics without doing a serious injustice to interpretation. This is not to say that all that happens in the bilateral relationship is the result of events that impinge upon these two governments from outside North America. Quite the contrary, often the most important stimuli to specific policies originate in the domestic spheres of one or both societies. In order to give the proper meaning to these policies, and in order to sense the dynamic underlying the evolution of relations between these two countries in the late twentieth century, one must adopt an international relations perspective that reveals the limits and direction of statecraft. If the relationship is treated in bilateral terms only, an impression is left that the two governments have a larger degree of freedom for their conduct of policy in some cases and a smaller degree in others, than is in fact true. Moreover, a primary focus on bilateralism

1

fails to provide clues as to why some policy initiatives have been disasters while others unaccountably have emerged winners on the basis of domestic support alone. U.S.-Canada relations are by no means a backwater unto themselves but are in most respects tied to developments within the international system; this has been particularly true during the last quarter of the twentieth century, when structural change within the international system has become so much more evident. If this relationship is unique, its uniqueness is put to a full test when evaluated from the international relations perspective.

A review of several questions regarding U.S.-Canada relations will reveal how the international relations perspective becomes essential to interpretation. In the years 1970-72, crucial initiatives emerged in each country's foreign policy towards the other. This was the period in which the Trudeau government announced the so-called Third Option policy of trade diversification and greater autonomy in the formulation and implementation of measures regarding foreign affairs. This was also the period in which the Nixon administration announced the end of the so-called special relationship between Canada and the United States. At about the same time, the United States applied an interest surcharge to capital exports, denying Canada for the first time its exemption from policies that are applied to other states. How are these initiatives to be interpreted? Was the dynamic contained essentially within the relationship between the two polities? The bilateral perspective suggests that it was: one government's policies were, in effect, merely rebounding off those of the other, as though the governments were two billiard balls isolated from the rest of the system. Is this episode simply another example of "reactive nationalism," in which domestic political forces and protectionism on each side were allowed to get out of hand and to undermine state interests? Was Canada, as Americans sometimes feel, succumbing once again to a fit of "uncontrolled" or controlled nationalism that had little basis in a relationship so benign and mutually beneficial as that experienced in North America? Was the United States, as Canadians sometimes feel, once again displaying the true harshness of its economic policies, now reinforced by the removal of the rhetoric of the special relationship?

Or, conversely, is there another way of looking at these events which is perhaps more deeply informed by the evolution of history involving powers outside North America and by the contemporaneous global crush of pressures and opportunities along the East-West and North-South axes? This international relations perspective suggests that shifting power relationships and the changing structure of the international system itself may have had something to do with both the timing and the direction of changes in the bilateral relationship. The international relations perspective is less surprised by outcome and less indignant about apparent motive in the formulation of new policy initiatives on both sides of the border. This perspective is also able to reveal more effectively the contradictions inherent in the policies both Ottawa and Washington formulated—policies whose consequences neither country may have seen clearly, because of preoccupation with a largely domestic and North American explanation for events. These contradictions of interpretation and initiative are untangled in Chapter 1 through the use of historical analogy and systems-wide assessment.

A second major application of the international relations perspective to the study of Canadian-American relations is made in Chapter 6 in conjunction with the struggle each government has made to cope with jurisdictional problems involving environmental betterment, fishing rights, and the law of the sea. It is popular in the United States to think of Canada as espousing a kind of ultranationalism in these matters, which is reflected in the zeal to extend fishing boundaries to 200 miles and to exclude foreign fishing fleets, to define Arctic pollution restrictions in innovative ways, to press hard for reductions on acid rain, and to guard jealously navigation rights and other rights along its coastal perimeter. It is certainly the case that despite early American interest in environmental matters and matters of the law of the sea, the United States more recently has taken a less assertive and less expansive interest in pressing for reform in these areas. From the bilateral viewpoint, Canada does appear to be out front of the United States in most of these jurisdictional disputes, leading in a direction that would directly benefit the Canadian national interest and would often harm the interests of other governments, especially, to some extent, those of the United States.

If one takes a larger international relations perspective, however, would one come to the same conclusions regarding the seeming disparity in Canadian and American proposals and outlooks? Must these differences be dismissed simply as the result of two alternative and somewhat opposed issue agendas? Or does a thorough explanation lie far deeper? Indeed, from the larger perspective are there any grounds for the assertion that the jurisdictional claims of Canada are any more nationalistic than those of the United States, or, for that matter, any more out of tune with developments in contemporary international law or global political preference? These are complex issues that receive illumination only when treated outside the strictly bilateral policy context.

A third principal application of the international relations perspective emerges in Chapter 7 with the discussion of energy policy and the significance of the Canadian National Energy Program (NEP) for Canadian-American relations. Is such a lengthy discussion of energy policy, especially the energy policy of one government in a single period, out of place in a manuscript devoted to analysis of the foreign relations between governments? Nothing could be less true. In the decade of the 1970s no other issue captured the attention of the industrialized governments as much as the issue of energy supply. Similarly, in the early 1980s, American preoccupation with the possible impact of the NEP on American-owned firms operating in the Canadian energy sector and upon general commercial relations between the two countries so dominated discussions that often little else could be accomplished. Hence, it is necessary to include an extensive examination of this much-obscured topic in any serious evaluation of bilateral relations for this period.

Additionally, the paradox of failing to treat issues in the larger international relations perspective is nowhere more eloquently portrayed than in the energy issue. Had the United States placed the dispute over energy policy and national treatment in the light of events following the initial Libyan takeover of concessions, of the 1971 Teheran Pricing Agreement, and of the factors that led to the two abrupt price escalations thereafter, the initiatives Canada took would have seemed neither so novel nor so inexplicable in international political and commercial terms. Indeed, the leading international oil firms were less nonplussed than the U.S. government, because they had been "closer to the oil fields" over a long interval. Had Canada viewed its own objectives in the light of considerations going beyond the North American setting—taking into account, in particular, opportunity costs, alternate strategies to achieve the same objectives, and, finally, the possibility that the greatest obstacle to the success of the NEP would be, not opposition in Washington or New York, but the impact of the world oil market on plans for Canadianization and megaproject development—large errors might have been avoided and a particularly nasty interval in the relationship between Canada and the United States might have gone more smoothly. The limits of a narrow bilateral focus on the relationship emerge clearly from this extensive case study. The energy issue is comparable to many other concerns that have all too frequently been examined as though they were operating in some type of North American vacuum. Regarding perhaps no other issue, however, has this persistent bilateralism of perspective had such direct and visible costs for each government in terms of its own policies and the atmosphere of constructiveness essential to progress across the issue agenda.

Although the international relations focus is neither methodology nor theory, I argue that it is nonetheless critical to the proper interpretation of U.S.-Canada relations. Without this focus, problems and initiatives appear distorted. Policy options seem too confined or too limitless. Relations between the two countries seem parochial and misleadingly simple. A correct analytic perspective does not guarantee rigor or depth of insight, but it does at least create an intellectual foothold for further study of this underexamined relationship, a foothold that makes subsequent analytic steps a lot safer.

THEMES AND THEORY

At a time when the code words, in Washington, are *interdependence* and *integration* and, in Ottawa, *independence* and *autonomy,* this manuscript asks a totally unfashionable and, for some people, embarrassing question. Are the two governments prepared to admit that partnership, even in its multilateral form and in the limited context of specific projects, is dead in North America? To some observers this question may seem antediluvian and out of step with informed opinion on each side of the border. To others the question may seem premature, more suitable for a future era of greater self-confidence and altered rules of participation. But for purposes of dialogue, if for no other, the assumptions underlying this question and the implications for policy of the various possible responses must be addressed. I take the view that if everyone else, in intellectual terms, is selling, the time may be ripe to buy.

A recurring theme of this book is that Canada and the United States have both taken recent actions that will make future management of the relationship more difficult. Americans persist in favoring an integrationist mentality that argues that ever-closer relations are better relations. Without being fully aware of this tendency themselves, Americans equate bigness with virtue and integration with harmony. Liberals no less than conservatives think in terms of the European experience when they utopianly attempt to transfer the formal idea of international economic integration to the North American setting. The consequence is that Americans unwittingly tend to deny Canada its own identity. The weaker such an identity is, the more grievous is the faux pas committed by the integrationist mentality. When either an individual or a society feels that its identity has been jeopardized or slighted, its response is distrust and anger. Americans have earned that response in the last decade by impinging more and more carelessly on the Canadian sense of identity and purpose.

Conversely, Canadians cling more and more to an autarkist mentality that tends to shut out external reality, especially reality that has anything to do with the United States. Regardless of whether genuine trade diversification, built upon more than diversion, is possible, and regardless of whether new political coalitions are available to replace the old, the quest for autarky goes on. At a time when an appreciable increase in relative Canadian capability is already evident and when the United States is already worried about strains within the Atlantic Alliance concerning America's responsibility to itself and to the alliance for security, the Canadian quest for greater autonomy is in danger not only of being misunderstood in the United States but also of being misrepresented as anti-American and as an unwelcome burden on the alliance itself. At a time when bilateral issues need greater American attention, the autarkist mentality seems to invite less. At a time when the United States ought to be reminded of its special responsibilities to a close neighbor, it is allowed to get off free.

The upshot is that the American integrationist mentality feeds paranoia and the quest for greater autarky in Canada, and the Canadian search for more operating room exacerbates the American penchant for selling closeness and harmony. Instead of recognizing that an independent Canada is likely to be a more viable trade and alliance partner, the United States sometimes appears to deny that room for differences of perspective and interest exists. Instead of diminishing American fears of alliance collapse and policy fragmentation through skillful Canadian manipulation of American sensitivities, Canada sometimes seems to believe that it can simultaneously challenge the Washington outlook directly and maximize benefits.

Hence, the very notion of partnership between two sovereign, asymmetrically powerful, but legally and representationally equal states is open to some question. From opposite sides, both autarky and integration challenge this notion of partnership. Whether the fundamentals of partnership are still workable, or whether partnership as a practical guideline for policy formulation has indeed been forgotten, provides the leitmotif for this study.

An unfortunate disparity exists between the importance of Canada to the United States and the amount of attention Americans devote to the relationship. If the presence of cross-border mobility and political friendship is not enough, the fact that Canada is by far the largest trading partner of the United States and the largest single locus of U.S. foreign investment ought to be a sufficient incentive to attention. Yet more attention is devoted to foreign policy matters involving countries a fraction the size of Canada and thousands of miles away than to those matters on the U.S. border. How is this disparity to be explained? The theoretical framework of this book, which is discussed later, is designed to elucidate this disparity between importance and attention and to discuss the implications of this disparity for the principal theme of the study regarding the viability of future partnership. Comprehending this disparity is even more difficult when one considers that in the first year and a half of office, President Reagan had an unprecedented five major contacts with Prime Minister Trudeau at a direct, personal level, and countless contacts between the governments occurred at the ministerial level, yet relations between the two countries, according to some observers, dipped to an all-time low.

Part of the difficulty is that contacts between two governments are not to be equated with attention if on either side there is insufficient preparation before, or insufficient follow-up after, high-level discussions. Another part of the difficulty is that in order to get attention to issues, Ottawa is obliged to raise its voice in the public press and in private exchanges. This may have short-term value for individual governments or representatives, but in the longer term this approach becomes the equivalent of "crying wolf" and eventually deafens ears in Washington. Calling relations bad in order to get legitimate attention to issues may also become a self-fulfilling prophecy: relations may worsen. Hence, because of its consequences, the disparity between the importance of bilateral issues to the United States and the attention they receive requires examination that goes beyond tactics and style.

In Chapter 2, the theory that frames the analysis in the following six chapters is explicated. This theory accounts for the disparity between the comparative importance of bilateral issues and their neglect in terms of the contrast between American and Canadian treatments of the principal lines of foreign policy analysis. According to this framework, foreign policy involving the two countries can be divided into three principal dimensions: the political-strategic; the trade-commercial; and the psychological-cultural dimensions. Whereas the United States places the highest priority on the political-strategic dimension, Canada tends to emphasize the trade-commercial dimension. Analytically, however, according to the arguments presented in Chapter 2, neither the first dimension of analysis, nor the second, is most critical to an understanding of relations between Canada and the United States. The third dimension—the psychological-cultural dimension—is of greatest centrality. It is therefore not surprising that agreement is often difficult between the two countries even when interests are not fundamentally opposed, inasmuch as the two governments weigh their foreign policy priorities so differently. Moreover, because the United States in particular seems to ignore the third set of foreign policy factors, the psychological-cultural dimension, the likelihood that a disparity will arise between the importance of Canada and the handling of American foreign policy toward it is scarcely astonishing.

Why do these differences of foreign policy priority exist between the two countries, and why does the United States persist in undervaluing psychological and cultural considerations in the relationship? In order to explore these questions in greater depth, Chapters three, four, and five each examines in detail one of the dimensions of foreign policy conduct and formulation. Using examples that are either historical or idealized, the theoretical insights from Chapter 2 are carefully applied and extended. Moreover, the conclusions drawn from the first chapter regarding the analytic importance of the larger international relations perspective are brought to bear repeatedly in these chapters; this analytic importance is also emphasized strongly in Chapter 6, which concerns the various jurisdictional issues, and in Chapter 7, which concerns energy policy.

Chapters 6 and 7 are detailed case studies of the two most important collective issues in Canadian-American relations during the early years of the 1980s. These chapters are essential to the perspective and major theme of the analysis. They highlight, on the one hand, the problems created for analysis when the international relations perspective is not applied, and, on the other hand, the problems created for policy management when the difference in policy priority between the two countries is overlooked.

Theory, developed in Chapter 2, explicates the relationship of the equilibrium among the three principal dimensions of foreign policy analysis to the emergence of the issue agenda and to the handling of individual issues involved in the decision process. Theory also examines the characteristics of the U.S.-Canada relationship which make it unique and not merely an example of the interdependence paradigm. Five characteristics of these relations stand out when compared to other pairs of states in the system: (1) high intervulnerability; (2) declining but still very large power asymmetry; (3) offsetting bargaining strengths; (4) an unusual degree of ambiguity of national interest; and (5) a long tradition of prudence in bilateral policy conduct. When combined with the tactics and style commonly employed in the U.S.-Canadian relationship, these characteristics make it unique.

In the final chapter of the book I return to the major theme of the study, namely, the prerequisites of partnership and the future direction of and tone of the relationship. The problem on the U.S. side, which is created by the imbalance between the amount of attention devoted to Canadian matters and the importance of the relationship to U.S. interests, receives special emphasis. Based on the foregoing analysis, conclusions are drawn regarding policy correctives that would help resolve some of the irritants and perhaps help eliminate what is sometimes viewed as the mishandling of initiatives. Thus, the book does not eschew policy prescription. Policy prescription emerges directly out of the foregoing assessment and is a product of both the perspective employed and the theory developed in earlier chapters. Partnership requires that the senior partner get its own house in order first.

AUDIENCES: PRETENDED AND INTENDED

Unlike the allegedly more mature social sciences, such as economics and psychology, with which political science sometimes jealously compares itself, political science is frequently ambivalent about its intended audience. Not unexpectedly, the field of Canadian studies may suffer from the same affliction. The scholar may write for a narrow audience of fellow Canadianists, thereby preserving the purity of tribal motive and approach. Or the scholar may seek a wider audience, including those who know less about Canada or the United States specifically but much more about world politics in general. Similarly, the scholar is torn between the purity of "analysis for the sake of analysis" and the temptation to write for audiences that are interested in policy prescription. This manuscript is a product of the heresy that the author need not, and should not, succumb to such a dichotomy.

Equally of interest to the Washington or Ottawa "insider," the college teacher, and the informed businessman, the study of U.S.-Canada relations ought to combine substantive analysis, guided by a proper appreciation of theory, with a set of conclusions that have some relevance to the policy process and to the government decision-maker. Prescription without prior analysis is impossible; analysis without impact on the decision-makers responsible in large part for shaping the political outcomes in the first place is arid and possibly distortive. Just as modern techniques of political analysis ought to be scrutinized by the government policy-maker in order that they be judged as to the contribution they make to a larger understanding of politics and society, so the assumptions and practice of the policy-maker in both the United States and Canada ought to face critical assessment at the hands of the trained academic.

These are, at least, the prejudices with which this study was embarked upon and which characterize it still. Multiple audiences are not easy to address; the relationship between Canada and the United States itself testifies to that. To deny, however, that such diversity and richness of interpretation is feasible, and indeed mandatory, is, in my judgment, to misread the obligations of the profession. Proclaimed audiences are sometimes pretended, but surely the same cannot be said for those that are merely intended.

ONE

Setting the Stage:
Problems, Proposals, & History

In the course of more than a century, the partnership between Canada and the United States has evolved into the close, interdependent relationship that exists today. This partnership is historical. In the annals of world statecraft it has few parallels in terms of scope or amity. It intrigues observers outside North America, who speculate on the origins of its intimacy and resilience. Democratic institutions, parliamentary on the one hand and presidential on the other, can take part of the credit for the record of benign interaction. At base, however, the political explanation lies at the level of the individual citizen on each side of the border. Regardless of governmental differences, the respect, with rare exceptions, of Canadians and Americans for each other has guided policy in the two societies, both of which were transplanted and which are, by European standards, still quite malleable and young.

Whereas Canadians are perhaps too well aware of the importance of the United States to Canada, Americans may still be oblivious to the importance of Canada to the United States. But statistics document the latter importance. In 1981, for example, U.S. exports of manufactured goods to Canada exceeded sales to Japan by a wide margin and, indeed, exceeded sales to the entire European Community.[1] U.S. imports of raw materials and manufactured goods from Canada in turn outpaced imports from every other country. Not only is Canada America's leading trading partner, however; more than one-fifth of all U.S. foreign investment resides in Canada. Canada is, moreover, rapidly becoming one of the largest foreign investors in the United States, with dollar holdings approximating one-quarter of those the United States has invested in Canada.[2] Apart from the socio-psychological and security value to the United States of the relationship with Canada, that relationship's economic value is matched by no other.

The concept of partnership, which I explore theoretically in Chapter 8, lies at the heart of Canadian-American relations. Partnership involves, at a minimum, the existence of two separate and sovereign entities, not necessarily of the same size, having a common agenda and sharing a sense of purpose. Interests may differ; power surely will. But the vision of shared purpose overcomes these differences without threatening either actor's autonomy or the viability of his own individual goals.

Despite the history of civilized exchange and interaction between Canada and the United States and despite the evident importance of each to the other, the partnership itself has lately come under stress. Although the foundations of partnership still remain firm, the superstructure has begun to tremble. Cracks are forming in some of the reinforcing tenets that have held the relationship together philosophically. Pessimists are even talking of serious erosion. Less strident observers express concern that on both sides some of the benefits of long-enjoyed partnership seem to have been forgotten. Likewise forgotten, perhaps, is the awareness of how difficult such an edifice as the U.S.-Canada relationship is to build and how simple it is to undermine. Forgotten also are the allowable limits of state action in the Canadian-American context and some of the costs that might accompany an actual collapse of the relationship if those traditional limits are insistently and repeatedly ignored.

Strains have been observed concerning diverse issues and in a variety of initiatives. Lacking a comprehensive examination of each problem, which might expose communalities and causes — a lack this study seeks to remedy — policy-makers and analysts have been uncertain how to respond to the obvious warning signs. I begin this chapter by considering some of the tactical proposals that have been advocated to strengthen the relationship. To evaluate the merit of these proposals and others, an examination of historical analogy is valuable. Although by no means identical, the relationship between Britain and Canada in the nineteenth century holds insights regarding changes in the relationship between the United States and Canada in the twentieth century. Historical analogies force the analyst to confront certain realities of politics that a too-close familiarity with contemporary details often tends to bury or mask. At the core of this examination, therefore, is this question: What is the causal basis for the changes we have noted in the relationship and for the tensions that seem to underlie it? By correctly identifying the source of change and of grievance, the policy-maker will be in a better position to advocate policy recommendations that address cause rather than symptom.

TACTICAL INITIATIVES:
CAN THEY WORK?

In response to a growing feeling of crisis regarding the U.S.-Canada relationship, a number of observers have recommended institutional fixes. According to this definition of partnership, a sense of common purpose can be restored through the creation of bilateral institutions. The Canadian-American Committee has recommended creating a per-

manent focal point for intergovernmental activities within the bureaucratic structures of each federal government.[3] This committee also
recommends that, wherever appropriate, states and provinces as well as
various nongovernmental groups ought to be brought into the policy
process in a more institutionalized fashion. Marie-Josée Drouin and
Harald B. Malmgren advocated establishing two bodies: a bilateral commission of specialists from the public and private sectors to assess problems, and a joint cabinet committee composed of members from the two
governments to review recommendations from the commission.[4] Maxwell
Cohen, the distinguished Canadian constitutional lawyer, proposed
setting up two functional bodies: a joint economic commission and a
joint seaward boundaries commission.[5] Writers, such as Anthony Westell,
have favored instead a standing joint committee of Congress and Parliament to monitor the relationship, because nonpolitical commissions, in
Westell's view, would carry insufficient influence to actually deal with
problems in a way that would command sufficient governmental attention.[6]

All of these ideas for institutional initiative are motivated by several
common objectives: to halt the slippage in the tone of U.S.-Canada relations through the introduction of mechanisms to regularize and coordinate policy making in bilateral matters; to remove the surprises and the
politicization that has characterized recent disputes; to enable specialists
in foreign policy and the functional areas to resolve disputes inside a
framework with established procedures for dealing with contentious
issues; and to eliminate some of the confrontational quality of the exchanges by creating channels through which resolution of conflicts is
possible and through which actual progress can be made on the real
issues—channels that circumvent the bureaucratic atmosphere often associated with more public diplomacy.

The objective of cooling disputes and of regularizing diplomacy is
laudable. The idealism expressed in the desire to create joint institutions
is precisely the kind of idealism necessary to remove some of the recent
tensions in the relationship, whatever the nature of the bilateral bargaining setting. It is interesting to note, however, that in his East Lansing
speech to the Association for Canadian Studies in the United States,
Allan Gotlieb, incoming Canadian ambassador to the United States, took
exception to this sentiment, noting instead the difference in the interests
of the two countries on foreign policy matters. This emphasis is an indication that Canada does not want interests sacrificed for an improvement
in tone.[7] At the same time, the student of Canadian-American relations
will note the proliferation of institutional initiatives that has marked the
relationship over the years. Bilateral institution-building is not new, and
neither are differences in interests and perspectives. The question must
be, How bridgeable are the current differences?

Since the founding of the International Joint Commission in 1909, by all standards the bellwether of such organizational developments, no fewer than a dozen joint committees and a half-dozen joint governmental commissions have been established.[8] Most of these committees and commissions emerged at a time when serious problems required focused attention. The most effective of these bodies dealt with narrow, technical problems that often became troublesome and politicized. Rarely did the commissions or committees cross issue-areas, and when they did, as the Canada-United States Interparliamentary Group did, the institutions were careful to act as review agencies only, offering few specific policy recommendations for governmental actions. The life expectancy of a number of these bilateral institutions was not great, either because the problems they were designed to deal with were resolved or because each government allowed the institutions to languish slowly as decisions were made around them. Part of the success of the International Joint Commission (IJC), in contrast to many of the other bilateral institutions, was that it had a very large research role, it accepted disputes that lent themselves to technical solution, and it conscientiously avoided the long-range, overarching disputes filled with manifold political and economic trade-offs. By addressing the disputes it could profitably address, in a fashion that both governments countenanced, the IJC has had a long and distinguished institutional career that is respected by diplomats in both countries.[9] By not asking the IJC to do things that it was likely to find institutionally impossible, both governments avoided embarrassment and lent credibility to this type of bilateral decision-making format.

At present the creation of bilateral institutions is attractive to many people in the United States because it appeals to several fundamental axioms of U.S. behavior toward Canada. These opinions have recently become more widely acceptable to Americans because many bilateral institutions were established during the World War II coordinated military effort in 1940 and during the parallel joint economic effort codified in the Hyde Park Declaration the following year. Few Americans would debate these axioms today:

    1. Increased economic interdependence with Canada is desirable and beneficial to the people of both countries.

    2. Increased economic interdependence is probably inevitable and may eventually lead to some form of tighter economic integration between the two countries.

    3. Open political conflict between the two governments is symptomatic of a poorly managed relationship and is possibly explosive.

    4. Greater economic interdependence, accompanied by greater bilateral institutionalization, is likely to stem the propensity for intergovernmental conflict.

Each of these axioms appeals to a society whose size and self-confidence enable it to distinguish between economic and political goals. These axioms are, in general, accepted in Europe also; they underlie the Treaties of Rome of 1957 and, thereby, the European Community of today. They emphasize efficiency and economic productivity while drawing positive conclusions about the capacity of external political institutions to buffer the member governments from the shock of crisis and conflict. They accentuate the virtue of harmony and the dysfunctional nature of confrontational politics. Although they correspond to the highest aims of liberal-idealist thought, they are, paradoxically, also very conservative in philosophical tone, because they seek to preserve the relationship between the two countries in an essentially unchanged form. These constructivist axioms seek to build and to reinforce rather than to tear down or to reverse that which the forces of history have evolved.

In contrast to this perspective, which is favored by many Americans, Canadians committed to a nationalist outlook, some of whom were members of the 1981-82 Liberal Cabinet, reject the liberal-idealism of these axioms in favor of a tough realism that is, paradoxically, radical in its intent. They believe certain levels of interdependence can be reduced and integration reversed in certain sectors, for example, broadcasting, without fundamentally harming the relationship to the long-term detriment of Canada. They reject the inevitability of closer economic integration. They do not find confrontational politics, especially against a larger but somewhat constrained partner, objectionable. Having matured in the trenches of federal-provincial political warfare, they consider battles with Washington to be less risky, more predictable, and perhaps even helpful domestically. Finally, those Canadians who accept this latter perspective do not believe that further creation of bilateral institutions can "paper over" differences of interest and strategy which they feel only time and greater political distance can alleviate.

Given this Canadian perspective, the axioms of U.S. behavior toward Canada in the post World War II period cannot provide much policy assistance. From this perspective—a perspective apparently shared by a significant number of Canadians—suggestions for the creation of additional bilateral institutions seem to move in the wrong direction. It is one thing to reject new institutions, of course; another to reject the history of partnership. Institutionalization of the true essence of the partnership would be, not the norm, but a departure from the norm for both governments.

When one recognizes the existence of this perspective, which challenges many of the assumptions of American statecraft toward Canada in the post-1945 period, the lack of official enthusiasm in Ottawa for President Reagan's North American Accord concept becomes more explicable. As initially outlined, this accord among Mexico, the United States, and Canada would seek to coordinate trade and commercial policy through the creation of a cabinet-level observer agency in Washington composed of representatives from the three governments.[10] Such an accord would, it was hoped, take some of the lumps out of regional economic planning and implementation.

From the Canadian perspective, however, such an accord looked like creeping integration. Ottawa rejected economic integration, and hence the accord, because it felt the arrangement would be inherently unequal, with no foreseeable safeguards to protect the interests of the smaller participants. Moreover, even if Canada's fears that the accord was motivated by America's desire to grab Mexican and Canadian fuel and nonfuel minerals—fears that a careful reading of the accord idea does not seem to justify—had been allayed, the accord would still have been unattractive to Ottawa because of the Canadian government's feeling of dependence and loss of decision-making control.

The timing of the accord idea could not have been more ironic, coming in the same interval as the Canadian National Energy Program.[11] In terms of the implications for U.S.-Canada relations, the philosophies of these two major governmental initiatives were 180 degrees apart. It is useless to explain the subsequent deterioration of relations between Canada and the United States in terms of alterations of policy. Both governments were merely putting into the form of policy assumptions about the relationship which each had harbored for at least a decade and which, moreover—provided there were no hidden costs—were extremely popular within domestic electorates. Not by chance, the essential elements of each plan were announced during the respective national campaigns.

The problem for American diplomacy, then, is to understand the dynamics of historical change in the Canadian-American relationship and within Canada itself. Timing and an understanding of the Canadian mentality are at least as important as the generation of a set of bold foreign policy strategies. Canadian foreign policy, like the speeding electron physicists have tried but failed to photograph, may unfortunately respond less to obtrusive strategies, such as the accord idea, than to gradual improvements in the general foreign policy environment. In other words, U.S. policies may become the source of their own ineffectiveness.

Indeed, the task for American foreign policy is to examine the history of American and Canadian interaction in order to unlock, if possible, the explanation for the problems of misperception which have aggravated the relationship on both sides. To what extent is the explanation for the emergence of a Canadian foreign policy attitude that rejects fundamental axioms of U.S. behavior to be found in the very momentum of the Canadian-American relationship itself? To what extent is the origin of Canadian misgivings about U.S. policy initiatives found, unwillingly perhaps, not in Ottawa's own foreign policy assertiveness but in the assumptions the United States has made regarding foreign policy purpose? To what extent is the conflict between Ottawa and Washington not so much a tactical conflict (which would be amenable to institutional initiative), or an explosive conflict (which would be subject to some law of escalation) but instead a strategic conflict, focused in the interests and political priorities of the two governments and therefore increasingly a fixture of Canadian-American relations?

A HISTORICAL ANALOGY:
BRITAIN AND CANADA IN 1846

Historical analogies are never perfect. Yet, treated with the proper circumspection, historical analogies can be highly instructive, both in terms of parallels for contemporary state behavior and in terms of the sources of divergence. In many ways, the nineteenth-century relationship between Britain and Canada with respect to power and trade is similar to the twentieth-century relationship between the U.S. and Canada. Although, as detailed elsewhere in this book, Britain was much closer to British North America in a cultural and formal legal sense than the United States could ever be to Canada, the contrasting effect of geographic proximities has been something of an equalizer. Although British commercial involvement in Canada emphasized portfolio investment, and U.S. involvement emphasizes private direct investment, the high levels and comparative exclusivities of the respective investment situations are quite similar. Although the British navy provided British North America with security in the nineteenth century, and the U.S. strategic nuclear deterrent provides Canada with security in the twentieth century, in each case Canada relied upon a friendly foreign power for the bulk of its peace-time defense requirements. But much more important than these observations about the static analogy between the roles played by Britain and the United States is the analogy between the possible *change* in these roles. The source of the change in the association of major and minor partner is, for the contemporary analyst of Canadian-American relations, by far the most instructive insight to be gained from the study of British and U.S. roles in Canada.

To examine the source of the change in the relationship of Canada to Britain in the nineteenth century, further investigation of some of my earlier questions about the changing relations between Canada and the United States is needed. Who was primarily responsible for altering the political and trade association between mother country and colony, Britain or British North America? Did British North America seek independence from Britain because of the demands placed upon Canada in terms of taxation or security contributions? Was Canadian Confederation in 1867 the result of the same forces that had led the thirteen American colonies to revolt nearly a century earlier? Was British North America attempting to sever the link with Britain because the terms of that linkage were too onerous? Or did the process of historical causation operate in the opposite direction, namely, through Britain's decision, for its own reasons, to gradually dissociate from its colony in faraway North America, a decision that resulted from Britain's changing view of the global trading system and of the British capacity to prosper and exert leadership within that system?

Answers to these questions, I believe, are found within the events that led to the repeal of the British Corn Laws in 1846, a set of events which the commercial elite in Montreal so dreaded that they flirted with the politically unpopular notion of annexation to the United States. To capture the full significance of these events, however, one must consider the nature of the commercial and trading system that had existed prior to the emergence of British free trade.[12]

During the eighteenth and early nineteenth centuries, Britain, like other European countries, advocated the doctrine of mercantilism. Mercantilism had many variations, some of which, like the limitless acquisition of monetary wealth, were, even on the surface, economically self-defeating. The mainstay of the mercantilist idea, however, was more complicated and less easily dismissed as totally counterproductive for the immediate participants if not for the system as a whole. In essence, mercantilism involved two considerations of major significance for Britain and British North America. First, mercantilism established an exchange of British North American raw materials for British manufactures. Second, mercantilism allowed Canada to enter the British market at a preferential rate, a rate not obtainable on the world market. Thus, mercantilism came to be accepted in Upper and Lower Canada and in Nova Scotia as an attractive way of doing business.[13]

An important, related aspect was that British North America could count on Britain for political and military leadership. Britain would continue to assume institutional responsibilities of a colonial variety, would mediate differences, for example, between Anglophone and Francophone communities (mediation that was continued after 1867 in the form of judicial review by the Judicial Committee of the Privy Council), and would continue to supply the material base for military security. This form of partnership would allow British North America as much flexibility and autonomy as it desired without fostering a break with British institutions of government.

Although this dual economic and political arrangement of partnership between British North America and Britain was not idyllic and free from strain, it offered certain benefits to both polities. It placed a premium on the bargaining capability at the government-to-government level rather than on entrepreneurship per se. It also created the appearance of prosperity and economic growth while maximizing the emerging comparative advantage displayed by each polity. Why then did mercantilism fail?

Mercantilism failed, not because of anything British North America did or did not do, but because Britain discarded the system for that of free trade. Britain discarded mercantilism because in the larger context of its world relationships it could no longer compete successfully with other European and rising world powers on the basis of the mercantilist philosophy. But conversely, global free trade began to offer Britain opportunities that it could no longer afford to disregard, especially given internal political pressures within British society for a more equitable and "consumer-oriented" system of exchange. The British middle classes rejected both protection of agriculture and the resulting higher prices during the years of bad harvests in the 1830s and 1840s.[14]

Increasingly, Britain discovered a manifold truth. The obligations of managing a global political empire through intimate administrative contact of the type required in British North America exceeded the resources available. Costs of manning fortifications and of constructing the proper infrastructure, such as the Rideau Canal, were themselves construed to be excessive. But detailed involvement in other people's affairs meant eventual involvement in their disputes as well, and Britain was loath to face these implications, even under the leadership of Henry Palmerston,[15] let alone under Robert Castlereagh or William Gladstone.

At the same time, mercantilism forced Britain to forego certain opportunities of trade with partners outside the preferential system. Although British ships carried much of the valuable maritime trade, concessions offered trading partners, such as British North America, to keep them inside the preferential trading system nonetheless became costly. "The apostles of the 'free trade' creed in the mid-nineteenth century favoured a more subtle kind of empire, a method by which," said a free trader in 1846, "foreign nations would become valuable colonies to us, without imposing on us the responsibility of governing them."[16] Britain began to recognize that the opportunity costs of mercantilism were excessive relative to the costs of a system of freer and more open trading relationships.

In short, Britain found that free trade offered more advantages than the older system with fewer of the responsibilities and dilemmas. Britain was able to continue the profitable exchange of manufactures for raw materials and primary commodities without having to assume the administrative and military burden of colonial government. Former colonies did not cease trading with Britain after separation; as the U.S. case revealed, they increased their trade. Free trade was a panacea for Britain from the economic as well as the political perspective.

Although free trade was attractive to Britain, it was interpreted as a catastrophe for British North America. The comfortable arrangement known as the Old Imperial System had many attractions. Established in 1821, the timber preference that Britain provided was an advantage to New Brunswick in the export of lumber and ships. Following the union of Upper and Lower Canada in 1841, Lord Sydenham extended a £1,500,000 imperial loan, which was ultimately used to expand and complete the system of St. Lawrence canals.[17] Hence mercantilism meant not only a guaranteed market for goods from the Province of Canada and elsewhere but also substantial access to scarce capital at preferred rates. Canadian merchants grew accustomed both to the ease of trade within the British Empire and to the availability of large amounts of capital so long as the imperial system's prohibitions against the establishment of manufactures that competed with those of Great Britain were observed. That these prohibitions and limitations channeled the economic development of British North America toward a pattern of commodity and raw-material exports that contrasted sharply with the situation south of the border seemed not to concern the commercial elite. Perhaps this was because industrial development in manufactures was so unfeasible at the time; perhaps this view was shaped by an awareness of the corresponding difficulties of competition under a regime of free trade. Whatever the source of the commitment, the commercial elite in British North America seemed to treasure the Old Colonial System.

Merchants in Montreal had an additional reason for favoring the imperial system — politics. A collapse of mercantilism was also likely to bring with it a gradual disintegration of political ties with Great Britain. This was already happening in the movement to obtain responsible government in Nova Scotia (achieved in 1848), Prince Edward Island (1851), Newfoundland (1854), and New Brunswick (1855). To the eastern merchant Tories, responsible government spelled the equivalent of a cultural and class revolution. It meant the rise of the French into government office, with a possible change of public attitude toward foreign commerce and trade as well as toward systems of public works and even toward taxation (Britain under Peel had reintroduced the income tax in 1842). Thus, for British North America, the mercantilist system as it operated in the early nineteenth century was more than a philosophy of trade; it influenced industrial structure, political preferences, cultural outlooks, and industrial life-styles. It was a way of life.

If British North Americans had wanted to rebel against Britain, and there is no evidence they did, they had little to rebel against. Whether Britain really believed it could transform the commercial and trade order, reduce security commitments, and cut administrative costs while still maintaining political control is dubious. In any case, such maintenance of political control was impossible, and the only question that mattered was avoidance of assimilation into the American union.

What was equally clear was that Britain was by action and intent pulling out of British North America. Canadian confederation emerged not so much from decisions in Halifax or Montreal as from prior decisions taken in London. Britain had undermined her own colony.

"In effect Great Britain had broken away from her own empire; and with the repeal of the Navigation Laws in 1849, the Old Colonial System, which had sheltered and nurtured the northern colonies through the whole period of their uncertain youth, came at last to an end."[18] British North America may have squirmed under certain aspects of British imperial rule, but by and large the empire looked better and safer than either free trade or independence. Yet the plight of the British resulted in both. Britain acted not out of particular disenchantment with her colony but out of a larger global self-interest and necessity. Canada was not the cause of the rupture in imperial ties with Britain but the product.

What lessons, then, does the British and Canadian experience in the mid-nineteenth century hold for the contemporary relationship between the United States and Canada? The nineteenth century, after all, was quite different from today. An international balance-of-power system prevailed instead of the present modified bipolarity. This system was far smaller and less global than today's. Technology was far more primitive. Yet, parallels between the British role in the nineteenth-century international system and the American role in the present system are scarcely over-drawn. Both periods were periods of considerable peace. Both governments faced the enormous costs of providing a network of extraterritorial security. Both governments administered a vast commercial complex of firms and transnational entities. Both governments struggled with, on the one hand, the responsibilities of maintaining world order and, on the other hand, increasing financial constraints caused by the size of the burden and by the unwillingness of the populace to continue to sacrifice for this purpose. Surely, though far from perfect, the parallels demand examination.

DEMISE OF THE SPECIAL RELATIONSHIP: AMERICA AND CANADA, 1971-1981

Although both Canada and the United States have regarded their foreign policy relationships with several countries as unique or special (Canada with Britain; the United States with Britain, Israel, and Saudi

Arabia, for example), the association between Canada and the United States in the postwar period had perhaps a larger claim to the term *special relationship* than did any other association. Often ambiguous in definition and content (an ambiguity I seek to penetrate in Chapter 2), the special relationship was, on both sides, nonetheless perceived as important.

To establish a proper historical perspective regarding current Canadian-American relations, it is necessary to highlight certain aspects of this special relationship and outline the conditions impinging on its demise. I do so fully aware of both the risk of oversimplification and incompleteness of explanation here and the cost of some repetition in Chapter 2, which seeks to unravel the complexity of the special relationship. Familiarity with the characteristics and the problems in historical perspective must precede development of a framework for analysis, and such a frame is in turn necessary for a thorough discussion of the problems.

Canada tended in the main to define the special relationship in terms of what J. L. Granatstein has called "exemptionalism."[19] Exemptionalism meant that Canada, because of its proximity to and economic interdependence with the United States, would receive exemptions from U.S. measures that were designed to harmonize its economic policies with those of its allies. Between 1963 and 1968, for example, in order to fight its growing balance-of-payments problems, Canada on three occasions sought exemptions from U.S. measures. The measures concerned restricted foreign access to U.S. capital; this was done through the Interest Equalization Tax of July 1963, the Voluntary Cooperation Program of December 1965, and the Mandatory Direct Investment Guidelines of January 1968. Each time, the exemptions were granted, and Canada enjoyed advantages not extended to other allies and trading partners.

In practice, however, Canada expected and received more from the special relationship than financial exemptions. In terms of trade, the convention tax arrangement enabled Canada to obtain approximately 100 million U.S. dollars yearly from Americans attending conventions at sites in Canada, because U.S. income-tax law treated these expenses the same as those incurred at conventions held within the territorial United States. Similarly, the United States did not press Canada as hard as some of the other NATO allies for military contributions to NATO. Canada came to expect that through the Bilateral Defense-sharing Agreement offsets in military procurement would further reduce some of Canada's military costs. The United States was able to get officials of the General Agreement on Tariffs and Trade (GATT) to wink at some of the provisions within the Auto Pact between Canada and the United States because of the special nature of the North American automobile industry and the special character of forward and backward economic linkages.

In contrast, the United States tended to define the special relationship in often unstated but nonetheless important commercial terms. Regard-

less of how unstable and hostile the investment climate in other countries
might be, Canada was viewed as benevolently disposed to foreign investment from the United States. Indeed, for many Americans—and this was
the premise upon which they invested extensively in Canada—the two
markets were essentially one. Canada and the United States were and
would remain separate countries with sovereign governments, but for
these Americans the special relationship meant that the economies were
open. By world standards, Canadians were free to invest and trade without
many restrictions in the United States; U.S. firms operated on the same
assumptions concerning Canada. This was indeed a special commercial
and economic relationship, a relationship enjoyed by few polities even
inside a Common Market, such as that of Western Europe.

Indeed, Americans seemed to be arguing that underlying the special
relationship between Canada and the United States was an implicit bargain. That bargain involved the extension of certain trade and financial
concessions plus strategic security, on the one hand, in return for a relatively open investment and trading situation, on the other. The United
States would provide security for Canada, as for itself, without attempting
to exact proportionate payment, and would grant Canada exemptions
from U.S. trade and commercial policies not granted to other states. In
short, despite the difference in size of the two polities, the United States
would not squeeze as hard as it could in the interest of preserving a long-
term relationship that was favorable to the United States. In turn, Canada
would view trade and commerce with the United States in terms that, if
not preferential, were at least not disproportionately adverse. Because
Canada needed capital and the United States needed safe outlets for investment and because each country benefited from a closely coordinated
defense relationship wherein the United States bore a far larger amount
of the financial costs as a percentage of GNP, as did Britain a century
earlier, the development of the special relationship was thoroughly
grounded in the enlightened self-interest of both countries. What could
change the way each country viewed its own self-interest and the per-
petuation of the special relationship?

In 1970, the United States began to initiate policies at the global level
which would diminish many of the benefits of the special relationship
from the Canadian perspective. In the same year, Canada announced a
new foreign policy emphasizing national interest, a policy that would
eventually serve to destroy some of the special character of the bilateral
association from the American perspective. In *Foreign Policy for Canadians,*
Canada asserted that its foreign policy would be the extension abroad of
domestic priorities, suggesting that "functionalism" and "internationalism" would take a back seat.

Partly because of the Vietnam War, partly because of longer-term
trends of history, the United States began to rethink its foreign policy in

the 1970s. The U.S. economy was not nearly so dominant in world trade as it had been in the 1950s during the European and Japanese reconstruction. By the 1980 presidential election, a former president could assert that the United States had slipped to number two in strategic military terms.[20] Surely the dynamics of global power seemed to support each of these observations. The extraordinary reversal of alliances that occurred between China and the United States at mid-decade—only a few years after Secretary of State Dean Rusk had accused China of acting as the real enemy in Vietnam—was a rapprochement that presaged the need that China and the United States felt, despite their ideological differences, to balance rising Soviet power. For the first time in the period after World War Two, rigid bipolarity collapsed, and a balancing mechanism re-emerged at the top of the international power hierarchy. This effort to balance Soviet military ascendancy was reinforced once again in Europe. Although the Reagan and Mitterrand governments were at odds in ideological terms, the United States and France were in agreement regarding the need for balance in the face of the Soviet military build-up. For the first time in the era after World War II, the United States really needed some of its allies in more than conventional military terms.

Similarly, on the economic side, the inability of the United States to continue to finance balance-of-payments deficits, which funded the trading surpluses of its allies and much of the growth of the postwar economic system, led to the transformation of the Bretton Woods monetary arrangement and the shift to flexible exchange rates. It was especially significant that this shift, like the long-term alterations in the Soviet-American military balance, had little to do with Canadian-American relations directly. Canada was not the fulcrum upon which these structural changes within the international system were to turn; yet Canada would soon feel their effects.

The United States summarized the political importance of the global alterations in international power in the framework of the Nixon Doctrine.[21] According to the Nixon Doctrine, the United States would continue to provide strategic deterrence through the U.S. nuclear umbrella. Henceforward, however, allies and especially friendly nonallied states would need increasingly to look to their own defenses for security. Vietnam taught the United States that it could not fight a ten-year war, albeit of a circumscribed variety, and still provide adequate supplies of both guns and butter. Inflation and a loss of public morale were the consequences. In the future, governments threatened at the conventional and subconventional level of external aggression would have to rely primarily upon their own defense capability and perhaps upon a more vigorous regional military balance.

The primary importance of these developments for Canada was that with the collapse of the Bretton Woods agreement and with the advent of the Nixon Doctrine, the United States was no longer capable, or felt itself no longer capable, of extending exemptions to its closest ally. Canada, according to Presidents Nixon, Carter, and Reagan, was to be treated like every other major polity. With its accession in 1975 to the club of the seven (including Canada) advanced industrial democracies, Canada was considered to be "on the varsity" and subject to the rules and understandings that prevailed within this elite membership. From the U.S. perspective, this was a far more mature association for the two countries to contemplate. It was one of greater visible equality and certainly greater formal diplomatic equality; it entailed larger responsibilities for Canada, but the status accompanying this new position was considered a sufficient offset. Canada, in this view, would act as a more equal partner in the ranks of world powers and presumably would benefit economically from the shift from dependence to greater interdependence.

From the Canadian perspective, however, none of these American assumptions were justified. Prime Minister Trudeau's response to the shifting global situation and to the new bilateral situation was to sponsor the Third Option.[22] The October, 1972 study of Canadian foreign relations by External Affairs Minister Mitchell Sharp advocated a diversification of trade and investment, largely directed toward Europe and Japan. A major internal debate on the Canadian military posture resulted in the reduction of Canadian troops in Europe. That these policy initiatives were not strictly coordinated and self-reinforcing did not belie the implications of the policies for the U.S. interpretation of the special relationship. The United States had previously declared the "special relationship" dead; these Canadian foreign policy initiatives seemed to confirm this conclusion.

Not until October of 1980, however, with the return to power of the Liberal government in Ottawa and the election of a new Republican administration in Washington, was the full significance of the disappearance of the special relationship clear. The National Energy Policy boldly attempted to deal with a unique situation in the oil and gas industry, in which profits and profit repatriation were large and rapidly growing. The way in which Ottawa sought to deal with this problem caught Washington's eye. Prompted by unparalleled levels of foreign ownership and control of Canadian industry, the new Liberal government decided to challenge firmly and directly one of the principal American assumptions that remained as a legacy of the special relationship, namely, the comparatively unfettered movement of capital across the border. This bold step was the final blow to the American notion that Canada was different in investment terms from governments elsewhere in the international system. It is fair to say that the equivalent of the Nixon shocks of 1970-71 were the Trudeau shocks of 1980-81. In each case, the political turmoil following the economic shock was great.

Given these developments surrounding the demise of the special relationship, to what extent are the roles played by Britain in the nineteenth century and by the United States at present similar? To what extent has history merely repeated itself as far as Canada is concerned?

WHO ABANDONED WHOM?

In both historical instances, the burden of foreign security arrangements and older financial and trading patterns became excessive for the major power. Britain found that the cost of building fortifications, of foreign administration, and of preferential loans to her older colonies exceeded the capacity of the crown to obtain revenue through the Old Imperial System. The United States found in the 1960s that the obligations of sustaining "order maintenance" nonselectively and world-wide and the efforts to finance continuing balance-of-payments deficits were obligations that the American taxpayer no longer could absorb.

Partly for domestic and political reasons, Britain replaced mercantilism with free trade. This eventually caused the downfall of British colonialism in North America. Britain expected to cut her financial losses while retaining most of her political control and the bulk of her trade and commercial advantages. But the demise of the Old Imperial System meant the coming of responsible government to the provinces and, within twenty years, to Canada as a whole. Thus, Britain did not and could not maintain the same political relationship with British North America once the rules of trade and commerce had changed significantly.

In 1971, the United States replaced the Bretton Woods system with that of flexible exchange rates in the only way it could — precipitously. This damaged the special relationship, because the United States signalled that Canada would receive the same commercial and economic treatment as all other major trading partners. Although the United States anticipated that this initiative would be well received in Ottawa, because Ottawa was familiar with the world security obligations the United States was carrying and the problems of chronic balance-of-payment deficits the United States faced, the Canadian response was quite different. Instead, Canada announced the Third Option idea, indicating interest in trade diversification and new commercial linkages. Implications drawn from the creation of the Foreign Investment Review Agency and the National Energy Program reinforced the American awareness that the old American assumptions concerning the special relationship no longer held. Canada and the United States were not to be considered as a single market, albeit within the framework of separate and sovereign governments. Britain and the United States discovered that once the perquisites of the Old Imperial System, on the one hand, and of the special relationship, on the other, had been removed, Canada began to seek other alternatives to an arrangement that, however attractive previously, had now collapsed.

In each case, the impetus for change seems to have come from the more dominant partner. This does not mean that pressures for change from within Canada were not present. Particularly in the more recent situation, members of the New Democratic Party had long advocated various measures to Canadianize the economy and to attempt to reorient Canadian foreign policy away from what was described as a "lock-step" association with the United States. Similarly, the more nationalist wing of the Liberal Party pressed hard for such reforms prior to the officially inspired demise of the special relationship. A long history of newspaper articles, scholarly debates, and party initiatives preceded the actual policy shifts that occurred in the early 1970s. Nonetheless, a single policy decision by the major partner in each case was responsible for unleashing far-reaching adjustments in Canada's external policy.

With the advantage of hindsight there can be little doubt that Britain, not British North America, precipitated events leading to a new kind of association between the two polities. Britain aimed at the empire but in the process struck British North America. Similarly, evidence suggests that the initiatives that led to a rethinking of ties between Canada and the United States originated in Washington, not Ottawa. Although economic nationalism has come to be regarded in the United States as a made-in-Canada phenomenon, perhaps the basis for that assumption must be re-examined. The nature of the response is certainly Canadian, but the impetus for change may well have been the awareness that the United States was in the process of deserting an arrangement that had become too costly for it to maintain.

An interesting aspect of both the historical and the contemporary situation is that the commercial elite in Canada was by and large opposed to a disruption of links with the leading trading country in the international system. The eastern merchants had grown accustomed to the rules of the Old Imperial System, unlike their Yankee counterparts, and accepted the restrictions of mercantilism. Why was Montreal more prepared to accept the prohibitions placed upon the development of manufactures that competed with British industry, for example, than was Boston? The answer may have been that the merchants of Montreal felt they had fewer alternatives than did merchants in the United States. After all, the domestic market was smaller in British North America, and much of the transportation access to the Eastern seaboard was more difficult. Free trade, moreover, may have looked more threatening to Montreal in the absence of much of a capacity either to protect domestic manufactures or to get them to a point where they could compete effectively without protection. But one is also struck by the impression that Montreal had grown accustomed to the ease of imperial trading channels, through which the comparative advantage British North America enjoyed in the fur trade and in the sale of timber, fish, and other commodities could be parlayed into immense fortunes inside preferential markets.

Likewise, the contemporary Canadian business community has been far slower to accept the arguments of Canadian economic nationalism than other segments of the community. The proximity and size of the North American market has been too attractive to replace it with the fortuitousness of European or Third World trade, for example. Similarly, the Canadian business community has been far less enthusiastic about Canadianization than some academic and political leaders, in part because business leaders are more aware of the financial costs and in part because they recognize that takeovers are likely to involve the federal government ever more deeply in the Canadian economy. In any case, the business and commercial elite has not in general been on the forefront of support for a reorientation of association away from the United States, even after the collapse of the special relationship notion.

Canadian political elites, on the other hand, have always regarded themselves as the caretakers of the common welfare, to an even greater extent than is true within some other parliamentary democracies. Conventional explanations include the harsh climate (despite the fact that the majority of the Canadian population lives in climatic conditions warmer than those of northernmost parts of the United States) and the contrast between the short north-south distance of the population band and the immense east-west distances, a condition that creates problems of transportation and administration. Thus, faced with a crisis of adjustment, the Canadian polity is likely to respond through its governing elites in a way that may be at odds with the perspectives of a number of its leading citizens.

Even if this interpretation of the origins of contemporary Canadian nationalism is found to be on the mark (the thesis will be examined again in subsequent chapters), the analyst must be careful not to exaggerate the pace of change. After all, the British North America Act was patriated only some 114 years following confederation. Relations between Canada and Britain remain close and warm. The contributions of British culture and institutions to the Canadian experience, such as the voluntary retention of the English sovereign as Canadian head of state, are evident to everyone. Indeed, but for the rapid British economic decline, trade and commerce with Canada might have enabled Britain to retain its share of the Canadian market even under an increasingly free-trade-oriented international regime.

Likewise, the pace of change in the transformation of U.S.-Canada relations ought not to be exaggerated. The proximity of the two countries, the extent of institutional ties, the depth of common political and security interests, the dictates of the North American market, and the sympathy that the population of each society has for the other all reinforce a status quo, highly interactive political and economic association. Indeed, no sooner was the special relationship consigned to obscurity than it was reviewed as a "unique" or "exemplary" relationship.[23] Its legacy is seen in many examples of reciprocally preferential treatment on each side of the border.

Yet, the climate of the Canadian-American relationship in the 1980s is not that of the 1960s. The concept of partnership enshrined at Hyde Park and enlivened both by military cooperation during World War II and by the post-war foreign investment boom, is no longer accepted without scrutiny. The assumption regarding the mutual benefits of untrammeled access to both markets is under siege. The sense of direction in alliance and global security is somewhat less certain and is troubled by some unwillingness to view security as indivisible and to share defense costs accordingly. Indeed, for a generation of Canadians and Americans not personally aware of the tumult and devastation of World War II and somehow unable to come to grips psychologically with the meaning of nuclear deterrence, the notion of partnership itself is less evocative of a sense of security and peace.[24]

At stake in contemporary U.S.-Canada relations is the notion of partnership itself. On each side the apparent privileges and obligations of partnership are currently being reassessed. In the remaining chapters of this book I explore the scope and impact of this reassessment for both countries.

TWO

A Framework for the Analysis
of U.S.-Canada Relations

Historically, one of the differences that was supposed to have separated the Old World of Europe from the New World of North America was the quality of North American politics. Governments in North America were supposed to be, or regarded themselves as, more enlightened than their European counterparts. This meant they quarreled less, they tended to isolate themselves within the hemisphere, they viewed the use of force with suspicion, and they concentrated on business rather than on the business of government.[1] The old European adage, "The neighbor of my neighbor is my friend" did not hold here. In North America, one's immediate neighbor could be one's friend.

It would be a mistake, however, to believe that this idyllic view of world politics, which is infused with a good deal of nineteenth-century liberalism, prevailed without strain or stress, particularly for smaller partners. Likewise mistaken is the view that politics in North America operated somehow exclusively of power relationships. Certainly by the end of the nineteenth century, if not before, no government in North America feared the use of force by any other on the same continent. In this achievement, North America preceded Europe by half a century. Nonetheless, despite the rhetoric, international power relationships existed, and they shaped the evolution of U.S. and Canadian foreign policies toward each other.

HISTORICAL EQUILIBRIA

One of the shortcomings of contemporary foreign policy analysis is its frequent depiction of Canada and the United States as a dyad, or pair, separable and separated from the rest of the international system. This conceals the origins of state action. It tends to oversimplify decision making and causes policies to appear as though they emerged from a political vacuum. At every point in history, the international system has impinged on U.S.-Canada relations and has shaped outcomes. Indeed, the historical equilibrium of global power has determined outcomes perhaps to a greater degree than any other single factor.

The year 1776 was a turning point in the historical equilibrium of power, not just in the ways that the American Declaration of Independence affected U.S.-British relations but also in the ways that independence affected all of North America. In a sense, 1776 was the French revenge for the British conquest of 1759, which left Quebec a French-speaking fragment under British colonial rule.[2] Although the creation of the Dominion of Canada in 1867 might have appeared a further event along the same trend line, in reality it was not. The transformation of British North America into Canada came as much out of commercial reaction to U.S. protectionism following the Civil War as out of a desire for greater Canadian autonomy from Britain. Britain needed Canada as a hedge against the too-rapid emergence of the United States as a world power; Canada needed Britain as a counterweight to the dynamism of the U.S. doctrine of Manifest Destiny.

Thus, the United States was born of the interplay between France and Britain; Canada evolved out of the interplay between Britain and the United States. Regional and global power balances were such that Canada would cling to Britain as long as Britain could reasonably offset the rising American power. But the power of Britain and the United States moved rapidly in opposite directions. It is instructive to observe how Canadian external policy was affected by this changing international equilibrium of power. Canadian trade patterns, for example, followed the trends of shifting power very closely. As British power declined, the British share of Canadian trade also declined (fig. 1); conversely, as American power increased, the American share of Canadian trade increased. Gradually the United States replaced Britain as Canada's principal trading partner.

Not until World War II, however, was the triangular relationship between Canada, Britain, and the United States strikingly changed. First of all, World War II transformed the military relationship between the United States and Canada, because of the need for close coordination in the North Atlantic and in continental defense.[3] The extent of this coordination was unprecedented for the two governments and was necessitated by the nature of the Asian and European threats and the demands of wartime efficiency. Both governments yielded some sovereignty, but, despite the magnitude and the importance of the Canadian wartime effort, Canada probably gave up more sovereignty in this arrangement than did its larger military partner. The comparative success of this coordination, combined with the effects of postwar demobilization on the one hand and the ascendancy of the Soviet Union on the other, prepared the way for even greater cooperation on issues of security between Canada

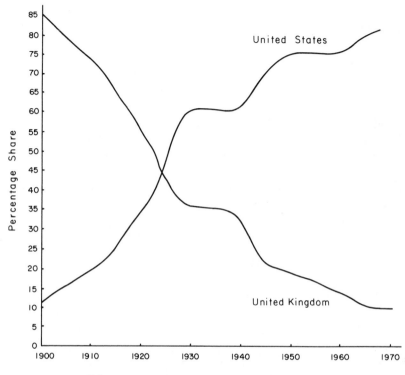

FIGURE 1.   British and U.S. Percentage Shares
of Total Foreign Investment in Canada

and the United States, cooperation that was evident after 1945 in the
NATO and North American Air Defense Command (NORAD) agreements.

Second, with increases in military coordination came growing interdependence in commercial and economic terms.[4] Not only was each
country soon to become the leading investor and trading partner for the
other, but the much larger size of the American population and GNP
meant that the weight of the U.S. economic presence in Canada was much
greater than that of Canada in the United States.

The striking aspect of these developments was how quickly they occurred, driven in particular by the exigencies of preparedness for World
War II, and how much they contrasted with the conditions of the late
nineteenth century. In a period of fifty years, Canada and the United
States had changed from mere neighbors to seemingly inextricably associated trading partners and allies. In all but a formal legal and constitutional sense, the United States had come to replace Britain as the dominant foreign political and economic presence in Canada.

This new equilibrium put peculiar pressures on the foreign policies of both Canada and the United States. For Canada, the search for a counterweight to the American presence and to declining British visibility became almost a fixation. Fear of being absorbed into American culture and republican society conditioned the writing and editorial thought of many Canadians.[5] Margaret Atwood, for example, captured this popular sense of neurosis in *Survival.* Much as the Quebecois had earlier felt abandoned by the French, English-speaking Canadians in particular felt abandoned by the British and, in some ways, found themselves in contention with Westminster over constitutional patriation. For all practical purposes, the triangular relationship had collapsed, leaving Canada in the lap of the United States, out of earshot of the British (Canadian) Queen.

Similarly, the United States had problems adjusting to the new equilibrium. No conscious design had lifted the relationship to this level of interdependence. Frictions in foreign policy were bound to intensify. The United States was obliged to provide evidence of good intentions and behavior on every occasion. All foreign policy actions would be held up to the scrutiny of America's near neighbor, and suspicions were easily aroused. While the United States found itself in the vulnerable commercial position of concentrating nearly one-quarter of its total foreign investment in a single country, it also found itself in the position of having to so constrain its policy statements that no hint of coercion or illwill would accompany its responses. Both countries spoke of "managing the relationship," but management became more difficult as tight interdependence precluded much room for diplomatic maneuver and instead generated tensions of its own. Yet there were obvious benefits flowing from the new equilibrium for both countries; the relationship would otherwise never have been permitted to proceed so far.

The dynamics of the new equilibrium were far from simple, however; misperceptions occurred on both sides of the border. In the postwar period, many Americans committed two kinds of error in their thinking about the relationship. First, they tended to respond as though the historical norm for the relationship was continental integration. To compare the diplomatic distance and type of commercial association of the nineteenth-century U.S.-Canada relationship with that of the twentieth-century relationship is sufficient to highlight the error in this perspective. Second, most Americans continued to misconstrue both the extensiveness of their own presence in Canada and the desire on the part of most Canadians to express their own cultural and political autonomy. These misconceptions, or misperceptions, regarding the Canadian-American dialogue complicated for the U.S. government the task of managing the relationship.

The misperceptions of the dynamic were, however, at least as great in Canada. Canadians often looked upon the 1945-56 interval (ending with Canada's peace-keeping initiative at Suez) as the high point of Canadian international status and influence. In a sense they were right. Canada ended the war in possession of one of the largest navies in the world. Europe and Japan lay in ruins, and only Canada and the United States were able to revive those countries, which they did through a variety of reconstruction plans and financial loans that built upon the strong and undamaged economic bases of the two North American countries. Largely because of Canada's prior military record and its status associated with postwar reconstruction, the Allies accepted important modifications of the NATO charter and incorporated the so-called Canadian article, Article Two of the charter, which broadened the purpose of the alliance in economic and social terms. Thus, alliance politics epitomized the significance of the Canadian presence.

Canadians were also correct, in a sense, about a relative decline in their international status, a decline that occurred because of subsequent Canadian military choices and technological developments in weaponry. Canada wisely chose to forego acquisition of nuclear weapons, but at the same time to drastically cut back its military spending relative to its wealth and economic capacity to support such spending. The effect of this decision was to release substantial productive resources for use elsewhere in the economy, where the effect of multipliers would be greater. But, inevitably, this reduction in military spending also reduced Canada's contribution to NATO and thus its significance, in terms of security, to its allies. In addition, the reduction also made Canada much more dependent upon the American security umbrella, not just in the nuclear strategic sense, which was unavoidable, but in all areas of conventional armaments as well. As a consequence of these changes in military defense, Canada experienced a decline in importance as a world power, from the security perspective, in about the same period that the United States rose to preeminence. The contrast in world roles, in responsibilities during crisis intervals, and in strategic planning was understandably felt deeply in Canada, yet this contrast was to some extent of Canada's own making.

National status is not, however, correlated solely with military power; nor is national capability merely the sum of various types and levels of military spending. Indeed, in the longer term the underlying determinants of military power are probably economic, technological, and territorial. In these areas (in a strictly military context) Canada has always looked better than other countries.[6] But the more important point is that in terms of overall relative national capability, especially in the context of the twentieth century, Canada's position in the world system is in reality far different from what many Canadians have perceived it to be.

Relative national capability combines the long-term underlying determinants of power, including GNP size, per-capita wealth, territorial and population size, resource availability, and various indicators of military power.[7] Critics may complain that this approach mixes apples and oranges. A plausible response is that it does and that the result is an index of fruit, or, to translate the analogy, national capability. National capability is considered relative in the sense that it is a ratio: for example, Canadian national capability relative to that of the international system of states or to that of any other single state, in this case the United States. Figure 2 presents the empirical results of this exercise.[8]

These results show that although Canada did experience an upturn in relative national capability in the World War II period, because of the size of its military effort (and, although not revealed by these dyadic data, because of the temporary collapse of the European and Japanese economies), Canada enjoyed its largest increase in relative capability in the most recent decade. Far from showing the decline that many observers instinctively felt, Canada has experienced a surge of economic vitality and growth, buoyed by the richness of its natural resources and its active international trade account. Far from being overshadowed by the supposed greater growth in capability of the United States in the post-1945 period, Canada has probably done better than the United States on many indices of national capability. Only if one focuses primarily on military spending and security concerns would one be likely to conclude the opposite.

Canada's superiority in relative capability in the postwar period is further reflected in the behavior of the non-Communist, advanced-industrial governments toward Canada. In 1975, Canada was co-opted into the club of non-Communist nations that have the largest industrial clout in the system: the United States, Japan, West Germany, France, Britain, and Italy. Although its entry was opposed by some of the members, on political rather than economic grounds, Canada's participation was strongly supported by the United States. Canadian membership in this elite economic club signified in world terms that Canadian economic importance could no longer be taken for granted. It was now formally recognized by all, including the United States.

Of course, one must not exaggerate the significance of the changes in relative capability for policy analysis. On many critical indicators, for example, an absolute disparity in size exists between the United States and Canada, amounting to a ratio of at least nine to one.[9] In absolute terms, the United States continues and will continue to cast the longest political and economic shadow of any single nation-state within the global system. Leadership within the Western alliance system will continue to come from the United States. Canadian-American relations will continue

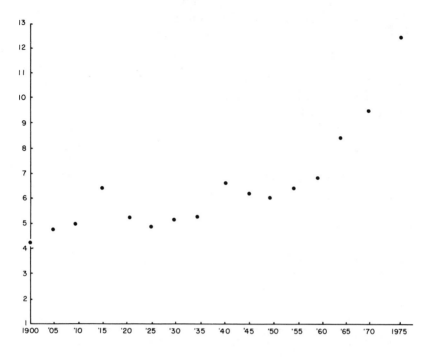

FIGURE 2.   Index of Relative Capability
(Canada-United States), 1900-1975

to reflect the existence of this absolute disparity in overall power in a
variety of ways, including the way the issue agenda is framed in the
approach to negotiations and perhaps—although this is more qualified—including certain outcomes.

Yet the myth that this dominance creates of an everencroaching
American imperialism ought to be dispelled by these empirical findings.
One cannot say with any certainty that the increase in the relative share
of each country's trade as a percentage of the other's total trade has
peaked; the more important statistic is that trade between the two countries continues to be of paramount significance to each country. One
cannot say with great confidence that the U.S. share of total foreign
investment in Canada has reached a plateau or that the Canadian share
of foreign investment in the United States is likely to continue to expand
rapidly; the more important statistics are that Canada and the United
States are each other's best investment partners. What is certain is that
neither relative capability nor relative levels of trade and commercial
interdependence have shifted against Canada in the last decade. Evidence
for the thesis of increasing imperialist domination of Canada by the

United States is nonexistent, and the indicators that might have fed such apprehensions are at least a decade behind the present reality of the relationship.[10]

Thus, those Canadians fearing an enormous erosion of Canadian global prestige and influence in the postwar period are misperceiving the dynamics of relative capability, despite the admitted decline in Canada's systemic significance in narrowly military terms. Like Americans, Canadians have had a difficult time accurately assessing these dynamics in a relationship that has in some ways become so close as to induce myopia and the loss of a proper sense of historical and analytic perspective.

The historical equilibrium of Canadian-American relations has thus been partnership on a single continent, not estrangement or amalgamation. For the most part, each has respected the other's sovereignty; force does not enter the relationship. Natural economic efficiencies of large market size and north-south linkage, plus the physical distance of other major trading partners, encourages interdependence. But the overall relationship remains that of equilibrium. In the nineteenth century it was an equilibrium in which Britain politically offset the United States. In the twentieth century, with the disappearance of Britain as balancer and with the emergence of the security imperatives that stemmed from the East-West struggle, the circle of actors operating within the equilibrium expanded but the space for diplomatic maneuvering actually shrank as the association between Canada and the United States became closer. For the present, Canada has rejected Europe and Japan as counterweights to the United States, while seeking Third World partners as balancers.

Just as Canada thought of herself as a "linchpin" between Britain and America during World Wars I and II, so Canada seeks today to act as the linchpin between the United States and the Southern Hemisphere. Regardless of the composition of the triangle as far as Canada is concerned, however, Canada occupies one corner, the United States a second, and a third actor (or actors) has always been sought to complete the equilibrium.[11] The equilibrium changes with respect to the identity of the residual membership and the closeness of the partners. But the premises of the historical equilibrium have never varied as to ethos or operation.

Dimensions of Analysis

Canadian-American relations can be assessed in terms of the factors that shape and determine the issues and the issue agenda. There are essentially three of these underlying factors, or dimensions of analysis: (1) the political-strategic dimension, (2) the trade-commercial dimension, and (3) the psychological-cultural dimension. These three dimensions can be regarded as basically uncorrelated sources of foreign policy explanation, with issues located at various points along these dimensions, depending upon the degree to which the issues reflect the content of the dimensions. For example, the dispute over television advertising possesses both psychological-cultural and commercial aspects, but the former are probably more important to most Canadians and the latter are undoubtedly more important to Americans. Similarly, the negotiations regarding the purchase of the F18-A fighter plane had political-strategic implications as well as trade-commercial significance for both countries, although Canada probably weighed the latter more heavily and the United States tended to emphasize the former. It was, however, the complex interaction of the two sets of considerations (that the planes were purchased from the United States perhaps caused it to view the demands of North American security with more toleration than if the purchases had been made elsewhere) that made the deal possible and eventually satisfied the objectives of both governments.

Thus, each issue has a different mix of factors associated with it; each government values these factors differently and will therefore view a particular issue in a unique way. Disputes can be resolved only when the underlying factors associated with an issue are fully understood by both countries and when bargaining proceeds accordingly. Negotiation must take the different assumptions and weight of objectives fully into account. The primary theoretical consideration in the U.S.-Canada relationship is that each government starts from different assumptions about international politics, and these assumptions in turn affect the weighting of the bargaining dimensions themselves.

Political-Strategic Dimension. Because of its role as focal point for a wide-ranging series of alliance systems, the United States assumes a global view of international politics, one that stresses security considerations. International politics has primacy in Washington because Washington not only must provide the bulk of the strategic security for the non-Communist world but also must broker the various interests and concerns of the member nations so as to maintain political harmony. These political functions go with the responsibilities of leadership and in many cases require that commercial advantage or benefit receive less attention. In the period after World War II, the United States has repeatedly been obliged to yield on economic or commercial matters in order to obtain cooperation on military and security matters. No country is able to subordinate all of its national interests to the larger international systemic interest of promoting order. Such behavior is sometimes regarded as patronizing or hypocritical—a form of enlightened despotism, perhaps. Yet, in the nineteenth century, Britain was able to act as the balancer, in part because it could dissociate individual state interests from the systemic interest and economic benefits from the larger military-strategic perspective. Similarly, in the latter half of the twentieth century, the United States has, at some cost to itself in economic terms, assumed the responsibility of sustaining the political order of the global system and of militarily balancing the Soviet Union. It is perhaps gratuitous to observe that the United States never sought these responsibilities and that periodic bursts of isolationist spirit belie any popular commitment to a perpetual world role, far less an imperialist course, for the nation. That global leadership was thrust upon the United States, however, does not mean that the U.S. government is less prepared to exercise leadership in this period or to make the necessary sacrifices attendant upon this role on behalf of a stable world system.

Conversely, Canada has been comparatively less interested in a truly global foreign policy. Repeatedly, high government officials argue that their principal foreign policy problems (and perhaps opportunities as well) involve the United States. If the United States tends to look outward toward the world system, Canada, because of its size and priorities, tends to look toward the United States. Because security considerations are by definition almost eliminated from the two-actor setting, and because Canada, for reasons to be explored later, does not involve itself directly in strategic decision making, Canada tends to de-emphasize the political-strategic dimension. When Canada does employ political-strategic argument, it normally does so through Washington, influencing global security by influencing Washington's orientation toward that security. When, for example, Lester Pearson, as Minister of State for External Affairs, challenged the doctrine of massive retaliation, he did so in a National Press Club speech in Washington and in personal meetings with Secretary of State John Foster Dulles. Although some Canadian commentators have been critical of this approach, because it seems to involve Canada too deeply in the domestic decision-making processes of its near neighbor and thus legitimizes a blurring of sovereignties, Canada achieves maximum influence by employing that kind of access to the highest circles of power in Washington which is only available to trusted allies.

All of this is not to argue that Canada is indifferent to global peace and to stability. What it does mean is that Canada cannot, or chooses not to, attempt to affect world peace and stability through conventional alliance structures and its own manipulation of armaments. Instead, Canada relies on other areas, in which its comparative advantage is higher.

Canada has employed the functionalist ideal not only because many proponents inside and outside Canadian government favor the liberal principles that underlie this concept of world order.[12] Functionalism embodies opportunities and safeguards that Canada, at this stage in the evolution of its foreign policy role, cannot afford to ignore. As a result of the functionalist policy, Canada was able to perform an important brokerage function in the U.N. General Assembly, as a middle power that understood the needs of Third World countries yet was itself inside the industrialized camp. More recently, Canada has been able to perform this same function outside the United Nations in the context of North-South conferences, such as that held in Cancun during the autumn of 1981. Canada's contribution is not only that it functions as a communicator between two groups of nations with fundamentally different perceptions of international politics but also that it has the ear of Washington. During President Reagan's trip to Ottawa in the spring of 1981, he gave Prime Minister Trudeau a qualified commitment that the United States would attend the North-South meeting in Cancun. Canada had thus done what possibly few other governments could have achieved, namely to persuade the United States to continue the North-South dialogue at a time when East-West preoccupations were paramount. Functionalism, with its emphasis on the role of foreign policy, enables Canada to take advantage of its political strengths by mediating quarrels and by getting potential opponents to communicate in a way that alienates no country and enhances Canada's international status.

Functionalism provides safeguards to Canada because of the principle that every actor is to be treated as sovereign, autonomous, and equally a subject of international law. Functionalism creates roles for countries today, as it did in the context of the British Empire and later the British commonwealth. Each government must perform its role properly if the international system is to function; thus, each country is partially able to dissipate the pressures associated with the rough and tumble of power politics. Functionalism safeguards the integrity and place of the smaller members of the international system.

The significant aspect of Canada's attitude toward the political-strategic dimension of foreign policy is not, however, that other considerations bulk larger in governmental priorities. Canadian preoccupation with federal-provincial relations and its focus upon bilateral U.S. relations tend to reduce the time and bureaucratic resources available for consideration of the larger realm of global politics; this, more than the personal predilections of the prime minister, accounts for Ottawa's emphases since 1968. Unlike the United States, Canada is not forced into the vortex of world politics by its power position; Canada can choose or choose not to adopt a mainstream posture. Given the broadly similar liberal, capitalist foundations of the two societies, they might have found their political-strategic outlooks reversed had history dealt them converse power positions.

Trade-Commercial Dimension.   Because both Canada and the United States are middle-class, commercially oriented polities, both value the trade-commercial dimension in foreign-policy making. But the weight given to this dimension varies for each government. For Canada this dimension is much more important than the political-strategic dimension in the overall genesis of foreign policy; for the United States it is less important. The reasons for this difference emerge clearly from a comparison of the countries' structures.

First, the propensity to rely on trade in the international system is inversely associated with the size of a nation's economy. Hence, foreign trade as a percentage of GNP is more important for Canada than for the United States. The United States is able to rely on its large domestic market; Canada is less able to do this, not only because of the smaller size of its domestic economy but also because of its low population density and the peculiar spatial distribution of this population along the northern U.S. border, a distribution that makes transportation costly.

Second, trade and commerce are valued more highly in Canada than in the United States because Canada, despite its wealth, regards itself as something of a developing country. Canada's industrial base is strong, but Canada still retains a comparative advantage as a producer of raw material. This means that its industrial sector is not developed as deeply as that of Japan, Germany, or the United States. Canada thinks of itself as having to "catch up" with a number of other industrial countries in developmental terms, despite its high per-capita income and high economic growth rate. This developmental preoccupation causes Canadian governments to seek ways of maximizing economic return and of using the international system to transform the character of the Canadian economy. Economic development becomes an end in itself rather than a collateral or secondary aim of statecraft. It means that the Minister of Finance has greater political clout within the Cabinet than the Secretary of State for External Affairs and that the economic impact of most decisions is contemplated before the political impact. In short, the condition of the Canadian economy becomes the primary raison d'être of Canadian external policy.

Third, the U.S. government in the post-World War II period has behaved toward the American economy as though it could generally manage itself. This proclivity was perhaps greater under Democratic than under Republican administrations and greater in the interval prior to the 1973 oil crisis than after that crisis. The consequence has been, however, that sophisticated economic problems have often been left to technicians and specialists rather than to trained political decision makers, and the knowledge of managers of foreign affairs has been greater in strategic and security matters than in matters of political economy. Given the U.S. propensity to emphasize free market processes, minimal government is considered good government. Minimal government is scarcely possible in the security sphere. In an ideal economic world, in which virtually all government intervention, except for basic monetary and fiscal functions, was prohibited everywhere, the private sector could manage itself in such a way as to maximize efficiency, if not always equity. In the real world of constant and widespread economic intervention by governments, the U.S. private sector, because of its strength, has still done a reasonably good job of holding its own without much assistance from Washington, the plight of the U.S. steel and auto industries notwithstanding. Managers of foreign affairs could certainly make the case that economic policy was less critical to the health of U.S. interests than was a sound security policy. That this viewpoint contrasted sharply with the observed policies of most other advanced industrial states was scarcely a convincing reason for altering the emphasis. This viewpoint went a long way, however, toward explaining the difference between the Canadian and American foreign policy outlooks.

Psychological-Cultural Dimension. The third dimension underlying the U.S.-Canada relationship—the psychological-cultural dimension—is probably more critical in explaining disputes between the governments and in explaining outcomes than either of the other two dimensions. It is also the dimension upon which there is the least consensus domestically, which is the most contentious externally, and which is the least understood analytically. In all of these respects, the psychological-cultural dimension is essential to an understanding of general Canadian-American relations.

The psychological-cultural dimension is manifested, at a somewhat superficial level, in the well-known American tendency to "take Canada for granted" and in the Canadian proneness to feel a mixture of envy and ambivalence regarding the United States. But the psychological mechanisms that lie beneath these manifestations are far more complicated than the manifestations themselves. Why do Americans assume they know more than they do about Canada? Why do Canadians exhibit so much ambivalence toward the United States? Part of the difficulty is bound up, on the one hand, in the Canadian effort to establish a separate and cohesive national identity and, on the other hand, in the American effort to overcome a deep sense of cultural insecurity by reducing all differences between themselves and others to extensions of Americanism. In trying to solve their own problems of cultural insecurity, Americans tend to deny Canadians their own Canadian identity. When Americans assert that Canadians are just like Americans, Americans think they are conferring an honor, or at least sharing something that is distinctive and valuable. But the real effect of such an assertion on the Canadian mentality is to take away the Canadian identity. By denying Canadians a feeling of national identity, Americans unknowingly elicit hostility, because a single, autonomous national identity has eluded Canada since its founding.

Conversely, when Canada rejects the proffered extension of Americanism, this not only offends American pride, it challenges something more fundamental — the American sense of well-being and success. Why would anyone want to reject what is viewed by some Americans as the cause of American greatness — not grandeur but greatness. Rejection of American values strikes at the core of the American need for cultural security and the need to affirm political legitimacy.

The psychological-cultural dimension would not be so compelling for the Canadian-American relationship if the countries were not so close physically and if all kinds of interdependence were not so binding. The United States may find Canadian complaints irritating; Canada frequently finds the American presence suffocating. Difference exists here in scope if not in kind. Americans simply do not understand how overwhelming the economic and population size can be.[13]

The psychological-cultural dimension explains a great deal that is important in the relationship. When a presidential or prime ministerial visit goes well, for example, it is because the psychological and cultural aspects of foreign policy have been correctly taken into account. Conversely, when things go badly in specific issue areas, it is often because Canada or the United States has not correctly handled the emotional and stylistic aspects of the negotiations. The United States tends to underestimate the significance of this dimension, because Americans often erroneously assume that Canadians "think like us" about foreign policy. Proximity and superficial cultural similarity elicit such mistakes. The difference in foreign policy roles of the two countries, if nothing else, should reveal how wrong such naive interpretations of the relationship can be.

Impact of Time on the Importance of the Dimension.   A multiplicity of considerations within the international system, both internal to Canadian and American societies and external to them, determine which dimension is most crucial to the Canadian-American relationship at which time. During the great international cataclysms of the first half of the twentieth century, for example, the political-strategic dimension was predominant to such a degree that the whole structural relationship of the two economies was transformed, almost as though the trade-commercial dimension had not existed. In periods of recession or depression, however, the trade-commercial dimension takes priority, overshadowing in particular the psychological-cultural dimension. But the psychological-cultural dimension does not become important only when economic prosperity gives Canada sufficient confidence to raise grievances with the United States that might otherwise remain dormant for fear of Canadian vulnerability. Domestic political considerations often shape the impact and timing of the psychological-cultural dimension. An election or referendum in Quebec or a policy of cutbacks in crude oil production in Alberta will affect Canada's psychological outlook toward its external relations; a change of administration in Washington or the advent of an important social movement, such as environmental activism, will eventually condition U.S. foreign policy toward Canada.

It is critical for Canadians to remember how much U.S. foreign policy toward Canada is affected by global developments. No dyadic model of Canadian-American relations alone can be anything but misleading. The trade-commercial dimension of the Canadian-American relationship became critical in the Nixon years, not so much because of the nature of the relationship per se but because of structural changes within the international economic system, changes that led to the collapse of the Bretton Woods agreement, large-scale stagflation, persistent balance-of-payments disequilibrium, and an impending energy crisis. The trade-commercial dimension rose to prominence not because Ottawa or Washington intended this outcome but because U.S. efforts to manage its global economic relations dictated that the trade-economic dimension would be highlighted.

Just as Canada and the United States may value a particular dimension differently, so a dimension may be more or less important to the relationship in a given period. Successful conduct of foreign policy requires a sensitive reading of changes in the relative importance of these dimensions in the attitudes of governments and societies on both sides of the border. The capacity to anticipate change is the capacity to generate a positive foreign policy climate; a positive foreign policy climate is essential to an effective foreign policy.

Issues, the Issue Agenda and
the Foreign Policy Decision-Making Process

Issues arise for a variety of technical, domestic political, socio-economic, or legal reasons. An issue becomes an issue when an action or inaction by one government is a matter of dispute and requires intergovernmental negotiation. The issue agenda establishes priorities among issues.[14] It also records the way each government estimates the costs, risks, utilities of resolution, and the available means of resolving each issue. Each individual issue, and the issue agenda as a whole, is largely determined by the interplay among the underlying dimensions of the relationship. When the two governments weigh the dimensions differently with respect to an issue, or when substantial information is lacking, so that an issue is poorly comprehended, a dispute is likely. If comparative agreement exists on the weighting of the dimensions underlying an issue, the issue is likely to be resolved quickly or demoted on the hierarchy of priorities within the issue agenda. For example, when the convention-tax issue was viewed by the Trudeau government as well as by both the outgoing Carter administration and the incoming Reagan administration as a matter of trade and commerce that might diffuse some of the pressures associated with the psychological-cultural dimension, U.S. tax law was modified to enable American convention-goers to deduct convention expenses from their income tax even when the convention was held in Canada.

In theory, at least, each government goes through a fairly rational process of decision making regarding the issues on the agenda. Simultaneous negotiation occurs on a variety of issues. Hence, the agenda itself is less important than the way each government views an individual issue. Despite the conclusions of a fairly extensive literature on setting an agenda, there is very little mystery about how an issue gets on the negotiation agenda; getting on the agenda, moreover, has little significance for how quickly an issue will be resolved.[15] Either government may put an issue on the agenda, although there is some misunderstanding among analysts about this.

Some analysts have suggested that the United States, because of its greater national capability, essentially establishes the issue agenda. Canada then becomes something of a price taker, merely responding to the initiatives made by the United States. Because, according to this view, there are advantages to setting the agenda, Canada is placed in the unenviable position of having to adopt a passive or defensive role that leads to more defeats than victories. Without commenting upon whether Canada or the United States has won more disputes in the last decade or so and without exploring whether a defensive or offensive strategy is more likely to be successful in the context of bilateral bargaining, we can state that the above proposed view of setting an agenda seems false. In general, Canada has taken the initiative on more issues than the United States. Canada has probably also shaped the overall agenda to a greater degree than the United States. Whether this means that both sides pursue initiatives with equal intensity is not clear from the argument so far advanced. This list of issues brought to the bargaining table by Canada is, however, usually longer than that submitted by the United States. This is not surprising. The United States, as the larger negotiating partner, is probably also the more conservative. Canada is likely to initiate more proposals and to take the offensive more often. The United States is likely to be more cautious and more passive.

The number of issues promoted by one government or the other says nothing in itself about the comparative justice or injustice of the issue agenda, or, for that matter, the equity involved in the overall foreign policy relationship. Although a government feeling a grievance will probably voice this grievance by formally "flagging" an issue for negotiation, a single major issue may be more troublesome for one country or the other than a series of minor issues. Similarly, "winning" a series of minor issues may amount to a mere diversion from the more central goal of foreign policy if a major issue fails to reach satisfactory resolution.

In theory, Canada and the United States go through roughly similar decision-making processes when formulating a strategy to obtain an issue objective, although the institutional procedures vary substantially. As in most other governmental decision-making processes, a threefold calculation is involved in making foreign policy decisions.[16] The principal variables are (1) the perceived utility of the issue objective, (2) the cost involved in obtaining that objective, and (3) the risk associated with failing to obtain the objective. Although actual decision making is normally collective, and these variables may be treated largely in an implicit, intuitive fashion, they nonetheless accurately frame the decision-making process.

The utility of the issue objective is of central importance in U.S.-Canada relations. One government may feel far more strongly about an objective than the other. If this is so, a decisive difference in capabilities in the opposite direction may fairly easily be offset. I suspect this was the case, for example, in the convention-tax issue, which ultimately was resolved in favor of Canada. Analysts sometimes miss this reality by focusing too narrowly on means. Determinations of the utilities of issues are affected by tradition, bureaucratic preferences, electoral penalties, interest-group pressures, and the personalities and ideological orientation of key decision makers. In a decision-making setting such as the Canadian-American relationship, in which the limits that define appropriate means are clear and restrictive, the utility of objectives becomes even more important, because this variable is simply more variable than others. When the utility of an objective carries great weight in the decision-making process for both decision makers, the possibility of mixed-motive outcomes and non-zero sum, or shared consequences, is likewise quite high, because cooperation itself, especially viewed in the longer term, carries a positive value for both sides.

The second critical variable in decision making is cost. Cost really involves the inherent cost of obtaining an objective, that is, the amounts of resources and time expended. Especially in the Canadian-American context, cost must also reflect a subtraction of the opportunity costs of not obtaining the issue objective; frequently such a cost is measured as a loss of party support in the United States or as a loss of Cabinet support or parliamentary governing margin in Canada. In operational terms, these opportunity costs may affect either the perceived utility of the objective or the estimated overall cost of achieving an issue objective. No foreign policy objective is cost-free; the magnitude of these costs will help determine whether an issue ever appears on the bargaining agenda. Each partner can, of course, affect the costs that the other will have to bear. Thus, for both actors, cost estimation and cost assumption interact to a large degree.

A third variable is risk. Risk is the probability that an objective cannot be achieved or resolved to the satisfaction of the government. Expressed slightly differently, risk is unity minus the probability that the objective can be achieved. Governments make choices about which issues to raise, and those issues end in outcomes that are partly determined on the basis of risks. Some governments are more averse to risk than others. A general observation is that both the United States and Canada are quite averse to risk, especially in terms of bilateral disputes. This fact, perhaps more than any other, makes Canadian-American relations appear placid to nonspecialists. The key consideration here is that of *comparative* risk, however, just as earlier we were concerned with comparative utility and cost. Both actors being comparatively averse to risk increases the number of issues available for consideration by the two polities but constrains the options available for the accomplishment of goals. This accounts for some of the highly interactive quality of the relationship. It also accounts for some of the actors' frustration; they may be dissatisfied with outcomes but unable to resort to means used by other governments to alleviate such tensions. Often almost unperceived by the political bodies of the two countries, these tensions are felt most acutely at the bureaucratic interface between the two governments, in the Department of External Affairs and in the Department of State. Tradition, competence, and a high degree of professionalization within both governments prevent such frustrations from spilling over into more serious confrontations.

Together, risk, cost, and the utility of an issue objective—treated comparatively by both Canada and the United States—determine the outcomes of disputes in U.S.-Canada relations. To some people, the mechanics of the decision-making process are less interesting than the limits established upon that process. To others, the unique institutions associated with the foreign policy decision-making process on both sides of the border appear most important.

Before leaving this discussion of issues, the issue agenda, and the foreign policy decision-making process, one significant practical element ought to be mentioned. In a relationship as interactive as the Canadian-American relationship, a great source of disputes is the failure of decision makers to consider the full external consequences of their actions. Surely this has been illustrated by domestic energy legislation in both countries. Some analysts in Canada have professed surprise at the degree of concern felt in the United States over provisions in the National Energy Program which were regarded by Americans as discriminatory and confiscatory. Certain analysts in the United States expressed amazement that Canada should resist U.S. energy legislation that subsidized the shift from oil to coal by Midwestern electrical utilities, legislation to which Canadians objected because it did not at the same time subsidize the use of stack cleaners or other technology to cut down the coal-fired plant emissions associated with acid rain. In neither case should the governments have found so shocking their neighbor's anxiety about such "strictly domestic" legislation. In the U.S.-Canada relationship, internalities become externalities very quickly; by focusing upon the external political and economic costs of domestic legislation, both governments could reduce the number of disputes on the foreign policy issue agenda and simplify the lives of their foreign negotiators.

Tone

The quality of the general foreign policy atmosphere is described as tone. Tone is not merely the sum of the various foreign policy outcomes in a period; it is not necessarily true that the fewer the unpleasant disputes, the better the tone. Yet, the number and the seriousness of the issues faced by the two countries will affect the tone of the relationship, and the overall tone certainly affects the capacity of the governments to deal with crises and problems of foreign policy. Tone improves when a particularly troubling issue has been resolved satisfactorily. In what, then, does tone consist?

The tone of the foreign policy relationship is largely the result of the kind of leadership provided on each side of the border and the degree to which this leadership is able to command a positive response in the opposite country as well as at home, regardless of what the issue agenda may look like. In a technical sense, this is easier for Washington, which has a greater command of the media and is able to capture the public mood more easily. In a practical sense, however, this seldom occurs, because Washington is unable to separate its projection of foreign policy toward Canada from its general pattern of international relations abroad. The U.S. policy of restricting the flow of arms into El Salvador, for example, raises fears in Ottawa of a possible military intervention on behalf of the junta; the American effort to get tough with the Soviet Union through a grain embargo rebounds in Canada, because Canada is also expected to comply with the embargo. Thus, improving the tone of Canadian-American relations is no easy task for either government, in spite of the positive legacy of resolved disputes.

Governments recognize, however, that although tone may be an end in itself, it is scarcely a sufficient end of foreign policy. If improved tone must come at the cost of state interests associated with specific issues, tone may be sacrificed. For tone to improve, both governments must contribute, although one may take the lead.

CHARACTERISTICS OF THE RELATIONSHIP

In this theoretical overview of Canadian-American external relations, we have so far considered how international systemic equilibria affect the relationship, how certain perceptual dimensions underlie the outlooks of the partners, and how the foreign policy decision-making process deals with issues and the issue agenda. Now we turn to an assessment of the central structural characteristics of the relationship, which give it political meaning that is, perhaps, unique among industrialized countries.

The Interdependence Paradigm

According to prevailing interpretation, the concept of interdependence best describes the relationship.[17] At first glance, this interpretation certainly appears apt. The relationship is definitely not one of power politics—a relationship normally construed as the antithesis of interdependence—because military force does not enter the relationship and does not determine, either in the passive or the active sense, the outcome of disputes regarding issues. Both economies are deeply interwoven in terms of capital flows, migration, and trade. Although many disputes arise, negotiation on various issues is vitually continuous, and, by world standards, the process by which these disputes are resolved is remarkably smooth.

Again by world standards, both governments are rich and highly industrialized, and both have highly developed bureaucracies that facilitate sustained negotiation and finely tuned regulation.

A fundamental improvement in the tone of the U.S.-Canada relationship is difficult to achieve if each partner weights the underlying dimensions of the relationship differently. Disagreement regarding the content and weighting of these dimensions of foreign policy tends to erode the atmosphere. If Canada emphasizes the importance of the psychological-cultural dimension, for example, or the trade-commercial dimension, while the United States tends to view the world in strategic and political terms, the discrepancy in viewpoints on specific issues is likely to be greater and the overall tone of the relationship is likely to suffer. Hence, when commentators talk of "improved relations," they imply either that certain difficult issues have been resolved or that the governments have juggled the weights associated with the underlying dimensions of foreign policy so as to make them more consonant on each side of the border. Resolving issues per se is a short-term panacea; bringing greater agreement to foreign policy outlooks is more difficult, but it is also more lasting. Such agreement will enable the governments to deal with specific issues more expeditiously and will also create an atmosphere in which many foreign policy problems are handled well and promptly enough that they never appear on the foreign affairs issue agenda.

Canada and the United States are also interdependent in that positive developments in one country, such as higher economic growth, tend to spill over into the second country through trade and other flows, contributing to prosperity in the second country; likewise, negative developments, such as inflation or the exaggerated use of monetary instruments to curb inflation, will have effects in both economies simultaneously. Despite these commonplaces of interdependence thought, however, there are a number of reasons to question the unqualified application of the idea of interdependence to the Canadian-American context.

First, if greater interdependence is to be equated with greater cooperation and less conflict, then the U.S.-Canada relationship is not purely interdependent, because, viewed over an interval of several decades of association, closer economic, cultural, and social ties have not reduced the number of issues in dispute between Canada and the United States. Prime Minister Pearson earlier anticipated this situation from the Canadian side with his famous comment on the postwar period: "The era of easy and automatic relations with the United States is over." Similarly, the United States has not found that issues involving Canadian sensitivity and self-interest have become easier to resolve either as a result of increased interaction between individuals and firms on both sides of the border or because public policy tends increasingly to affect both peoples simultaneously.

Interdependence is sometimes assumed to create a greater need for joint coordination of policy; this may indeed occur, but to suppose that such coordination will in fact occur because an atmosphere of cooperation will also emerge, an atmosphere that will facilitate that policy coordination, is probably mistaken.

Closer relations may create greater acrimony, which in turn may lead to more distance in the relationship, followed by a corresponding reduction in tension. This pattern has probably repeated itself many times in the Canadian-American context. As I argued earlier, the tone of the relationship (roughly the ratio of cooperation to conflict) is by no means a strict function of the number of issues at stake, the seriousness of those issues, or the overall closeness of integration between the two economies; all of these things matter but they do not entirely determine the tone. When two sovereign governments are involved, a simple correlation between increased interdependence and improved tone in the foreign policy atmosphere is not likely unless other considerations are also present: better congruence among the underlying dimensions of foreign policy understanding; adroit foreign policy management; and the emergence of institutional buffers that help insulate governments from the friction produced by closer and more frequent interaction.

A second questionable assumption of interdependence in the U.S.-Canada context is that an equality of national capability exists—that the difference in size of the two countries, if recognized, is not relevant politically or is at least psychologically unimportant to the smaller partner. Canadians often feel overwhelmed by the large population of the United States. A simple "thought experiment" highlights this point. If 10 percent of the Canadian population visits the United States at least once during a year, approximately 2.5 million Canadian visits will have occurred. Set against the U.S. population base of 225 million, this welcome tourist inflow will have scarcely been noticed on an individual basis, except perhaps in those few areas, such as Plattsburgh, New York, or Florida, where concentrations of visits may occur. Conversely, if 10 percent of the American population were, by some chance, to visit Canada during a similar interval, on average, one out of every two people in Canada would carry a U.S. passport! Although this might do wonders for the Canadian current account, it would not do wonders for the cultural and political dimension of Canadian-American relations.

Hence, the concept of interdependence must somehow encompass the feelings of dependence that many Canadians feel in numerous areas, including that of environmental affairs, for example, in which the greater size of the U.S. economy creates an inertia of process, if not of policy intent. Excellent neighborly intentions notwithstanding, the United States will continue to produce the bulk of the sludge that enters Lake Erie and the majority of the acid rain that devastates ponds and streams in Quebec. Such technical dependence is a reality that Canadians ask Americans at least to admit; the current notion of interdependence seems to minimize such dependence. But the minimization is less apparent to observers in the United States, where some of the strongest defenders of interdependence reside; this situation creates accusations of hypocrisy against the United States. Despite the idealism of the interdependence thesis, interdependence looks a bit like a subterfuge for dependence to those in the smaller polity.

Third, interdependence notions often convey a sense that cooperation between governments is an outgrowth of structural necessity rather than conscious choice.[18] In this emphasis upon political inevitability, the interdependence theorists are more realistic than the so-called philosophical realists. But how realistic *is* this notion of structural necessity? Surely the presence of high inflation may inspire willingness to coordinate monetary policies more closely, so as to mitigate the global effect of this mutual problem; but the effort to cope with inflation may also stimulate enthusiasm for flexible exchange rate regimes that are self-policing but are also in a way far more autarkic than were the former fixed rates. The existence of a problem does not itself precipitate enthusiasm for joint solutions.

A converse problem with the structural "necessity leads to cooperation" thesis is that it de-emphasizes the human effort and conscious choice involved in improving relations between countries. Governments must work to sustain the tone of the relationship. The myth of interdependence suggests that governments are bound by close ties to improve relations. But the reality of interdependence is that many more things can go wrong than could if governmental policies were less intertwined. The burden on governments who are attempting to conduct policies is appropriately greater with interdependence, not less. More crises develop, more bureaucratic tempers flare, and outcomes are often more precarious in highly interactive situations than in situations in which a bit more foreign policy distance allows pressures to defuse. This does not mean that interdependence ought to be reversed; it does mean that better foreign policy management is critical to the success of the interdependence environment and that such success ought not to be uncritically assumed as a concomitant of structural necessity.

Fourth, interdependence is often taken to mean the absence of the use of power in politics. But absence of military force as an instrument of policy from Canadian-American relations does not mean that political power considerations are totally absent. Insofar as considerations of political power are evident in other areas of U.S. foreign policy and in Canadian federal-provincial relations, for example, this presence raises the question whether power could disappear entirely from the relations between the two governments. If power is the capacity on the part of either government to get the other to do what it would not otherwise do, then the use of power is surely evident in the relationship. For example, when the coast guard of government C arrests the crew of A's fishing boat for trespassing in territorial waters, C has exerted power, especially if the purpose of the action is to obtain a change in A's overall fishing policy. Similarly, if the response on the part of government A is to threaten to cut off imports of fish from C until the boundary situation is clarified, power has again been exerted. I could cite many other examples of the use of economic or political power—some as subtle as leaking a news story to an influential newspaper—to substantiate the claim that power is very much in evidence in the relationship. But what is comparatively unusual about U.S.-Canadian relations by the world standard is how relatively seldom, and with what considerable reluctance, the two governments resort to the use of power to decide outcomes.

Interdependence allegedly precludes transferring the benefits of power use from one issue area to a second. In particular, theorists of interdependence have in mind the seeming difficulty, in the nuclear age, of transferring any meaningful degree of power from the military sphere to other areas of foreign policy activity, such as the economic sphere. Although the nuclear stalemate may have placed constraints on the transference at the highest force levels, transference at the conventional level and below is very much more feasible. When one speaks of the nonforce aspects of power, transference of effects from the political to the cultural or the economic sphere and back again is common.

In the Canadian-American context, for example, the voyage of the S.S. *Manhattan* through the Northwest Passage had as its immediate purpose the demonstration that crude oil could be shipped via this route as an alternative to some combination of pipe lines and West Coast shipping. But the U.S. government might also have seen in this energy venture a transfer of benefits to jurisdictional questions wherein the Northwest Passage could be regarded in certain respects as an international waterway. Conversely, by legislating the Arctic Waters Pollution Prevention Act, which had as its immediate effect the preservation of the northern marine environment, Canada also sought to transfer benefits to the jurisdictional area, thereby demonstrating certain types of national control over the flow of traffic in these waterways. In each case, the respective governments sought to transfer influence from one issue area to others, albeit gradually and implicitly.

Similarly, although the National Energy Program has as its formal justification the promotion of Canadian self-sufficiency in terms of energy as well as other economic motives, both domestic and external, the NEP has equally important political objectives. In other words, the NEP is an economic instrument designed to obtain political ends. One of these domestic political ends is to assist the shift of power from Alberta to the federal government or, at the very least, to forestall the shift of political power in the opposite direction. One of the external political ends of the NEP is to demonstrate a bit more political autonomy between Ottawa and Washington (that is, increased Canadian control) by unilaterally reducing the level of U.S. foreign investment in the energy sector.

Thus, interdependence in the Canadian-American context has not prevented the governments from transferring power effects from one sphere to another. Interdependence may even have facilitated the transfer: first, as in the latter example, by creating a justification for the transfer; or, second, by creating a web of relationships so complex that it necessarily crosses normal economic, cultural, and political categorizations.

Finally, interdependence in the North American setting is scarcely irreversible, despite the doctrine's implications to this effect. Interdependence is as much a normative process as it is a technical or behavioral process. Interdependence may have emerged for technical reasons, but governments permitted this emergence, and governments could, under changed circumstances, limit or reverse the trend toward greater and greater interdependence.

Interdependence exists in equilibrium with a complex of other social and political processes—dependence, co-dependence, autarky, integration, and fragmentation.[19] Interdependence is in competition with all of these other social forces for the sympathy of societies and the attention of governments. Nothing guarantees that, over an interval of several decades, interdependence will triumph over the other processes with which it is in contention. Hence, the friends of interdependence must safeguard and promote the notion, for interdependence is not a proposition that can survive outside the proper intellectual climate.

If the objective is to analyze U.S.-Canada relations (as opposed to using these relations as a canvas upon which to sketch the principles of interdependence), interdependence is a useful metaphor but hardly a sufficient one. U.S.-Canadian relations are both less and more than interdependence implies: less because the total elimination of power politics has not been achieved, and cooperation is not an inevitable structural outgrowth of the network of interaction; more because the relationship is far richer and more dynamic than interdependence alone suggests, far more the result of traditions that are perhaps unique and foreign policy competences that are highly developed than the result of some type of automatic social process. An alternate theoretical framework that is at once truer to the details of Canadian-American politics and more properly focused on the centralities of the relationship thus becomes essential.

A Revised Model of U.S.-Canada Relations

A commonplace of thought about international relations is that because governments find themselves closely entangled in each other's affairs in the latter twentieth century, they are obliged to coordinate policies closely. Although this is certainly descriptive of Canadian-American relations, these relations involve additional characteristics that tend to complicate, if not completely transform, the simple interdependence paradigm. These characteristics are (1) intervulnerability, (2) asymmetry, (3) offsetting bargaining strengths, (4) ambiguity of foreign policy interests, and (5) a tradition of prudence in foreign policy conduct. The theoretical implications of each of these characteristics are important.

Intervulnerability. Because of the scope, closeness, and frequency of intervention at all levels between Canada and the United States, each polity is much more vulnerable to the policy initiatives of the other than they were when interactions were less tight. What is intervulnerability?

Intervulnerability is the cost to partners of one's own domestic policy choices. In a sense, intervulnerability is the opportunity cost of a policy choice, but it is an opportunity cost borne by one's partner. Intervulnerability, in the economist's sense, is a measure of policy externality. It is a bonus, but a negative bonus. Moreover, intervulnerability suggests that, within a two-state relationship, susceptibility to the external impact of the other state's domestic policy choices is mutual. Neither polity can avoid the external impacts of its neighbor's policies, enjoying only the benefits of its own domestic policies. In short, in the age of intervulnerability, there is virtually no distinction in many spheres between domestic and external policy; most policy today has both domestic and external effects. To ignore these effects is to injure one's foreign policy environment and to encourage one's neighbor to do likewise. To comprehend these effects is to improve one's foreign policy environment and thus to encourage one's neighbor to consider possible negative external effects in its decision making about domestic policy.

Essentially, three types of intervulnerability exist in the Canadian-American context. They differ in terms of who bears the costs and of how far the process of cost shifting proceeds.

Type A intervulnerability involves actions by one state which have the effect of improving its welfare or position at the cost of the other partner. Such a consequence may be the intended or unintended result of a domestic policy initiative. The external consequences for the other actor are, in any case, the same. The costs are likely to be both direct and immediate, although more protracted and obscure effects are also possible. Recent policy examples, which are discussed at greater length elsewhere in this book, come to mind.

On the Canadian side, the National Energy Program had some of these features of intervulnerability. Although the official purpose of the NEP was essentially domestic—namely, invigoration of the Canadian oil and gas industry, combined with a more sustained drive toward petroleum self-sufficiency—a number of the provisions of the NEP were discriminatory toward foreign investment, the bulk of which was American, and partially expropriatory in terms of transference of control and ownership of investment already in place. The international criticisms of the NEP were not directed at divestment per se, which is totally acceptable under international law, provided reimbursement is immediate, adequate, and effective, but at the mode that divestment was taking. By discriminating in terms of taxation against foreign-owned companies and by changing the terms of ownership after investment was in place (for example, the NEP stipulates that the federal government will receive 25 percent of revenues generated by foreign-owned companies in the oil and gas industries), Canada was attempting to increase its own share of the oil and gas industry operating in Canada by means of a squeeze on foreign industry. A domestic fiscal and ownership policy thus had immediate negative external effects on a neighbor.

On the American side, the proposed policy of offering incentives to accelerate the conversion to coal of oil-field electrical utilities in the Midwest without insisting upon the use of the latest air pollution technology is an example of this kind of intervulnerability. Although the policy had the acceptable domestic objective of shifting to a more plentiful fuel in an energy-scarce age, it also had the negative side effect of creating more air pollution, much of which might descend upon eastern Ontario and Quebec in the form of acid rain. Whereas the United States was able to save costs in terms of fuel and to avoid a further subsidy to encourage the application of the proper air pollution equipment, Canada was likely to have to absorb the resulting costs of environmental damage to its lakes and streams.

These examples reflect how the attempt to increase one's own welfare may become a cost to a neighbor. Domestic benefits to one polity may translate into external costs to another.

Type B intervulnerability concerns actions by one state that have the effect of improving its welfare or position primarily at the cost of world order or the global economy. A number of security-related examples fall into this category of intervulnerability. In the early 1970s, Canada attempted to withdraw all of its troops from Europe. This was seen inside Canada as a measure of financial prudence; it was perhaps also a signal to the United States and to Western Europe that the cold war was over, international political relationships were more fluid, and Canadian foreign policy was more independent. From the perspective of Western security, however, the proposed withdrawal was viewed somewhat differently. Not only were Canadian troops probably the best trained in Europe, but they performed the function of a "tripwire," revealing the commitment Canada felt toward collective defense and guaranteeing additional support from Canada if Western Europe were threatened by a conventional Soviet attack. That only eight thousand troops were at issue mattered less than that the principle of collective security was upheld. If Canada withdrew its troops, other countries might do the same, and NATO itself might experience a serious erosion of responsibility. Hence, the reasonable Canadian domestic objective of cutting costs spilled over into the regional security system, with potentially damaging consequences.

Similarly, if the United States government succumbed to domestic pressures from certain quarters by slashing financial commitments to the United Nations because of what are viewed as perpetually unfavorable votes within the General Assembly, this would symbolically and perhaps substantively undermine the structure of world order that was established after World War II. Once again, the objective might be to save costs or to increase bilateral influence. But the cost in terms of the erosion of confidence in multilateral institutions could far outweigh the savings to the individual member of the system.

Commercial actions that establish precedents for undermining the Organization for Economic Cooperation and Development (OECD) or the pattern of generalized trade preferences within the GATT may become extremely damaging to the global trading system. Inasmuch as both Canada and the United States are regarded as leading trading nations within the non-Communist system, unilateral actions by either state are always viewed as an index of commitment to the total system of trading arrangements which has evolved since 1945. Incremental unravelling of commitments can ultimately become as damaging as isolated large-scale attacks on the system as a whole.

Type C intervulnerability involves actions by one partner to improve its welfare and position which result in a corresponding action by the other partner, leaving both partners worse off in relation to each other and to the remainder of the international system. This type of inter-vulnerability is the most striking, if only because the mutuality of costs is clearest. Here, efforts by one state to obtain an edge in trading or com-merce are immediately countered by another; the initial action harms the second state, and the subsequent action harms the first state. Conse-quently, both states are now worse off with respect to each other and to the rest of the global trading system than at the onset of the initiatives.

A case in point is the oft-noted dilemma that Canada faces regarding its need to develop more semiprocessing facilities in order to capture a larger portion of the "value added" that accompanies upstream manu-facture. The major obstacle to the location of more semiprocessing in Canada is the structure of U.S. tariffs, which discriminate against manu-factured products but allow raw materials to enter the U.S. market duty free. If these tariffs were to be removed, however, the United States would expect similar tariff removal on Canada's part, for Canada has imposed almost identical tariffs to protect its own industry. Because Canada is unwilling to forego this type of protection, the United States is unwilling to eliminate its own impediments to the free flow of manufac-tures and semimanufactures. In consequence, fewer semiprocessing fa-cilities are built near the source of extraction, where, in some cases, efficiency would be greatest. Hence, both trading partners suffer from impediments to trade which, for varying reasons, neither has the courage to eliminate entirely.

In the current period, the application of various nontariff barriers is far more troublesome than tariffs per se. But the dynamic of reciprocal application is similar. If Canadian utilities, for example, insist on pro-visions that require only Canadian-made (or province-made) materials and equipment to be purchased, the United States is likely to do the same, sometimes in fields that may be more problematic for Canadian exports. If the United States temporarily inhibits the flow of capital into Canada for balance-of-payments reasons, Canada may feel justified in placing restrictions of various kinds on the patriation of profits from U.S. owned enterprises, when such patriation could create balance-of-pay-ments problems for Canada. Similarly, if the United States drags its feet on pipe-line development that is in the medium-term interest of both countries to put into operation, Canada may be encouraged to resist future extension of pipe lines through its territory when the initiative comes from the U.S. side.

Type C intervulnerability is peculiar in that reciprocity exists in the same area as the original initiative. Once reciprocity occurs, both actors are worse off than they were before the initiatives and responses, because the total amount of trade between the countries is reduced; the total flow of capital between the countries is restricted and must be augmented in the Eurodollar Market or elsewhere at a higher interest cost, or the efficiency of joint enterprises, such as pipe-line development, must be foregone; any of these consequences places the Canadian and American economies at a global disadvantage. Attempts at escaping the lesson of this kind of intervulnerability are less tolerable because type C intervulnerability is so obviously compelling for both partners; type C intervulnerability cannot be avoided through concealment or subterfuge. Too much information exists in the Canadian-American context for such tactical evasions to be successful. Careful monitoring of all legislation and executive decision making in both capitals means that the reciprocal character of intervulnerability is reinforced and made virtually automatic.

In short, intervulnerability is a major key to understanding Canadian-American relations. Type A leads to one-sided allocations of costs; type B leads to transference of costs to the Western security or global trading system; type C leads to a situation where costs become reciprocal for both partners. The reason that Canada and the United States must repeatedly bear the costs of these respective vulnerabilities is that they tend to view initiatives in narrow domestic terms rather than considering the true costs for the region as a whole. Because both Cabinet and Congress are more responsive to political representation that is internal to each polity than to that which is external, and because the Department of External Affairs and the Department of State are often left to negotiate outcomes after domestic legislation is in place, the full meaning of intervulnerability is not always conveyed to domestic elites and decision makers soon enough.

One step in reducing the negative consequences of intervulnerability is to improve the monitoring functions in each capital and to decrease the interval between the time that a foreign government first notes legislation that is inimical to its interest and the time that the legislators responsible are informed of the objections. Because foreign interests will never be as fully represented internally as the interests of constituents and domestic pressure groups, regardless of the respective diplomatic corps, the lessons of intervulnerability must be learned again and again. As new governments and administrations come into office, the relearning process must recur. History, in the U.S.-Canada context, is potentially an excellent teacher, provided that analysts of the relationship accurately and systematically convey their information. Nevertheless, the costs of intervulnerability may still have to be experienced from time to time for intervulnerability to seem real.

Asymmetry.   Although broad cultural orientations must always be qualified at the level of the individual, differences between the attitude toward authority found in Canada and that found in the United States are reflected in the respective forms of government—republic as opposed to monarchy. Canadians are more deferential toward authority than Americans; Canadians value order more than Americans and equate liberty less often with freedom.

Given these value preferences, and given that Canada is the smaller polity—in terms of population size, economic size, defense spending, or technological development, if not in terms of territorial size or wealth —Canada is likely to be far more sensitive to the asymmetry of the relationship than Americans. Americans easily identify with equality. They speak of "equality and justice" in the relationship in a sense that seems to go beyond mere equality as subjects of international law. Yet Canadians instinctively perceive the difference in the national capability of the two polities as the primary characteristic of the relationship.

Why do Americans minimize asymmetry while Canadians tend to exaggerate its significance? At base, the United States is a liberal, pluralist culture that views authority somewhat uneasily, and that often exercises power with an accompanying sense of guilt. Americans tend to deny the existence of that with which they are uncomfortable. Conversely, Canada is a much more hierarchically organized society in which the existence of authority is assumed. Given the enormous technical disparities in power between the two countries, Canadians tend to assume the worst about its application in the relationship.

Whether its existence is denied or exaggerated, however, an asymmetry of power between Canada and the United States is present. Americans need to recognize this fact so as to avoid justifiable accusations of hypocrisy. Beyond this recognition, the analyst must decide how important this asymmetry is in determining the nature of outcomes.

In reality, asymmetry is probably much less important than Canadians think and much more important than Americans are willing to admit. On the one hand, the vast disparity in power between the two countries shapes the role of foreign policy decisively. It places the United States at the center of the international political universe and Canada somewhat on the periphery. It means that the United States gets more publicity for its foreign policy than it would like and that Canada gets too little. It means that the United States is the acknowledged leader in many interactions between non-Communist states and, particularly, in interactions with the Soviet Union, and it means that Canada tends to be an acknowledged follower.

On the other hand, in bilateral relations between Canada and the United States, the split in outcomes does not suggest that Canada comes away the perpetual loser, as the disparity in raw power and the Canadian press occasionally suggest. Rather, the split is much more even. The United States tends to prevail on those issues in which it has the greatest stake and about which it feels most strongly affected.[20] These issues typically fall in the military-strategic area. Canada tends to prevail on those issues on which it demonstrates the greatest tenacity and feeling, namely, trade and commercial questions. But neither actor wins all of the outcomes even in its favored set. The United States has not convinced Ottawa of the need to increase its defense spending by a significant percentage; Canada was unable to persuade the United States to push the East Coast Fisheries Treaty through a reluctant Senate even though the negotiations became highly politicized. On those dimensions that Canada and the United States traditionally value strongly, however, the chances of foreign policy success are higher than on the less-favored dimensions.

One of the reasons the disparity in power does not count for more in Canadian-American relations is that Washington has learned to distinguish between the short-term and the long-term goal in making foreign policy with its closest ally. Rarely is a foreign policy goal worth a loss of tone and substance; a prolonged fight would risk serious damage to the relationship. Like the price leader in an oligopolistic, industrial setting in which survival is valued above short-term price maximization, the United States would in most instances prefer to yield or compromise rather than to push a dispute to an extreme conclusion.

Foremost in the mind of U.S. negotiators ought to be an awareness that it is not in the long-term U.S. interest to squeeze as hard as is possible. This is perhaps the most important principle that new administrations in Washington must learn about the relationship. In general, Republican administrations tend to define the U.S. interest more sharply than Democratic administrations, although the matter of competence and the nature of the issue agenda intervene as well. But regardless of partisanship, the United States must continue to recognize that the long term is more important than the short; good and loyal allies have a right to treatment above that accorded the average polity.

Another explanation for why the disparity in power does not appear to have a bearing on outcomes is that Canada sometimes takes this disparity into account implicitly in framing its agenda, especially on multilateral issues. With the reserve of the taciturn counselor, Canada pretends to demand much of the United States but often anticipates obtaining rather little. Canada's true expectations are seldom out of line with its actual capabilities, which is the mark of well-coordinated foreign policy. Disputes tend not to get out of hand, because the stakes are realistic from the beginning. This shrewd assessment of the U.S. position and of the art of the possible is in keeping with the Canadian domestic motto of peace, order, and good government. Even when the United States wanders far from the spirit of this motto, in the estimation of most Canadians, Ottawa has learned to modulate its criticism with a large measure of northern forbearance. Disparities in power never seem to have an effect in such milieux, because the opportunity for testing them is skillfully obviated. Canada's century or so of experience in statecraft as a colony and then as a dominion makes dealing with a mere large neighbor something less than a series of catastrophic events.

Nevertheless, the United States should never forget (as Canadians have never forgotten) the anxiety associated with being politically dominated. This anxiety must be managed, diffused, placated, and otherwise displaced; it can never be eliminated entirely. Moreover, if the United States wants "good relations" and "cooperation," it must recognize the limits of foreign policy concession which a sovereign and autonomous polity can tolerate. The United States ought also to recognize that it must keep in check the full weight of policies stemming from disparities in power if the relationship that the United States idealizes over the long term is to be sustained.

Offsetting Bargaining Strengths.   Academic writers in Canada and America sometimes do not understand that Canada enjoys a number of bargaining strengths that tend to counteract the reality of asymmetry. First is the manner in which each government focuses its foreign policy attention. Because the United States perceives its responsibilities in global terms, it tends to focus upon events that threaten world order or that shape global trade policy. This focus draws the United States directly into disputes in Africa, the Middle East, and Asia that are extremely time consuming and demanding of foreign policy energies. Conversely, Canada tends to define its relations with the United States as its major foreign policy "problem." This means that Canada's foreign policy energies are concentrated on a single target rather than diffused, and its attention is comparatively unbroken by the shifts and vacillations of international events. Because foreign policy attention is finite, and because the competition among issues allows only a few issues to occupy the top levels of governmental thought at any one time, Canada is at a considerable advantage in dealing with the United States. The full weight of Canada's attention can be employed in its negotiations with the United States on fisheries agreements, for example, whereas U.S. attention is often much more inconsistently applied. Distracted by events such as the hostage crisis with Iran, the United States may be more prone to err in negotiation. Greater concentration usually leads to better results at the individual as well as the governmental level.

Second, resources are distributed in a way that often favors Canada in bargaining. For example, the Canadian embassy in Washington is far larger than the U.S. embassy in Ottawa, by a ratio of perhaps four or five to one, which allows for greater specialization, more complete development of reports, and more effective monitoring of issues. At the same time, matters involving the United States are probably handled at a higher bureaucratic level in Canada than are matters involving Canada in the United States. This means that Canada is able to apply more political leverage inside its own government to deal with bilateral issues, thereby obtaining more bureaucratic responsiveness and providing its negotiators with the edge of flexibility. The comparative efficiency of the two civil services in processing of bilateral issues is well known; Canada can alter its terms in a negotiation with far more rapidity and certainty than can the United States, in part because the cabinet form of democracy facilitates this type of decision making. The government that devotes more bureaucratic resources to bilateral issues and enjoys more flexibility in decision making is likely to be at an advantage in many bargaining situations.

Third, Canada can often bring more evidence of constituent support to the bargaining table than the United States can. During political negotiation, the capacity to demonstrate the support of one's public is very helpful. It suggests legitimacy. Indeed, perhaps the best example of this is the contrast between the durability of Canadian governments in the twentieth century and the considerable fluctuation in the leadership of U.S. administrations, especially in the last two decades (Eisenhower was the last president to complete two terms of office). But a demonstration of public support can also be used to argue that one's "hands are tied" and that one cannot back down on a negotiating stance. In contrast, the American public is less involved in bilateral matters than the Canadian public, which often allows Canada to point out that because an issue has become of national concern in Canada and not in the United States, it is apparently more important to Canada. Because the U.S. electorate is often less informed and less concerned about bilateral issues than the Canadian electorate, Canadian government negotiators can confront Washington on grounds that seem to justify greater U.S. concessions.

In short, the disparity in national capability between the United States and Canada is often offset in actual negotiations by greater Canadian institutional and political bargaining strengths. These strengths help further explain why, in practice, the outcomes of negotiations between the two countries split rather evenly.

Ambiguity of National Interests. American observers of Canada frequently make the mistake of believing that Canadian and American interests are identical. This conclusion is a natural outgrowth of geographic proximity, of the superficial similarity between the characteristics of the two populations, and of the congruence of popular tastes. What this assessment of national interest neglects is the fundamental difference in cultural outlook between the two countries, the difference in institutional and historical ethos (despite equally strong commitments to democracy), and the difference in foreign policy role.

On the other hand, Canadian observers of the United States sometimes draw the equally erroneous conclusion that the interests of the two countries are largely opposed. This conclusion stems in part from the temptation to define Canadian interests in terms of the interests of the United States rather than in terms of self-standing factors that are authentically Canadian. Canadian interests, in other words, are sometimes erroneously regarded as everything that American interests are not.

Observers may also draw a false disparity between Canadian and American interests by assuming that if the two governments reach the same conclusion, the United States must have applied pressure to get Ottawa to change its views. This notion is as much a misunderstanding of power as it is of interest. Power is the capacity of one actor to get a second actor to do what it would not voluntarily do. If Canada happens to come to essentially the same conclusion as the United States regarding an international event, the agreement is in itself no indication that power has been exerted in the relationship; it is not impossible that the Canadian interest should occasionally approximate the American interest.

Despite some differences in nuance, the two countries view their interests in similar ways. A more genuine difference in outlook stems from the attitude toward means. Both governments stress the commitment to a stable world order. Both support the liberal international trade system and have important commercial interests abroad. Both believe in democratic values and defend these values in international forums as well as at home. Both governments are committed to the defense of North America and have demonstrated twice in this century that they regard their own security as ultimately inseparable from that of Western Europe. But here the nuances begin to become important.

Canada is far more conscious of the need for political order domestically and abroad than is the United States, yet Canada seems far less prepared to use force to back up this preference. For example, Canada has taken a lead in most international disarmament conferences and opposes the use of military intervention to resolve disputes. Canada has also been much more avant-garde in its relations with China, Cuba, and Eastern Europe than has the United States, opposing U.S. sanctions against some of these regimes and anticipating U.S. recognition in other cases. How can these apparent differences in state interest be explained?

In explaining the different attitudes toward means, one need not go much further than to consider the effect of asymmetry on state interests.

Asymmetry determines that Canada, a middle power, will occupy a different foreign policy role than the United States, the principal actor in the non-Communist alliance system. More dependent upon the security of others, Canada is more aware of the tenuousness of nuclear deterrence. More flexible in its role as a middle power, Canada can be more innovative in its foreign policy. The United States must adopt a more conservative stance because greater responsibility falls on its shoulders not only in times of crisis but also in the generation of a security policy that is acceptable to all of the members of NATO and to principal bilateral alliance partners, such as Japan.

In broad matters of security, the United States must take the lead, whereas Canada can afford to assume the role of critic and counselor. It is in Canada's interest to find a diplomatic stage upon which it can best perform. Previously, the United Nations provided such a stage, because Canada could act as a mediator between East and West on arms-control issues and could perform peace-keeping functions on behalf of the legitimized authority of the United Nations. But with the decline of the global peace-keeping function in the face of greater regional assertiveness and with disappointments associated with maintaining a seemingly perpetual military presence in such locales as Cyprus and the Sinai, Canada has sought other foreign policy roles that are still in keeping with its overall state interests.

To some extent, the shift in voting majority within the U.N. General Assembly toward the Third World has both taken a prior responsibility away from Canada and created a new responsibility. This shift means that Canada can less usefully mediate East-West questions, because these are fought less and less often on U.N. turf. But the gap between the North and South perspectives within the system is approaching the gap that existed decades earlier between East-West perspectives. Canada identifies with the plight of many Third World countries because of the resource focus of its economy and its experience with industry that is controlled from abroad. Yet Canada is an advanced industrial country and a member of the non-Communist industrial club. Canada is thus poised to interpret Third World grievances and to communicate these to the leading industrial nations of the North.

To some extent, the different attitudes toward means in foreign policy are explained by the means that are at a country's disposal. In terms of foreign policy instruments, Canada has an advantage shared by virtually no other middle power. Because of its proximity to the United States and because of the similarity of its state interests, Canada has the confidence of the United States. This confidence can be parlayed into influence on the world stage by getting the United States to adopt a perspective on multilateral issues that it might, by itself, not acquire or might acquire only belatedly. Although Canada chooses to use this leverage with discretion, its power to do so still counts for a great deal in world politics today. By assuming a position on a number of security-related issues which makes it appear the villain, the United States creates an opportunity for Canada to appear far more ethical and enlightened in its own initiatives. Some of the same type of moralism that exists in the thinking of many Canadians (which, at its best, is capable of producing the highest ideals of collective diplomacy) is very much an element of American social and political thought as well. Is it too much to suppose that if the asymmetry of power were inverted, the diplomatic roles of the two countries would reverse? And if the roles reversed, is it implausible to speculate that the United States would then become the critic of the use of force, intervention, and of the strategies of maintaining order that Canada, in turn, might have chosen to use in this same post-World War II period? Such hypotheses are untestable, but students of statecraft have, in any case, an obligation to reflect upon such counterfactuals.

State interests are ambiguous guides to foreign policy conduct, especially in the bilateral setting. They are particularly ambiguous because Canada and the United States choose to distort them. But this distortion has itself become one of the characteristics of the relationship. A key tension in the relationship is the conflict between the U.S. struggle to deny that any difference exists between the way the two countries view means and ends and Canada's struggle to show that the difference is so fundamental as to be, in some cases, unbridgeable. I argue that the propensity for distortion of state interests is perhaps more important analytically than the nature of the state interests themselves, for they are, by world standards, rather commonplace. Distortion is just as important as political reality, because when distortion or misperception shapes policy, it becomes reality. This is as true for Canada and the United States today as for any other dyad of countries in the system.

Tradition of Prudence in the Conduct of Foreign Policy.   U.S.-Canadian relations have not always been as pacific as they now are, but a longer tradition of unbroken peace exists in North America than in Europe, Asia, or Africa. Since U.S. independence, the United States and Canada (British North America) have exchanged blows only once with any consequence—during the War of 1812. During the primary incidence of the Fenian Raids, 1858-66, a few U.S. citizens disrupted the peace of Canada, and during the Civil War, a few Canadian citizens took part in the belligerency. But with these exceptions and for more than a century, force has not seriously entered the strategic calculations of either government toward the other. The Alaska boundary dispute of 1903 was the last earnest border disagreement; its settlement established forever the boundaries between the two countries in clear and legally recognized terms. Part of the tolerance the two governments have shown toward each other stems from the eventual formal acceptance of these boundaries, boundaries that were themselves sometimes arrived at in a stormy political atmosphere. Demilitarization of the Great Lakes and the St. Lawrence has helped perpetuate the nonbelligerent quality of the relationship in a physical sense. But the key to the peaceful character of the relationship lies deeper in the cultural heritage of the two peoples.

In terms of its attitude toward lawful behavior and conflict resolution, Canada is one of the most civilized countries in the world today. Canada's lack of a revolutionary past, its inculcation of the principles of responsible government, and its careful balancing of regional and Anglo-French interests all contribute to a firm but controlled approach to government. Although the United States experiences far more domestic political turmoil than Canada and relies upon the application of force more consistently in its foreign policy, neither of these characteristics affects its relationship to Canada. For many Americans, this pacific outlook toward Canada stems from the ironic belief that "Canadians are just like Americans." Because one does not consider using force against oneself, the use of force by Americans against Canadians becomes unthinkable. The outlook also stems from an awareness that Canada presents no security threat whatsoever to the United States. Thus, neither Canada nor the United States presently conceives of a situation in which force could enter the relationship.

Prudence in the conduct of bilateral relations has, however, a still deeper origin. Without concealing its foreign policy preferences, Canada has been careful not to challenge American sensibilities too vigorously on multilateral issues, while reserving the greatest candor for bilateral disagreements. This emphasis is understood in Washington. By downplaying multilateral disagreements, Canada obtains greater leverage in Washington on bilateral issues. Although all of this is implicit, it is nonetheless effective. An immediate quid pro quo for the Canadian assistance in the Iranian hostage crisis, for example, was neither required nor expected. Such an expectation would have been much too crude and obviously self-serving. Yet the hostage crisis, like other multilateral issues, created an atmosphere and a political chit that later—perhaps much later—would have considerable value in bilateral negotiations.

Not all multilateral issues possess this quality of transferable influence, however; only those issues on which the Canadian interest differs from the American interest have this quality. Great confusion seems to accompany this point, especially in the Canadian press. The United States, for example, could scarcely regard mutual pressure on the Soviet Union with regard to the Afghanistan invasion in the same light as the hostage crisis. Except for the international legal implications concerning rights of diplomatic immunity, the hostage crisis was primarily an issue involving U.S. interests. In contrast, the Afghanistan invasion imperiled all of Western security to the same degree, Canadian equally with American. Canada could not expect (and the Canadian government did not expect) special recognition from the United States for supporting action that warned the Soviet Union of the seriousness of its aggression. The matter of advance consultation about the nature of appropriate action was a legitimate concern for Canada. But an understanding of how each polity views its own interests is critical to analysis regarding whether bilateral influence is likely to emerge from a particular policy stance.

Anxiety in the United States over the strength of Canadian unity has caused the American government to walk softly during periods of internal Canadian tension. Ottawa has not always sought to ease the American anxiety. The normal prudence in the conduct of foreign policy of the two actors thus acquires an even more silent quality in periods when federal-provincial relations are most stormy. A measure of the impact that the Quebec Referendum issues, for example, had on Washington was the abnormal reluctance of U.S. high officials to comment even privately on the political significance of this matter for the bilateral relationship.

When the federal-provincial struggle is noisiest, Ottawa is least disposed to press hard on its bilateral foreign policy interests; this pattern of behavior is nicely paralleled in Washington, for similar reasons, in terms of U.S. interests. The fear of some Canadians that Washington would try to take advantage of Canadian weakness in periods of Canadian political disunity is a serious misunderstanding of how American foreign policy is actually conducted and of American long-term priorities.

In sum, the U.S.-Canada relationship can be analyzed in terms of five characteristics: intervulnerability, asymmetry, offsetting bargaining strengths, ambiguity of foreign policy interests, and an enduring propensity, by world-wide standards, to conduct foreign policy with great prudence. This places the interdependence paradigm in a somewhat different light, because we emphasize the function of both tradition and rational choice rather than emphasizing structural determinism in explaining, at a theoretical level, the peculiarities of Canadian-American relations. These peculiarities themselves require further assessment, however, because the uniqueness of U.S.-Canada relations is often debated.

TACTICAL TOOLS OF STATECRAFT

Linkage

Newcomers to U.S.-Canada relations tend to look fondly upon the idea of using linkage as a means of obtaining greater leverage in foreign policy dealings with the opposite partner. Linkage appears as a supposedly untried but promising means of accelerating the flow of benefits in the bargaining setting. In the formal sense, linkage is the explicit effort to tie progress in one issue area to progress in a second, completely separate issue area. Unless benefits are obtained from a partner in the first area, no concessions will be forthcoming in the second. Thus linkage attempts to cross issue areas and to transfer the bargaining process from a focus within issues to a focus between issues. Linkage looks like an inexpensive technique to multiply political benefits and to constrain political costs.

The reason newcomers to Canadian-American relations seem more interested in linkage than more experienced observers is manifold. First, they are frequently unaware that linkage is in fact a comparatively old idea, with a history of some application. Recently, for example, the U.S. Congress tied U.S. concessions on the convention-tax issue to Canadian concessions on the Canadian television-advertising issue. Canada had disallowed tax breaks for Canadian companies who advertise on U.S. television stations that reach Canadian viewers and had deleted U.S. commercials on cable television.[21] After years of comparatively fruitless negotiation, the United States finally obtained concessions on Canadian taxes in another area (a reduction in the tax rate on revenue earned by U.S.-owned companies in Canada) in return for solving the convention-tax problem, but no concessions were made to U.S. media advertisers on programs broadcast to Canadians. Other examples of linkage appear from time to time, promoted in most cases by enthusiastic domestic interest groups.

Second, newcomers fail to recognize that linkage is being touted on *both* sides of the border as a panacea. But linkage works, if it works at all, only if it is practiced on one side at a time. If it is attempted simultaneously on both sides, especially when the issue area at stake is tied to completely different issue areas on opposite sides of the border, linkage becomes a recipe for chaos.

Third, those who are new to the relationship fail to understand how debilitating linkage is in the long run for both partners. Linkage is a formula for the absence of progress in negotiations, not for the furtherance of progress. Governments ought to use linkage in negotiations with opponents when the objective is to stall negotiations—linkage may enable one to assert that one's hands are tied—not among friends when genuine progress is sought. Linkage is a technique to frustrate negotiations for a variety of reasons, not to accelerate them.

One of the reasons that linkage slows down negotiations is that diplomats have a difficult time dealing with interest groups from different issue areas. How can a State Department officer explain to a labor union lobbyist that benefits in automobile employment have been traded for progress in East Coast energy exchanges? Similar problems may occur in Canada, although, because the political process is more hierarchical and closed in Canada, interest group trade-offs may be less climactic than in the U.S. Congress.

Large-scale deals such as linkage demands, inevitably force the losers on each side of the border into public and embarrassing positions, forcing them to protect their legitimacy by putting more pressure on government elsewhere. Linkage is the kind of process which attracts newspaper coverage; high visibility of this type in time reduces the flexibility available to negotiators.

In general, the tactic of linkage may create short-term advantages for the United States, but may do so at long-term costs. More levers to apply linkage exist on the U.S. side of the border than in Canada, although high-ranking government officials in Canada have also occasionally advocated using linkage. In the longer run, the United States will not benefit if the tone of the relationship suffers because of the use of linkage and if a backlog of issues develops, which is possible because linkage in effect brings negotiation to a standstill.

Linkage works well in a legislative process in which vote trading is a well-established tradition and in which personal contacts among legislators facilitate the creation of complex deals. But in the more arms-length negotiations across borders, in which publicity intervenes and national pride as well as sectoral and regional competition become obstacles, linkage is much too complicated and bruising a process to lead to consistent success. An overt practice of linkage is likely to further erode the traditions of mutual respect and orderly procedure which have long been a part of the Canadian-American relationship.

This analysis is made more precise in theoretical terms by distinguishing between bargaining in one issue area that is explicitly, as opposed to implicitly, tied to another issue area and bargaining that involves demands for concession, as opposed to simple offers of concession. The most objectionable kind of linkage is *mandatory linkage,* in which the connected issues are explicitly stated, bargaining has become thoroughly routinized, and governments make any concessions on their part depend on satisfaction of specific demands for concession on one issue area. *Voluntary linkage* is less objectionable because concessions are "voluntarily" offered by one partner to the other, although bargaining on linked issue areas remains routinized and is therefore still a complicating mechanism and a negative precedent.

Much more acceptable are arrangements in which no specific ties between issue areas are identified. In *open issue trading,* demands on a variety of issues are articulated and the partner is left to decide how to mix and match these across issue areas (implicit bargaining). Even more desirable is *accelerated bargaining,* a situation in which a government offers concessions in several areas simultaneously if the partner is willing to make corresponding concessions of his own choosing. Accelerated bargaining does not carry the sting of demands, nor does it legitimize and routinize the process of bargaining in linked issue areas. Instead, it is an approach that tries to place a series of issues on the agenda simultaneously to clear the agenda more quickly and to improve the overall tone of the relationship. Concessions are not unilateral; they must be matched in order to become effective. But the concessions come in the form of offers, rather than in response to demands, and any bargaining on linked issues that takes place is voluntary and left to the partner to interpret in causal terms. Accelerated bargaining operates using "package deals" and is completely compatible with the ideal of noncoercive and open negotiating processes, an ideal familiar in the Canadian-American relationship.

In short, simultaneous negotiation on a series of fronts is traditional and acceptable. Progress in one area will lead to a general improvement of the overall political atmosphere and possibly to progress in other areas. But linkage that is mandatory and specific as to demands is likely to generate more stalemates, bad publicity, irritation, and feelings of being dominated than do other more proven negotiating techniques. Linkage is not for the experienced tactician of U.S.-Canada relations, whatever its merits in bargaining with the Soviet Union or other similar governments.

Politicization

When *Principles for Partnership* appeared in 1965, that report, better known as the Merchant-Heeney Report, after the names of its American and Canadian authors, advocated "quiet diplomacy."[22] Ironically, Canadians have endorsed the idea of quiet diplomacy less confidently than Americans, even though quiet diplomacy describes the procedures of responsible government rather than those of presidential democracy. In Canada there was a sense that quiet diplomacy meant strictures on expression and that Canada might come out the loser. Canadians worried that the recommendations to handle disputes through private diplomatic channels might serve to muzzle opposition to American diplomatic initiative. Periodically, proponents on both sides of the border have sought to use the press and public opinion to further diplomatic initiatives. But politicization as a hypothetical tool in U.S.-Canada relations has generally held more appeal in Canada than in the United States. How can one explain this differential appeal?

Part of the explanation for the difference of views may be that Americans, because of the nature of presidential democracy, have had more experience with politicization, particularly with its negative aspects, than have Canadians. A negotiating tactic may have more appeal in the abstract than in practice.

According to the model of those who advocate this approach, politicization is supposed to enable the negotiator to use press coverage, noisy legislative debate, and ultimately the weight of public opinion to gain leverage in negotiations. Most of this activity is supposed to occur in the home country. But if the negotiator can also demonstrate the degree of concern the citizens of his own country feel regarding an issue by means of favorable press coverage in the opposite country, public opinion in the opposite country may become more sympathetic; more sympathetic opinion abroad may generate pressure on that government to become more lenient in negotiations or to act with more dispatch. If this is the model that proponents of politicization have in mind, it is flawed in numerous respects.

First, the spectacle of public outcry against the policies of a neighbor is not likely to induce sympathy within that neighbor's body politic for one's own policies. Such an outcry induces nationalistic impulses that are difficult to control and consequences that may have the opposite of the intended purpose. It creates hostility with respect not only to the particular issue at hand but also to totally unrelated issues. It makes compromise politically far tougher for both sides, not easier. In this sense, politicization becomes the antithesis of good negotiating procedure, because it forecloses options and forces governments into more belligerent stands.

Second, because of the proximity of the two countries and because of the high degree of information flow between them, politicization that originates within the general population and that is therefore a genuine factor to be considered politically can easily be distinguished from politicization that is contrived by government leaks or other sponsorship. One government cannot fool the other by manipulations of public opinion when no genuine groundswell of opinion is at work. Politicians on both sides are experts in the fine democratic art of sensing the public mood; they are likely not only to discount false opinion but also to move against a government that attempts to mislead in this fashion.

Third, two can play the game of politicization. Whereas Canadians are likely to be more easily aroused by issues of a bilateral nature than Americans, American institutions lend themselves to politicization more readily than the Canadian. Moreover, the American press is admirably suited to spread alarm concerning hostility to U.S. policies abroad. Once aroused, however, U.S. opinion is not easily controlled and may end up stimulating Congress to take actions that are clearly not in the long-term interest of either Canada or the United States. Protectionism, for example, is always a possible defensive mechanism in answer to perceived hostility abroad.

Thus, politicization is scarcely useful as a technique to demonstrate how strongly a polity feels regarding an item of bilateral negotiation. For this purpose, politicization tends to backfire. Politicization does, however, have one useful subsidiary value, which has been used on occasion for circumscribed political advantage and which is therefore tolerated for this purpose by the political leadership in both countries. If local elites become too vociferous in political criticism of their own diplomatic representatives, a few widely publicized "tough" speeches in the local press may do a lot to restore confidence. This action is not self-serving; it is sometimes a necessary part of the legitimization process during a period of protracted negotiations, when local politicians and the press tend to oversimplify solutions and to become frustrated at the slow pace of negotiations. Such an effort to restore credibility at home is always tolerated in a sophisticated bargaining setting. Politicization within limits is thus permissible if not overused. But as a general tactic to put pressure on a bargaining partner, politicization is a mistake not only because it will fail but also because it is harmful to the underlying traditions and norms of the relationship.

Reciprocity and Retaliation

Apart from occasional outbreaks of altruistic passion, Canada and the United States behave toward each other less like saints than like publicans. They tend to return good for good and evil for evil; seldom do they respond with good regardless of the nature of the initiative on the other side. Outright malevolence is also absent. For our purposes here we characterize the exchange of good for good as *reciprocity* and the exchange of bad for bad as *retaliation*. Both reciprocity and retaliation have long been descriptive of tactics in the relationship.

Reciprocity has acquired the too-narrow connotation of reciprocal tariff reduction under the banner of liberal free trade. In reality, the tactic of reciprocity is a far broader phenomenon. Reciprocity covers the range from executive to legislative actions and from political to commercial actions. Reciprocity is characterized by, for example, the willingness of each polity to accept the political and economic fugitives of the other. Canada, of course, accepted Loyalists in large numbers after the American Revolution and U.S. "draft dodgers" during the Vietnam War. The United States has accepted large numbers of Canadians during periods of severe economic depression in Canada. The United States also gave de facto temporary sanctuary to Louis Riel and William Lyon Mackenzie when they were political fugitives.

Reciprocity was evident in the old Reciprocity Treaty, which was abrogated in 1866 and which established tariff conditions between Canada and the United States.[23] The nature of tariff negotiations in 1911 also gives evidence of how reciprocity proceeds. Canada favored a tariff agreement in natural products only; the United States wanted to include a comprehensive list of manufactures. The United States relented by accepting a specific rather than a comprehensive list of manufactures; Canada relented by including manufactured as well as natural products. Concessions on one side yielded concessions on the other. When reciprocity works properly, the overall tone of relations improves markedly.

Retaliation is not a more common tactic than reciprocity, but it is more highly publicized. Examples of retaliation are familiar in various contexts. In 1974, Canada banned American beef exports to Canada on the grounds that the chemical DES had contaminated American beef.[24] When negotiations led to a certification program but the Canadian ban still was not lifted, the United States declared a ban on Canadian beef exports. When Canadian government officials took the East Coast Fisheries debate to the press in the spring of 1981, a U.S. government official responded by sending a letter that emphasized the U.S. position to a prominent Canadian newspaper. When, set against the backdrop of constraints on U.S. investment in Canada, Canadian investors attempted, in several highly publicized efforts, to take over American firms, the U.S. government signaled its displeasure by changing the rules concerning margin requirements for borrowing purposes, making the rules the same for both foreign and domestic investors. Other examples of direct or implied retaliation also exist. When Nova Scotia gave a grant in 1975 to the French Michelin Tire Company to locate in Nova Scotia, the United States placed countervailing duties on Canadian tires entering the United States, because, it was argued, the primary purpose of the Michelin decision was to export into the American market.

In most cases, retaliation is technically easier for the United States to implement because its greater relative size gives it more opportunities and somewhat lower vulnerability. On the other hand, Canada is much more efficient at reversing policies or implementing new policies. This tactical flexibility gives Canada advantages in bargaining, because it can demand much more at the beginning of a negotiation, knowing that subsequent concessions can be accommodated by the greater discipline exercised by its political institutions. If U.S. retaliation carries greater clout in some areas of the relationship than does Canadian retaliation, this is not necessarily true in matters concerning private foreign investments.

Because the United States has so much more investment in Canada than Canada has in the United States, U.S. foreign investment in Canada is held hostage. This is quite the opposite argument from that heard among Canadian economic nationalists, who assert dependence on the United States because of foreign ownership and control. High concentration of U.S. foreign investment in Canada has made retaliation against this investment quite feasible. Even the threat of retaliation against U.S. firms operating inside Canada is effective. Of course, in a linkage situation or in a situation with or without linkage in which escalation of retaliatory acts proceeds, the United States is likely to prevail. But such a sequence of events might so poison the diplomatic setting that ultimate outcomes would look foolishly costly to both parties. Thus, the full weight of retaliation is probably not likely to fall in matters of foreign investment; at the margin, U.S. foreign investment remains vulnerable to Canadian government pressure.

The United States may have advantages in terms of how necessary the U.S. market is to Canadian exports—the exports of manufactured goods being especially and increasingly important—but both Canada and the United States must recognize how damaging the use of retaliation is in the eyes of the average citizen abroad. Repeated use of retaliation is likely to worsen diplomatic relations in a way that isolated or occasional use will not. Retaliation establishes the limits to unilateral action and therefore is probably functional, provided that it is not used excessively. Certainly, neither Canada nor the United States can expect a major initiative that has a negative impact on the other partner to go unanswered. But reciprocity is a far firmer basis for improved relations between the two countries than is retaliation. Retaliation may achieve a reversal of specific policy, but the cost may be an erosion of the general political atmosphere. A relationship primarily preoccupied with the repeated use of retaliatory tactics is likely to grow tense and unproductive of mutually beneficial initiatives.

Why does retaliation occur at all? Two explanations are plausible. First, some legislators, cabinet officials, or ministers of state may think narrowly in terms of domestic political interests, and because external actors are incapable of employing electoral sanctions, their interests can safely be ignored. Isolationist wings of political parties and spokesmen for nationalist perspectives will always find external interests, even in a close partnership (or perhaps especially in such a partnership), easy to sacrifice. Retaliation is thus often precipitated when domestic elites attempt to get governments to view the national interest in an untraditionally chauvinistic fashion.

Second, retaliation occurs when government officials themselves try to slip a particularly heavy-handed item of legislation past the other partner without consultation. This is not a case of a government being forced to bow to powerful internal interest groups. Instead, it is a situation in which an assertive bureaucracy, which is perhaps somewhat new to the way in which the relationship has evolved, attempts to outwit counterparts abroad by tactics more suitable in political contexts in which information flow is less complete and in which norms of external conduct are less well established. Having exhausted other techniques, the other partner feels retaliation is the only way it can register its sense of unfair treatment.

Reciprocity and retaliation have become commonly accepted, although seldom-discussed, tools of the relationship. They symbolize a single monumental reality. In the present context of intervulnerability, neither government can pass domestic political legislation or adopt diplomatic procedures without full regard for the impact of this legislation or these procedures on the other partner. To some extent, this rule prevails for all members of the global trading system today, especially for the non-Communist members of the system. But reciprocity and retaliation are, in particular, a reality for the governments that are politically sovereign yet closely interdependent in economic terms. Since no other pair of actors in the international system combines these attributes of political sovereignty and economic interdependence to the degree that Canada and the United States do, it follows that reciprocity and retaliation are likely to be indigenous to the relationship. Once again, however, we are confronted with the question of how unusual the U.S.-Canada relationship really is and whether its difference from other relationships is perhaps one of degree only.

HOW SPECIAL IS THE SPECIAL RELATIONSHIP?

Part of the confusion that surrounds the special relationship idea stems from definition and content. One can conceptualize the special relationship in essentially two ways: either as structure or as policy. Although policy can generate structure and structure may facilitate policy, the two theoretical categories do not overlap.

At the structural level, the U.S.-Canada relationship can be thought of as special because of the scope and depth of the interactions between the two countries. Scope refers to the number and variety of activities that emerge in one polity and impinge upon the other. These encompass the entire range from cultural and linguistic activities to economic and military-strategic activities. Not only is the scope broad, but the interactions are usually not trivial. They reach down into the fabric of each society, especially the Canadian. This depth of interaction makes bilateral relations all the more difficult, because of the intervulnerability of the two political systems. Scope combined with depth means that large sectors of the populations of both countries are affected by these interactions all of the time.

Over time, the issues that come up for attention shift, because neither the scope nor the depth of interaction is static. Yet, because the scope and depth of interaction have perhaps increased, the number of issues that the two governments must resolve each year has not declined. Fisheries questions, for example, have been on the agenda at least since the Treaties of Utrecht (1711), which ended the wars with Louis XIV, yet the nature and geographic focus of these questions changes. As the territorial waters are extended, even the border issue itself returns, although in a different form with regard to new types of jurisdictions. The major point is that few other countries can demonstrate a scope and depth of interaction that matches that found in the Canadian-American relationship.

Another structural aspect of the special relationship is the pacific nature of the relations, which was mentioned earlier. It would be difficult to assert that no other pair of proximate countries has enjoyed as long a period of nonviolent interaction. The range of candidates, however, is probably limited to South America. Although South America has, in general, a magnificent record of peaceful coexistence among countries, its record of orderly governmental procedure within countries is just the opposite. Canada and the United States have combined peaceful relations between the governments with orderly internal governmental procedures, although the U.S. record, based on its own cultural and social peculiarities, is marred by the Civil War and one other factor: the United States has suffered one of the worst records of presidential assassinations and assassination attempts of any modern country. Although the consequences of this problem of violence may unavoidably have impinged upon the Canadian-American relationship, the problem is of itself only of comparative interest.

In terms of cross-border violence, U.S.-Canada relations have not been marred by any significant use of force since 1812. Although Mackenzie King may have been right to challenge the authenticity of the "undefended border" as envisioned in the Rush-Bagot Agreement of 1817, few immediate neighbors can demonstrate such a degree of political openness.

A further structural justification for the label *special* is the extensiveness of bureaucratic and private-sector activity. The political significance of this extensiveness is that a large portion of the decisions that are normally funneled to the top of the governmental decision hierarchy are dealt with instead, in the Canadian-American context, either by lower-level governmental officials or by the private sector on both sides of the border. This means that fewer disputes come to the attention of the Cabinet or the White House. It also means that the prime minister and the president must share, implicitly, some of their decision-making authority with the private sector and with career civil servants. A great deal has been made of how responsive governmental officials are, in Canada and in the United States, to discussions over the telephone. If one were to calculate the amount of transgovernmental business that is handled through informal contacts outside formal channels, the results might surprise both governments and analysts. None of this is unique to North America. But the weight of the lower-level bureaucracy and of the private sector in most matters of cross-border trade, commerce, and political interaction is not paralleled elsewhere. Although it is interesting to speculate about whether

Canadians or Americans make the largest use of this truly extraordinary decision-making network, I suspect that both sides use this network about equally. Communications can sometimes become snarled if formal channels are circumvented, but by and large Canadians and Americans have added an enormous amount of efficiency to the relationship by pragmatically relying upon these large, informal communications and transactions networks.

Finally, at the strategic level, the relationship is special because of the existence of so many institutional buffers. By institutional buffer I mean the more than 180 bilateral treaties that regulate every manner of transboundary exchange and the dozen or so commissions, working groups, and committees that serve to protect the sovereignty of the two countries while providing a continuum of discourse. The most famous of these buffers, the International Joint Commission (IJC) (1909) is also among the oldest and most institutionalized. But other functionally specific buffers with greater or lesser degrees of permanence have also emerged: International Pacific Halibut Commission (1923); International Boundary Commission (1925); International Pacific Fisheries Commission (1937); Committee on Trade and Economic Affairs (1953); North American Defence Command (1958); Senior Committee on Defence Production / Development Sharing (1958); Balance of Payments Committee (1963); and the Canada-U.S. Interparliamentary Group (1959); as well as a number of others.

At least two principles seem to underlie the creation of these buffers, as epitomized by the International Joint Commission. First, the tasks of these institutions are narrowly defined and limited to a single functional area. The objective is not to try to create superagencies that encompass broad areas of jurisdiction with major legislative powers. Second, Canada and the United States have legal and operational equality on these boards and commissions. This is important because the recommendations have a voluntary character and must reflect accurate and fair assessments of problems and solutions.

I am not suggesting that other countries do not participate in bilateral arrangements of various types. Nor am I suggesting that these institutionalized buffers are determinative of overall Canadian-American foreign policy decision making. What I do argue is that the number and variety of commissions and boards contributes to the special nature of the relationship in that they impart to the relationship a commitment to equality and pragmatic specificity that is missing in a number of other bilateral settings.

At the structural level these four elements lend a special quality to the Canadian-American milieu. Change affects structure slowly. These structural elements are the constants, or "givens," that theoretically set the relationship apart from other seemingly comparable bilateral associations.

At the policy level, a cluster of government behaviors further supports the claim that something within U.S.-Canadian relations warrants the adjective *special*. These behaviors are really governmental expectations about how the relationship ought to work. The expectations are not held equally by both actors; nor are they as little subject to change as the prior structural considerations. On the other hand, analysts have in general been more prone to justify the term *special* when assessing these policy expectations than when discussing structural considerations. In this view, the specific policy expectations about how the relationship is to be managed are special.

First among these policy expectations is that of consultations. Much of the institutional machinery that has been tested in the postwar period has had the objective of improving consultation.[25] For consultation to be effective, each government must keep the other informed of policy changes. Once this information is in place, the governments have the responsibility of discussing policy alternatives and the implications of policy choices with counterparts. Consultation implies prior discussion of policy choices, with at least the potential that contrary recommendations from the opposite government will be considered in making policy decisions. Otherwise, consultation amounts merely to selective, ex post facto notification of policy decisions, notification perhaps made prior to the time that such information appears in the newspapers.

Obviously, people who believe that consultation is the unique aspect of the relationship must show that consultation between Canada and the United States has been somehow more consistent, more reliable, or more complete than that occurring between other pairs of governments. This is not an easy burden to assume. Not only is the record of consultation difficult to assess, because of its unavailability and complexity, but also the record of consistency and reliability has been quite variable. About the best the analyst can do is to note some of the highlights of the consultation effort and then attempt to assess trends.

One can more easily identify the failures of consultation than the successes, because the failures are more broadly reported. Canada was critical of the United States in the Cuban Missile Crisis of 1962, because Canadian air space was threatened by U.S. initiatives vis-à-vis Cuba which had not been extensively discussed in advance with Ottawa.[26] Similarly, U.S. quotas on Canadian oil imports came as a shock to the Trudeau government in March of 1970. The United States, for its part, rejected Canada's unilateral decision to extend its territorial sea to 12 miles and its environmental controls to 100 miles through Territorial Sea and Fishing Zones legislation and the Arctic Waters Pollution Prevention act respectively. The Canadian decision in 1974 to ban American beef exports to Canada on the basis of alleged DES chemical contamination was also precipitous. Both the Nixon administration's New Economic

Policy, with its accompanying 10 percent import surcharge, and the Trudeau government's Third Option policy were essentially unilateral in nature, the governments having done little, if any, prior consultation.

Such examples of negligible or nonexistent consultation fail to reveal, of course, a broader historical sweep of more successful consultation and the general background of issues upon which consultation was extensive even during periods of controversial unilateral decisions. But the gap between policy announcements, especially during summit conferences, and the actual practice of consultation appears to be quite wide. Perfect consultation, of course, does not exist even within one government—between regions of a country, for example. So the standard of consultation by which we are measuring the Canadian-American relationship is high.

The multitude of institutional buffers set up to improve consultation reveals good intentions on the part of the two governments, intentions that are accompanied by some slippage in practice. The number of these institutional arrangements that have grown obsolete is witness to this slippage. Yet, one of the reasons for the high failure rate of the consultative institutions is not so much that they were ineffective or were ignored by decision makers as that their functions were probably already being performed elsewhere in the relationship or were subsequently usurped. Very seldom, in my opinion, is information completely lacking about what one government is doing or is planning to do vis-à-vis the other, though this scattered information is often available only in the press and in private circles. Elaborate intelligence-gathering is scarcely necessary. Canada and the United States can complain less that they lack information about the plans of their counterpart than that those plans may have a large self-interested component. This component may simply not be very susceptible to change in the direction that the other government would like. As I discussed earlier, domestic pressures on governments are often stronger than external pressures and these domestic pressures may be reflected to a greater extent in unilateral initiatives than in initiatives based on consultation. Indeed, the more distasteful a governmental initiative is likely to be to one's foreign partner, the less likely advanced consultation is to occur, especially if the effect of such consultation would be to undermine or otherwise weaken the initiative. Conversely, the less controversial the proposed legislation, the easier it is for government officials in Canada or the United States to discuss the legislation beforehand with counterparts in the other country.

The key question remains, however, Is the quality and the frequency of consultation better between Canada and the United States than between other partners? I doubt that on issues of high priority Canada consults less with Britain than with the United States or that in security matters, for example, the United States consults less with the German Federal Republic and Japan than with Canada. On medium- and low-level issues, the amount of consultation between Canada and the United States is probably unparalleled. But the quality and frequency of consultation varies enormously with the personnel at the head of each government and with the historical interval. Overall, consultation in the post-World War II period has been far greater than was true in the prewar period; consultation was more consistent in the 1976-80 interval than in the 1970-76 interval, for a variety of reasons both internal and external to the relationship. It must also be remembered that consultation is not the equivalent of compromise; and compromise does not automatically translate into effective policy. This is perhaps the most recent lesson to have been learned regarding consultation in Canadian-American relations.

A second major set of policy expectations descriptive of the relationship has been identified as exemptionalism. In the post-World War II period, Canada repeatedly sought and obtained exemptions from the external impact of U.S. economic legislation. That such exemptions were requested and received was considered special because other countries did not obtain such favored treatment; the grounds for granting the exemptions were that the two economies were inextricably intertwined.

The process of exemptionalism essentially began in April of 1948 when President Truman permitted recipients of U.S. Marshall Plan aid to make purchases in Canada as well as in the United States. President Nixon's New Economic Policy of 1971 canceled this process for the first time by denying Canada an exemption to the 10 percent import surcharge.

The exemptions had an economic impact of some significance, but perhaps the psychological awareness that Canada and the United States were unique economic partners was even more telling. The exemptions gave Canada a special "break," a fact that had undesirable overtones of paternalism and dependency, but more than that, they created in Canada a sense of economic confidence and security. Come what may, Canada would not be subject to the full weight of U.S. economic pressure. Regardless of other factors in the relationship and regardless of Canadian behavior toward the United States, the United States could be counted on to provide special economic treatment to its closest and best ally. This attitude is what made the Nixon denial of the exemption on the U.S. import surcharge such a crushing event for many Canadians.

Surely the abruptness of that denial, the lack of advance consultation and discussion, and the disregard for prior practice epitomized what was undesirable in the relationship. Any doubt, however, that exemptionalism was at an end was dispelled by President Nixon's speech to the Parliament on April 14, 1972. "No self-respecting nation can or should accept the proposition that it should always be economically dependent upon any other nation. Let us recognize once and for all that the only basis for a sound and healthy relationship between our two proud peoples is to find a pattern of economic interaction which is beneficial to both our countries and which respects Canada's right to chart its own economic course."[27] The demise of exemption seeking was echoed by then External Affairs Minister Allan MacEachen, although with qualification, and again by Secretary of State Henry Kissinger. What were the conditions that underlay this precipitous decline of exemptionalism?

Those people who were shocked by the revelation that new economic circumstances had intervened had failed to note the changing dynamic of history in the period preceding the decline of exemptionalism (see my summary of this changing dynamic at the beginning of this chapter). Two things were strikingly different. The first, indexed by the collapse of Bretton-Woods, was that U.S. dominance had declined from its peak in the interval of European and Japanese reconstruction; the United States was no longer able to make the generous, unilateral concessions it had in the past, because its relative position in the system, had brought it more nearly to equality with the other great economic powers, especially Japan and the European community. In terms of the dynamics of relative capability, the United States was no longer as competitive in economic terms as during the 1950s, nor did it comprise as large a share of the world's trade and total economic product. In other words, the power of the United States had declined to the point that it could no longer ignore significant economic pressures on its balance of payments.

The other important development was the emergence of a more vigorous, more diversified Canadian economy. Canadian growth and economic prosperity were obvious to all. Thus, as U.S. dominance declined vis-à-vis the world economic system, Canadian prominence became more evident. In 1975, this prominence would be symbolized by Canadian entry into the elite club of non-Communist advanced industrial countries. As I discussed earlier in this chapter, overall Canadian capability relative to that of the United States was increasing, particularly in the decade of the 1970s. Under these circumstances, Washington could no longer bring itself to consider the Canadian economy as less stable or less competitive than that of Italy or France. Because the United States took a global, comparative view, Canada no longer appeared to deserve special treatment on the basis of a lack of sufficient economic size, wealth, growth prospects, or maturity.

What this American view failed to recognize, however, was that Canada continued to think of itself, not in terms of this broader, global, comparative view, but in terms of its bilateral relationship with the United States. And what appeared from America's global perspective to be justifiable treatment appeared from the Canadian view to be the "selling-out" of America's closest friend and ally when the economic going got tough for the United States.

Thus, in summarizing this conception of the "special relationship," at least two considerations ought to be kept in mind. First, if exemptionalism was all that the special relationship involved, then MacEachen and Kissinger appeared to be right that the special relationship was dead. But because the term *special relationship* probably meant, and means, much more than the granting of exemptions, others were correct to challenge the meaning of Nixon's New Economic Policy as it applied to Canada. In other words, the special relationship continued to thrive in ways other than exemptionalism.

Second, subsequent behavior called into question whether, even in the narrowest policy sense, the special relationship was indeed dead. This behavior involved the convention-tax issue. The decision of the Carter administration and Congress (which was supported by the incoming Reagan administration) to unilaterally reinstate these convention-tax privileges, thereby making the Canadian hotel industry again competitive for U.S. convention business, is in fact a partial return to the practice of exemptionalism. Mexico is the only other government to have received this exemption. Whether such exemptions will occur as broadly as before, and whether the United States will expect more quid pro quos from Canada in return, perhaps in other areas, remains to be seen. But even in the narrow sense of exemptions from the external impact of American economic legislation and in spite of official statements to the contrary, some aspects of the special relationship seem to live on.

Finally, the special relationship may be conceptualized at the policy level in terms of investment security. Just as Canadians have conceived of the label *special* largely as a promise of exemption from the impact of U.S. economic policy, Americans have conceived of *special* largely as a guarantee of a safe and secure arena for U.S. private foreign investment. Americans have imagined Canada as a country uniquely hospitable to investment from abroad, especially American investment. Although Americans have been quick to observe differences between the two countries, in terms of legal norms and cultural perspectives, and have acknowledged the sovereignty of the two governments, they have also tended to view the economies as being part of a single large market. Multinational corporations, whether based in Canada or the United States, have always been "continentalists" in that the similarity of tastes and the geographic proximity and increasing economic homogeneity have enabled them to treat the Canadian and the American economies as part of a single large market area. Americans have, perhaps naïvely, been prone to this type of economic thought without concluding at the same time that the societies were any less Canadian or any less American because of this synthesis of markets. Although it is a member of the European Community, France in this view is no less French than if France were outside the community. This is surely the average American's view of the political impact of market synthesis on Canada and the United States in North America.

According to this view of the special relationship, other governments might exclude foreign investors, discriminate in various ways in favor of their own industry, and otherwise erode the investment climate, but Canada was always held to be a special case. Just as Texas was not likely to discriminate against capital from the northeast section of the United States or from Canada, for that matter, so Canada, in this idyllic view, was not likely to act toward foreign investment in the way that a number of other governments, especially Third World governments, had acted.

Perhaps the first challenge to this conception of the single market came in 1963, with the proposals of Walter Gordon, Minister of Finance in the Liberal government of Lester Pearson. He recommended a 30 percent tax on the value of Canadian firms that were taken over by U.S. subsidiaries and a tax on dividends which would vary with the degree to which a firm was owned by foreigners. Although these proposals were not enacted by Parliament, they sharply challenged the American conception of the special relationship. Subsequently, the creation of the Foreign Investment Review Agency (FIRA), the provincial efforts to expropriate the potash industry in Saskatchewan and the asbestos industry in Quebec, and finally, the ambitious National Energy Program all began to reverse the American view that there was much that was special about U.S.-Canada commercial relations. Indeed, a trend seemed to be emerging to make these commercial relations conform more and more to the global norm of increased hostility to foreign investment, hostility that existed everywhere outside a handful of countries within the OECD. Inasmuch as this hostile perspective was the opposite of the view Americans held toward the flow of Canadian investment into the United States (despite the very different relative levels of foreign investment in each country), the special relationship conceived in investment terms looked less and less attractive.

What the investment conception of the special relationship failed to take into account was that most of the Canadian hostility to foreign investment occurred in the natural resource sectors. Moreover, by world standards, Canada was more receptive to foreign capital than many countries, even more than some members of OECD. The American view of the special relationship also neglected to note that U.S. shares of many Canadian industries had become so high as to overshadow not only other foreign investment but also Canadian investment, in some cases perhaps even overshadowing the immediate potential for rapidly increasing Canadian investment.

Undeniably, however, Canada looked far less attractive as a site for increased U.S. investment in 1981 than in 1961. In the energy sector Ottawa did not appear to behave toward U.S. investment much differently than did a number of countries belonging to OPEC, although Canada's pace of discrimination and takeover was somewhat more incremental. Outside the area of resources, the fruits of the Tokyo round of tariff talks further reduced the incentive to locate outside American borders, because other markets could now be as easily serviced from the home market; but this was a reduction of multilateral incentive, not bilateral incentive. Canada was affected no more or less than a number of other possible investment locations. Again, the Canadian-American relationship looked less special from the commercial perspective than it had a decade or two earlier.

In short, two answers seem to arise in response to the question, How special is the special relationship? At the structural level, the Canadian-American relationship continues to appear unique or special, because no other pair of countries can demonstrate the combination of close governmental interaction, institutional ties and buffers, pacific conflict resolution, and extensiveness of cross-border bureaucratic and private sector activity. On the other hand, at the policy-making level, the factors that have made the relationship special in the past—consultation, preferential economic treatment for Canada, and a secure, hospitable atmosphere for U.S. investment—have all begun to erode. The analytical problem is not so much to explain why the special relationship is considered special; the problem is to determine where the trend in bilateral foreign policy is taking the two countries. If the special relationship deteriorates sufficiently in terms of policy, change will occur at the structural level as well. A close, complex structural relationship between the two countries may not alone have the capacity to offset the deterioration at the level of policy. Some indications exist that neither government is prepared to contend with the domestic political inconvenience of perpetuating policies of advanced and detailed consultation. Some indications also exist that the decline in U.S. sympathy for special exemptions for Canada in the economic sphere has paralleled the Canadian unwillingness to treat U.S. private foreign investment much differently than many other countries have treated it. None of these trends are consciously interactive; indeed, government leaders themselves may not be fully aware of the history of the relationship or of the encompassing nature of current trends. But the negative impact on the notion of the special relationship is the same; Canada and the United States, despite scattered evidence to the contrary, seem to be drifting apart for a variety of reasons, some of which are at the heart of the way the special relationship has traditionally been regarded.

Thus, in theoretical terms, change in the historical equilibrium between the two countries, new weights for the underlying structural dimensions of Canadian and American foreign policy, the manner in which the strategic characteristics of bilateral foreign policy now mesh, and the emphasis on tactics in Ottawa and Washington all point to a new overall definition of the relationship. Can it be described any longer as special, or is this label rapidly becoming a distinction without a difference? If a new equilibrium is evolving between the two countries, affecting the issue agenda and the tone of the relationship, where will this equilibrium of power and economic circumstance settle, and with what consequence for the future of bilateral relations in North America?

These are the questions that this theoretical survey seeks to highlight further. Theory may not lead directly to conclusions for policy making, but it can guide analysis to a more focused understanding of the nature of policy choices—choices that Canada and the United States must make, perhaps within the present decade, regarding the meaning and direction of their historical partnership.

THREE

The Psychological-Cultural Dimension

Of the major dimensions underlying the U.S.-Canada relationship, the psychological-cultural dimension is the most important, because it is more determinative of outcomes than the trade-commercial or the strategic-political dimensions and because it is the most complex. The psychology of Canadian-American relations defies the conventional assessment provided by the literature on foreign policy perception.[1] Despite the shared traditions of the two polities and the interdependent character of their economies, government-to-government interaction is often highly sensitive. This sensitivity is noted in the historical outlooks of each society toward itself and toward the world. Placed alongside such a psychological ethos, the mechanics of interaction become almost incidental. To understand the relationship, one must understand why each society holds the values and beliefs it does. One must also understand how these values and beliefs shape the way each government attempts to define its purpose, for this purpose is what ultimately determines the feasibility of partnership.

In the current phase of each country's historical evolution, the sense of collective purpose displayed by each is somewhat different. The historical phases themselves are not identical. Regardless of numerical age, Canada is a somewhat younger polity than the United States in terms of economic differentiation, bureaucratic autonomy, and international political leadership. Canada's major preoccupation is the development of its own unified sense of political identity. This preoccupation currently overrides all other goals, and it conditions every Canadian foreign initiative and response. It establishes priorities for Canada regarding domestic legislation that will have an external impact, and it sets limits on what tasks Canada can undertake in the international field.

Preoccupation with political identity implicitly shapes the nature of Canada's multilateral agenda and determines the timing of its thrust into the international spotlight as broker between the nations of the North and the South. Prime Minister Trudeau could not embark on major global initiatives until after the May 20, 1980 Quebec Referendum had affirmed that Quebec would remain within the federation. Conversely, the effort to orient the agenda of the 1981 Economic Summit Conference toward North-South relations slowed the U.S. drive toward primacy for East-West matters and toward emphasis of closer North American ties. For the international community, the timing of the discovery of North-South grievances effectively differentiated Canadian foreign policy from American foreign policy and served to generate in internal sense of esteem regarding the uniqueness of Canadian achievement.

Canada seeks to use its foreign policy for domestic ends, whereas the United States tends to use domestic policy for external ends. The Reagan Administration, for example, cut domestic social expenditures in part to expand military spending. For Canada, foreign policy must generate feelings of domestic unity and pride in the nation-state; it must divert the gaze of citizens from internal squabbles over energy, income redistribution, or culture. But the Canadian preoccupation with political identity is twofold. Although it must create a sense of societal purposiveness and cohesiveness by overcoming internal divisions and confrontation, the preoccupation with political identity must also lift Canada out of the shadow of the United States. Canada must obtain its own identity, not an ersatz identity borrowed from south of the border, but an identity that is "made in Canada."[2] Canadian foreign policy serves domestic ends by helping to create that identity, both by fostering a new internal sense of unity and by shifting the focus away from American things.

In contrast, the major preoccupation of the United States is with its global responsibilities. Internal problems of unity were solved long ago, not very peacefully but with finality, at Appomattox. Whatever its sense of political identity, America does not feel politically overshadowed by any other power. In this sense, the American political psyche is mature. What the United States agonizes over are its responsibilities abroad, especially now that the international political system is undergoing greater change than at any time in the preceding two decades. The United States worries that its power is slipping in an interval when its international political responsibilities are growing.

One kind of response to this dilemma is exemplified by the Nixon doctrine, which sought to reduce America's foreign responsibilities, to put allies on notice that they must assume a larger share of their own security, and to inform the global system that the United States could no longer act as world policeman (an unofficial but implicit role that the United States had not sought). Another kind of response is exemplified by the Reagan administration's policies that are built on the selective Middle East policies of the Carter doctrine. The Reagan administration sought unilaterally to expand military spending at the strategic and conventional levels in order to bolster containment of the Soviet Union and to reassert U.S. leadership within the Western alliance.

Although these policies, coming at opposite ends of a decade, seemed contradictory, they were not. Both policies attempted to deal with the same problem from different sides. The Nixon doctrine attempted to reduce responsibilities; the Reagan policy attempted to increase capability. What neither set of policies could do, of course, was to change the relative stature of the United States in the global system, or, in the context of the larger problems, to lessen significantly world poverty, hunger, unemployment, or the disaffection of the Third World countries with respect to the values of democratic pluralism or the market economy. Despite the new realism about the limits of its foreign policy, however, the United States emerged in the aftermath of Vietnam as a more self-confident prime minister in the cabinet of non-Communist governments.

Although the preoccupations of Canada and the United States did not coincide, they also did not come into conflict. The destinies of the two countries seemed to carry them in different directions. In the 1980s, Canada, in search of a larger political identity, and the United States, in search of a way to balance its world responsibilities against its capabilities, are like friends passing in the night on divergent paths. Hence, the collective psychology of the two countries, which underpins these respective state interests, will determine to a large degree whether partnership is in danger of splintering or is still possible.

TORY-TINGED LIBERALISM
VERSUS POPULIST-COLORED DEMOCRACY

In the popular mind, there is very little difference between a Canadian and an American in terms of value and outlook. Many Americans believe this to be true; many Canadians fear that it is so. Stories abound, for example, concerning Canadian students traveling in Europe with a Canadian flag sewn to the back of their shirts in order to let Europeans know they are not Americans. Except for a slightly different pronunciation of "house" and "about," even the use of English is often the same. Of course, regionalism in Canada contributes to these impressions, because at various points along the border differences between Canadians are often greater than differences between Canadians and Americans. Everyone can identify the Newfoundlander, the Quebecer, or the resident of Kingston, Ontario as authentically Canadian, albeit very distinguishable in regional terms. But the similarity between citizens of Vermont and New Brunswick, Minnesota and Manitoba, Montana and Alberta may be greater than the similarity between groups living within different regions of Canada as a whole. Hence, regionalism in both countries, particularly in Canada, contributes to the mythology of sameness.

When one contrasts the larger political ethos of Canada with that of the United States, however, unmistakable differences in value and outlook emerge, differences that affect the conduct of foreign policy. Canadian liberalism, for example, has a quality that is scarcely conservative but certainly displays a Tory cast.[3] The Liberal party of Canada, for example, can be simultaneously more socially progressive and more commercially nationalistic than the American Democratic party. Canadian liberalism is comfortable with hierarchy, formality, and title, yet it encompasses a broad spectrum of society and is tolerant of great diversity. Like British values, Canadian values do not seek to homogenize and are quite tolerant of eccentricity. Indeed, a bit of eccentricity is looked upon as a relief from the boredom of the middle-class life-style, a life-style that is as characteristic of Canada as of any other Western society.

Responsible government, meaning cabinet government, is also responsible in the sense that Canadians, despite their loud complaints, tend to trust government (whether federal or provincial) on fundamental political issues more than do other peoples. Although ultimate sovereignty may philosophically rest with Parliament, Canadians have allowed the executive branch more extensive powers and far greater authority than the executive branch has in a presidential democracy.[4] Canadians expect the federal government to govern even though they often criticize it for exceeding its authority on a host of regional and constitutional issues. But whether the authority is federal or provincial in origin, Canadians are respectful of authority for the most part and believe in the phrase from the British North American Act, "peace, order and good government." Domestic tranquility contrasts sharply with the social disorder and lack of personal safety often displayed in the "noisy republic to the south."

Canadians are not as uncomfortable with secrecy as Americans. Power, political or economic, has always been more closely held in Canada than in the United States. The press has acted in a fashion that is far more constrained—that is, less as a critic than as a participant in the policy process. Because public surveillance of government activity is not as tight as in the United States, far more freedom of maneuver is possible at the top. Political participation is more indirect and not as assertive as in the United States, which again gives government a larger opportunity to appear efficient and to act with efficiency. Such a set of political values creates a climate in which the bureaucracy (headed by the so-called mandarins) is able to exert more influence in daily policy making than is true for many other modern democracies.

What is perhaps most puzzling to Americans is the relationship of the private to the public sector in Canada. Although the Progressive-Conservative party is more reflective of private-sector thinking than are either of the other two leading political parties, as the battle over the fate of Petro-Canada during the Clark interregnum indicated, all of the parties are supportive of the concept of the Crown, or government-sponsored, corporation. Yet, the relationship between the public and the private sectors in Canada is much closer than even the Crown corporation notion suggests. Historically, much Canadian investment has occurred in large government-sponsored projects, such as railroads, utilities, and mines, in which the private and public sectors become virtually conterminous. Because of its resource production and need for massive investment in infrastructure as well as its distinguished tradition in the sphere of investment banking, Canada has found that a large government role in investment decision making was often desirable, if not mandatory.

Another explanation for the close association between the public and the private sectors is the question of size, especially the relative differential in size between the Canadian and the American economies and, similarly, between Canadian firms and American firms. The adversary character of relations between government and firm that has grown up in the United States is simply absent from Canada, as it is from most other non-Communist, advanced-industrial states. In Canada, with some qualifications, the bigger the firm, the more desirable the firm. This is true regardless of the effect of domestic constraints on competition behind tariff walls, because larger firms can compete more effectively abroad, especially with American firms. The object in Canada has been not so much to regulate or control the competition among Canadian firms as to enhance, by political and fiscal means, their capacity to grow in size.[5] Consumer protection and incentives to consume were less important than producer incentive and incentives to invest. Although helpful in the early stages of a firm's development, tariffs were a mixed blessing, because tariffs tend to encourage permanently "infant" industries. Yet, ever since the advent of Sir John A. MacDonald's National Policy, tariffs have to some degree been seen as a developmental tool in Canada. But as Canada participated actively in the postwar rounds of GATT, Canadian industry, much of it foreign owned, was increasingly exposed to the full blast of international competition. Yet Canadians esteem large corporate size and the policies of "Canadianization," for example, and continue to promote this government objective.

Thus, ties between the private sector and the public sector have remained close, a marriage supported by broadly held political values within Canadian culture. But to some extent, the closeness of public- and private-sector policy coordination in Canada has left less room for farm and labor participation and hence has contributed to the advent of prairie radicalism in Manitoba and Saskatchewan and to the drive of the trade-union movement to find greater political representation within the New Democratic party.[6] One consequence is that the range of party ideology in Canada is broader than in the United States. To be sure, populism in both societies is reflected in the political process, but whereas, after 1896, the populist program in the United States was absorbed into both the Republican and the Democratic party platforms (especially into the latter), populism in Canada found fertile ground in the creation of new political parties that led eventually to the establishment of the New Democratic party (NDP). Much of the strength of the NDP is not ideological, however, but results from the omnipresence of the Liberal party in the twentieth century. For those Canadians who could not bring themselves to vote Conservative, NDP became the symbol of opposition to the Liberal party-dominated federal government.

The United States stands out against this Canadian backdrop as a populist democracy *in extremis.* Public participation is valued over governmental assertiveness. Interest group pressure is tolerated in an atmosphere of low party discipline. The average citizen fears political and corporate bigness and concentration of power. Public and private sectors have adopted adversarial roles, witnessed in particular in antitrust proceedings. Press freedom and other freedoms are emphasized to a degree that Canadians equate with license. The whole character of American government, which is based on the principle of checks and balances, appears in the Canadian view to encourage political diffusion, chaotic administration, and demogoguery. Some Canadians would be tempted to brand presidential democracy as "irresponsible government," especially in view of its lack of capacity to provide for personal safety and public order.

At the heart of the Canadian critique of American democracy is the fact that, despite its debt to British institutions, American government is very non-British in its republican origins. American democracy is far more homogeneous and egalitarian than its Canadian and British counterparts. American society is likewise assimilationist in character, something that Canadian society can never be. America is a land of minorities, as Lyndon Johnson reminded his critics, with no cultural enclave permanently dominating society. Canada, on the other hand, is described as a cultural mosaic and a racial pyramid, where pluralism enters only around the edges and where minorities cling to their traditional values and prerogatives.[7] If immigrants to the United States strive to shed their linguistic and cultural baggage as quickly as possible, so as to be accepted as truly "American"—that is, English speaking and middle class—immigrants to Canada often attempt to re-create a version of the home country in Canada, or, alternatively, they gradually learn to coexist with one or another of the two separate indigenous cultural groups.

Canadians secretly envy the exuberance with which Americans uphold patriotic symbols and accept the American national values of the great mass of their assimilated immigrant forefathers. Americans are noisy about their patriotism and confident of the supremacy of their political and social values. But the pace of American life, the volatility of American passions, the startling upward and downward mobility of American political careers (for which prior experience in foreign affairs, for example, is clearly no prerequisite to the presidency and in which the media play a larger and larger role on both the electoral and the administrative levels) also leave Canadians a bit dismayed and frightened.

Given these large differences between how Canadians and Americans view politics and the political system, disparities in the way the two countries conduct external affairs are not surprising. But these disparities occur not in diplomatic style alone; they lie at the base of how decisions are made and how policy is interpreted. Because the image that each country projects abroad is heavily influenced by that country's image of itself and by its own preferred political values, Canada and the United States look at the world differently.

Canada views the global system at once more benignly and less tolerantly, with a greater craving for political order, than does the United States. The United States, paradoxically, is more prone to use force to settle disputes (just as domestic political violence is more acceptable as a fact of life in the United States) and more tolerant of large vacillations of alliance structure and public order (one year Egypt and China are "enemies" of the United States, the next year they are "friends," and traditional allies are sometimes neglected). In some ways, Canada is far less politically pragmatic than the United States with regard to diplomatic instruments, but at the same time, Canada is far more comfortable with ideological diversity. Americans tend to reject unfamiliar political values and ideologies, whereas Canadians tend to minimize or ignore different values and ideologies (the pluralist, assimilationist outlook versus the vertical mosaic outlook). In general, Canada expresses in its foreign policy far more confidence in governmental institutions, including supranational institutions, and far less confidence in the private sector than does the United States. In part because their foreign policy roles and degrees of power are different and in part because their domestic political elites emphasize different sets of priorities, Canada and America weigh differently the political-strategic and trade-commercial dimensions of statecraft.

In short, tory-tinged liberalism and populist-colored democracy generate different claims on foreign-policy decision makers. These claims prop up state interests in a different fashion and cause both governments to explain the foundation of world politics in different ways. Part of the reason that the Canadian and the American world views diverge is that the domestic elite in each country has been socialized in ways that often appear superficially similar but in fact have been quite disparate.

UNITED STATES: THE CLASH BETWEEN
THE VALUES OF EQUALITY AND LEADERSHIP

In dealing with a polity, such as Canada, in which both asymmetry and intervulnerability prevail, the United States often seems troubled by conflicting pressures in terms of goal-orientation. These conflicting pressures stem from a deep ambivalence regarding certain American political values. Historically, the United States has been committed to a far-reaching egalitarianism of legal status and opportunity. Such egalitarianism stems directly from the absence of a feudal tradition and from the competition among new and old immigrants. In the United States one had the right to succeed or to fail. There were few privileges that guaranteed wealth or success and few safety nets for people on the downward side of mobility. This was an egalitarianism of achievement, not of birth or heritage.[8] Most of all, it was an egalitarianism of status and power, in which the capacity to make money was the "great equalizer."

Ironically, and in contrast to societies with a strong Marxist orientation, American egalitarianism had little to do with an administered equalization of income and wealth. The evolution of the welfare state and of progressive taxation came late to the United States. Yet, the individual capacity to acquire income and wealth was absolutely critical to both the myth and the reality of the American brand of egalitarianism.

The problem that the philosophy of egalitarianism posed for American foreign policy toward middle powers was that although egalitarianism extended the ladder of upward political mobility to all states capable of themselves climbing the rungs (for example, Iran and Brazil), it also transferred to the exercise of power, for many Americans, a sense of solicitude and guilt. Why were all states not equal, if free, and if free, not equal? If the fundamental discriminator among individuals was money, not status or political power, then how was one to explain outcomes in international society, in which differences of status and power seemed to be the sine qua non of statecraft? If, in domestic political terms, one could soften the discrepancies of wealth by the niceties of informality, personalism, and voluntarism, then why did these values seem to fail so repeatedly when applied to international politics? Most of all, how could the requisites of political leadership be squared with the American version of egalitarianism?

Unlike in Communist societies, in which egalitarianism was limited to the economic sphere and was offset by an austere inegalitarianism of party structure, or in societies like Canada and Britain, which displayed a tory cast and possessed a bias in favor of authority, in the United States, the philosophy of egalitarianism served internally to decentralize, to diffuse, and to counterbalance power in a complex way; abroad, it served to undermine the exercise of power. The United States could seldom square its desire to treat everyone in the same fashion, as "equals" and as "friends," with its evident preeminence within the global system and with the gradation of association that the complex hierarchy of international relationships demanded. The United States was often more concerned with being liked than with being effective in the conduct of foreign policy; more concerned with showmanlike displays of amity and good feeling than with securing specific objectives that would be capable of underpinning world order in a concrete way.[9] In particular, the American public often experienced guilt and anxiety regarding the exercise of power and regarding the need for governmental action in the context of a highly inegalitarian hierarchy of power and status abroad. It mattered not that the United States had grown into this system and that the system was not of American choice or making.

The United States still lamented the auspicious inequality of power in international relationships and, as a result, often appeared awkward in discharging its responsibilities. Far from reinforcing international stability, such hesitance to accept the reality of differences in power and to work through them led to knee-jerk responses in crisis situations (created by the attempt to quickly shore up perceived weaknesses) and to opportunities for opponents to challenge the fitfully applied U.S. leadership.

America's struggle with egalitarianism in a world of political inequality contributed to a sense of political uncertainty among its allies. America's brand of preferred egalitarianism sometimes weakened consultative mechanisms, because of the American feeling that the United States was no richer and not much more powerful than some of its allies and was, after all, acting on behalf of its ally's interests. As a result of this attitude, some Americans felt that elaborate consultation, in addition to being laborious and unpleasant, was often in the final analysis unnecessary.

U.S.-Canada relations suffered from the tensions between leadership and egalitarianism in several ways. First, effusive friendship sometimes seemed to replace positive action. Canada felt that protestations of good intent and of equality sometimes seemed to take the place of favorable initiatives in the bilateral relationship. American leadership appeared on occasion to treat Canada as though it had no state interests other than those that were conterminous with American interests. Because the two societies were proximate and equal, there was, in this view, perhaps no need for a separate definition of interests. America's propensity for egalitarianism and neighborliness had blinded it to differences of outlook and position between Canada and itself.

Second, the tension in the United States between professing a doctrine of egalitarianism and exerting sustained political leadership was brought home to Canada during changes of U.S. administration. Political leadership based on the rather amorphous values of professed equality and well-being tended to zigzag on issues without much warning. Would a new administration look more favorably on pollution abatement or would it emphasize energy trade-offs? Would such a new government continue policies of preferential tax treatment or would Canada be lumped in the same category as other allies? The American brand of egalitarianism and good feeling almost seemed to act as a cover for the exercise of state interest, especially changing state interests. Canada found it very hard to read the foreign policy signals in such a context. Many Canadians accused the United States of hypocrisy—when in reality there was no such hypocrisy—because of the difficulty of interpreting shifts in U.S. foreign policy. Indeed, as far as Canada was concerned, Canada might as well base its own policy on what was happening in terms of American *domestic* politics, because these developments were a better indicator of policy toward Canada than was the general outline of U.S. foreign policy itself.

Finally, American uncertainty and tentativeness about assuming leadership for fear that such leadership might appear hegemonic sometimes generated hegemonic leadership. If Canada and the United States were to be the closest of allies, then, before charting a course that affected both partners, the larger partner had the obligation of providing adequate information to and of requesting advice from the smaller partner. Full consultation meant that the opinions of both partners would be taken into consideration; contrary to the ideology of egalitarianism, however, this did not mean that each opinion would always carry equal weight. Weighting would depend upon how deeply interests were affected and how many resources each partner was willing to contribute to a common task. Sharing a burden equally always earns an equal voice. Even when neither interests nor resources were equivalent, however, consultation nonetheless necessitated reflecting the opinion of both partners, whatever the relative weights, in the final decision. Canada did not want to hear for the first time about a policy decision that affected its interests by reading the morning newspaper.

The problem for Canada was that the American philosophy of egalitarianism held out the promise of excessively full consultation, whereas the practice of American leadership sometimes involved narrowly unilateral decisions. Bridging the gap between the need Americans feel to preach political equality and the responsibility they have to exercise political leadership is not something that Americans find easy.

CANADA: STATUS DISEQUILIBRIUM

A burden that Canada must shoulder in its relations with other nations is expressed in terms of status disequilibrium. International status disequilibrium has a number of operational forms, but in general it is characterized by the pains associated with life as a middle power. A country's status disequilibrium is caused by a number of factors. In some ways and with regard to some indicators (territorial size, per-capita income, resource base), the nation is classified as a major power, but in other ways and with regard to other indicators (military spending, GNP, population) it displays the capability and perspective of a small state or regional power. This inconsistency is said to nurture anxieties and uncertainties regarding the perception of its true position relative to others in the system.[10] Such an equivocal status position is difficult for any nation to rationalize and adopt.

In what sense is Canada in status disequilibrium with respect to how other states view it or with respect to its own perception of its place in the international status hierarchy? One contradiction involves territorial size and population size, two conventional indicators of national power. In terms of territorial area, Canada is the second largest country in the world, yet in terms of population size, it ranks among the small states (having scarcely 25 million people). This disparity is compounded by the fact that more than 80 percent of the population lives in a narrow band located along Canada's southern border, a band that is 100 miles wide and 3,000 miles long.

Status disequilibrium is also evident in the economic and commercial spheres. Canada's economic size has earned it a place among the top seven Western nations at each of the economic summit conferences since 1975. Yet, as the elite's newest entrant, Canada has known this prestige only very recently; Canada is the most prosperous of the "developing" polities, the youngest of the advanced-industrial elite. Such rapid change is dizzying for leadership and citizen alike. In terms of per-capita income, Canada is even more prominent, but the nation is uncertain amidst all of this economic success. It fears that too large a fraction of this wealth is attributable to resource extraction and that resource endowments will be depleted. It also fears that, despite this wealth, too large a fraction of these receipts is seeping out of the economy through domestic investments owned by foreigners and through foreign investments owned by domestics. Thus, although it is very rich, Canada is troubled about not being rich enough or about not being permanently rich.

Similarly, in commercial terms Canada is a great trading nation. But despite very positive balances of trade and large earnings on exports to foreign countries, the nation is unhappy about the composition and direction of that trade as well as, perhaps, with the relative size of the foreign-trade sector. Three criticisms are leveled at the character of foreign trade. First, too large a portion of exports is in commodities and raw materials and too small a portion is in manufactured goods, where the "value-added" is supposedly much greater. Second, too large a fraction of total trade (both exports and imports) occurs with a single trading partner, the United States, thus creating subordination. (The inverse of the relationship—that too large a share of U.S. foreign investments is in Canada—is also true, as is witnessed by U.S. vulnerability in the areas of petroleum and natural gas; this vulnerability is, however, offset somewhat, in relative terms, by the enormous size of the American GNP.) Third, Canada would like to become more self-reliant, producing more goods at home and importing fewer from abroad. The size of the overall foreign-trade budget is thought to be too great relative to the total production of Canadian goods and services. Canada is far from convinced that the volume and composition of its foreign trade—which is the envy of most countries in the world today—is necessarily in its own best interests, an uncertainty that adds to its sense of overall disequilibration.

Regarding military power, Canada again experiences the tensions associated with conflicting pressures. The nation displayed a brilliant military record in World Wars I and II, despite initial reluctance to get involved in European quarrels. In World War I, Canada made a greater military contribution to the allied effort than did the much larger United States (Canada sustained more than 43,000 battlefield-related deaths); this is partly because Canada entered the war two and one-half years earlier than the United States and partly because of the great periodic intensity of engagement. Today Canada ranks among the top ten military powers in the world. Yet Canada feels itself squeezed between the two military giants on its borders, the United States and the Soviet Union (it is the only nation in the world with such dual contiguity). Although it is one of the top ten countries militarily, Canada is totally dependent upon the United States for its national security. Such dependence creates anxiety, especially in situations in which U.S. military power is used, such as the Cuban missile crisis, and in which, therefore, Canadian territory might come under increased risk of attack. Canada is perpetually nervous about its dependence upon another friendly power for its security, lest the use of force entangle it in quarrels abroad, particularly with the Soviet Union. Consciously abjuring nuclear weaponry, Canada has also gradually reduced its manpower commitment to Europe and has had doubts about the value of its antisubmarine force within NATO.

Set against the historical record, its present military potential, and its ambivalent military relationship with its two giant neighbors, Canada feels conflicting pressures from its need to preserve territorial security and its feeling of helplessness regarding the selection of the appropriate means to assure that security.

Although it may not be a prevailing view in Canada, many Canadians believe they have no enemies, because relations between Canada and other countries are seemingly so warm and benign; hence, they feel that their greatest risk is getting dragged into a conflict between the United States and the Soviet Union. Canada also pays for this condition of dependence, however, in terms of anxiety, frustration, and a profound sense of alienation that at times spills over into its relationship with the United States.

Finally, with respect to foreign policy interests, Canada is more than a regional power but less than a global power. The Trudeau government, for example, in keeping with the opinions of much of the general population and of the elite, attempted to de-emphasize the American connection and to expand links with Europe. It wanted to strengthen the Canadian association with the advanced-industrial club, to which Canada certainly legitimately belongs, but it would also like to act as one of the at least symbolic leaders of the Third World, with which it identifies as a primary commodity producer struggling against the domination of the super-powers, Japan and Old Europe. Yet Canada finds the dual roles of, on the one hand, being a regional and global power with membership in the world's industrial elite and, on the other, being a would-be chief polity in opposition to that elite seemingly impossible to fulfill. The desire to pursue conflicting and ambiguous roles is a characteristic of status disequilibrium, because of the insufficient reinforcement associated with old roles and the compunction to demonstrate a capacity to assume new ones. Canada is not yet confident of its new position.

One of the strongest props to nationalism is the bias against foreign involvement or intrusion. This is sometimes described as ethnocentrism or "negative nationalism." Liberal political theory often deplores this attitude for the valid reasons that its dark side may be discrimination against foreigners and, in some cases, even internal repression. But the reality is that feelings of hostility toward governments abroad may give a powerful thrust to nation-state unity. Such feelings are not sufficient for unity and may not even be necessary, but they can catalyze a spirit of political unity that might otherwise remain dormant for a long period. On the other hand, a policy of cultural resistance to the United States is possible and indeed necessary from the Canadian point of view. Such resistance may have nothing to do with anti-Americanism and may simply be part of the Canadian protective instinct in the face of perceived cultural pressures from abroad.

In the present-day context, anti-Americanism serves as a catalyst for Canadian identity. The problem for U.S.-Canadian relations is, of course, that what catalyzes Canadian identity may severely strain the relationship between the two countries. Americans may fail to understand the instrumental value of anti-Americanism for Canada, taking such attitudes too seriously and too personally. Conversely, some Canadians may begin to believe that the rhetoric has a basis in substance and that the substance therefore warrants dissociation. An external policy tinged with anti-Americanism requires great subtlety of implementation if it is at the same time to invoke the language of Canadian-American cooperation and to deal appropriately with issues that are long term, broad in conception, and without immediate pay-off.

ABSENCE OF AMERICAN CULTURE VERSUS
THE PERVASIVENESS OF THE U.S. CULTURAL PRESENCE

Americans, for a variety of reasons, do not take their own culture very seriously. Indeed, Americans, for the most part, could not care less about that which is termed *high culture* or about the dispersion of American cultural values. Americans are quick to defend their country's political institutions and concept of political freedom, but many Americans believe that culture—in the valuational, or linguistic, sense that the French, for example, treasure it—will take care of itself. Critics often equate this attitude with the absence of culture, an observation that hardly bothers most Americans, even though it is not entirely correct.

The explanation for Americans' extreme confidence, or indifference, to the American cultural impact is manifold. First, America epitomizes the development of spontaneous, mass culture that is petite bourgeoisie in origin and not yet self-conscious. Most members of the society have struggled too hard for material betterment to spend much time on the luxury of cultural reflection. Culture is to be created and to be enjoyed for its own sake, but, for the most part, not to be studied or disseminated. Second, American culture is synthetic. It is a nascent amalgam of all of the influences that its widely diverse members have brought to it; in an effort to quickly attain full standing in American society, second- and third-generation Americans have unfortunately attempted to shed many of these influences. Finally, American culture is technical in orientation. The Smithsonian Air and Space Museum is more typically "American" than perhaps any other museum in the country. Technical preeminence, whether in polio research or space flight, does tend to "speak for itself." These are some of the reasons why Americans are so oblivious to the conscious expression of American culture, even though Americans from Ernest Hemingway to Frank Lloyd Wright have made their imprint on the world cultural outlook.

Given this lack of awareness of American culture, it is not surprising that most Americans are unaware of the magnitude of what is termed the "American cultural presence" abroad, especially in Canada. Americans tend to ignore the potential impact that American television programming has on a large Canadian viewership; or the impact that textbooks published in the United States and exported to Canada can have on learning; or the effect U.S. advertising can have on Canadian purchasing habits; or the effect an American tourist infusion can have on Canadian provincial parks and natural areas. Americans do not think of themselves as leaving a cultural imprint upon any other society; Canadians feel this imprint, however, largely because of the disparity in physical size between the two countries and the highly visible, seemingly ominous centricity of the U.S. world role.

Part of the disparity of perception is, perhaps, explained by the difference between *Americanism* and *post-industrialism*. Some Canadians fear that the influence of American culture will mean the disappearance of a simpler, more personal way of life and the substitution of a life-style that is faster paced, more urbanized, and more interdependent, yet more technocratic. This is not American culture anymore than it is German or Japanese culture. It is post-industrialism, with an emphasis on high technology, bureaucracy, standardization, cost efficiency, and service orientation. Fast-food chains may have come to the United States first and may often carry American corporate names, but the reason they germinate and take root in Teheran, Hong Kong, and Vancouver is that they offer a standardized menu at low cost, with little loss of time to the customer. Post-industrialism may be accepted or rejected, but it is a fact of historical development, not a facet of American culture.

On the other hand, part of the Canadian fear is legitimate. The United States influences Canadian culture far more than Canadian culture influences the United States. This is not merely a matter of exchanging ice hockey for American football (as adapted by Canadians) or baseball. It is a problem for a society worried about its own cultural unity as a nation-state and its own political autonomy as a separate actor within the global system. Concerned about the dependency of its economy on the United States, Canada is equally determined not to acquire a political and cultural dependency.

Perhaps the greatest faux pas committed by Americans regarding Canada, however, is the seemingly irresistible American tendency to deny Canadians their own political and cultural identity. It has become such a caricature of American cultural indifference that members of the American intellectual establishment no longer allow themselves to fall into the trap of saying that "Canadians are just like Americans" in the belief that they are extending a compliment to Canada. But American scholarship and political analysis still asserts the inevitability of Canadian cultural assimilation into the American orbit.[11] And the word *continental* does not have the same negative connotation in the United States that it does in Canada. Americans still prefer to emphasize the similarities between Canadian and American tastes and institutions without fully realizing the damage this does to the relationship they want to preserve.

The problem of the American denial of the Canadian identity is manifold. The denial hurts in particular because it cuts to the core of Canadian uncertainty regarding the nature of the Canadian identity. Canadians are thus forced to examine their own historical development and social ethos; the denial forces them to contend with the question of bicultural or separate-national identity. American denial of the Canadian identity also demands of Canadians an assessment of what their preferred relationship is with the United States. But to assert that the Canadian identity is little more than a facsimile of the American identity is infuriating to Canadians, first, because it is factually and historically incorrect, and second, because it seems to condemn Canada to precisely the perpetual subordination that most Canadians reject.

The inadvertent American denial of the Canadian identity also hurts because it comes from a society that is supremely confident — to the point of indifference — regarding its own cultural resilience and coherence. Because many Canadians are somewhat more elitist than Americans, cultural comparisons between the Canadians and the British and French are regarded as flattering, whereas comparisons between Canadian and American cultural perspectives are regarded as demeaning; these comparisons seemingly relegate the Canadian cultural position to a mass-population outlook, one with a rather plebeian set of values. Set against these discontents is the reality that in some important ways the Canadian and American cultural outlooks, for reasons of parallel historical evolution and proximity, *are* similar.

If an emotional bomb confronts the U.S.-Canada relationship, it is the problem of the Canadian identity and the way Americans respond to this identity. Anti-Americanism, when it is something more than a strategic political instrument, is, in my opinion, directly a response to the American tendency to erase or to subordinate the Canadian identity. A national identity is the collective personification of the individual ego at the nation-state level.[12] When this ego is abused or challenged, its natural response is to strike outward at the challenger. Because, in some cases, Americans have been careless about how they approach issues involving the Canadian political and cultural identity, they have earned the kind of anti-Americanism they are surprised to discover.

As Americans become more aware of the nature of this psychological problem and of their part in creating the problem, the resentment some Canadians feel toward American institutions and values is likely to diminish. Similarly, as Canadian political institutions and sociocultural outlook mature, Canadians will feel less sensitive about their own identity problem and will relate to the United States more positively. Underlying all identity problems is the necessity for self-esteem and confidence. A better external environment would help resolve the Canadian identity problem: in other words, as the United States becomes more aware of Canada as a truly separate political actor on the world stage and becomes more aware of how to relate to Canada in a way that elicits confidence and respect, the Canadian sense of well-being, unity, and stature will improve. But the largest part of the task of improving the Canadian sense of political and cultural identity is, of course, a Canadian task. No country can build a sense of nation-state cohesiveness, especially in a polity that will necessarily remain binational, in a generation or two. Yet both internal and external challenges to the Canadian political and cultural identity can leave the polity stronger, not weaker, and can provide a foundation that is both unique and durable.

ANGLOPHONE AND FRANCOPHONE PSYCHOLOGICAL OUTLOOKS TOWARD THE UNITED STATES

Americans are often puzzled regarding the true attitude of Canadians toward the United States. Americans visiting Canada, especially during the height of the referendum crisis in Quebec, have sometimes heard Anglophones complaining bitterly about the attitude of Francophones toward Canadian politics or Francophones complaining bitterly about the Anglophone attitude toward federation. This experience normally leaves Americans a bit unnerved and curious regarding how each group of Canadians views the United States. Added to this curiosity is the mythology regarding which group of Canadians relates best to the American mentality.

A great deal of interest, and perhaps some misunderstanding, seems to attend this latter question on both sides of the border. It has been suggested, for example, that Anglophone diplomatic representatives to Washington are more effective because they relate better to Americans and can communicate more easily. If it is the case that Anglophones outperform Francophones in Washington (and I know of no evidence for this assertion), it is most likely not a consequence of a better ability to relate to Americans or, perhaps, even of language similarities.

Surely the difference of language creates some problems for Francophones who do not speak English well, or for Americans, the great majority of whom do not speak French. On the other hand, Americans often appear to esteem things French more than they do things English. French names are associated with luxury and panache, with the finest perfumes and the best food, and French culture to Americans means a highly cultivated life-style with a touch of the romantic. Hence, Francophones from Canada meet an image in the United States that, no matter how partial or distorted, is nonetheless very favorable.

The language congruence of English-speaking Americans and Anglophone Canadians is, to be sure, an important asset in business and in personal relations. But it is a mistake to assume that, in North America at least, language is the primary determinant of cultural attitudes toward societies abroad. The true relationship is far more subtle and complicated.

To an extent, an inverse process is at work here psychologically, a process in which the sense of national identity is a key variable and in which language has the opposite of predicted consequences. Because Francophone citizens of Canada enjoy a language barrier that preserves their cultural and perhaps political identity from the American influence, Francophones who speak English relate easily to Americans on a personal level. Francophones seldom feel defensive socially in the presence of Americans. The confidence that their own sense of linguistic separateness provides enables them to act in a way that is extroverted, personable, and, most importantly, informal, all social characteristics that Americans admire. Americans can thus relate to the charm and natural warmth of Quebec society, in part because it is forthcoming.

Conversely, despite the similarity of English-speaking language and traditions on both sides of the border, Canadian Anglophones, especially those most influenced by a British educational or social outlook, often find a personal relationship with Americans more difficult. For Anglophones this stems in part from the very similarity of the two cultures and from the absence of a language difference to bolster the Canadian identity. The absence of an obvious external key to national identity often constrains Anglophone-American relations at the personal level to the same extent that the presence makes relations easier for the Quebecer. Thus one ought not to suppose that all Anglophone Canadians have an easier time than Francophones at relating to Americans and to American culture.

In response to the broader question regarding how Anglophone and Francophone Canadians relate to the United States, two observations are foremost. First, on average, regarding matters such as the attitude toward U.S. private investment in Canada, the perhaps surprising discovery is that language differences seem to count for very little. Canada is far more unified in its attitudes toward many aspects of the relationship with the United States than perhaps either Canadians or Americans are aware.

Secondly, regional differences in Canada are probably more important attitudinally than linguistic-cultural differences. Albertans in general are surely more "pro-American" than Ontarians; Newfoundlanders may look upon the United States in some regards more favorably than Quebecers. These regional attitudinal differences result from a host of internal political and economic circumstances, including immigration, that have deep historical roots. These differences also relate in some cases to current and historical interactions across the borders of the two countries, again along regional lines. Hence, deep-seated regional attitudes have been shaped for a complex of both intra-Canadian and Canadian-American reasons, and these regional differences serve to blur and sometimes reverse attitudes that might otherwise have had a primarily linguistic-cultural base.

The conclusion of these assessments of psychological outlook, however, is that for Canada, generalizations from the broad, social level to the specific, individual level are far more difficult than for most societies and should be attempted only with the utmost care. The wonderful diversity of Canadian society makes this particular variety of analysis potentially far more misleading for studies of Canada than for studies of many societies, precisely because each group in this heterogeneous society influences other groups. Indeed, Canada's peculiar blend of cultural heterogeneity and homogeneity gives Canadian society one of its most distinctive qualities and sets it apart from the United States in another fundamental way.

PSYCHOLOGICAL IMPACTS ON POLICY

The psychology of the relationship is not of interest as a mere artifact of cultural curiosity. It is of interest because it controls the issue agenda and determines how readily individual issues will be resolved and with what political consequence. The psychology of Canadian-American relations is as complex as any two countries can experience. The role this psychology plays in the relationship can be exemplified in three policy contexts.

Two-Audience Problem

Canada has a two-audience problem of its own in that French and English Canada often respond differently to the same information from Ottawa; or, alternatively, Ottawa feels called upon to try to address each segment of Canadian opinion, not just in a different language, but with different substance and strategy. But the two-audience problem that affects Canadian-American relations most directly is the one Washington and Ottawa themselves underwrite vis-à-vis each other. It is the problem each country has when it attempts to speak to its own constituency and is overheard abroad or when it speaks to its partner's society and government and is overheard by its own constituents. The problem is grave when accusations are made that the same message is not left with both audiences, either because the message, for understandable political reasons, was different, or because, although the message was the same, it was interpreted differently by the two audiences.

The first reason the two-audience problem is difficult for Canada and the United States is that both countries are democracies and are subject to the pressures of public opinion, especially in election years in the United States and especially regarding critical issues that might threaten a parliamentary majority in Canada. Second, the physical proximity of the two countries, the fairly perfect flow of information across the borders, the alert private sector in each country, and the fact of intervulnerability all contribute to audiences in each polity which are sensitive to what is said at home and abroad. Moreover, these audiences also have good short-term memories and have demonstrated a willingness, with the help of the press, to hold their governments accountable.

For reasons that are obvious to policy makers, a government must, from time to time, leave different messages, or different interpretations of the same message, with a domestic and a foreign audience. If, for example, in a period of a hardening U.S. line toward instability in the Caribbean, Canada feels conflicting pressures from its interests and public opinion, it may encounter the contradictions of the dual-audience problem. If Ottawa yields to Canadian public opinion by challenging U.S. Caribbean policy, Canada runs the risk of severely damaging its bilateral relations with the United States, to the point of sacrificing state interests for a multilateral principle. Conversely, if Canada supports U.S. policy in the Caribbean, thereby strengthening its hand in bilateral relations with the United States, the Canadian government risks alienating important elite groups in Canada and embarrassing itself before the Parliamentary opposition. Under these circumstances, high Canadian government officials, while in Washington, are strongly tempted to tell the American audience that "Canada has no vital interests in the Caribbean" (later corrected to mean Central America). Unfortunately, if the Canadian press reports such statements back in Canada, the furor regarding the direction and purpose of Canadian foreign policy can become quite unpleasant. There are many other examples involving U.S. as well as Canadian policy statements that carry a different ring when made abroad than when made at home.

What are the consequences of the two-audience problem for the psychology of the relationship and for policy? First, the two-audience problem results in more tightly defined limits of diplomatic maneuver in Canadian-American relations than elsewhere. Ottawa and Washington must be more careful of the wording of public statements regarding policy when that policy affects the other country. Second, in domestic political terms, the cost of diverging interests to governments in Ottawa and Washington is likely to be greater than in other relationships of similar magnitude, because those divergences cannot so easily be softened or blurred through the proper use of diplomatic language. The domestic elites monitor the relationship too closely to permit the kind of governmental double-talk that is often the stuff of international politics. Third, the two-audience problem is most serious with respect to credibility. How reliable are government statements? Governments are likely to lose credibility, both with the important domestic decision-making elites and with foreign governments, when they run afoul of the two-audience problem.

Perhaps the overall effect of the two-audience problem on the Canadian-American relationship is to drive policy discussions into secrecy. What happens behind closed doors becomes more important than what is said to the press, regardless of where public statements are made.

The two-audience problem encourages governments in Ottawa and Washington to tolerate a certain amount of stage management for the benefit of the other country's local elites at the cost of one's own public image. Because of the closeness of the relationship, each government must become more sensitive to such domestic political requirements of the other government and must learn to discount accordingly the importance of public statements as policy indicators. The irony of the openness of democracy and a free press is that secret diplomacy becomes more common and more essential in order to avoid the political contradictions imposed by the two-audience problem.

Regional Policy Perspectives

Suppose the government of Alberta sent a trade delegation to Washington. What would the proper reception be, in diplomatic terms, and how would Ottawa perceive this initiative and response? This kind of practical application of the psychology of the relationship to policy making appears constantly in Canadian-American relations. Regional policy perspectives continually feed into the overall management of the relationship.

At a formal level, because the province of Alberta does not have diplomatic status as a sovereign international actor, certain diplomatic activity and recognition is automatically precluded. But the United States must be careful not to alienate Alberta because, after all, the province has considerable political and economic autonomy within the framework of the British North American Act. On the other hand, the United States must avoid giving the wrong signals to Ottawa regarding the American position on Canadian unity and federal-provincial relations. In particular, Washington must avoid falling into the trap of giving Ottawa the impression that the United States is lobbying on behalf of provincial interests. This is especially problematic when the U.S. position is closer to the actual provincial position than to the Canadian federal position on an issue, such as tariff reduction or energy policy.

The rules for dealing with such regional matters are not merely defined by what is correct diplomatically; the psychology of relations is at stake as well.[13] In general, the more regional these matters can become on both sides of the border—that is, provincial-state in character—the easier relations will be to manage at the federal level. Although the United States may at various times sympathize with the positions on issues held by one or another province, all negotiation must occur either at the province-state level, or, if at the federal level, through Ottawa.

Negotiations between Washington and a particular province are likely to become troublesome for all concerned. Negotiations between Ottawa and a particular state create fewer problems for the obvious reason that the same anxiety that exists in Canada over sovereignty and control does not exist in the United States, although conflicts between Washington and the border states over the handling of issues inevitably will occur.

To some extent, regional issues are regional if treated that way by both governments and national if treated that way by one or both governments. Geographic location alone does not establish whether an issue is regional or national. Is the Alaskan Pipe Line agreement regional merely because it passes through a portion of the United States and Canada? Such a designation would mean that only a few national security and multilateral issues have a truly national character.

Moreover, it is a misunderstanding of the psychology of the relationship to suppose that validly regional issues are necessarily any less acrimonious than national issues. Again, the key is how these issues are treated by each government. Careful management of issues will ensure that the tone of the overall relationship is not sacrificed in defense of content. But if messy regional or national bilateral issues are allowed (and perhaps encouraged), for whatever reason, to become highly politicized on one or both sides of the border, they are likely to ruin the tone of the relationship, with potentially far-reaching consequences. Thus, regional grievances and the way such grievances are handled will determine tone, and the tone of the relationship when the federal governments are involved has national and international consequences.

Unsynchronized Policies

A puzzling aspect of the psychology of U.S.-Canada relations is that each country can favor the same policy involving bilateral relations, but at different times. Lack of synchronization thus dooms mutual acceptance and implementation of the policy. This perverse tendency to adopt similar policies at dissimilar intervals may owe its explanation to tactics (see earlier theoretical discussion). Governments may manipulate timing and avoid having to accede to policies that are substantively acceptable but that would create too great a loss of sovereignty. Or, conversely, the governments may actually want the outcomes but may be unable at the last moment to get the various interest groups and constituencies to agree to policies that each country separately finds plausible and beneficial. Or, the actual policies may be a function more of a set of internal forces than of external negotiation; this set of internal forces follows a cycle of its own. When one government is at the point in its cycle where it is prepared to negotiate, the other is at some other point in its own internal decision-making cycle, and negotiation, for the time being, is impossible. Somehow, the two governments fail to bring these two cycles into harmony. I find this third explanation the most plausible. It can be illustrated by a brief look at the history of tariff negotiations.

In contrast to prevailing wisdom, Canada was historically a low-tariff country, and the United States was a high-tariff country. But in the period of approximately sixty years between the autumn of 1849 and the winter of 1910-11, each country shifted its position on tariff negotiations many times. Following the collapse of the Old Colonial system and the advent of British free trade, Canada was driven to consider other alternatives to a preferential association with Britain. The merchants of Montreal, fearing isolation and bankruptcy, signed a manifesto in 1849 that advocated annexation of Canada to the United States, a manifesto that was virtually ignored in New York and Washington, as it was elsewhere in British North America. Yet, Canadian sentiment for closer commercial association with the United States would never be stronger.

The two domestic decision cycles involving tariff reduction came together temporarily in the Reciprocity Treaty of 1854, which established reciprocal free trade in coal, fish, and agricultural and forest products. But with the defeat of the low-tariff South in the Civil War, the American North rejected the previously determined terms of reciprocity and introduced a new program of protectionism. This American disinterest in partial free trade was reinforced in 1874, when the U.S. Senate rejected Alexander Mackenzie's offer, through George Brown, to accept a quid pro quo of a Canadian concession on inshore fisheries for a treaty establishing mutual free trade in manufactures of wood, iron, and steel, as well as some commodities.

By 1875, MacDonald had converted this American disinterest into a new Canadian national policy that would create "incidental protection" for Canada's manufactures and a solid backlog of votes from Ontario citizens for the Conservative party. By the turn of the century, the United States was looking for new markets for its manufactures, and its farmers were feeling less pressure with regard to price than before 1896, the year of the titular collapse of the Populist movement, which had had a strong protectionist overtone. This new American enthusiasm for tariff reduction found a friendly audience in the government of Sir Wilfrid Laurier. Negotiations resulted in a package that involved tariff reductions in selected manufactured goods as well as in commodities and natural products. But the treaty languished in the Canadian Parliament in the winter of 1910-11 for want of closure on debate and was lost entirely later that year with the defeat of the Liberal party in the federal elections, a defeat based partly on the issue of reciprocity.[14]

How can we explain the vacillations in attitude toward tariff reductions that took place on both sides of the border during this critical period of industrial development? My own assessment is that the politics of rapprochement between the two countries rest on a very thin psychological edge. Rapprochement is dependent upon support from domestic political groups, which must themselves fight for ascendancy and position. There is no guarantee that these political groups will prevail electorally and, indeed, some suspicion that, on average, they will not. Moreover, the timing of their ascent and decline has little to do with factors external to each country. Hence, only by luck and by dint of enormous subsequent diplomatic effort will groups that advocate policies congruent enough to lead to productive negotiations come to the fore politically at the same time in both countries.

Among the forces that were influential during this period in tariff negotiations, regional forces clearly were important: forces in the southern United States and in the Maritime provinces and western Canada. Similarly, political parties—the Democrats, the Liberal party and groups within the Republican and Conservative parties—determined whether a proposal for a tariff reduction would ever get a hearing domestically. Bold leadership was also important and was as specific as the commitment of Sir Wilfrid Laurier or William Howard Taft. But the public mood in each country was as much a factor, and that mood could become overpowering, as the landslide in favor of Sir Robert Borden in the 1911 Canadian elections demonstrated. Thus, to quite an extent the Canadian-American relationship was and is hostage to the domestic political outlook and to domestic leadership on each side of the border. If, for some reason, a hardening of negotiation terms occurs or painful issues arise, and these circumstances are useful for electoral or parliamentary purposes in Washington or Ottawa, no amount of diplomacy can reverse a psychology in the relationship that is apparently extraordinarily vulnerable to such manipulation.

One of the similarly fascinating long-term changes in the political psychology of Canadian-American relations is the way that political parties can shift their focuses regarding the utility of closer binational coordination. Between 1911 and 1981, the Conservative party and the Liberal party exactly reversed their postures toward the United States; the Liberal party now advocates the more protectionist, more trade diversionist point of view, whereas the Conservative party is now sympathetic to more bilateral cooperation. The responsibilities of governing as well as the changing nature of constituent support in the twentieth century have contributed to these changing party outlooks. Only through an examination from such a historical vantage point can one hope to unravel the dynamic changes in the collective psychology of modern Canadian-American relations.

FOUR

The Trade-Commercial Dimension: Neutrality versus Reciprocity

Just as the principle of comparative advantage determines to some extent what a nation will trade by encouraging a country to use most intensely those factors of production it possesses most abundantly, so comparative advantage determines which of the overall theoretical dimensions will figure most strongly in the foreign policies of Canada and the United States. What this means is that Canada has traditionally emphasized the trade-commercial dimension, whereas the United States emphasizes the political-strategic dimension. Canada has a comparative advantage in trade and commerce because such a large relative share of its GNP is tied up with external trade and because private foreign investment figures so significantly in its economic development. Although the United States stresses political-strategic factors, it is not uninterested in international trade and commerce. In recent years, U.S. export trade as a percentage of GNP has increased to roughly 12 percent. Although the corresponding figure for Canada is 30 percent, American economic relations with Canada have nonetheless become more significant in the last decade. A few statistics bear out both these absolute and relative levels of significance.

Although each country is the other's most important trading partner, as our discussion on intervulnerability explained, there is marked asymmetry in the relationship. In 1977, Canada accounted for about 21 percent of America's export trade, whereas the United States accounted for about 67 percent of Canada's foreign exports. Turning to foreign investment, if the official statistics were reported properly, each country would be the other's most important source of foreign investment.[1] But again asymmetry is pronounced. In 1978, about 22 percent of America's foreign direct investment was located in Canada, whereas Canada had concentrated about 39 percent of its direct foreign investment in the United States.[2] The United States has about four times more direct and portfolio investment in Canada than Canada has in the United States, but the rate of U.S. investment in Canada is decreasing, while the rate of Canada's investment in the United States is increasing. Canadian investment in U.S. manufacturing, energy, real estate, and construction industries is growing at a rapid pace. Based on this quick review of the bilateral economic situation, a number of things can be noted regarding how this dimension is beginning to affect the whole foreign policy relationship between the two countries.

First and foremost, each country is undeniably the most important single economic partner of the other. This fact in itself conditions the entire relationship and sets it apart from all others for both countries. Each country is capable of providing benefits to the other. A decline in the level or intensity of economic interaction is also likely to hurt both trading partners. These are the simple realities of intervulnerability.

Second, some asymmetry exists in the foreign trade relationship. Foreign trade, in an overall sense, is less important for the United States than for Canada. Canada has a far higher percentage of its total foreign trade involved with the United States than the United States does with Canada. If trade diversification and self-reliance are important politically (and in an interdependent world this may be more questionable than it seems historically), then the United States is somewhat freer of obligations in this economic sense than is Canada. These findings also seem to uphold the hypothesis that Canadians emphasize the economic dimension more than do Americans.

Third, in contrast to the implications of the prior observation, the enormous absolute concentration of U.S. foreign investment in Canada leaves that investment highly vulnerable to pressures of various sorts. This high local concentration of U.S. investment generates potential influence for Canada because of the hostage character of the investment. If the policies of the two countries diverge, and one or both countries resort to power politics in the economic sphere, this enormous bloc of U.S. investment is subject to manipulation by the Canadian federal government or by the provinces. At the margin, in terms of amounts of recent annual investment, the two countries are balanced, which somewhat offsets the effect of the hostage character of the larger total U.S. investment base in Canada. The hostage status of U.S. investment, which is created by its high concentration relative to the size of the Canadian industrial base, is nevertheless further reinforced by the locus of the investment in the energy industry, which Ottawa has marked for Canadianization, and in a few other industries. Thus the asymmetry favoring the United States in terms of trade is fairly compellingly offset by the asymmetry favoring Canada in terms of investment. The conclusion is that, in more general terms, intervulnerability within the Canadian-American relationship is convincingly supported.

From the analysis so far presented, an initial conclusion is that the attitude each government adopts towards the economic dimension is critical to the relationship. If the overall economic and commercial philosophies of the two governments are congruent, the respective asymmetries are unlikely to make much difference and the fact of intervulnerability will be impressed upon both governments. If, however, the philosophies of foreign trade and investment policy begin to diverge, coordination may grow more difficult.

An assessment of some of the prevailing historical economic outlooks of the two countries will be helpful at this point. On the basis of this historical view, it will then be possible to examine the present outlooks and draw some conclusions regarding how those outlooks are likely to shape future trade and commercial policies. Conclusions can also be reached about how these commercial policies themselves are likely to affect the overall foreign affairs relationship that has been the hallmark of governmental behavior within the U.S.-Canada partnership since 1945.

TRADE AND COMMERCE
FROM THE U.S. PERSPECTIVE

U.S. trade and commercial policies in the twentieth century have become sympathetic with liberal international trade policies. However, the United States has not always been a defender of tariff reduction, and in 1816, Henry Clay's "American system" imposed tariffs of 30 to 40 percent on certain iron products, cotton, and wool.[3] These tariffs were later extended and became the basis of the attack of the southerner John C. Calhoun on the "tariff of abominations," which he claimed was a scheme to enrich Northern manufacturers at the cost of agriculturalists in the South. On the heels of the stock market crash, the highest tariff in U.S. history — the Smoot-Hawley tariff of 1930 — was imposed. The commercial consequences of this tariff taught the United States two lessons that entrenched liberal trade policy in the post-World War II era. First, it became clear that protectionist pressure from labor and industrial management was greatest during recession or depression in industries that had the greatest difficulty in competing abroad because of relatively low productivity. Second, the use of tariffs reduces the world volume of trade, world economic output, and employment and leads to retaliation by other trading partners. No international trade order could maximize efficiency or equity through countenancing the widespread use of tariffs and quotas. Thus, the disasters of the 1930s, more than any other single event, encouraged the United States to take a leading role in the formation of the General Agreement on Tariffs and Trade in 1948 and in the successive efforts at multilateral tariff reduction known as the Kennedy and Tokyo rounds. U.S. trade policy toward Canada must be seen in the light of this larger U.S. commitment to the ideal of the liberal international trade order.[4]

A second aspect of the U.S. economic outlook is the support for the comparatively free movement of capital and labor. With regard to labor, the United States has always favored liberal immigration policies, by international standards, in part because of the low density of the U.S. population and in part because such an immigration policy is considered one of the principles upon which the republic was founded. The U.S. attitude toward immigration from Canada has been even more favorable, welcoming flows of workers, students, temporary residents, and permanent citizens. Indeed, in some cases, immigrants found that U.S. citizenship via Canada was easier than direct immigration to the United States itself. Like most other democracies, the United States also permits unfettered exit from the country; like Canada, the United States permits virtually unrestricted movement back and forth across the Canadian-U.S. border.

Movement of capital, in either the direct or the portfolio form, has been a principal stimulus to U.S. economic development in the nineteenth century and continues to be at the core of U.S. commercial policy toward other countries in the twentieth century. The U.S.-Canada relationship has become a symbol of this concept of unrestricted capital mobility. Although each multinational corporation has its own objectives in making investments abroad, including greater profits, market diversification, offsets to competition, and an assured supply of raw materials, U.S. capital as a whole has historically been attracted to the Canadian market for several broad reasons. First, Americans believe they know the Canadian market, and they are comfortable with the Canadian people. Ease of communication and transportation also increases Canada's attractiveness as a locus of foreign investment. Second, the existence of comparatively high Canadian tariffs in the past encouraged American manufacturers to locate inside the tariff walls, in order to service the Canadian market via American branch plants. (But the Tokyo round of tariff reductions has freed up all but about 20 percent of the trade between the two countries, and thus the rationale for U.S. investment in Canadian manufacturing is less compelling, because more of the Canadian market can be supplied from the excess production capacity of American-based plants.) Third, U.S. direct investment in Canadian mineral extraction provided the capital for rapid development while diffusing risk over large, worldwide operations. Successful development contributed to vertical integration and therefore to both efficiency and assured supply.

Finally, American capital was attracted to Canada because American firms regarded Canada as possessing a favorable political climate for foreign investment. The risk of political instability was virtually nonexistent. The attitude toward capital repatriation was satisfactory, and until the late 1970s, with the toughening of screening procedures for the Foreign Investment Review Agency and the advent of potash expropriation activity in Saskatchewan and the provincialization of asbestos production in Quebec, the threat of expropriation or creeping expropriation was thought to be minimal. Canada stood out among countries as a place where American firms could do business. The result was the very high level of American investment in Canada, including investment in key industries that received high visibility.

A quid pro quo for Canada was that Canadian investors were welcomed to the United States. This did not mean that takeovers of U.S. firms, for example, would be easy or that the impact of Canadian investment on American institutions and society would be the same as the impact of American investment in Canada, even if the amount of Canadian investment in the United States were the same as the amount of U.S. investment in Canada (which is true only at the margin). After all, the Canadian GNP is only one-ninth that of the United States. Nonetheless, the principle of equivalent access for Canadian investment was well-established and was honored by the U.S. government and by the state governments, with few exceptions.

In broad terms, then, the American outlook toward economic matters was not strongly oriented toward free trade, because many barriers still stood in the way of the perfectly unrestricted flow of goods, services, labor, and capital across boundaries; instead, the United States adopted a liberal trade attitude founded on the norms of reciprocity and nondiscrimination. Third World countries were allowed to discriminate to some extent. Third World countries benefited from the most-favored-nation clause of the GATT, enjoying the same trade concessions as the advanced industrial nations without having to make concessions in return. The key provision of trade liberalization was that, insofar as possible, liberalization would lead to equivalent increases in exports and imports for all the multiple trading partners. Most Third World countries were not expected to become members of the GATT, but they would enjoy the benefits of tariff reductions anyway. Of course, if no tariff reductions among the advanced-industrial trading partners occurred in areas, such as textiles, where Third World production was concentrated, the benefits of trade liberalization for them would be less appreciable. On the other hand, for countries like Hong Kong, Taiwan, and South Korea, which had consciously export-oriented growth and development plans, the increasing liberalization of the trade order did seem helpful. For a country like Canada, rich in resources and possessing the proper mix of skilled labor and capital, the liberal international trade order was regarded by many trade theorists as highly propitious. Large size was, of course, extremely valuable for a country, because it enabled firms to take advantage of a local market and of more economical, longer production runs. Consumers, too, benefited from greater product specialization and a wider selection of products and lower costs.

According to the American conception, the liberal international trade order was important precisely because of the problem of the differential size of economies. Because small countries were not able to enjoy the same diversity and low cost of goods as could the larger economies, reliance on international trade was more critical for them than for the bigger countries. Indeed, in countries with smaller economies, the ratio of foreign trade to the size of the GNP is larger. Because international trade is so important for countries with smaller economies, according to this argument, this trade should occur among countries that discriminate as little as possible against each other if collective gains from trade are to be maximized. Of course, the actual distribution of the gains from trade is less easy to specify or guarantee.

Size was not everything, however, even in the context of the trade order that existed during the 1960s. A small country like Sweden, for example, had on average lower tariffs than Japan, Britain, the United States, and the European Community, ranked in that order. Further multilateral tariff reductions stood to benefit all trading countries largely according to the degree that they participated in world commercial trade. Moreover, when the United States was, from time to time, reminded of the trade wars that had occurred in the 1930s and of the existence of nontariff barriers that still inhibited trade, this concept of the liberal trade order, properly accompanied by trade incentives for Third World development, gained favor. In any case, no other proposal appeared more workable or offered more widespread appeal.

TRADE AND COMMERCE
FROM THE CANADIAN OUTLOOK

Historically, British North America was not a high-tariff country, at least in the context of trade relations inside the British Empire, where it participated in the system of imperial preference. The system of exchange was essentially that of mercantilism: British North America traded fish, lumber, and other raw materials for finished goods from Britain. As Britain shifted toward free trade, British North America furtively sought other arrangements with the United States, ultimately in terms of the protectionist policies of Sir John A. MacDonald's National Policy. Although the National Policy was publicized as a revenue measure, its real immediate purpose was to protect Canadian manufacturers from foreign competition and to garner votes for the old Liberal-Conservative (or simply Conservative) party.[5] Subsequently, however, the National Policy had larger implications in developmental and regional terms.

First, the National Policy and protectionism (and here protectionism includes the notion of subsidies and nontariff barriers) became equated in the public mind with nation building. Nation building was essentially a political rationale for restrictionist economic measures, but the political rationale was ultimately more persuasive than the economic. Whenever protectionism has been advocated, including during its periodic appearances in the United States, the movement has obtained the greatest public support when it sounded the most patriotic. In the Canadian context, however, nation building was a far more compelling theme, because of the unevenness of population concentrations, the combination of cultural and linguistic differences and regional homogeneity, and the enormous spatial distances; nevertheless, the use of protectionism as a tool for nation building may have been no more justified and successful here than efforts to use protectionism for this purpose have been elsewhere.

Nation building had two elements. First, nation building, through the use of protected markets, was designed to foster economic and political bonds between the eastern and western sections of Canada. The key was to establish a vigorous industrial core in Ontario and Quebec. Montreal and Toronto, reinforced by the corridor between them, were to evolve as the principal metropolitan centers of the industrial heartland. Outlying areas of Canada, including the mountain, prairie, and the Maritime provinces, would provide markets and sources of farm products and raw materials. This did not mean that farm products and raw materials were always unavailable in the industrial heartland itself or that industrial development was to be discouraged by governmental action when it flourished outside of the designated areas. The National Policy came to be interpreted as a means to strengthen ties between the eastern and western sections of Canada by creating an industrial core that was large and concentrated enough to enable Canadian industry to survive international competition. Because this concept meant industrial development was to be encouraged where the bulk of the labor force lived, the eastern and western regions were necessarily at some disadvantage. At the polls, however, the government was reinforced in the wisdom of its strategy, because the National Policy coincided with the interests of the majority of the voters, who happened to live in the regions that benefited most, in terms of growth, from protectionist policies.

Second, nation building was designed to disrupt economic bonds between the United States and Canada. Although this was not clearly stated as an objective, it was implied. Many of these north-south transactions were more efficient, because distances were shorter and economies of scale kept the U.S. costs of production lower; goods produced in the United States were therefore sometimes difficult for Canadian manufacturers to undersell. For similar reasons, Canadian farmers and mine owners could ship to buyers in the United States and often receive a better price than if they relied on markets within Canada. Manitoba wheat producers sometimes found the Minneapolis or Chicago price more attractive than the Toronto or Montreal price. Trade in manufactured goods between Vancouver and Seattle and between Toronto and Cleveland made as much sense economically as trade largely within the interior of Canada. Thus, from the viewpoint of protectionists, north-south trade had to be diverted into east-west channels in order to overcome the natural attractiveness of the U.S. market.

From this perspective, it was particularly important that nation building offset regional trade across the border. Too close an identification between British Columbia and the Washington-Oregon area, for example, or between Alberta and Montana, held implications that intense but randomly dispersed north-south trade did not hold. These implications carried strong political overtones that went far beyond a simple fear of the continental market notion. From the Canadian nation-building point of view, such implications came close to sedition, because they tended to encourage regional autonomy within Canada itself. Regional autonomy was an even greater threat to Canadian unity than was too close an economic association with the United States as a whole.

Nation building via a protectionist course also had the larger objective of diffusing institutional ties between Canada and the United States that might grow up around trade itself, ties that could eventually spill over into the political realm. Thinking was (and is) unsettled regarding the seriousness of this problem. But the proponents of protectionism who used the nation-building argument feared the impact of north-south trade on buying preferences, banking habits, recreational choices, and even voting behavior. If north-south interactions were allowed to flourish unimpeded, it was feared, the importation of institutional associations and cultural preferences would be such that Canada would have trouble maintaining its distinctness at the popular or mass level, regardless of the resilience and loyalty of the governing elites. Protectionism would enhance nation building, in this view, by disrupting some of the north-south traffic and by halting some of the effects of attitudinal contamination.

A second major argument on behalf of protectionism in Canada was the well-known argument concerning infant industries. This argument justifies protectionism on the basis that it shields fledgling industries from foreign pressures until they are able to mature. Although Japan has shown that the argument may have some plausibility when applied to firms in a so-called leading sector, in which future demand for products will be very high because a new market is emerging that is "up for grabs" globally, the argument has flaws in virtually every other context. Protectionism cannot create new industries where there were none (France, for example, could not use government subsidies and protection to build a viable computer industry) any more than protection can eliminate industrial inefficiency when there is a great deal of it. But the principal problem that Canada has found with this argument, a problem that has been encountered everywhere the infant-industry rationale has been tried, is that it serves to keep infant industries infant; that is, these industries fail to mature precisely because they are not forced to become efficient enough, through innovation and expansion, to compete internationally.

Why, then, has the infant-industry argument been perpetuated? It has survived in part because Canadians sometimes think of their economy as sharing the characteristics of a Third World country; that is, a high proportion of the national income arises from the export of farm commodities, pulp and lumber, and minerals. New firms and new industries are thus eligible for protection because the economy as a whole has had such a difficult time diversifying. In economies, like those of the United States or the European Community, in which greater diversification is present, the flaws in the infant-industry argument are easier to accept as unsolvable.

A third argument for protectionism involved the trade-off between growth and development. Many Canadians are willing to sacrifice some economic growth for a more diversified economy obtained through protected markets. In other words, protectionism may inhibit growth, but at least it facilitates a broader economic base, which may in turn provide a more stable income. These Canadians would prefer a protected and comparatively inefficient chemicals industry to no chemical industry at all. But which industries are to be regarded as essential and how much inefficiency is to be regarded as tolerable?

The alternative of maximizing economic growth by concentrating in those fields in which Canada does best is not attractive if those fields do not include firms in the leading economic sectors of, for example, electronics, petro chemicals, and high technology. Moreover, there is a feeling that the "value added" is greatest in the processing and semiprocessing industries, not in the fields of mineral extraction, farming, and forestry. Thus, somewhat slower, more stable growth that includes the prospect of creating a diversified economy—even if that economy is not as efficient as it could otherwise be—is an acceptable proposition to many Canadians.

Finally, there is a trade-off that supports the use of tariffs or, if tariffs become sufficiently unpopular internationally, government subsidies or other types of nontariff barriers. This trade-off occurs between national income, growth, and individual wealth. By and large, Canadian public policy has sacrificed individual wealth and consumer preferences for investment and increases in national income. To an extent, Canada followed a "supply-side" economic policy before the Reagan administration made the phrase popular in the United States. Canada has encouraged saving and investing over consuming through appropriate personal and corporate income taxes and generous depreciation rules; government subsidies and nontariff barriers that assist Canadian industry but place extra cost on the consumer also operate to the same end.

Thus, the individual Canadian subsidizes the government and the Canadian private sector. Adjustment costs are thereby avoided and some unpleasant inter-regional disputes, for instance, disputes over the fate of declining industries, are also diffused, if not permanently resolved. But the key observation is that the average member of Canadian society is apparently more loyal to the federal government than the average American citizen is to Washington; a measure of this is the way that the average Canadian tolerates transfers from consumers to government or to the private sector through the admittedly often rather invisible mechanisms of protection and government subsidy. Loyalty is also increased through the high level of government service and middle-class welfare provided by Ottawa.

A philosophy of protectionism and subsidy is well established in Canada; it is at odds with the American philosophy of liberal international trade. The paradox here is interesting. The United States began its economic development as a high-tariff country but now defends liberal international trade and low tariffs. Canada began its economic development as a comparatively low-tariff country but now defends various restrictions on international trade. It is important to examine further some of the costs associated with the economic path Canada has decided to follow before considering how these two philosophies of trade and investment affect current bilateral trade and commercial policy.

One reality of the protectionist approach is that at least half of the political strategy has backfired. Although protectionism may have safeguarded Canada from too close an economic and political association with the United States, protectionism has not fostered closer east-west ties within Canada. On the contrary, the National Policy to some extent planted the seeds of regional economic disunity in Canada, despite a far-sighted policy of economic transfer payments to the poorer provinces which, until recently, was financed primarily by the industrial heartland. The National Policy may have strengthened east-west ties in a narrowly economic sense, but it also worsened political fragmentation. It raised the specter of industrial exploitation by Ontario, because the outlying areas had to purchase industrial goods at inflated costs from either Ontario or foreign countries, and in some cases, they received lower prices for their commodities and farm products in return. Thus, the political tension surrounding Canadian economic policy could scarcely be considered a source of political unity even after tariffs with the outside world were lowered following the Kennedy and Tokyo rounds. Memories of real and imagined exploitation remained in the western regions, for example, contributing to the poor electoral showing of the Liberal party west of Winnipeg. Western citizens' suspicions of the federal government on trade and commercial policies was reinforced by the government's attempt to create an industrial core in east-central Canada, especially as the financial power and, more slowly, the population began to shift westward.

A second negative consequence for Canada of the protectionist course was the encouragement given to foreign direct investment to jump tariff walls. The consequences of protectionism in this regard were twofold. On the one hand, protectionism accelerated the quantity of investment that would normally have flowed into Canada, because this was the only way foreign firms could gain access to the Canadian domestic market. On the other hand, protectionism also catalyzed the tendency to create "truncated branch plants" or plants designed to make essentially the same products as those made in the United States but at lower economies of scale, rather than to manufacture goods for re-export globally.[6] One characteristic of this trend was that much less research and development was necessary in a branch plant than in a firm attempting to compete globally for markets. Patent rights, for example, could be acquired, for a fee, from the home office. This tendency to construct branch plants was a direct consequence of the tariff structures. Had tariffs been lower, the branch plants, like Canadian domestic firms, would have been forced to compete internationally and to rely on innovation to establish new markets and to keep costs down. Indeed, the tariffs had a remarkably similar effect on both foreign-owned branch plants and domestic Canadian firms: both were producing largely for the domestic Canadian market behind tariff walls that sealed out the pressures that would have encouraged technological and administrative dynamism. Just because a domestic firm was domestic did not mean that it automatically acquired a different outlook than a foreign-owned facility. Under these protectionist circumstances, the domestic firm was as likely as the foreign-owned facility to rely on the comfortable security of the Canadian market and to avoid the clash of harsh competition in export markets abroad.

A third drawback of the protectionist system was that government interventionism in terms of investment had implications for the matter of management risk and capital availability. Insofar as Canada pursued an interventionist course, this would affect the amount of political risk that foreign investors perceived, not just in the industries, such as energy, which were marked for intervention but in other industries as well. Fear of nationalization or "creeping nationalization" would increase the cost of borrowing in bond markets and would reduce the willingness of foreign investors to enter the Canadian market, because no way existed to compartmentalize risk and to show that the risks of increased governmental intervention were restricted only to certain areas.

Nonetheless, these drawbacks are qualified by the realization that

Canada has traditionally been viewed as a far more attractive site for U.S. investment, in particular, than other countries. Indeed, U.S. investors historically have tended to regard the Canadian market as no more risky than the U.S. market, because both governments were thought to treat investment similarly, treating domestic and foreign investment equally. But government intervention against foreign investment in energy took the "glamour" away from Canada as an investment location, not just in areas where foreign investment was purposefully shunned but in other areas as well, because of the spill-over effects of fear and risk. Interventionism carried a cost that was bearable from the interventionist point of view: nonetheless, the cost was real and measurable in terms of lowered bond ratings, higher interest rates on borrowed money, increased overall caution on the part of foreign investors, and the depressing effect on the Canadian dollar.

Finally, the policies of protectionism, subsidy, and government intervention created an additional cost for the Canadian consumer: the generation of local monopolies. The purpose of these Canadian commercial and trade policies, which began as far back as the National Policy, was not to enrich some Canadians at the cost of others or to inhibit competition in the Canadian marketplace. Neither was the purpose to slow down the growth of output or productivity. Yet, the generation of local monopolies was a side effect of protectionism, albeit an unwanted one, and it tended to have some of these consequences.

In the attempt to create larger firms and a stronger industrial sector, Canada has, in some cases, allowed monopolies and monopoly practices, such as price coordination, to arise. Existence of large amounts of foreign investment in an economy is by itself no measure of competition between firms. If the objective of foreign investment is to get inside a protected market so as to earn an unusually high profit, as domestic firms are earning, the presence of foreign capital is no shield against monopoly practices.

Similarly, the rapid growth of a firm—growth designed to allow the firm to take advantage of economies of scale—may not be helpful to the welfare of the average consumer if the bulk of that firm's production (regardless of whether it is a domestic or a foreign-owned firm) is directed at the local market and is subsidized or otherwise protected by governmental policy. Output and productivity gains will be smaller under conditions of monopoly.

Thus the trade-off between the size of a firm and its efficiency has been an unpleasant one for Canada. The high cost of consumer goods in protected or subsidized industries indicates the price Canada has paid for a more interventionist route to economic growth and development.

Apart from these internal costs associated with a more protectionist trade and commercial philosophy, a large potential external cost may also exist. Canada has increasingly become a net exporter of capital, as noted earlier, especially to the United States. Also, as I observed in Chapter 2, because the tactics involved in the Canadian-American relationship include, in extreme situations, the threat of retaliation, any large increases in protectionism by either trading partner invite the erection of similar barriers on the other side of the border. The consequence amounts to Type C intervulnerability. Both partners lose, in strict economic terms, with respect to their own interests and with respect to the system as a whole. If protectionism increases, some analysts may argue that Canada will enjoy the political benefits of greater isolation from the United States or the confidence associated with a more diversified economy. But the economic costs associated with possible retaliation by other trading partners, including the United States, would surely dilute the net benefits of protectionism, if any, to Canadian society.

Conversely, because, as we have seen in the theoretical discussion, liberal trade expansion characterizes the relationship, the expanding benefits of the GATT negotiations have enabled Canada both to diversify its trade somewhat, because of the rule of reciprocal trade preferences, and to strengthen its economy relative to that of the United States. Far from encouraging greater inflows of foreign investment into Canada, the Kennedy and Tokyo rounds have stimulated all of the non-Communist advanced-industrial governments to rely to a greater degree on trade (insofar as the effect of nontariff barriers has not offset the effect of tariff reduction). Thus, liberal trade expansion is likely, to some extent, to have the opposite impact on Canada, and on its trading partners, from the effect its opponents envision. Multinational firms are likely to contract foreign operations, not expand them, as the international economic universe becomes more oriented toward trade and less toward foreign investment.

PERSPECTIVES IN COMPARISON AND IN CONTRAST

In considering the origin of the difference between the Canadian and the American trade and commercial perspectives, the perceived importance of economic size has certainly been critical. To some extent, the United States, because of its economic size, has been locked into a continuation of past policies, because any major change would affect other economies so sharply; movement toward flexibile exchange rates, for example, was postponed to the last minute. Liberal free trade is the one approach to international economic relations that minimizes to a tolerable degree the disparity between the economic self-interest of the United States and its responsibilities to the global international economic order.

For Canada, asymmetry—that is, the contrast between the size of the

Canadian GNP and that of the United States—has been an overwhelming determinant in its trade and commercial outlook. The idea that "good fences make good neighbors" has never been far from Canadian economic thinking. An offset to the predominant economic influence of the United States has always been sought, usually in the form of subsidy or protection, through governmental initiative.[7] From the Canadian point of view, if Canada had been ten times larger in economic terms, or ten times more geographically distant from the commercial heartland of the United States, unrestricted free trade would have looked a lot better.

Governmental interventionism against the weight of foreign investment near the end of the twentieth century, in a period when foreign capital is perceived as less essential to some areas of Canadian economic development, is thus the natural counterpart of trade protectionism at the end of the nineteenth century. Both the National Policy of Sir John A. MacDonald and the National Energy Program of Pierre Elliott Trudeau involve governmental intervention into the Canadian economy. Both seek nation-building by limiting outside economic influence and by accentuating east-west links. But by protecting trade, the National Policy induced a large and sustained inflow of foreign investment into Canada, principally from the United States. Discrimination against foreign investment, such as that implied by the National Energy Program, is an effort within a single industrial sector to stem the flow of investment from abroad. This one set of interventionist policies seeks to reverse what the earlier set of policies inadvertently started. Although Canada has participated fully in the Tokyo round of tariff talks, which eventually freed up 80 percent of the trade between Canada and the United States, it has in the same period sought to protect a sector of its industry through proposed "buy Canada" legislation and investment discrimination. Canadianization is, from the interventionist viewpoint, the inevitable counterpart to protectionism on the trade side. Although investment in resources followed a more complicated rationale than did strict tariff inducement, without the initial policy of trade protectionism there would have been less incentive for Canadianization. But with protectionism came the need the Canadian government perceived to constrain foreign ownership, especially in the energy-producing industry, which was likely to earn increasing rents as the Canadian domestic oil price approached the world price.

In a way, the real economic objective of both Canada and the United States has been to overcome the restrictions of insufficient market size: the United States through specialization via liberal free trade; Canada through governmental intervention in support of economic diversification and enhanced domestic ownership. To some extent, doubts about both of these approaches prompted then-candidate Ronald Reagan to propose the creation of a continentwide customs union involving Mexico,

Canada, and the United States.[8] This union would create a new trade area with a collective GNP, in 1979 terms, of 2.5 trillion U.S. dollars and a combined population of 312 million. North America would have an economy twice the size of that of the European Community and two and one-half times that of Japan. It would be largely self-sufficient in most food and resource production. It would also have a rapidly growing industrial base.

The problem with this approach to increased global economic competitiveness from the point of view of Canada and Mexico, however, was that the inequality in size among the trading partners created the fear of potential U.S. domination of decision making. Despite the apparent economic advantages of such a union to all partners and regardless of whether the energy component was included (most customs unions, in fact, exclude energy policy from joint decision making), Mexico and Canada continued to experience doubt with respect to the arrangement. But a customs union involving the three countries was an alternate path to increased competitiveness in North America which avoided the pitfalls of additional protectionism while going beyond the limited benefits that further multilateral tariff reduction alone could provide.

Perhaps the real difference between Canada and the United States in trade and commercial perspectives, however, is rooted in more fundamental societal values and is not merely a function of the differences in economic size. In a middle-class community that must struggle to maintain unity, a slight tendency toward collectivism holds appeal. In a middle-class community where unity seems assured, individualism is allowed to flourish. Herein lies a key difference in values, and ultimately in perspectives, between Canada and the United States. The liberal trade outlook with an emphasis on a strong private sector is the product of an individualist ethic. Governmental intervention in the economy is the product of great faith in governmental initiative. Myths in both countries stimulate these respective tendencies. In the United States, government is often regarded as incompetent and inefficient, whereas the private sector (although no guarantor of equity) is regarded as both competent and efficient: both government and the private sector sometimes live up to these expectations. In Canada, the private sector is often regarded as weak and stagnant, whereas government is the place where true entrepreneurship is found; again the private sector and government often measure up to these standards. In administrative and entrepreneurial terms, in North America one gets to some extent what one anticipates. Myths sometimes become self-fulfilling, even though individuals make an effort to struggle against the stereotypes. Although the analyst should not exaggerate the differences in values and cultural perspectives of the two societies, nor in their preferred approaches to commerce and trade, insight into the origins of behavior on each side of the border helps explain why Canada and the United States do not always share identical economic outlooks. Different economic outlooks raise the question of whether the economic futures of the two countries are convergent or divergent, and to what extent.

ASSESSING BILATERALISM
AND THE NEW INDUSTRIAL POLICY

Although at the time of this writing Canada's new industrial policy is still being debated in Cabinet, bits and pieces of the loosely structured policy are already evident in the areas of energy, education, scientific research, and regional development. An attempt to revive the Third Option, bilateralism has economic aspects that are well-defined and that seem to be congruent with Canada's New Industrial Policy insofar as the outlines of that policy are already visible.

In an important statement of contemporary governmental outlook, Allan Gotlieb, under-secretary of state for external affairs, and Jeremy Kinsman, chairman of the policy planning secretariate of the department of external affairs (later Canadian ambassador to Washington and minister-counsellor, respectively), observe the following:

> The nature of the Canadian economy and society has required governmental involvement to channel aspects of long-range development in beneficial ways. Similarly, it is axiomatic that the benefits of development have to be worked at by Canada. They will not fall out of a free trade, free investment, free-for-all continental economy. This is not an option for Canadian development. Benefits for Canadian industry, however, do not necessarily mean a cost to US private interests, but Canadian policy needs to adopt a strategic approach to succeed. How do we use the levers we have?[9]

This is an interesting statement when set against the prior discussion of the contrast between the Canadian and American trade and commercial outlooks. The phrase that rejects "free trade, free investment, free-for-all continental economy" confirms the dichotomy of views. Canada favors a nationalist approach. Canadian development is to be planned and strategic in nature. As the authors note further, "business interests often need representation at the governmental level." The American preference for a semiadversarial relationship between government and business is rejected. The Canadian government will provide support to Canadian business, presumably to counterbalance the kind of support foreign business interests operating on Canadian territory will receive. Canada will seek "to use the levers we have," which suggests the application of political power on behalf of economic interests.[10] Interdependence is secondary. Functionalism is rejected for a more activist, more power-oriented, approach to international economic relations. As the authors state further, the overall objective of these policies will be to "strengthen control over the Canadian economy and reduce its vulnerability." Thus, the arguments that underlaid much of MacDonald's National Policy regarding trade are echoed today regarding ownership within the Canadian private sector.

Bilateralism has, however, a more explicit meaning that extends and makes specific the policy of trade diversification recommended under the Third Option. But unlike the Third Option statement, the more recent statement of Canadian foreign policy views mentions the United States repeatedly as the target of policy-making activity. In this sense, 1981 finds Canada far more self-assertively critical of economic relations with the United States than did 1971. As the Gotlieb and Kinsman statement puts the matter, "the greatest foreign policy challenge is the relationship with the United States."

Bilateralism explicitly seeks to diversify trade, moving away from the United States, not toward the other advanced-industrial countries, such as Japan and Western Europe, as the Third Option advocated, but toward the "high-growth" partners—Brazil, Mexico, Venezuela, Algeria, Saudi Arabia, South Korea, and members of the Association of Southeast Asian Nations (ASEAN), plus Australia and New Zealand.[11] Why the change of focus? It is partly the result of a problem Canada faces and partly the result of an opportunity Canada sees. The problem involves the trade-off between economic development and political autonomy. Trade diversification, seen from the Canadian point of view, could achieve increased political autonomy. But trade diversification also ought to promote economic development, or at least not hinder that goal. Canada's problem in attempting to diversify trade toward Japan or Germany, for example, was that these countries wanted to exchange their own manufactured goods for Canadian raw materials. The United States, in contrast, bought a far higher proportion of Canadian manufactured goods, in part because the United States, like Canada, is a major exporter of agricultural commodities and raw materials. Thus, to diversify trade toward Japan and Europe meant to drift back into a less diversified set of exports. New trading partners did not mean new industrial markets, it meant somewhat of a return to an earlier era of mercantilism, albeit in a modern trade setting. What Canada seeks is greater political autonomy *and* economic development, not one goal at the cost of the other.

Canada also sees in trade with Third World countries an appealing opportunity. Third World markets are rapidly growing. These countries are interested in Canadian investment both because it provides needed capital and because it offsets the investment efforts of Japan, Europe, and the United States. Trade diversification for Canada means trade diversification for the Third World countries as well. Structural outlooks concerning the role of the middle power in world politics—a role that Canada and the Third World countries all play—are also strikingly similar in some cases. Finally, many of these countries are willing to purchase Canadian manufactured goods. Yet, some difficulties attend this new set of initiatives as well.

Foremost among these difficulties is the diversity of this set of countries in terms of political outlook, geographic location, and cultural composition. A single set of commercial policies is scarcely feasible for so heterogeneous a group. Second, competition is keen and the rate of economic growth, although rapid, still does not yield an actual magnitude of GNP growth that approaches that of the advanced-industrial countries, especially the United States. Third, these markets must be penetrated in large part by the Canadian private sector, far from the shores of Canada. The American market is closer, is familiar, and has far more appeal to the average Canadian manufacturer than do the largely unknown and uncertain markets advocated both by responsible policy makers and by individuals who in some cases have little practical business experience. Finally, apart from export subsidies, special borrowing provisions, information, and other special tax arrangements, the federal government in Ottawa can do little either to divert trade specifically to these destinations or to guarantee that once Canadian foreign investment finds these locations, trade will be secure and profitable. Thus, the prospect of Canadian trade diversification under the rubric of bilateralism may be little more attractive than the experience of government-sponsored trade diversification in the last decade. If one discounts the increase in market share of Japan and Western Europe by the losses to Canada due to commodity concentration, and if one corrects absolute figures for inflation, the Third Option was not very successful. Some trade diversification is already occurring, largely because of the large market share of Canadian trade accounted for by a single country, but such incremental diversification would probably have occurred anyway for sound commercial reasons that are apart from governmental policy.

On the other hand, until bilateralism has had an opportunity to take effect, it is premature to draw conclusions about its ultimate impact upon Canada's trade patterns. Although it is aimed at reducing the U.S. share of trade with Canada, bilateralism is attempting to achieve this in the positive fashion of opening up new markets, rather than suppressing old ones. In this respect, the term *trade diversification* does a disservice to the concept of bilateralism, because it evokes an image of trade diversion rather than trade creation. Trade creation is what all governments wish to encourage, although some market-oriented countries, like the United States, West Germany, and Hong Kong, may leave the task more or less to the private sector, because the feeling is that individual firms are far better at making the critical judgments necessary than are governments. Certainly the United States should have no objection to this form of trade creation so long as discrimination against U.S. trade is not involved. It is up to each individual country to choose its own trading partners, just as it is up to each individual firm to determine its own investment decisions, provided that discrimination, and therefore actual trade diversion, is not at the source of altered trade ties.

More at issue for the United States than the policy of bilateralism is the effect that certain aspects of the new industrial policy may have on U.S. foreign investment in Canada, particularly that in the energy sector. Although I leave a more complete examination of the National Energy Program to a subsequent chapter, I consider some of the investment implications here.

According to one of the clearest and strongest official defenses of the impact of the NEP on U.S. foreign investment, a defense by Ambassador Peter Towe, the United States government should not respond to the demands of the industrial critics of the NEP for a number of reasons.

1. Canada remains an extremely attractive site for foreign oil-industry investment. For every dollar spent on exploration in the federally controlled areas, the after-tax cost for firms with 75 percent Canadian ownership will be seven cents, and for firms with 100 percent foreign ownership the cost will be twenty-eight cents.[12] The Canadian government continues to absorb the bulk of the exploration costs for both foreign and domestic oil firms.

2. The level of foreign control, ownership, and repatriation of capital in Canada is unparalleled in the world and is no longer acceptable to Canadians, as, in converse circumstances, it would not be to Americans. In 1979, for example, 72 percent of the Canadian oil and gas revenues went to foreigners; seventeen of the twenty-five largest oil and gas producers in Canada were foreign-owned and controlled; capital outflows in 1978-79 including dividends and interest amounted to 3.7 billion dollars.[13]

3. The National Energy Program merely corrects an inadvertent discrimination against smaller Canadian firms that had no taxable income against which to get a tax credit. Because the foreign-controlled firms already had the best acreage and oil-sands leases, something had to be done to correct this inequity.

4. Canada had no intention of nationalizing firms, and sales, such as that of Petro Fina's interests to Petro-Canada at 120 dollars a share, were openly negotiated at prices above the market. Firms will not be forced to sell against their preference.

5. Canadians are "surprised" at American calls for retaliation against Canadian proposals for a moratorium on Canadian investment in the United States energy companies. Such retaliation calls into question whether bilateral norms regarding investment openness have been changed.

6. Efforts at retaliation will fail to persuade the Canadian government to further modify the NEP, and such efforts could even amount to "counter-productive endeavor."

7. "In the American context, measures which restrict foreign investment do not appear to serve US national interests, economic or political."

8. Although the NEP does discriminate in favor of domestic firms, sales of assets have occurred because investors have responded to attractive purchase offers.

What this assessment and others indicate is that Canada is establishing a new set of rules for foreign investment, unilaterally and without consultation, although not without prior warning. The key aspect of these new rules is that the government of Canada will discriminate sharply and openly against foreign investment. The purpose is to Canadianize investment by squeezing foreign firms into selling their Canadian holdings, either because of the tax provisions already apparent in the NEP or because of anticipated actions on the part of the Canadian government that could further bolster discrimination. Purchase prices for these holdings have been at or above prevailing market prices, however; compensation therefore meets the criteria established by international law for cases of divestment.

Beneath the surface of the discussions regarding Canada's New Industrial Policy lie two further considerations with import for U.S. policymakers. The NEP is something of a test case for these considerations. First, the primary intent of Canadianization is to reduce U.S. ownership, just as the intent of bilateralism is to diversify trade, moving away from the United States in trade relations. Yet there is nothing in the NEP provisions that discriminates exclusively against U.S. investment. This is the brilliance of the Canadianization package. It employs the predominance of U.S. investment against itself. The greatest number of foreign sales will be American because the bulk of foreign investment is American. In the process of adjustment, the effect could even become disproportionate, thus changing the actual foreign investment mix, although that would happen only if some of the largest foreign holdings in the oil and gas industry were sold.

Second, if the simple expedient of a change in tax laws which alters revenue prospects for foreign investors works in the petroleum industry, why should the same expedient not work in other industries, such as mining or the processing of forest products, in which a net outflow of revenue from the investment is occurring? And, if the application of tax discrimination works elsewhere at very low political cost to the government of Canada, in situations where both able Canadian manager-owners are available and sufficient portfolio capital abounds, what prevents Ottawa from enacting such policies? Thus, concerning the treatment of foreign ownership, the oil industry is perhaps a special case more in concept than in practice.[14]

Outright expropriation, such as Saskatchewan employed in the potash industry, is not necessary, because Canada can achieve the same objective with far less coercion. Some coercion is of course necessary, but it can be more subtle and constrained, depending on the requirements of the individual industry, financing situation, and interval of the business cycle. As far as Ottawa is concerned, the critical management problem is to avoid a situation in which either the NEP does not seem sufficiently coercive to foreign investors to encourage them to sell otherwise attractive oil and gas holdings or the turmoil is so great in the Canadian oil and gas industry that very little actual exploration occurs in Canada, either in Alberta or elsewhere. Such a stalemate would mean a defeat for the NEP perhaps more serious than foreign objections and would probably lead either to the cancellation of much of the NEP or to the imposition of even more coercive regulations to accelerate the process of divestment.

Canada perceives the utility of much of the foreign investment in the Canadian oil and gas industry to be at an end—not all of it (the investment that brings with it skills or technology needed, for example, in the development of the oil sands is still valuable), but much of the investment. From the Canadian viewpoint, foreign capital was desirable when the Canadian oil and gas industry was not self-financing. But the enormous increases in the world-wide price for energy changed all of this, creating the possibility of moving against the largely U.S.-owned energy industry in precisely the fashion that OPEC pioneered. Although the architects of the NEP would probably reject any strategic analogies comparing the NEP with the programs of Libya, Iran, or Saudi Arabia and would probably claim a larger degree of originality for the methods of the NEP, in fact Canadianization of the foreign-owned oil and gas industry follows an already familiar pattern.[15] Canadianization is perhaps the most recent effort since 1973 by a government to transform the nature of the international oil and gas industry. Given this reality, the U.S. government must chart its own course, not just in the bilateral context or in the context of a single industry but in terms of a more general strategy for managing its foreign investment situation in the 1980s.

NEUTRALITY VERSUS RECIPROCITY
IN THE CANADIAN INVESTMENT SETTING

In assessing its response, if any, to the NEP, the United States faces a difficult choice between the principle of neutrality in foreign investment situations and the practice of reciprocity (i.e., retaliation) which has often emerged in U.S.-Canada relations. Points 5 and 7 in the summary of Ambassador Towe's address reveal a full awareness of how difficult this decision is for the United States. Neutrality implies that although the United States supports open movement of capital between countries, it will not come to the assistance of its corporations when they encounter some type of discrimination or coercion abroad.[16] Retaliation implies that if other governments do not honor the unrestricted movement of capital in the way the United States does, the United States will attempt to impose restrictions of the kind they impose. In order to clarify the nature of the choice between neutrality and reciprocity, we must examine the Canadian oil and gas situation in more detail.

When the Ministry of Energy, Mines, and Resources formulated the provisions of the NEP, it calculated that the United States would observe the principle of neutrality or, if the United States did not, that the costs of retaliation would not exceed the benefits of Canadianization. Why was Canada confident that the United States would observe the principle of neutrality? First, in general, the United States views private sector transactions to be at arms length from the core of foreign policy decision making. The ethos of liberal trade favors a system in which firms operate independent of government involvement, through an interval process of regulation but not of sponsorship or support. Second, the United States government did not intervene significantly in any of the disputes over the nationalization by the OPEC nations of U.S.-owned oil and gas properties. Nor has the United States expressed more than its unhappiness in many other investment disputes, for example, the massive nationalization of American-owned properties in France after the emergence of a socialist regime. Why, then, should the United States respond negatively to actions that ensure full compensation and that use much less coerciveness than did nationalization? In particular, for example, if the United States did not more than verbally oppose the nationalization by a government it despised, of its foreign-owned interests in Libya, why should it oppose something far less drastic than nationalization on the part of a government as friendly as Canada?

Third, according to the argument that the United States was unlikely to respond, the old law of the significance of insignificance applied. Canada could slip out from under the umbrella of any American investment norms, because the United States would not want to take any actions that would become a precedent, possibly upsetting its commercial relations with its other OECD trading partners. The leadership responsibilities that the United States has had to assume in defending the liberal international trade order in the post-1945 period simply would not permit it to take exceptional action in the Canadian case. Canada's comparative insignificance in terms of trade and commerce, set alongside America's other interests and obligations, would enable Canada to escape reciprocity because the United States would not want to initiate an action that could be disruptive if broadly applied among OECD countries.

Fourth, if the United States did attempt to retaliate within the same narrow category of foreign investment in oil industry, the United States would not be able to generate much of a response. All of the vulnerability lies on the American side, because the United States has several times more capital invested in Canadian oil and gas than Canada has in U.S. oil and gas. Restrictions on the flow of Canadian capital into the United States would hurt Canada less than additional Canadian restrictions on U.S. foreign investment in Canada could hurt the United States. In addition, strictly parallel legislation could not be effective unless it were focused directly on Canada, because Canada comprised so much smaller a fraction of the total flow of foreign investment into the United States. Under these circumstances, Canada could argue, as it has, that this potential American counter-response would be discriminatory, because it would apply solely to Canada, whereas the Canadian action applied to all foreign investment (even though the United States bears the brunt of the action because of the larger relative size of its Canadian investments).

Finally, in this Canadian view, the United States would not respond because the United States would not want to prejudice its overall political relationship with Canada on behalf of support for firms in the private sector. Given the observation made in Chapter 2 that the United States values the political-strategic dimension over the trade-commercial dimension, the United States would not challenge Canada in a fashion that threatened the positive tone of the relationship. Instead, it would accept the economic consequences with a stiff upper lip, spreading out the costs of "creeping nationalization" over the possibly much larger benefits to the political relationship of doing nothing that Canada might find upsetting.

In view of this array of arguments that seem to support a compliant American policy in the aftermath of the NEP, the United States must reflect upon what its strategic response, if any, to such acts of commercial discrimination ought to be and how such a response fits into the larger pattern of its relations with Canada.

As the basis of its response, the United States must first decide whether the trade and commercial relationship with Canada is to be considered unique or special. If the relationship is not unique or special, then the United States has far less of a moral foothold from which to argue that interference with flows of capital is improper. The moral foothold is tenuous in the absence of the special relationship notion because foreign governmental interference has long occurred with a feeble U.S. response, perhaps for both philosophic and practical political reasons. On the other hand, if the trade and commercial relationship with Canada is to be considered special, inasmuch as North America shares a single huge market divided up among three sovereign and autonomous polities—a market that has unique attributes of intervulnerability and communality—then the United States can argue that reciprocity holds here, as perhaps in only a few other places, such as Western Europe. Just as the United States honors Canadian investment in the United States, so Canada has traditionally honored U.S. investment in Canada. This unrestricted flow of investment funds back and forth has been a cornerstone of Canadian-American relations, giving these two countries much of their impetus for growth, productivity, and efficiency. Obstacles to the movement of production factors across the border will necessarily cause each government to reassess the meaning and nature of the present trade and commercial partnership.

Second, in the midst of the turbulence of discussion, the United States must keep its eyes on the actual issue at stake. The issue involves whether one or another trading partner can unilaterally impose discriminatory terms on the investments of the other. If such a policy becomes generalized among the OECD countries, then foreign investment is likely to be strongly inhibited. If domestic capital is favored over foreign capital, the same kind of inefficiencies are introduced as in the case of trade using tariffs or quotas. The total output of the system is constricted. Indeed, if the international economic system were to rely only upon trade for the exchange of goods and services, a large part of the dynamism that the system has experienced in the late twentieth century would probably disappear; surely adjustments to new opportunities would not occur as quickly and neither economic growth nor development would be what it is today. Thus, the unilateral imposition by one of the leading seven advanced-industrial countries in the non-Communist system of discriminatory practices that favor domestic investment is likely to establish a precedent that others will follow. At least, this is a concern which the United States must voice and against which all of the leading commercial partners must guard.

Third, the argument that high levels of absolute or relative investment in an industry are justification for discriminatory action in favor of domestic investment is highly questionable. Does this mean that if Canada enjoyed an investment share by its firms within another country of greater than 50 percent, say, in the aluminum industry, Canada would be prepared to advocate tax discrimination in favor of the local industry against its own firms? Moreover, what level of foreign investment is acceptable and by whose judgment? Is the mere fact of repatriation of capital an indication that a firm has lost its utility to the country in which it operates and that it is thus to become the subject of discriminatory tax legislation? Or, instead, is the foreign firm to be encouraged to invest as much capital as possible until the time when it begins to repatriate earnings, whereupon it becomes a target of coercion by the government that invited it into the country in the first place? Clearly, the rules regarding such treatment of foreign investment appear somewhat arbitrary. The rules also approximate the use of power politics in the marketplace, thereby demonstrating how thin the web of interdependence is when domestic electoral factors intervene. Canada may very shortly find itself in the position the United States is today vis-à-vis a third commercial partner; after all, Canada is a rapidly growing capital exporter. Canadians thus establish precedents that may be used against themselves at subsequent points in time.

Fourth, a government surely has the right to exclude capital from certain industries for national security or other reasons. Of course, it must be prepared to accept the same type of exclusions, regarding its own investment, imposed by other commercial and trading partners (i.e., the creation of one Foreign Investment Review Agency [FIRA] may justify the creation of other FIRAs abroad). What is less justifiable is a major change in the investment rules after the investment is in place; this is akin to entrapment. Insofar as all parties understand the rules of the investment situation in advance and a decision to go ahead with the investment is made, the firm making the investment has no cause to complain if the investment is unprofitable or if unforeseen problems cause the investment to fail. ITT's abortive investment in the Quebec paper industry might serve as a case in point. Neither Ottawa nor Quebec City was responsible for a series of problems that cost the American firm nearly 1 billion dollars over a period of several years and ultimately led to the collapse of the project.

Conversely, however, if a government does change the rules once the investment begins to become very profitable, this appears to be an attempt to remove the return on an investment once the investor has successfully assumed the risks. But even such a policy might be valid under certain circumstances of extraordinary profitability or rents, if the policy were applied even-handedly and affected both domestic and foreign investments according to the OECD investment code. In general, applications of new investment rules once foreign investment is already in place are likely to be regarded in international circles as a breach of faith and contract.

Finally, the Canadian assumption that Canada somehow has the right to use political power to advance the interests of the Canadian private sector, whereas the United States either cannot, or ought not to, do the same vis-à-vis the interests of U.S. direct foreign investment, seems curiously one-sided. Either both governments ought to refrain from promoting or inhibiting direct private foreign investment in the other polity or both governments ought to be able to do this. The principle of neutrality may be superior to the principle of reciprocity, but when one government practices a nationalist policy in the economic realm, the other has a difficult time adopting an internationalist posture, if for no other reason than that the press and constituents hold the second country accountable for the actions of the first country.

Every government has the right to determine for itself whether to adopt a strategy of increased domestic ownership; Canadianization is neither implausible conceptually nor unacceptable in terms of international economic discourse. It may appear costly in strict financial terms, but if the domestic political benefits outweigh these costs, the program ought to proceed. What *is* damaging, however, is a policy of nationalization that employs coercion to achieve its ends. Once a clear policy is established to favor domestic investors over foreign investors through tax procedures, subsidies, protectionism, or other techniques, a government will have a difficult time limiting preferential treatment to firms within a single industry. Moreover, once one trading partner applies these techniques, other trading partners will face a series of domestic political pressures to give the same type of preferential treatment to local firms. Perhaps the lagging economy, combined with a new realization regarding some of these external implications, was responsible for the changed tone of the 1982 Canadian budget, which pledged to shelve some of the proposed, more restrictive investment provisions.

There is some validity in the American view that if Canada wants to play "on the varsity" in the club of seven, then it must play by the rules of the advanced-industrial countries; it cannot seek the concessions allotted to Third World countries while maintaining the facade of advanced-industrial status. Private foreign investment is to be treated as domestic investment, and vice-versa, according to OECD rules.

An irony of the debate over preferential treatment of local firms is that opposition among the elite has arisen to Canadian investment in the United States, opposition that should not have, and probably would not have, emerged in the absence of the NEP legislation. There are several social costs to both Canada and the United States. In some cases, antitrust rules and margin requirements that had their origin in sound public policy were relaxed because of the "threat" to national integrity. In the interest of greater national economic autonomy, a net transfer of wealth occurred within societies, causing substantially greater inequality. Government support became, in some cases, the vehicle for making large personal fortunes even larger. For strong economic nationalists on the political left, the trade-offs must have been extremely uncomfortable.

More paradoxical than some of these consequences of preferential treatment to local investors, however, was the identity and character of "local" investment. When family firms were involved, for example, in some cases one member of the family carried an American passport while another member carried a Canadian passport. Tracing whether the funds involved were Canadian or American therefore proved impossible, because other investment locations, such as the Netherlands, Bermuda, and Geneva, also figured in the transfers. In almost all cases, refinancing involved a shift from direct to indirect investment, some of which was raised in New York. None of these international financial dealings are surprising in the U.S.-Canada context. What perhaps *is* surprising is that some decision makers began to think in terms of "national capital" and "national firms." By its nature, international capital flows easily across borders and carries a national label only at tax time.[17] Thus, shifts in the identity of national ownership were often more ephemeral than genuine and more an artifact of an accountant's record book than a reality of international finance.

U.S. policy responses regarding capital were signals to Ottawa, not indications of actual anxiety about capital inflows. Canadian capital is needed in the United States and should always be regarded as warmly welcome.

This financial complexity corresponds to the enormous complexity of Canadian-American relations, the interpersonal and intrafirm character of many transactions, and the inevitable mobility of both capital and persons across the 49th parallel. When governments intervene in the private sector, especially in a fashion that attempts to discriminate among sources of finance, a whole new set of financial opportunities is created which may or may not be in the interest of either society as a whole, regardless of how governments may rhetorically label these transfers and exchanges. This question, perhaps more than questions of neutrality or reciprocity, ought to come to the attention of political decision makers in Ottawa and Washington.

Having considered the different economic traditions in the two societies, the different economic outlooks of their governments, and the different positions that have been taken on policies regarding direct foreign investment, I conclude this assessment with some perceptual considerations that are related to the arguments raised in the last chapter. In the economic dimension of the relationship, each society appears to have a peculiar blind spot. The United States seems to take for granted the unusual character of its economic relationship with Canada. Canada, in turn, seems to ignore the privileged nature of its association with the United States at the individual, private, and public levels of discourse and interaction, assuming that regardless of discriminatory policies, all beneficial ties will remain. Unless these blind spots are acknowledged and corrected, the future of partnership may be in jeopardy.

For its part, the United States often acts as though its economic position in the Canadian economy is invulnerable. Worse, it sometimes acts as though Canada were a feudal estate. Indifference that verges on arrogance sometimes colors American attitudeš toward Canadian enterprise. Most Americans are unaware of the magnitude of U.S. investment in Canada and of the importance that Canada-U.S. trade has in the vitality of the American economy. The Canadian role in the economic partnership sometimes receives deprecatory comment. In short, the United States is often oblivious to Canadian pride and self-interest in matters of trade and commerce. Part of the explanation for the extraordinary indifference to the economic association with Canada is that Americans have been slow to realize that Canada is a separate polity, with separate traditions and a separate need for nation-state identity.

For its part, Canada sometimes seems to have a blind spot regarding what might be described as American "good will." The concept of "good will" is sometimes considered naïve and empty in a supposedly sophisticated world of *realpolitik*. On the other hand, in the business arena, good will is a legal concept that conveys important attitudes of marketability and identity; it carries significant financial value. It is this latter notion of good will that is important in the Canadian-American context. Canada, on occasion, seems to believe that the American capacity for good will is either virtually without value or virtually limitless (one condition perhaps contributes to the other).

In terms of the relationship, the American sense of good will toward Canada is indeed unique in scope and character. It extends from the individual to the collective level and from the private to the public level. An individual Canadian historian, for example, may find U.S. records and government correspondence open to him but not to anyone else other than an American. A Canadian businessman finds that receptivity to Canadian investment in the United States, notwithstanding the effects of the NEP, is unparalleled among advanced-industrial countries and is particularly open to Canadians. Canadian government officials have an ease of access to American officials at all levels which is not normally obtained elsewhere and which Americans do not grant ubiquitously. The United States is the most powerful actor in the current international system, yet Canadians are able to penetrate the U.S. decision-making hierarchy with remarkable ease and often with marked effectiveness, in part because Americans think of Canadians as "like themselves." A Congressional hearing devoted to "getting tough" with Canadian investment policy breaks down at the end in sentimental statements regarding personal friendships and familial associations with Canadians, a visible outpouring of "good will" that serves to negate the intent of the hearing.

Large as it is, American good will toward Canada is easily dismissed as sentimental and immaterial. Yet this is probably a serious misunderstanding of the American character and the American political process. Without this good will, American attitudes tend to slip toward paranoia, and the hostility associated with the paranoia is projected onto others, thereby reinforcing the original sense of paranoia. Employed shrewdly by Canada, the American feeling of good will toward Canada and things Canadian can yield a host of benefits, economic and political. Allowed to slip away, this sense of good will can leave a less pleasant and less productive association in its wake.

Americans do not understand the combative politics some Canadians play so well—the kind of feisty competition seen in the House of Commons (the best late night show on Canadian television) or in the highly publicized debates between Ottawa and the provinces. Americans tend to take such combat personally, and they tend to interpret it as an erosion of tone in the relationship rather than as a healthy bargaining tactic that relieves boredom and sharpens wits. Both Canadians and Americans must reiterate the limits of tactical posturing.

As the United States inevitably begins to give more attention to U.S.-Canada relations, the capacity for American good will is likely to receive further tests. This good will is real; it can be experienced, exploited, amplified, or abused. But it is neither trivial nor infinite. It can survive temporary upsurges of economic nationalism, but a permanent use of the politics of anti-Americanism is likely to strain the American sense of good will toward Canada beyond plausible repair.

In sum, both Americans and Canadians have blind spots that impinge on economic ties and that could threaten the overall relationship in a more serious fashion. The dual reality is that each country, although proud of its autonomy and identity, is also subject to the norms of economic intervulnerability within a single large market. Canada is likely to view the dimensions of this market in a different way than is the United States, favoring interventionist policies in many instances rather than unrestricted mutual access. But however the equilibrium is found, constructive management of the economic interface remains a constant.

CANADA'S REAL ECONOMIC
PROBLEM IN THE 1980s

In public affairs, perceptions frequently lag behind reality. Government responsiveness often lags behind public or elite perceptions. Government proposals in 1980 to tighten FIRA provisions, since withdrawn, were perhaps more attuned to the perceptions of the 1960s and the 1970s than to the actual economic problems facing Canada in the 1980s. The dilemma for Canada in the 1980s will not be an excess of foreign ownership or even primarily the concentration of foreign investment in the wrong areas or categories. Increasingly, the major economic dilemma will be how to retain the foreign investment that Canada already possesses in, for example, the manufacturing and processing sectors.

This change of circumstances has several origins. The principal explanation, however, is that by 1987 the full effects of the Tokyo round of tariff reductions will become visible. Foreign firms with branches in Canada will have less incentive to continue operations when the following conditions prevail: (1) the Canadian market can be serviced as easily and cheaply from excess production capacity in plants abroad; (2) labor or operating costs are higher in Canada and are no longer offset by the artificially high profits created by the presence of tariffs; (3) collateral pressure on management to increase research or to increase the Canadian content of their products cannot be met through simple reallocation procedures but actually begins to cut into profit margins. Under a combination of these circumstances foreign firms planning investment in Canada are likely to rely on trade instead. New investment will be postponed or eliminated, and old, inefficient branch plants are likely to be phased out entirely.

How will these developments impact upon Canada? On the positive side, this reorganization of the market will create opportunities for well-funded, aggressive Canadian entrepreneurs who can step into the areas vacated by foreign capital. On the negative side, to the extent that a net transfer of capital out of Canada occurs and to the extent that foreign trade replaces local production as a source of supply, Canadian employment will suffer. Loss of Canadian jobs could be the central consequence of these changes of market structure. Just as American labor opposes U.S. foreign investment because it creates jobs abroad, allegedly at the cost of jobs at home, so the reduction of that investment abroad with a reliance on trade instead will be construed as something of an employment panacea in the United States. The converse, of course, will be the case in Canada if branch plant operations close down and Canadian jobs disappear.

In terms of policy, the implications are that investment, whether foreign or domestic, is likely to be increasingly sought after both in Canada and in the United States. The prospect is good that the decisive decline in the ratio of foreign investment to total Canadian capital assets which has been experienced in the last decade will continue through the 1980s. Public and elite opinion in Canada will eventually become aware of the shift in investment patterns, trade, and employment, however, and will probably beseech Ottawa to do something to alter the trend. Planning in advance of these developments while acknowledging the power of the marketplace to sort out these diverse pressures will certainly ease the task in both Washington and Ottawa of finding accommodation under the shelter of partnership.

FIVE

The Political-Strategic Dimension

From the American foreign policy perspective, nothing exceeds the importance of the political-strategic dimension; from the Canadian foreign policy perspective, this dimension is secondary to the economic and commercial dimension. This difference in valuation means that the United States tends to look at the U.S.-Canadian relationship through the lens of global politics, whereas Canada tends to look at global politics through the lens of its relations with the United States. In consequence, the United States sometimes looks at Canada in smaller than real terms and Canada often looks at the United States in larger than real terms. Each distortion carries a penalty.

Partly because of its dyadic preoccupation, Canada is led from time to time to think of the United States as "its greatest foreign policy challenge" or to think of certain bilateral issues, such as the East Coast Fisheries Treaty, as Canada's "greatest foreign policy problem with any country." Such a perspective is hard to understand in Washington. American involvement in East-West questions, the wars in Asia, Middle East crises, and the security of energy supply make fisheries problems, for instance, appear pretty tame. On the other hand, this "security mentality" means that the United States tends to undervalue continuity, loyalty, and predominantly economically oriented issues and relationships. Paradoxically, the allies that are most trustworthy and the ties that are most critical to the long-term U.S. power position may receive the least attention. By failing to give attention to relationships that "really count" in terms of long-term power, the United States may undermine the very foundation of world order which its emphasis of the political-strategic dimension is intended to support. Hence, if the United States wishes to retain the loyalty of its allies and the solidarity of its political associations in the face of external threat, it must give attention to the kind of bilateral issues that Canada, for example, finds most critical. Neglecting to give attention to resolving intraalliance conflicts can be as debilitating to Western alliance strength as can neglecting military preparedness.[1]

Conversely, the "greatest challenge" on the strategic-political dimension to American leadership in the late twentieth century is the need to communicate the imperatives of collective defense. After more than a third of a century of comparative peace, governments and societies alike tend to become complacent. The notion that force use has become somehow outmoded and that war in large areas of the system is now obsolete appeals to many observers, especially those in the ideological center. It is a wish bred of hope that expansionism is dead and fear that governments are hostage to the advance of weapons technology. The generation of leaders with personal knowledge of the Great Depression and World War II is disappearing. The new generation of leadership in Japan and all of the western countries, including Canada, tends to assume the robustness of interdependence and the supremacy of North-South questions while practicing a kind of neonationalism that the prior generation of leaders more realistically abhorred.

To some extent, Afghanistan saved the Western alliance system, because it gave the lie to Soviet territorial saturation. But the task for the United States in the context of Canadian-American relations is to remind Canada that security goals are mutual goals. Disagreement can arise over matters of style, tactics, timing, and the extent of prior consultation, but there can be no disagreement about the substance and purpose of action. European security is as much Canadian and American security as it is German or French security. Stability in the Middle East is as much in the interest of a petroleum importer like Canada as it is in the interest of petroleum importers like Japan or the United States. A resolution of development problems and the achievement of a moderate political outcome in Nicaragua and Central America is as much in the Canadian interest as it is in the American interest. The two governments may from time to time disagree about means, but that does not indicate that they can afford to disagree about ends. What the United States ought to avoid at all costs is the impression that the United States is acting unilaterally on behalf of interests that are solely American. This message is not always understood in Ottawa, partly because, despite good intentions on the part of U.S. administrations, the multilateral character of the action sometimes appears compromised. Canada does not like to read in the morning newspaper that in the aftermath of Afghanistan, for example, it has joined a grain embargo of the Soviet Union, even if under suitable conditions of prior consultation Canada would have found the action completely justifiable.

Before I examine the security aspects of the relationship, I must examine three sets of problems that confront the political-strategic dimension: (1) the problem of the centralization of authority; (2) the problem of safeguarding political and cultural autonomy; and (3) the problem of adjustment to a new Canadian-foreign policy style.

THE LACK OF CENTRALIZED AUTHORITY

In foreign policy conduct one needs to know with whom one is negotiating. The more specific the identification of the source of authority, the better. The question, Who is in charge here? always precedes the question, What do you want? This does not mean that on tactical grounds ambiguity with respect to one's own authority arrangement is always detrimental. It is frequently useful to plead the necessity of consulting with higher authority before proceeding with bargaining or to excuse inability to conclude an agreement on the basis of foot-dragging by an individual, institution, or government over which one does not hold authority. But it is imperative to avoid falling into these traps when they are set by the opposite government and to know as precisely as possible where effective authority lies. Moreover, in a bilateral relationship the principle applies that negotiations in general will proceed more smoothly when each partner knows the nature of authority relationships on the other side and whether each partner actually possesses sufficient authority with which to negotiate.

A major problem of negotiation in the Canadian-American setting is the lack of centralized authority. The United States is often hindered in its formulation of bargaining initiatives by the awareness of the critical split between the authority of Ottawa and of the provinces. Canada is frequently disappointed in bargaining outcomes because of the split in authority between the President and the Congress. U.S. policy vacillates between intense concern regarding initiatives that might further splinter the federation and quiet speculation about initiatives that might improve the U.S. position if addressed more specifically to the interests of Quebec or Alberta. Canadian policy alternates between chastisement of the U.S. Senate for desultory action on Canadian issues and the development of a lobbying campaign that would carry the message of Canadian concerns directly to legislators.

Thus, some parallelism exists in the Canadian and the American attitudes toward problems of centralized bargaining authority. In general, these splits are looked upon as contemporary dangers to bargaining effectiveness. They are viewed as transitory but serious impediments that require a strategic response. When each political system returns to its normal equilibrium, these problems will, it is assumed, vanish; but for the present, ad hoc solutions must be found either to hasten the end to fragmentation or to persuade delinquent parts of the respective systems to act more in accord with the interests of the opposite negotiating partner.

I would like to argue here that this perception of the problem of centralized authority as it relates to negotiation capacity is fundamentally misplaced. Part of the confusion is that each government expects a coherence in the other's institutions that cannot be forthcoming. This expectation is bred of generalities, stemming from each government's own institutional experience, that are in turn projected onto the other polity. At the same time, there is a tendency for each government to minimize the difficulties within its own authority structure as essentially inconsequential for the relationship. The superficial similarity between presidential democracy and the Canadian form of parliamentary democracy worsens the confusion. Only by examining the nature of authority, both theoretical and actual, within each system, can we sort out the reasons for this confusion and form the basis for a more realistic set of expectations regarding the partnership.

In theory, the Canadian system—responsible government—locates authority in the Parliament. The Cabinet of Ministers, in which the prime minister is first among equals, is responsible to parliament and can fall if the governing party, either as a majority party or as a principal minority party in a coalition, is defeated or loses a vote of confidence. In practice, the ways of authority in Canada are somewhat different.[2]

First, the Canadian prime minister is not first among equals, he is merely first. Despite the new "envelope system" of government in Ottawa, which has introduced some decentralization of power through the creation of Cabinet-level committees and other reforms, the power of the prime minister towers above that of the other ministers. It is true that after reelection Prime Minister Trudeau delegated great authority to his deputy prime minister and minister of finance, Allen MacEachen, and to his intimate inner circle, including minister of energy, mines, and resources, Marc Lalonde, and minister of justice, Jean Chretien. It is also true that members of the prime minister's office and of the privy council have significant procedural and administrative powers. But in the last analysis the prime minister is the one who takes responsibility for ultimate decisions. By the standards of Western parliamentary governments, Canadian prime ministers are truly at the apex of the authority pyramid.

Second, although in a technical sense Parliament may "decide," in practice the government party wields enormous influence inside Parliament, notwithstanding the daily grilling of the opposition parties during the question period, some of which occurs before nationwide television cameras. Rarely has a government lost the confidence of Parliament. This is in part because party discipline in Canada is far higher than in Britain or the United States, for example. The career of an M.P. is not helped when he "crosses-over" on a critical vote.

In addition, when the majority party is also the dominant party in the country's two most populous provinces, Quebec and Ontario, as has been the case for much of the post-World War II period, the government party has a strong electoral base. Such a base probably further ensures parliamentary stability and the durability of party control. Surely the long average tenure in office for Canadian prime ministers attests to the apparent appeal of the prime minister and his governing party, the hold they have on the institutions of government, and the apparent validity of their interpretation of the will of the Canadian people at the federal level.

Third, a member of the House of Commons is not as subject to interest group pressures or demands from his local constituency as is the average U.S. Congressman. Interest group pressures are registered, but at a very high level within the Cabinet or the authority apex of the governing party. Because the prime minister is less vulnerable to reelection worries than the American president, he has less need to "go to the people" directly, either to pass legislation or to obtain campaign monies. Because the Canadian Senate is so much less powerful vis-à-vis its parliamentary opposite than is the U.S. Senate, once again greater unity of authority structure exists in Ottawa than in Washington. The American system of checks and balances and adversary proceedings creates greater opportunity for what Americans call "political participation" than does the Canadian system.

Part of the apparent fragmentation of authority at the federal level in the United States may also stem from the greater role of the judicial branch as a law-making as well as law-interpreting force. A good share of the seeming fragmentation results from the larger size of the U.S. government and the increased opportunity for bureaucratic intervention or resistance to executive branch decision making, intervention that is less frequent in Ottawa, although the bureaucratic "mandarins" are an important factor in Canadian politics, especially regarding the administration of day-to-day policy.

The conclusion of this analysis is that the Canadian federal government is highly unified, by Western parliamentary standards, with a high concentration of power at the top, at the discretion of the prime minister. When this institutionalized pattern of authority is combined with the actual political stability of the system and with the historical durability of Canadian prime ministers in office, the extraordinary strength of the Canadian federal government in terms of cohesion and resilience becomes understandable.

On the other hand, the very centralization of authority in Ottawa and the durability of government leadership, especially Liberal party leadership in the twentieth century, has meant that individuals, associational and regional groupings, and ethnic communities, which in Canada, for various reasons (apart from the ethnic and linguistic homogeneity of the two respective founding peoples), form a mosaic, have a relatively difficult time gaining political participation at the federal level. As a consequence, the ten large provincial governments provide a far more immediate sounding board for local grievances. And because the British North America Act allocates very substantial sovereign powers to the provinces, the capacity of the provincial governments both to listen to the electorate and to deliver is appreciable. More than this, however, the provincial governments create the natural rivals to federal power because of the degree of centralization of federal power, the incomplete nature of electoral participation within the federal governing party, and the capacity of the provinces to provide many services to local constituents. In the Canadian system, the natural cleavage between power centers is that between the federal government and the provincial governments. The place where bargaining, vote trading, and brokering of interests takes place is not Parliament, as it is in, for example, Britain, France, or West Germany. Instead, the lines of tension in the Canadian system are inevitably drawn at the interface between Ottawa and the provinces—at first minister conferences, ad hoc and one-time meetings, and in continual premier-prime-ministerial interchanges. Because political participation is cut off at the top in the highly centralized federal structure and because the Parliament is so dominated by the governing party, the Cabinet, and ultimately the prime minister himself, interest aggregation takes place for the most part at the provincial level and not in the federal Parliament. Under these circumstances, the provincial premiers do not need to grope for power; they find power thrust upon them. A natural adversarial relationship emerges between the power centers at the provincial level and the power center in Ottawa. The cleavage between the outlook of the prime minister and that of the premiers is not so much contrived as ordained by the highly centralized nature of the Canadian authority structure in Ottawa.

Although the Conservative party has advocated a reduction in the power at the federal center, the rejection of this political solution by the Grits (Liberals) is understandable. In addition to wanting to protect the Liberal party power base from deterioration, the Liberal party perspective recognizes that a correct diagnosis does not automatically lead to solid prescription, much less to an immediate cure. In circumstances of intense regional and cultural fragmentation, rapid decentralization of authority in Ottawa could further accelerate the trend of fragmentation. It is better that fragmentation approach its limits prior to a reduction of authority at the federal level. Of course, the Liberal bias is probably toward an increase of federal authority rather than toward its diminution, regardless of what might occur at the level of the community. But the question of the temporal ordering of priorities is certainly relevant. It may be, as John Meisel has argued, that a united community can tolerate decentralized governmental authority, whereas a fragmented community needs more centralized governmental institutions at the federal level.[3] But the real, dynamic question is, How does one assume adequate representation and cultural autonomy at the local level while allowing for sufficient governmental authority to administer well at the federal level? Moreover, how does one proceed from a situation, such as exists presently in Canada, in which there is both too much fragmentation at the local level and too much centralization of authority at the federal level? The long-term answer must involve both imagination and flexibility. After fragmentation is temporarily foreclosed, a program of selective decentralization of authority probably must ensure that the Canadian federal Parliament becomes a truly representative body that has sufficient autonomy from the executive that it can properly act as an aggregator and broker of local interests throughout Canada.

But in the short term, outside observers must not mistake the noise and turbulence within Canadian federal-provincial relations for imminent institutional collapse. Canadian power brokers are too adept and the average member of Canadian society is too calmly sensible to allow such a collapse to occur. Given the institutional characteristics we have examined, the cleavage between the two levels of government is politically inevitable. The cleavage does not signify disaster for the Canadian political system. It does not suggest regional separation. Most emphatically, it does not indicate serious political instability or the prospect of violence. Federal-provincial relations supply, in a louder and more public forum, some of the functions provided in federal parliaments in other democratic systems. This tension is thus politically normal and, under the circumstances, even necessary and politically healthy. The federal-provincial cleavage is all-important in Canadian politics, and until major transformation of authority relations occurs (if it ever does), this cleavage will remain highly visible. It is not a transitory phenomenon as some American political observers seem to think; nor, at its most intense, is it a barometer of precipitous collapse, as some of Canada's more astute external negotiators have sought to argue in periods of critical bilateral negotiation. Federal-provincial relations in Canada are simply at the heart of the contemporary political process, and this situation of continuing confrontation is likely to endure for some time.

Conversely, in a society that has fought a civil war over the issue of states' rights, it is not surprising to discover horror at the prospect of Canadian federal-provincial bargaining and tension. Likewise, in such a society as the American society, it is not surprising that political institutions have evolved so as to place the heart of the political process in the relations between the president and the Congress. Here is where everything that is important to the external conduct of affairs ultimately gets introduced, vetoed, compromised, or otherwise decided. It is from this enormous procedural and institutional complexity, with its high degree of political uncertainty, that outcomes eventually emerge. In a society that is as open, mobile, participatory, and adversarial as the American society, the complexity and uncertainty of presidential-congressional relations preserve the characteristics of interest aggregation and compromise necessary to make a political system work. It would perhaps be premature for Canadian analysts to conclude that intervention into this quagmire of politics will lead to more favorable political outcomes for Canada. Although the margin of authority in foreign-policy making shifts between the president and Congress, particularly the Senate, in response to external events and the domestic political effort to adopt and influence, it is perhaps optimistic to anticipate that outside governments can do much to affect the trend of these events.

Just as the natural interface of power in Canada is between Ottawa and the provinces, the natural interface of power in Washington is between the executive and legislative branches. Just as authority within the Canadian federal government is highly centralized, authority in Washington is quite decentralized. This means that the United States will continue to lament the uncertainty of federal-provincial outcomes and Canada will continue to lament the seemingly perfidious role of the American Senate. These institutional and authority relations are not impermeable to change, but neither are they likely to change significantly within a decade or so. Rather, adjustment to these structural circumstances and a capacity to work within the limits remain the key to successful conduct of foreign policy on both sides of the border.

PRESERVATION OF POLITICAL AND CULTURAL AUTONOMY

Unlike the United States, which because of its size and international political centrality gives little thought to matters of political and cultural autonomy, Canada gives a foremost place to these concerns. Because Canada takes these concerns so seriously, the United States must also attempt to understand the concerns, not only because the United States figures so deeply in the Canadian self-image but because successful U.S. foreign policy toward Canada depends upon a better understanding of these concerns. As some Canadians see the situation, the problem *is* the United States. Although this is scarcely a helpful diagnosis, the United States should reflect upon the significance of the American presence, because so many Canadians are troubled by the scope and alleged impact of this presence on Canadian values, institutions, and diplomatic flexibility. A Canadian problem becomes a problem for the United States.

Economic Interdependence and Canadian Autonomy

According to well-established functionalist theories of integration, integration proceeds by steps.[4] The first steps are technical or task oriented, such as joint scientific cooperation, cultural exchange, and trade development. The next step is economic integration through the creation of a free trade area or a common economic market. The final step is the formation of single political union. Spillovers occur from prior steps to later steps. This is the theory of integration that is the basis of the European Community's efforts to overcome nationalism, and it is the theory that many Canadians have in the back of their minds when they reflect upon their association with the United States.

There is a double irony regarding the functionalist theory of integration, however: it has not worked in Europe where sympathetic government leaders have attempted for twenty years to make it work, yet, conversely, there is an intense Canadian fear that it might work in North America despite the fact that both Canada and the United States oppose its political implications. How can we explain these apparent anomalies?

European integration has not proceeded beyond the economic stage for many reasons: agricultural protectionism; traditions of monetary independence; the desire to maintain autonomous foreign policies; dissimilar cultural traditions; and the general reluctance to relinquish sovereignty to centralized political institutions. Yet since the Treaties of Rome of 1957, Europe has been officially committed to progress toward eventual political unity. What Europeans have discovered is that an enormous gap separates progress on the economic level and progress on the political level. Despite whatever benefits economic integration may have bestowed on Europe, spillovers are far from automatic. Many defenders of the functionalist notion now acknowledge that the political sovereignty of separate European nation-states is here to stay.[5]

Why do some Canadian analysts fear the application of a theory of integration in North America, where no one wants integration, when the same theory is failing in Europe, where political union is actively promoted? The answer is that Canadians often erroneously believe Americans still believe in the doctrine of manifest destiny. Canadians sometimes fear that Americans have retained an impulse to annex, not by force but, perhaps, by political and economic subterfuge. Moreover, Canadians fear that even without actual integration, enormous damage could be done to Canadian values and institutions by too close an association with the United States. This speculation is based partly on awareness of the different conditions prevalent in North America and Europe.

First, unlike Europe, North America is composed of only three countries, Canada, Mexico and the United States; thus, there are fewer balancing powers and there is the potential for less flexibility within any resulting political configuration. Second, the disparity in power between the United States and the other two partners is unparalleled by any such disparities in Europe. This means, in the Canadian view, that the weight of U.S. dominance in decision making would necessarily exceed the weight of any single corresponding member of the European Community. Efforts to set limits on the decision-making authority of the largest polity in any new North American confederation, monetary union, or economic common market would in this view be unavailing. Third, political structures and cultural attitudes have taken centuries to form in Europe, but they are much more nascent and fragile in North America. Canada is thus concerned that U.S. values and institutions would tend to undermine the indigenous Canadian national character. Any consequent political configuration would be more reflective of U.S. values and cultural norms than those of Mexico or Canada. Unlike Europe, which would theoretically witness a balanced reduction of nationalism by all members, while not sacrificing any of the cultural integrity of the various societies, North America, some Canadians fear, would witness a lopsided reduction of nationalism, and the cultural integrity of Canada would be seriously infringed.

Hence, the critical obstacle to a North American accord, for example, are these Canadian anxieties regarding the loss of political and cultural autonomy. Indeed, in many respects, trends in Europe and North America are the opposite of one another. In Europe, governments are seeking ways to reduce nationalism in the aftermath of the excesses of nationalism experienced during the first half of the twentieth century. In North America, some of the governments appear to be attempting to increase nationalism, in part because they see nationalism as a means of preserving political and cultural autonomy and in part because they have not experienced many of the costs of nationalism in political or military terms. Paradoxically, Europe may be more sympathetic to the premises of the North American accord idea than is the region for which the idea was conceived.

One of the problems with analyzing the impact of interdependence and economic integration on political and cultural autonomy is that so little research has been done on the question. What impact some type of accord would have on North American perspectives is open to speculation. Most of the research in integration done so far has approached the question from a single direction, that of trying to determine what is required to obtain a reduction in political and cultural autonomy on the path to full political union. Little attention has been given to the opposite question—can one obtain the benefits of larger market size, greater more difficult to achieve. Here was the crux of the Quebecer's anxiety. What would happen if Quebec were cut adrift, alone, in an Anglo sea? How much of Quebec's evident prosperity would suffer? How much personal income would each individual Quebecer have to forego on behalf of a cultural and political ideal that he or she nonetheless shared? A clear trade-off between the preference for cultural and political autonomy, on the one hand, and for continued economic prosperity and security on the other, influenced enough Francophone voters to witness the defeat of the nationalist dream.

But how real was this trade-off in economic and political terms? Were Quebec voters unduly pessimistic about their economic prospects outside Canada, assuming that the rest of Canada was not bluffing in its stated opposition to the negotiation of a new legal and political pact with Quebec? Or were Quebec voters revealing a deep insight into the laws of economics and politics when they painfully came to the conclusion that, whatever its considerable merits, the parti Quebecois could not deliver an acceptable economic arrangement with Ottawa and that economic isolation itself would prove intolerably costly to the province (although it would in no sense threaten Quebec's actual survival)?

If one examines the relationship of economic size to external dependence in various polities within the international system, it is apparent that the perception of a significant fraction of the Quebec electorate on this point was right on the mark. However burdensome they might have found dependence upon Ottawa, reversal of this dependence would come only at significant economic cost to Quebecers collectively and individually. Indeed, the attempt to reduce formal cultural and political dependence through declared sovereignty might lead to greater economic and commercial dependence, not less. The justification for this conclusion is evident from the following brief empirical exercise.

In broad theoretical terms, three types of economic and commercial dependency affect Canada and, derivatively, Quebec.[10] The first and primary type is a measure of how important trade is to the polity and is indexed by the percentage of GNP which is accounted for by trade. As noted earlier, Canada's reliance on foreign trade is far larger than is America's, for example.

Second, commercial and economic dependence is indexed by the degree to which this trade occurs with a single trading partner or a small number of partners. By this index, Quebec is extremely dependent upon the other Canadian provinces, especially Ontario, and Canada is highly dependent upon the United States.

Third, economic and commercial dependence is indexed by the degree to which trade is concentrated in one or a small number of commodities. On a world scale neither Quebec nor the Canadian federation is very

economic efficiency, and better consumer choice through increased economic interdependence and integration *without* constraining the political and cultural autonomy of the members? In the North American context, the latter question is more relevant to actual policy-making and may, for various reasons, receive an affirmative response. Increased integration and interdependence may have little, if any, determinant impact upon cultural values and political structures. At most, the impact is probably very selective. The cultural and economic dimensions of foreign policy are quite independent of each other. But the necessary effort has not been made to test these assertions.

Why is there theoretical reason to believe that increasing interdependence in North America is no threat to the political and cultural autonomy of Canada and Mexico? First, if, political autonomy is equated with the capacity to increase autonomy (whether that capacity is actually exercised) and if, during a period of increasing interdependence, that capacity increases appreciably, then the analyst is justified in arguing that interdependence is no threat to political autonomy.[6] Whether an actual effort is made to exercise political autonomy is not the consequential point. A government that has increasing capacity to exercise greater political autonomy may on a variety of grounds choose not to do so. Other benefits may flow to a polity that does not choose to dissociate itself from its trading partners. Indeed, knowledge that the capacity to increase autonomy exists may be a sufficient comfort for many policy makers. Capacity for autonomy that is held in abeyance acts as a kind of deterrent to decisions from abroad that might threaten sovereignty. In sum, if it can be demonstrated in this post-World War II interval of increasing interdependence between Canada and the United States that the Canadian capacity for political autonomy (despite the fact that this capacity has not been substantially exercised), has also increased significantly, interdependence could scarcely be much of an impediment to growing Canadian power.

During the 1945-1980 interval the underlying base of Canadian national capability, relative to that of the United States, increased significantly. In the last decade, in particular, Canadian power has been on the rise. This reality should lay to rest the assertions, frequently heard among Canadian analysts, that the United States is increasing its dominance in the relationship. Nothing could be more inaccurate in political, strategic, or economic terms. In strategic terms, for example, the decline of the bomber threat has made NORAD less and less meaningful; the numbers of American military personnel in Canada, never large, are so small at present as not to merit mention. Moreover, Canadian power is growing, and this growth has come in a period of increasing economic interdependence between Canada and the United States. Interdependence has been no threat to the economic growth experienced in either country. Instead, interdependence has been an important catalyst of that growth in GNP, welfare, and political capability.

Similarly, the argument that increasing interdependence or economic integration will damage cultural integrity or cultural sovereignty is far from proven.[7] Emulation of foreign life-styles and cultural preferences can follow from personal contacts, commercial advertising, and exposure to foreign media. But this effect is surely selective. Just as the cultural and linguistic authenticity of 6.5 million Quebecers is scarcely in doubt, especially at a time when pride in the arts and letters is at a peak in French Canada, so the cultural identity of 24 million Canadians as a society is not seriously at issue. Of course, elements of the Canadian identity may evolve in a fashion that parallels the development of the American identity. Canadian regional heterogeneity will assure that some parts of Canada, more than others, will adopt outlooks strongly influenced by events and perspectives south of the border. But just as likely is the emergence of a reaction against values and institutions that are American in origin. Some Canadians will reject outlooks or value positions based less on their merits than on whether Americans hold the same positions. Hence, for these Canadians the impact of increasing economic interdependence with the United States could be to drive a deeper cultural wedge between the two societies.

For the majority of Canadians, however, cultural and political autonomy is not something that is planned, certainly not planned in reaction to the American cultural ethos; for these Canadians, cultural autonomy is something that merely happens. An emerging Canadian cultural identity is not something that has to be cultivated; it is something that is generated spontaneously and without reference to any other single culture or to the economic dimension of foreign policy. Neither imitation nor alienation is a substitute for creative authenticity. This later interpretation—that Canadian cultural and political autonomy grows through spontaneous and indigenous development—is the healthiest and the most durable view. It is also the most feasible.

A Case Study of the Boundaries of the Possible in the Search for Autonomy: The Quebec Referendum

Victory for the parti Quebecois on November 15, 1976 shocked most Americans and some Canadians, for it demonstrated at the ballot box what Rene Levesque and others had been saying for a decade, namely, that the possibility of qualified French separation was real. Yet, the defeat of the 1980 referendum that proposed a mandate to negotiate sovereignty for Quebec combined with economic reintegration with the remainder of Canada (sovereignty-association) seemed to reverse the

fortunes of secession. How is this sudden upsurgence and decline enthusiasm for the ideal of greater Quebec cultural and political a tonomy to be explained?[8] A variety of explanations will come to t mind of those observers familiar with the details of Quebec politics this period: (1) the ambiguity of the sovereignty-association notion (2) the success of the political counterattack waged by Pierre Trudeau Jean Chretien and others at the federal level and by Claude Ryan within the Provincial Liberal party, (3) the electoral impact of the Anglo minority in Montreal and elsewhere; (4) the age-group split among Francophone voters on the issue of autonomy; (5) both in the 1976 election and in the 1980 referendum defeat, the masking of the sovereignty-association notion by other issues, such as the campaign for good government and the personal popularity of M. Levesque, which tended to mislead some analysts about outcomes; and (6) a host of technical issues regarding the peaking of campaigns, campaign strategy, the disproportionate representation of rural votes, and the like. But the theoretical proposition that I would like to set forth here is somewhat different. It highlights in a special way the dilemma facing all efforts at increasing national autonomy in a world that is growing more and more interdependent. It also holds implications for the political relations between Canada and the United States.

This proposition regarding the movement on behalf of greater Quebec autonomy is twofold. First, regardless of the impact of the foregoing complicating factors, which tend to enrich but also to obscure interpretation, I shall argue that Francophone voters were on the whole far more enthusiastic about enhanced Quebec cultural and political autonomy than the defeat of the referendum seems to reveal.[9] Of course, older voters and less-educated voters were apparently less enthusiastic than their opposites. And of course Anglophone voters tended to vote against the idea of sovereignty-association because it would have had the effect of further isolating them. But in general the desire for self-expression, in both the political and cultural senses, was very strong in Quebec throughout this period. Although this need Quebec nationalists felt for greater autonomy has waxed and waned throughout the history of confederation, the level of this feeling was quite high in the late 1970s and, if anything, was probably underrepresented in the actual referendum voting.

Second, Quebecers were severely pressured by a competing set of concerns. The effect of this pressuring was to undermine the solidarity with the nationalist ideal. Quebecers favored greater political and cultural autonomy for themselves provided that this ideal did not cost too much in economic terms. But here was the most powerful argument in the federalist arsenal. Prime Minister Trudeau repeatedly pointed out that Quebec could obtain sovereignty easily but that some form of economic reintegration (association) with the remainder of Canada would be far

dependent; each is relatively industrialized and produces a wide variety of products for home consumption and export. But each is also a major exporter of raw materials and semifinished products. Economic development implies increasing diversification of the economy and perhaps a larger output share for finished products. If the argument is valid that finished products yield a greater "value added" than raw materials or semiprocessed goods, then movement away from raw materials export makes sense. Conversely, if advanced-industrial economies benefit from the stability provided by a broad export base, including the export of raw materials and farm products, then both Quebec and the Canadian federation, like the United States, will benefit strongly from the maintenance of a mixed economy. In any case, by this index of commercial and trade dependence—namely, the degree to which trade is concentrated in one or a small number of commodities—both Quebec and Canada as a whole are among the least dependent of the world's economies.

In sum, for Quebec, and for Canada as a whole, the first and second forms of dependence are much more important than the third. About one-third of the Canadian GNP is associated with world trade, for example, and of this volume (in 1980) slightly more than two-thirds occurred with a single trading partner, the United States. A very important norm marks external dependence relations. This norm seemingly conditions all trade relations, especially those in a system of highly unequal states. An inverse correlation exists between external commercial and economic dependence and population size. This means that large states, such as the Soviet Union, China, and the United States, regardless of their ideological complexion, trade with a variety of partners, export a variety of commodities and manufactured goods, and devote a comparatively small percentage of their goods and services to foreign trade. Small population states, on the other hand, particularly, but not exclusively (e.g., Kuwait), those that are also poor, such as the Dominican Republic, regardless of geographic location or political organization, display a significant overall external dependence. Large states can rely on their huge domestic markets to obtain the benefits of economies of scale, learning effects, adequate availability of capital, and market leverage. But smaller states possess none of these advantages and must therefore disproportionately expand trade abroad. In short, the norm regarding external dependence reads as follows: the smaller the country in terms of population size, the greater its external trade and economic dependence.

Canada ranks among the small- to medium-sized states in terms of population (24 million) and hence reflects moderate external dependence as well. Primarily because of its high concentration of trade with certain trading partners, however, Canadian dependence is somewhat greater than that of other polities of similar size. But in general the external dependence that Canada faces is, given its market size, wealth, and level of economic development, similar to the dependence other polities of similar size experience.

In the light of the norm that seems to underlie global international relations—the smaller the polity, the more dependent upon other governments that polity is likely to be—Quebec's search for greater political and cultural autonomy takes on additional significance. Had the referendum on sovereignty-association passed, Quebec would have faced an enormous hurdle to workable separation. Although the objective of sovereignty-association was to increase political and cultural independence from Ottawa, sovereignty without association would have caused the opposite effect in the trade and economic realm. Sovereignty without association would have deepened Quebec's trade and economic dependence upon its neighbors.

Empirical evidence suggests how Quebec's increased economic and trade dependence after separation (provided no workable common market arrangement emerged) was likely to happen. By splitting the Canadian polity, Quebec would have increased its external dependence upon its neighbors by an estimated 60 percent or more. Although dependence would also increase for the English-speaking fragment of Canada, this increase would be less severe because of the proportionately greater size of English Canada. The cost of separation for Quebec could thus be measured in hard economic and trade-related terms. Separation would lead to greater external dependence for Quebec, not less. Quite possibly Quebec would exchange apparent political sovereignty for real trade subordinance within the larger North American economy.

From this perspective, the decision of the Quebec voter to reject the sovereignty-association idea, despite the attractiveness of greater political and cultural autonomy, was highly perceptive and rational. It was not a rejection of greater political and cultural autonomy in itself, it was a decision based on a perceptive awareness of the opportunity costs imposed by the quest for increased political and cultural autonomy in the economic area. This decision to forego independence, however, strong as the sentiment is among the young and among professional groups, could be reversed under the right circumstances of grievance and high politicization.

In the event of separation, the only way greater economic subordinance could be mitigated would be through one or more unlikely strategies. Quebec would have to reduce its ratio of foreign trade as a percentage of GNP, perhaps through arbitrary tariff barriers or some other form of enforced trade and commercial isolation; or some technique would have to be devised to rapidly expand the composition of domestic production. Alternatively, Quebec could seek to diversify its trade pattern, perhaps through closer ties to France, the rest of Western Europe, or to Francophonie. Yet, natural economic advantages seem to lie with Quebec-U.S. or Quebec-English Canadian relations, and forced diversification could result in the subsidization of inefficiency. Equally difficult would be the attempt to rapidly broaden the composition of trade beyond the iron ore, asbestos, pulp, and certain manufactured goods that are presently exported. Independence for Quebec would not be likely to strengthen this effort at lessening commodity concentration in trade unless it could be demonstrated that Ottawa had been, in the past, acting to increase trade concentration, a very improbable proposition. Hence, each of these proposals to counter the effects of escalating external dependence following Quebec separation seems problematic. In rejecting such strategems by defeating the referendum, the Quebec voter once again appears to have pursued his or her natural economic self-interest.

A number of further difficulties reinforce the bleak picture of growing external dependence after Quebec separation. First, because of market familiarity and low transport costs, the bulk of Quebec trade after separation would continue to take place with English Canada and the United States as before. Even if a common market arrangement emerged (association), the political benefits of trade diversification and the economic benefits of trade creation would likely be slight. In fact, the effort to speed industrialization of the Quebec economy after separation might tend to integrate Quebec with each of the other economies even more tightly than before, but on less equal terms.

Second, although varying estimates abound regarding the net value of transfer payments to Quebec after federal taxes, whatever this value, it would be lost after separation. Between 1974 and 1978, financial subsidies provided by the federal government climbed from about one-half billion dollars to more than two billion dollars. In addition, the federal government created an estimated forty thousand jobs in Quebec, primarily for Francophones, through programs that would end with separatism and might or might not be continued by Quebec City.

Third, because Quebec possesses a number of labor-intensive, increasingly inefficient industries, such as textiles and shoe manufacturing, which have benefited from Canadian tariff protection at the expense of the Maritime and western provinces, separation would have a disruptive impact on employment in those Quebec industries and localities. No other trading partner would be likely to suffer these market impediments for the privilege of entering the Quebec market. Indeed, despite the great effort to modernize these labor-intensive industries, an important reason other Canadian provinces have tolerated the inefficiencies for so long has been the desire to bolster national unity; after separation, of course, this rationale would no longer hold true.

Thus, the Quebec voter accepted with some misgivings the death of sovereignty-association (defined by the Quebec government as political separation combined with economic coalescence in a common market) while keeping a firm eye on the prosperity and economic advantages Quebec enjoys within the union. Although ideological purists may deprecate the Quebec voter for such a pragmatic choice, the realistic analyst must respect that voter for comprehending the trade-offs and conflicting pressures at work during this exciting period of Quebec history.

The larger issue involved in this case study of the referendum struggle also remains clear. Size is critical to true economic and trade flexibility. Interdependence shrinks into a form of self-imposed dependence when arbitrary barriers restrict market size and efficiency in pursuit of other values such as greater political or cultural autonomy. Tariff and nontariff barriers, subsidies, quotas, restrictions on capital mobility, and other inhibitions on trade and commerce serve to promote this reduction in market size and efficiency, sometimes in the name of increased political and cultural autonomy. But the true irony is that although the loss of political and cultural autonomy may be real and important, there is little evidence and virtually no respectable analysis that demonstrates the negative impact of increasing interdependence on political institutions and cultural values. Thus, trade and commercial restrictions imposed for the purpose of achieving greater political and cultural autonomy may have virtually no positive influence in helping to achieve this objective. At the same time, these very same restrictions may lower the productive efficiency and overall performance of the Canadian and American economies.

Such an outcome would conform to Type C intervulnerability (as described in Chapter 2), in which not only are governmental policies unable to promote a situation in which one partner improves its position but also both partners are worse off vis-à-vis their prior positions and the international system as a whole. This is the most destructive form of intervulnerability, because it is both the most short-sighted and the most far-reaching in its overall effects. Political and cultural autonomy must be preserved, but neither the trade nor the commercial pathways to this objective provide hopeful shortcuts. Indeed, because a proper sense of Canadian identity and autonomy is highly subjective in nature and deeply psychological, careful examination may reveal a far greater capacity for sustaining these values on the part of Canadian society as a whole than the more fearful among analysts have admitted.

Mirror-Image Power Balances

A fascinating characteristic of U.S.-Canada relations is the extent to which these relations reflect the rules developed in Canadian federal-provincial politics. Balances of foreign political power often reflect domestic Canadian power balances. The response of Ottawa to Washington on bilateral foreign policy frequently resembles the response of Quebec or Alberta to the Canadian federal government on public affairs issues. Provincial criticism of federal government leadership (for example, allegations of arrogance, insensitivity, too little consultation) is similar to Canadian criticism of Washington's handling of specific foreign policy matters. Strategies used by the provinces to enhance their own power positions are similar to strategies employed by Ottawa to deal with Canadian grievances vis-à-vis the United States. In short, the political-strategic dimension involves balances of power at the international level that closely resemble mirror images of balances of power at the federal-provincial level within Canada.

What is the reason for this curious parallelism of style and strategy? In general, this parallelism involves jurisdictional struggles and conflicts over political turf. The provinces frequently seek to enlarge their spheres of responsibility while inevitably arguing that they are merely trying to retain interests guaranteed them by the British North America Act (in section 92) and also by constitutional convention. The federal government is made to appear as if it is infringing upon the rights and duties of the provinces.

Conversely, in bilateral Canadian-American relations, Ottawa sometimes creates the impression that Canada is merely responding to American initiatives and is therefore in a defensive posture strategically. Closer to the truth, in the most recent decade at least, is that Ottawa has been the principal initiator of bilateral policy in the areas of the law of the sea, fisheries negotiations, air pollution abatement, and even in the energy field. Although the United States has taken the lead in defense policy and in limited functional areas, such as the auto pact, Canada has often pressed harder for action on a variety of other important bilateral matters. Part of the reason for this greater Canadian activism may be that the list of Canadian "irritants" is simply longer than the American list. A better explanation is that just as Quebec, for example, has sought to reverse the power balance in domestic Canadian politics, so Ottawa has sought to transform somewhat the nature of the external power balance vis-à-vis Washington.

An excellent address by Deputy Prime Minister Allan J. MacEachen to the *Financial Post* Offshore Canada Conference on June 23, 1981 highlights some of these dynamics. After outlining the provisions of the National Energy Program which will ensure larger Canadian participation in east-coast offshore exploration and a far larger share of the purchases of material and equipment for Canadian firms, Mr. MacEachen notes pressures from the provinces for a larger role.

> Now that there are definite signs of commercially viable oil and gas reserves off the east coast, the provinces have become active in vary-

ing degrees in expressing their demands for control of the resources.
. . . It is part of a pattern of requests from particular provinces for
increased economic power: control over fisheries; control over communications; control of both interprovincial and international trade
in natural resources; maintenance of procurement policies that give
preference to local residents. Some have already withdrawn from the
corporate income tax collection agreement with the national government. And provinces want to own the east coast offshore resources
located on Canada Lands. I ask you: How far can you go in dismantling the economic role of the national government before you
cease to have an economic union, let alone a country in the political
and cultural sense of the term?[11]

The parallelism is evident. The provinces seek to expand ownership
and jurisdictional rights at the expense of the federal government. The
Canadian federal government in turn expands its demands internationally, most of which fall upon the United States, because of geographi-
cal proximity and historical closeness of commercial interaction. The
Canadian federal government rewrites its procurement policies in order
to increase the Canadian share of oil field equipment and purchases; the
provinces change their procurement policies in order to increase local
employment and to force the federal government to accept a larger
provincial economic role.[12] The federal government increases indirect
taxes so as to transfer a larger share of revenue from foreign (primarily
American) firms to the Canadian fiscal system; the provinces attempt to
levy higher indirect taxes on energy so as to divert funds from both the
federal treasury and the foreign firms. Hence, the competition between
federal government and province is transferred to the external sphere,
and the competition within the external sphere is used to mollify domestic
disputants.

Ottawa thus seeks to assert its leadership at the international level by
giving its policies a highly visible and unified national outlook. At the
same time, Ottawa is attempting internally to offset the demands of the
provinces for larger power and revenue by reminding the provinces of
the minimum of federal authority necessary to coordinate policies at the
nation-state level.

In attempting to maintain its position vis-à-vis the provinces, Ottawa
is often driven to make larger demands on the external sphere. This has
two purposes. First, it often provides the basis for future needed revenue
in the tax field or in resource jurisdiction at a time when the domestic
Canadian competition for this revenue is intense. Second, it creates an
image of leadership and defense of the Canadian national interest which
is essential if the federal government is to have credibility in the eyes of
the average Canadian citizen. But conversely, the demands on the ex-

ternal sphere often impinge directly on U.S.-Canada relations and complicate the implementation of crisis-free foreign policy.

Perhaps an even better way of understanding how Canada's external relations with the United States reflect the internal power equilibria of Canadian domestic politics is seen in the context of Quebec politics. To the surprise of many, Premier Levesque survived the defeat of the referendum on sovereignty-association, to which the parti Quebecois was devoted, and was reelected to a subsequent five-year term in the spring of 1981. To some analysts, this reelection seemed self-contradictory, because Quebecers had rejected only a few months earlier a proposal into which M. Levesque had invested a great deal of personal prestige. Once again, the answer to this puzzle indicates the complicated nature of power equilibria at the provincial, nation-state, and international levels.

Quebecers wisely prefer to have the best of two worlds, the federal and the provincial. They wish to have a powerful Francophone in office in Ottawa to ensure that the interests of Quebec are not trampled on by the other provinces. They also wish to have a powerful figure at the head of the Quebec government to lobby vigorously for local interests at the cost of the federal position. By establishing an equilibrium between the federal and the provincial leadership, they hope to maximize the benefits to the province. More importantly, perhaps, through this equilibrium they are able to maximize their own political and cultural autonomy in an atmosphere that is as free from insecurity as possible.

Given this understanding of Quebec politics, one can quickly see why the referendum had to be defeated and Premier Levesque had to be reelected. The referendum on sovereignty-association had to be defeated because the referendum threatened this entire system of balance of power politics. It introduced a whole new set of political risks into the game; it went too far without promising a sufficiently certain return. On the other hand, M. Levesque had to be reelected because, apart from his personal charm and skill, he was viewed as a stronger and more proven defender of provincial rights than his opponent, M. Ryan. By sacrificing to some extent his commitment to a renewal of the sovereignty-association ideal, Premier Levesque removed the final obstacle to his reelection. In the eyes of most Quebecers, this made him a stronger defender of the Quebec position inside the federal-provincial power equilibrium, not a weaker defender, because his commitment to work inside the system meant that he could place larger and more credible demands on Ottawa, especially on an Ottawa that would eventually see a non-Francophone at the head of the federal government.

The concept of equilibrium also applies at the international level. On the one hand, Canada wants to see a strong America capable of defending Western and non-Communist interests against Soviet challenge and against regional political upheaval, for example, in the Persian-Arab Gulf. If anything, because of domestic tradition, Canada is more concerned about the maintenance of a peaceful and noncoercive world order than is the United States. Canada is more in favor of "law and order" in global terms than are many other parliamentary democracies, because of its civilized outlook toward politics in general. In this regard, the Canadian government lives up to the Athenian ideal of citizenship, in which each individual limits his or her own action so as to maximize collective freedom.

At the same time, however, Canada seeks to exploit the global power equilibrium to its own advantage in bilateral relations by placing demands on the United States which cannot easily be made reciprocal. For example, Canada favors the use in some areas of procurement policies that discriminate against foreign firms—all foreign firms. But because most of the firms supplying the Canadian market are American, in effect the prohibitions apply mostly to American firms and interests. The United States cannot apply a similar provision in order to retaliate because it would either have to apply the provision across the board, thus angering its other trading partners (and further subverting the liberal trade order) or it would have to discriminate against Canada alone, thus escalating the process of discrimination. Canada can therefore, in some cases, press its interests with respect to the United States in a fashion that neither seriously undermines the American global strategic position nor creates a possibility for bilateral economic retaliation. In effect, the United States is a prisoner of size and global responsibility.

Just as Quebecers want to see both a strong representative of Quebec society in office in both Ottawa and Quebec City, so Canadians wish to see their own interest in world peace represented by the United States at the global level while Canada maximizes economic advantages wherever possible in bilateral relations with the United States. Just as Quebecers see no contradiction in wanting a strong representative of the Quebec outlook at both levels of government, most Canadians see no contradiction in wanting both a strong America, in terms of global strategy, and increased Canadian bargaining strength in bilateral economic relations with the United States.

Of course, the possibility of a contradiction does logically exist. If the balance of power is upset, the risks of the strategy to the participants become serious. If American strategic preeminence should become too dominant, or, conversely, if Canadian deprecations of the American economic base should become too debilitating of American strength, the external balance could be upset. But because the room for error in these calculations seems large, and the two balances seem quite stable, Canadian estimates of balance of power politics seem sagacious. In any case, the training and outlook that Canadian governments acquire in domestic struggles between provinces and federal government serve them well in their negotiations with the United States. In each case the objective of the actors is to press advantage as far as is feasible without threatening the traditional equilibrium itself.

Periodically, however, the limits of the equilibrium are tested. Partnership demands that such probes not go too far, that the provinces understand the prerequisites for federal union and not press beyond these limits, and that the allies of the United States understand the ultimate bond between strategic military preparedness and the economic capacity to finance that preparedness. Historically these assumptions have not been seriously challenged and thus the internal federal-provincial balances of power and the external Canadian-American balances of power have operated with tolerable efficiency and success.

SECURITY DILEMMAS

The third and final section of the discussion of the political-strategic dimension in U.S.-Canada relations deals explicitly with security concerns. As a percent of GNP, Canada spends less on security than any other member of NATO except Luxembourg. No other statistic so highlights the apparent difference in the Canadian and the American foreign policy perspective. Smaller allies tend to spend disproportionately less on defense than larger allies, but Canadian defense expenditures fall below even this pattern for the alliance as a whole.

How can so great a disparity of viewpoints on military expenditures be explained? At least four hypotheses purport to supply an explanation. I shall examine each hypothesis in turn to see whether it accounts for the apparent Canadian opposition to a larger defense effort.

According to the first hypothesis explaining the diminished security effort, Canadians may fail to perceive any significant contemporary threat to international security, or, if such a threat is perceived to exist, the origin of the threat may not be the kind which Canadians feel NATO can address. This hypothesis would, of course, account for the present attitude toward defense spending in Canada, because if there is no internal agreement regarding the nature of the military threat, there is not likely to be agreement about increased military spending. Although a propensity exists in some government circles to consider the North-South dialogue as more important in terms of world order than is the East-West confrontation, this is a statement about the long-term outlook for international politics and not an explicit judgment about Soviet military capability or intent.[13] Of course, contained within this outlook is a budgetary preference for a certain distribution of expenditures, and this preference does not favor current large military budgets. Canadian foreign aid as a percentage of GNP is higher than the corresponding figure for U.S. aid, but this figure is down from its high of the 1960s, suggesting that other factors are at work besides the desire to substantially increase spending in the Third World.

The commitment to internationalism ebbs and flows within all democracies. Measured by expenditures in the foreign realm, the Canadian commitment may be ebbing. Part of this tendency toward a kind of neo-isolationism may stem from the pull of domestic disputes and struggles. It is difficult for any government or any society to concentrate attention on foreign matters when the domestic claims on that attention are monumental. With the temporary easing of tensions about cultural issues between Quebec and the federal government and tensions about energy issues between Alberta and the federal government (following a resolution of the pricing issue), and with the patriation of the Constitution on terms that are at least marginally acceptable to a majority of Canadians, Canada will have far more opportunity to address external policy questions. But when that time arrives, it is debatable whether increased security commitments will be among the priorities.

Clearly, Liberal governments tend to interpret national threats much more broadly than Conservative governments, and because Liberal governments have dominated the Ottawa political scene in the post-World War II period, party politics have had much to do with the current levels of Canadian defense effort. On the other hand, Liberal governments have, for the most part, held a public mandate. The public has not opposed the stand these governments have taken in security matters. Indeed, though one can interpret the public controversy surrounding John Diefenbaker's refusal to accept nuclear weapons as resulting from a widespread Canadian belief that Canada was not living up to its obligations, national security has only more recently become a major political issue in Canada when security is perceived as costing too much. Thus, one cannot ascribe the Liberal focus on defense spending merely to the partisan preferences of the current political leadership; the explanations for the Canadian outlook on security must lie deeper.

Despite involvement on an important military scale in both world wars, Canada continues to think of itself as buffered from confrontations in Europe and Asia by the two oceans. Of course, Canada is aware of the changed technological nature of warfare which tends to entangle all nations, nuclear as well as nonnuclear, in armed conflicts, and of course Canada is cognizant of the effects of interdependence in transforming all major regional problems into global problems. But a residue of geographic isolation still colors Canadian foreign policy thought with regard to security matters, for example, the debate over the stationing of Canadian troops in Europe. Some of the arguments for reducing Canadian troop commitments to Europe suggested that Western Europe could and should look after its own security needs and that these needs might not be identical with those of Canada.[14] Despite sporadic discussion to the contrary, this differentiation of security outlooks never went so far as to seriously question whether Canada should remain within the North American Alliance.

In contrast to the United States and in consonance with some of the European governments, Canada has never feared Communism as much of an internal or external menace. Naturally, attitudes differ enormously within a population as heterogeneous as that of Canada, especially between diverse immigrant communities. Moreover, the commitment of Canadians to parliamentary democracy is as firm as that of any other people. But Canadians as a group do not fear the inroads of communist activity in the Third World the way some Americans do, nor do they fear the impact of the participation of major Communist governments in world politics. Canada takes a broadly liberal view toward the significance of ideology in international relations, neither challenging the right of other societies to adopt a competing ideology nor wasting much time in concern about the strength of Canadian allegiance to democratic welfare-oriented values.[15]

As a consequence, Canada sometimes appears to Americans to conduct its foreign policy as though it has no enemies. This characterization is scarcely fair. Canada leans strongly toward political association with non-Communist nations. Although it has taken a lead within the alliance in recognizing and trading with Cuba and China, Canada's primary affiliations are uncompromisingly on the side of the non-Communist countries, whether developing or advanced-industrial. Canada merely accentuates the liberal bias in favor of communication and trade with all countries, regardless of their internal ideological outlook. In committing itself to this broadly liberal principle, however, Canada indicates that it does view the nature of its security situation somewhat differently from the United States.

In the Canadian view, for example, Cuba presents less of a threat to the stability of Africa and Central America as a trading partner and full member of the international community than it does as an outcast or as a totally dependent ally of the Soviet Union. Canada saw, sooner than the United States, the cracks in the Sino-Soviet alliance and recognized that the greater threat by far to Canadian security stemmed from the Soviet Union. But viewed from the perspective of the Canadian polity as a whole, how much of a threat is the Soviet Union to North America? This is perhaps the most critical security question of all for Canadians to answer and the most difficult perceptual question for us to assess.

However much Canadians reject Marxist-Leninism as a philosophy of government and however much they lament the Soviet arms build-up as a danger to global stability, Canadians do not seem moved either by the idea that the Soviet Union has aggressive designs on areas outside its present borders or by the idea that a careful military balance with the Warsaw Pact must be maintained to offset Soviet pressures.[16] Although individual Canadians will indeed express these views, the Canadian public as a whole seems to fear at least as much the outbreak of major war from a variety of other possible causes, not primarily from calculated intent on the part of the Soviet Union. Moreover, the notion of the balance of power itself is conservative and is somewhat at odds with the liberal outlook of greater institutionalized progress toward world order. The balance of power emphasizes the immutability of power relationships between nation-states; the liberal idealist notion favors reform through supranational institutions, such as the United Nations, and through limitations on force, rather than reliance on efforts to balance force through the deterrence doctrine.

The view that military balance is a prerequisite to political stability on a global scale sits much less well with many Canadians than does the idea that a major attempt at nuclear disarmament might be far more meaningful for long-term security. In a word, more analysts in the United States, knowingly or not, subscribe to the conservative theory of international politics, whereas in Canada more analysts believe in the liberal theory.

Canadians, perhaps because of their North American ethos, are, however, much less motivated by contemporary neutralist impulses than are the protesting western and northern Europeans. In contrast to those leftist groups in Holland, Denmark and the German Social Democratic Party (SPD) who demonstrated or lobbied against the American production of the neutron bomb, Canadians have accepted the neutron bomb decision with apathetic nonchalance. Perhaps because the left is not as strong in Canada as it is in Western Europe, the liberal center of the population is less threatened and neutrality has less appeal. With respect to the neutron bomb, awareness that Europe, not North America, is the logical site for potential future use may have quieted some Canadian fears as well. No decisive shift in Canadian opinion is discernible against American leadership in NATO or against the basic principles for which NATO stands. Because in Canada the dependence upon NATO for military security, narrowly conceived, was never as strong as it was in, for example, the Federal Republic of Germany, so near the Soviet Army, shifts in the world balance of power have not been as shattering and have not raised as many doubts for Canada as they have for Germany.

One is left with the impression that Canadians tend to agree with Americans about the origin and direction of international security threats; they are associated with the massive Soviet military build-up. But Canadians simply feel less intensely about this threat. The ideological differences between democracy and totalitarianism are less of a spur to Canada than to the United States. The possibility of accident, escalation of Third World disputes, and breakdowns of communication are more worrisome to Canadians than to Americans. A collapse of NATO or ultimate Soviet military superiority seems less likely to Canadians, and therefore, perhaps, Canada has been less willing to take steps to avert these consequences.

Of course, the spectrum of opinion is wide in Canada, as it is elsewhere, with respect to defense questions. The Canadian military, for example, regularly adopts positions that are not very different from the official U.S. position on the nature of the security threat. But to analyze these positions is not to illuminate the reasons why Canada has made such a small commitment to military defense. The answers lie deeper in the psychology of elite and general public opinion and reflect the attitudes of those who are not necessarily called upon to consider defense on a day-to-day, professional basis. For many Canadians, world war scarcely seems imminent. Although the Russians are not to be trusted, they also appear comparatively docile. After all, a third of a century has passed since the world has experienced a major war. A new generation that knows nothing of such war is approaching power. For this generation in Canada, as elsewhere, the formulation of the security threat is extremely difficult. Because war appears remote, the preparations necessary to prevail in an armed confrontation are easily postponed or shifted elsewhere. Lacking an intense fear of military defeat or occupation, Canada is less motivated to find ways to avoid such an outcome. If not pressed too far, this difference in perception explains some of the disparity in proportionate military expenditure between Canada and the United States.

A second hypothesis for the disparate defense behavior of the two countries is that although Canada, in general, recognizes the Soviet Union as the major potential source of international insecurity, Canada relies upon the United States to deter that threat. Because Canada is so confident in the efficacy of this deterrent and defense potential (the view that in defending itself the United States must defend Canada as well), Canada sees no need to mount an appreciable military effort of its own.[17] In some ways, this is a more compelling hypothesis than the earlier one. Respected Canadian military analysts note that continental defense is not an option for Canada, it is a foregone conclusion. The issue of access to Canadian air space is often raised in this context, both by advocates of NORAD—to demonstrate a further Canadian military contribution to joint defense —and by detractors—who view access as a derogation of Canadian sovereignty. But realists acknowledge that mutual access to Canadian and American air space is necessary if continental defense is to remain workable. Canada may have more air space, but the United States has more military capability; availability of both is required in a crisis setting. And it is precisely in a crisis situation that the greatest difference of opinion may arise regarding how air space and military capability are to be used.

Notwithstanding this problem of coordination during a crisis, when threats are indirect and open to judgmental interpretation, a direct attack on Canada would necessarily be viewed in Washington as an attack on the United States. So in this regard, the security of Canada is guaranteed by the American arsenal of nuclear and conventional weapons.

If Canadian security is automatically guaranteed, then what incentives does Canada have to provide a greater military defense of its own? The answer is that it probably has very little incentive to divert expenditures away from more productive investments, inasmuch as its security is already guaranteed.

Almost unique among countries, Canada is thus in the peculiar position of having a location next to one of the superpowers without having to fear expansion on the part of that country or aggression from any other. From the perspective of Canadian immediate self-interest, to devote scarce resources to defense when national security is already guaranteed is virtually redundant. What makes more sense from this perspective is to expand resources in other international areas, such as foreign economic assistance or the export of private foreign capital. By becoming a "free rider" on American security, Canada frees its resources to achieve other objectives that would otherwise be unobtainable.

One problem with this type of security arrangement, however, is that although its security against external attack or occupation is assured, its capacity to avoid entanglements that it would prefer to abjure is not certain. To some extent, the burden of this arrangement is that Canada has only partial control of its security. In a crisis situation not of its own making and of which it wants no part, Canada may still become a target. If a potential aggressor concludes that Canada is an easier target of coercion than is the territorial United States, then Canada could become more vulnerable in a crisis situation than if it were not so closely allied to and militarily dependent upon the United States. Of course, it still would receive full military support from the United States. Moreover, any potential aggressor would have to regard an attack on Canada as the equivalent of an attack upon the United States. If it were more militarily self-sufficient, Canada might still get dragged into a dispute between the United States and another country, but the "free rider" approach to military security virtually assures that Canada will become a target in all major disputes in which the United States itself is involved.

For this reason, it is not surprising that Canada appears more concerned about "crisis situations," such as the Cuban missile crisis and the October War nuclear alert, than about the prospect of direct Soviet aggression on its borders. Like the Soviet Union itself, Canada relies on its enormous territory and its climate to discourage an aggressor contemplating occupation. What Canada is much more worried about is the prospect of an armed clash between the United States and the Soviet

Union. As an entangled ally, Canada could not escape the same fate that the superpowers themselves face; but unlike the superpowers Canada would have almost no voice in the outcome because it has contributed so little of the military capability employed in the confrontation. This is why Ottawa is likely to be far more nervous than Washington in any given dispute. Not only is Canada subject to the same penalties as the United States; it experiences the further disadvantage, in its current dependent status, of having less information than Washington and of having very little leverage over outcomes in any foreseeable dispute.

Inasmuch as Canadian security is fully supplied by the "free rider" arrangement, the bulk of its defense concerns are met. It will not have to submit to attack unless the United States itself is a target of attack. The United States will deter possible aggressors and will defend Canada if deterrence fails, not just because Canada is a loyal ally of the United States but because in order to defend itself the United States must defend Canadian territory. Awareness of this logic is like a giant sedative. It may not cure serious illness but it certainly takes away much of the pain. By removing the pain, this security arrangement with the United States also removes much of the incentive other governments have felt to acquire nuclear weapons. But the security arrangement is so compelling that it has removed much of the Canadian desire for providing strong conventional armed forces as well. The very success of the American nuclear deterrent is a large part of the reason that Canadian and American relative military expenditures are so disproportionate.

A third possible explanation for disproportionate military expenditures is, however, that even if Canada chose to increase its own defense preparedness, this increase would not necessarily add very much to the global military defenses of Western allies. Because Canada can affect Western defense decision making so little, according to this hypothesis, Canada has very little incentive to increase its present level of military preparedness. This third hypothesis is often heard in debates over Canadian military spending. It is coupled with the argument that Canada is, after all, a middle power with a rather small population. Relative to population size, Canada's defense effort looks larger. But according to this hypothesis, no matter what Canada attempted to achieve militarily, their efforts would be overshadowed by the U.S. defense program. If increased military expenditures would not in the end count for very much, why make the effort in the first place?

This logic was evident in the Canadian debate regarding whether to withdraw the remaining troops from Europe. Fewer than ten thousand soldiers could scarcely make a visible impact compared with armies that numbered a half million or more. Better perhaps to remove these troops and to divert the expenditures elsewhere, where the return to the national interest and to humanity is measurably larger.

What this logic failed to acknowledge, however, and what current levels of Canadian military spending belie, is that collective defense must be truly collective to be effective. The hypothesis that Canada can do little may help explain Canadian thinking on defense matters. But unlike the prior hypothesis, this one is flawed by a certain shortsightedness about the fundamental assumptions underlying NATO.

If each of the smaller allies adopted the same principle, namely, that their own military contributions were so inconsequential that these contributions ought to be terminated, the effect on NATO would be devastating. First, the actual level of military preparedness would decline significantly. Although the collective GNPs of the smaller allies equal that of the United States, their aggregate military expenditures amount to only three-fifths of the U.S. expenditures. But the collective defense contributions of the smaller NATO members, even by these standards, are by no means inconsequential. Their manpower commitments are far more critical.

Second, the concept of collective defense is as important as the actual level of present military expenditure. If the smaller members of NATO begin to subvert this notion by reducing their commitments, this process begins to undermine the solidarity of the alliance. Domestic critics of alliance participation in one country receive reinforcement from domestic opposition elsewhere. Military partnership within the alliance could begin to unravel from the bottom upwards. Should this occur, the first to feel the bite of increased military vulnerability could be some of the smaller members themselves. Thus, the idea that because an alliance member is small it is incapable of meaningful military contribution is very damaging to the concept of collective security.

Third, small military deployments may not be significant in themselves as a defense against attack, although, as the prior argument reveals, they will always possess symbolic value. But their real defense significance is as a tripwire. No responsible government will tolerate the sacrifice of its troops without purpose. In case of an overwhelming attack on Europe, Canadian soldiers in Europe, like American soldiers, act as a "trip wire" for greater subsequent military participation by these countries. Such deployment is a down payment on collective defense. These troops and material are hostage to European security. They act as a promise to the Europeans that Canada and the United States will come to the aid of Western Europe if it is attacked militarily. The credibility of this commitment is critical. Neutralist impulses and pacifism within certain groups in Holland and Germany today stem directly from doubts about the credibility of the conventional commitment in NATO—if this commitment is adequate, why is there a need to rely on weapons such as the neutron bomb to balance the Soviet superiority in tanks and manpower? Thus, if Canada and the United States want to avoid the twin dangers of a weakening of the alliance because of a loss of confidence in itself, and a greater reliance upon nuclear arms and the defenses of the United States alone, then a continued high level of conventional preparedness on the part of all members of NATO is essential until such time as the Soviet Union is willing to accept balanced and enforceable arms limitation.

The validity of this third hypothesis as a means of understanding Canadian thought about security is incontestable. Canadians feel they have less and less to contribute militarily to NATO. But what is perplexing is the evident contradiction within this mode of thought. If one feels that one's contribution is nonessential, one is not likely to increase one's contribution; by failing to increase one's military preparedness, one is likely to generate a sense of further helplessness and frustration regarding the operation of the alliance and the purposes of military defense. Why is this contradiction not more evident to the Canadian government and people? Is something missing from the arguments so far expressed which would erase this apparent contradiction and would complete our understanding of the Canadian outlook regarding international security? This brings me to the fourth and final hypothesis concerning the Canadian defense perspective.

The sense of incapacity to make meaningful contributions to defense tends to create a feeling of political helplessness. This feeling of helplessness in turn creates anxieties about manipulation, hierarchy, and lack of adequate consultation. But the key to both greater confidence about defense arrangements and greater involvement in actual decision making is an increased level of military participation. Greater relative military contributions earn greater participation in collective military decision making. Declining levels of military contribution suggest that a government is not interested in defense matters and is comparatively indifferent to strategy and tactics. Declining relative military contributions suggest that military defense planning ought to be left to someone else, because these decisions are less important than other matters on which a government tends to devote greater amounts of money and attention. The avenue to greater decision-making influence within a collective defense arrangement is greater military contribution such that one's participation becomes indispensable.

Canada may be at one with the United States on the nature of the international security threat, and, given the critical response to the third hypothesis above, Canada may recognize the need to augment the NATO strategic and conventional deterrence umbrella. But according to the fourth hypothesis, the problem may be that Canada is unable to find a satisfactory defense role within the current alliance structure. This is a complicated argument, but one which should not be dismissed without careful examination.

As I elaborated at length in Chapters 2 and 3, to outsiders, Canada is a mystifying country, profoundly committed to a larger role in world affairs, but to what role? Canadian foreign policy has evolved out of a liberal tradition composed of a mixture of idealism and pragmatic adjustment. Functionalism has also shaped Canadian foreign policy thought. Each country had a place in the system, a function to perform. By performing this function well, Canada earned the support of the other members of the system, including the more powerful members. It justified its existence as a nation-state. It also demonstrated its usefulness to the international system and thereby obtained a measure of self-esteem and security. But functionalism also created the pssibility of painful incongruities. Canadian membership in the United Nations and NATO was one such incongruity. Membership in the U.N. appealed to the Canadian sense of supranationalism and progressive institution building, but this membership could not provide immediate security. Participation in NATO provided a greater sense of immediate military security, but it threatened to split the universal membership of the U.N. and to orient the international system toward a conservative outlook concerned with the balance of power; Canada felt less safe in this ambience than within the liberal focus. It was difficult for Canada to make a functional contribution to both the U.N. and NATO because functionalism in these two contexts were at odds.[18]

But in the post-1945 era both the international system and Canada have changed, making functionalism in strategic terms even more problematic. The system has changed in two ways. First, the advent of nuclear weapons has made specialization in this mode of military capability more difficult, expensive, and dangerous. Canada has wisely foregone the acquisition of nuclear weapons, although it could have been among the first of nations to produce them, concentrating instead on the peaceful production of nuclear energy. Canada has thus become something of a model for the practice of nonproliferation. But the advent of nuclear technology has made functionalism more difficult despite Canada's self-abnegation; division of decision-making responsibilities in time of crisis has become almost impossible. Certain circumscribed vetoes over the use of nuclear weapons are about all that is possible on a predetermined basis.

Second, security responsibilities inside NATO have become more rather than less asymmetric over the years, with the United States assuming a larger share of the planning and implementation functions. This means that Canada has found carving out an acceptable role harder and harder to do.[19] If the United States is going to assume major mutually beneficial defense responsibilities in its own self-interest anyway, why should Canada attempt to perform the same functions? But the more the United States assumes these military functions, the less cooperation it gets from its allies, including Canada, and the more concern these practices seem to engender regarding the credibility of the American security commitment. Paradoxically, as America assumes a larger and larger part of the defense burden, it is labeled more and more isolationist. Because it is said to be isolationist, its commitments are, especially in the aftermath of Vietnam, said to be of less and less value. Yet hidden beneath this accusation is the fear that the United States might take its commitments *too* seriously and might act precipitously leaving Europe in rubble.

On the other hand, Canada has itself changed in this interval. Canada wants less and less to follow the functionalist dictum. Although Canada feels conflicting pressures in this regard, younger neonationalists want Canada to adopt a more power-oriented policy, at least in the economic realm. Canada has likewise taken unilaterally self-assertive steps in negotiations concerning the law of the sea and in the field of energy. Many Canadians would like to see a larger role for Canada which is more in keeping with the status of a great power. Functionalism does not permit such an expansive conception of foreign policy. To date, however, Canada has pursued this more power-oriented concept of foreign policy only within the confines of the economic and the legal-political realm. *Realpolitik* in the traditional sense has certainly not been part of Canadian thinking. It remains completely at odds with the Canadian liberal-idealistic outlook on international relations.

Thus, as this hypothesis suggests, the problem in the defense arena may be that Canada has not been able to define an acceptable security role within NATO. Having voluntarily given up the option to develop nuclear weapons and having recognized its peculiar security advantages in North America, Canada has no entry point into the security framework. Conventional forward defense was unsatisfactory along the central front, because the Canadian contribution was "swallowed up" by the contributions of the larger allies. Very little that was distinctive accrued to the Canadian defense effort. To some extent, therefore, the responsibility lies with the United States to create an adequate security role for the smaller allies; this role would go well beyond simply increasing the level of overall military spending, as the United States has recommended. If the allies are to approach their security potential within the alliance, they must be able to see more clearly how their contributions bolster overall defense capabilities as well as their own individual security. In attempting to find a new security role, Canada faces a number of difficult trade-offs.

One trade-off involves the general increase in military preparedness versus the choice of greater specialization.[20] The problem with a general increase in preparedness is that it is very expensive and Canada will probably not be able to match the level of expenditures of the larger allies. The problem with greater specialization is that it will reduce the balance within the Canadian armed forces and create greater vulnerability to technological obsolescence. On the other hand, through specialization Canada could make an indispensable contribution to the overall NATO defense effort. The Canadian military input would thus demand greater allied attention. Canadian influence over defense planning and decision making would correspondingly increase. Canada would then have greater control over its own security situation and that of its major allies, because without the Canadian input the allied defense effort would be appreciably weakened.

Another trade-off exists within the specialization route. Canada could choose to emphasize the following types of specialization: (1) defense of a particular area (2) technological expertise, or (3) service-oriented contributions. If, for example, Canada took primary responsibility for security within a single geographic area, such as the high arctic or a major section of the North Atlantic, this would enable Canada to maintain balanced military development and deployment in the other two types of specialization. Conversely, if Canada emphasized a technological form of specialization, as to some extent was done in antisubmarine warfare, this would enable Canada to pursue a form of technological expertise and development to the fullest while relying upon the efforts of allied development in other areas. Spillovers of a scientific sort might be considerable from a concerted effort of this type. Agreement from other NATO allies to purchase and deploy the resulting weaponry might be difficult to obtain; on the other hand, NATO itself would benefit from this form of specialization and standardization.

Finally, Canada might choose to emphasize naval development at the cost of the army or air force. This would enable Canada to police its coastal areas more effectively and to begin to protect its trade routes and fishing areas more fully. The cost would be a further decline in expenditures within the other armed services. But such a form of specialization was what the European great powers Britain and Austria-Hungary employed in the nineteenth century. The idea that governments can maximize their defense capability at a given level of military expenditure by simultaneously and equally emphasizing all the branches of the armed services is perhaps a prerogative only of the superpowers, and even the United States and the Soviet Union are finding the cost unacceptable. In any case, this is one more type of specialization that could extend Canada's military contribution at the present time and thereby increase its influence over allied decision making.

Of course, the coordination of highly specialized armed forces contributions would become even more critical than is the coordination of more balanced military efforts. Moreover, the United States as the leader of the western alliance system would have to provide incentive and encouragement to this type of defense effort if it were to succeed. But unless new roles are found for countries like Canada within the alliance structure, these countries will remain "free riders," notwithstanding appeals for them to transform their military efforts and come to the aid of the alliance as a whole.

Canada is not so much indifferent to the vulnerability of NATO as it is uncertain of how to proceed in order to make a truly effective contribution. Surely Canada can be forgiven for not wanting to merely replicate the defense preparedness of another country in a way that is redundant and perhaps already obsolescent. Alliance leadership requires seeing not only the nature of the external threat but also the problem of effective military response, from the perspective of each individual alliance partner as well as from the perspective of the alliance as a whole. Canada has a unique opportunity to increase its military effort without reducing its immediate security, and it can do this in a way that would maximize its influence within alliance councils. But Canada is not likely to do this within the context of present military planning. By recognizing that Canada is seeking a new foreign policy role and by attempting to help shape this role within the context of NATO, the United States may be able to strengthen the Western alliance system while providing Canada with a new sense of purpose in its foreign policy. A certain amount of imagination is required, however, both in Ottawa and in Washington.

Thus, all four hypotheses offer something to our understanding of why Canada has allowed its relative military effort to diminish. Only the fourth hypothesis, however, contains opportunities for the United States to take initiatives that will perhaps help Canada reverse the pattern of "free riderism." By creating a framework in which the Canadian government can formulate a new defense role for the Canadian armed forces, the United States will reinforce the Canadian desire to participate in the Western alliance system while shoring up some of the weaknesses that that system has increasingly revealed in the last decade.

ADJUSTMENT TO THE NEW
CANADIAN FOREIGN POLICY STYLE

Foreign policy style is the product of historical tradition and culture; it is also the result of intellectual preference and conscious cultivation. Style emerges, but it is also shaped. Foreign policy style conveys meaning and content. When a change occurs, the change has implications, particularly for governments that have grown accustomed to an older pattern of interaction.

Traditionally, Canada has recognized the uniqueness of its relationship with the United States but has treated it in a proper, formal manner. Canada has always been suspicious of the "hands-across-the-border" rhetoric that comes easily to American lips and is apt to be devoid of much substance. Although it accepts the language of interdependence as genuine and compelling for both partners, Canada has often sought to use bilateral institutions, such as the International Joint Commission, NORAD, and the Permanent Joint Board on Defense, as a means of aggregating information and, less frequently, of resolving disputes. But the real purpose of this style of negotiation was to safeguard Canadian sovereignty through the buffer of intermediary institutions. Similarly, Canada has traditionally sought, wherever possible, to soften the rough edge of U.S. policy-making initiative by multilateralizing agreements and by avoiding situations in which negotiations could become highly visible in the American press or highly politicized in the U.S. Congress. *Quiet diplomacy* was the phrase coined for aspects of this approach, but whatever the label, the style was considered to be in the Canadian interest. It not only fit the personal style of many Canadian diplomats, which was often intellectual and somewhat formal (for example, Canada's former Ambassador to Washington Hume Wrong) with an emphasis on "good drafting" and efficiency, but also corresponded to the nature of Canada's political institutions, which facilitated decorum, a modicum of secrecy, tactical flexibility, and discipline.[21]

In contrast to the preference of many of the members of Canadian society in the post-World War II period, a society that was often inward looking and isolationist, the style of Canadian diplomacy was self-consciously internationalist. It emphasized a strong commitment to international institutions, such as the United Nations, and to the activities of the specialized agencies. It was task oriented and specific as to purpose in terms of peace keeping, food assistance, public health services, and educational exchange. The drive for status was subordinated to the drive for human betterment. Outsiders tended to envy the liberal idealism that much of Canadian foreign policy, during the long Liberal tenure, seemed to radiate. At times this liberal idealism became moralistic and patronizing toward others who had greater responsibilities and fewer opportunities for reflection. And of course, liberal internationalism was very much in the Canadian interest. As a rich middle power, Canada sought to preserve a posture of maximum social responsiveness to the system of nations, and through this posture it achieved a greater sense of self-respect and apparent autonomy.

In the early years of the postwar system, Canada never spoke openly of functioning as a broker within the United Nations on arms control measures between East and West or, subsequently, on matters of international economic reform between North and South. Yet this broker role was implicit in the style that Canada adopted as the privileged intermediary—privileged because Canada thought it could understand the perspectives of the East and the South better than some of the other advanced-industrial non-Communist countries and because Canada also had the ear of the most powerful member of the international system.

Liberal idealism seeks to close the gap between "what ought to be" and "what is." It is not always a satisfying task. The gap frequently resists closing. Foreign policy victories were hard to come by in this liberal-idealist mode, in part because objectives often exceeded capabilities. Yet the Canadian foreign policy style was distinctive. Its image abroad was positive. Canada's self-abnegation regarding the acquisition of nuclear weapons, for example, gave significant moral weight to its advocacy of arms control, secure though others recognized Canada to be under the American nuclear umbrella.

Inside the secure perimeter established by the liberal-idealist style, however, Canada worried about an image of playing "second fiddle" in an American symphony. Despite the enormous differences in foreign policy style between the two countries, and despite the differences, for example, in economic and commercial outlook, many Canadian policy makers worried that the real image Canada was projecting abroad was that of a "little America." Dissatisfaction with the style of liberal internationalism mixed with the discreet coordination of policies—not always harmoniously generated—on a bilateral basis, led to a serious rethinking of Canadian foreign policy in 1971, which culminated in the advent of the Third Option, and again a decade later, in the emergence of bilateralism. But style was beginning to change more rapidly than substance. A tougher edge to Canadian foreign policy became apparent. A greater assertiveness was evident in communiqués and bilateral statements. The press was becoming an attractive instrument through which both to defend policies and to shape Canadian opinion toward a more unified nation-state outlook on world affairs. The lessons of federal-provincial dialogue and controversy became useful in tactical and verbal combat over "irritants" with the United States. Again and again the Canadian public was reminded that foreign policy ought to "serve the national interest." This was the denouement of many aspects of the liberal-idealist perspective in Canadian foreign policy.

Canada was growing more powerful. As Canada flexed its muscles, the older diplomatic style looked, to some observers, a little feeble, a little tarnished, and more than a little outdated. New arguments were to summarize changes in the Canadian diplomatic style which would deeply affect the relationship with the United States.

Essentially three changes in style were proposed.[22] First, decisions that affected Canadian "development" were no longer to follow the task-oriented, functional approach to diplomacy. They were to be given a more centralized strategic focus. This would allegedly assist in management of the relationship.

Second, "within very broad sectors," linkage of issues was considered a useful negotiating device. The idea that the bigger partner had the advantage in linking issues was rejected. Linkage was considered particularly useful in dealing with legislators. It would call their attention to the importance of Canadian interests in their own areas of expertise or within their own constituencies. Linkage was also regarded as useful in demonstrating how short-term bargaining outcomes would shape the long-term relationship between the two countries.

Third, Canada was more open to "institutional structures" than before, especially those conceived on a sector-by-sector basis. "Joint issue management groups" might find a larger role. An extension of this search for new "structures" was the need, as Canada saw the relationship, to project Canadian policy interests onto Congress and onto U.S. public opinion.

In contrast to the old Third Option statement, which was only implicitly directed at the United States, the new statement of revival was directed at the United States in a far more explicit way. Indeed, this fact describes the change in the style of Canadian diplomacy in the 1980s better than any other. Statements of the new policy have in common the commitment to focus on matters of state interest and economic policy. They are essentially pragmatic rather than ideological. Gone is much of the overreaching, multilateral idealism associated with Canadian participation in the United Nations or its peace-keeping or arms control efforts. The new statements invite other North American and non-North American states to address concrete issues of trade and commerce in a direct and bilateral fashion.

What are the implications for the United States of this new Canadian foreign policy style? On the one hand, the United States is increasingly able to interact with a more self-confident Canada, a Canada that considers itself more equal in terms of bargaining. This is seen in Canada's willingness to employ some form of linkage between issue areas and to dispense with functionalism as the primary doctrine guiding Canadian foreign policy. Canada is less likely today to exhibit the "touchiness" that Americans have sometimes observed in the past, because Canada considers itself a more able negotiating partner.

Willingness to consider new bilateral structures that go beyond the institutions presently in existence opens up a very important panorama of economic possibilities for both countries. It means that Canada wants to participate in the efficiencies obtainable on a sectoral basis from larger markets. It means also that the increasingly diverse set of day-to-day problems along the border can perhaps find accommodation in joint management on a "package" basis. The concept of joint management is not new, nor is it easily implemented, but there is a positive tone in the Canadian willingness to experiment with such structures and to innovate.

On the other hand, the new Canadian foreign policy style may require more in the way of adjustment than is conventionally assumed. The dropping of functionalism as the beacon of Canadian foreign policy implies more than centralization of decision making. Functionalism built toward something that Americans unequivocally interpreted in positive terms. It built toward a more peaceful and a more integrated world order, step by step in terms of specific tasks. What Americans fear is that the revived Third Option may inadvertently build only toward a richer and more powerful Canada, not toward a more viable international trading system. In the American view, idealism of the type found in the speeches and policy statements of Louis St. Laurent or Lester Pearson is being replaced by a more focused interpretation of Canadian self-interest.

I have already discussed the theoretical complications associated with the use of linkage in negotiations between highly interdependent actors (Chapter 2). Insofar as the proposed new Canadian negotiation techniques correspond, however, to what was described there as accelerated bargaining, in which a number of issues are placed on the bargaining table at one time, this approach has a good chance of achieving success. Congress might indeed respond to the prospect of clearing up a series of irritants at one time, and a number of congressmen or senators might respond simultaneously because they find that their regional interests are affected. Although the analyst should not attempt to claim too much for accelerated bargaining, this benign form of linkage may have some heretofore unexplored advantages that warrant its use.

A final aspect of the new Canadian style which will require American reflection and perhaps adjustment involves the American assumption that the only matters at issue in Canadian-American relations are a few minor irritants or border conflicts. Beneath the new Canadian style is the implication that the Canadian economic system and the continental economic association itself are in transition. This implication may not be novel for most Canadians, but most Americans will find it quite a shock. It suggests that the two economies may not be as interdependent as some have thought and that economic structures may diverge rather than converge. It also suggests that, when necessary, the Canadian government will use leverage to promote restructuring.

CONSEQUENCES OF THE NEW FOREIGN POLICY STYLE

The next chapter explores issues such as the Law of the Sea, fisheries, and the environment. Why should one use matters of foreign policy style to bridge the more theoretically-oriented and the more issue-oriented chapters? The answer is that one cannot understand the origins of Canadian policy-making in these areas in this period without examining them in the context of Canada's new overall approach to foreign policy conduct. Style may conceal substance, but it may also be used to convey substance. This latter sense is the sense in which foreign policy style was important to Canada in the jurisdictional area.

The foreign policy review that the Trudeau government made at the onset of the 1970s set the tone of Canada's foreign relations for more than a decade. The essence of the review was that domestic political priorities would determine foreign priorities. Canada would define its national interest carefully and would conduct its foreign policy on the basis of that interest.

Canada was prepared for a less than ardent reception to such initiatives. As Ivan Head observed in 1972:

> Canada cannot expect universal congratulations for pursuing policies of these sorts, however enlightened they appear to liberal elements within this country. Population pressure elsewhere in the world and escalating US demands for energy will undoubtedly cause Canada to be described from abroad as a selfish and self-indulgent country more concerned with protecting the high standard of living of its citizens than of sharing its space and resources with the needy of the world. . . . It will not be easy to counter these claims.[23]

On the other hand, many Canadians felt that the Canadian self-interest had sometimes been overshadowed by the idealism of international organizational involvement. According to this viewpoint, Canadian claims required more forceful expression. Even when these claims countered those of the United States or other principal allies the claims still had to be heard. Expression of Canadian self-interest in public international forums was not something Canada had to conceal. Indeed, through politicization of issues, skillful international lobbying, and other forceful statement, Canada hoped to achieve far more than it had via a less aggressive style of foreign policy leadership.

Canada chose to pursue this style of leadership at a time when the divisiveness of domestic regional politics might have undercut a vigorous foreign policy. Thus, the architects of the new foreign policy style had two objectives in mind. First, the new style warned those countries that might have attempted to take advantage of a Canada caught up in regional turmoil at a time when federal-provincial relations monopolized the attention of the prime minister and his principal advisors. The new style held possible intruders in abeyance. Canada demonstrated that it could contend with its own internal problems while at the same time conducting an active foreign policy in pursuit of its own interests. Perhaps the best defense in foreign policy, as in football, is a vigorous offense. Although the motive of the new foreign policy was in part to prevent challenges on the Canadian flank, the style of conduct was to press forward on a series of matters that would keep possible adversaries cautious and at arm's length. Under such circumstances, an attempt to exploit Canadian internal weakness would be less tempting, because other governments would first have to deal with the tough-minded initiatives that Canada placed on the bargaining table.

In other words, by taking the lead in foreign policy conduct, Canada sought to determine the foreign policy agenda. By setting the agenda, Canada could force other countries to address first those issues that were of primary Canadian interest, thus avoiding a situation in which Canada was in a defensive posture; and by avoiding a defensive posture Canada would be less vulnerable to external manipulation because of the major internal disagreements between the federal government, Alberta, Quebec, and a number of other provinces over the future of confederation.

Second, a strong foreign policy could redound directly to Canadian internal advantage. The 1970 foreign policy review statement had asserted that foreign policy could be used for domestic purposes. A strong, even combative, foreign policy could enable Ottawa to assert national leadership. Canadians could be proud that Ottawa was defending the national interest in a way that the provinces could not. If rivals had not existed abroad, they would have been created. The struggle for increased national jurisdiction was a symbol of what strong federal leadership could achieve. It was also a symbol of the continued need for centralized leadership. the struggle diverted attention from domestic political turmoil and thereby took pressure off the federal government internally. But the struggle for enhanced jurisdiction also created substantial benefits to the Canadian polity as a whole and thus demonstrated the utility of a self-interested Canadian foreign policy in an immediate and concrete sense. Canadian foreign policy thus proved its worth as an instrument of domestic political purpose.

How Canada and the United States adapt to these new ideas will determine much about the condition of future Canadian-American relations. Provided that the United States is able to accept the implications of the new Canadian foreign policy style, policy coordination should not suffer. Similarly, should Canada soften some aspects of the style and alter some of the tactics that would seem to follow from the overall strategy, the tone of the relationship is not likely to deteriorate. But if neither acceptance nor alteration is possible, the new Canadian foreign policy style could generate much heat in Washington.

The new foreign policy style is likely to bring the valuation of the political-strategic and the trade-commercial dimensions more closely together as Canada gives increased weight to the former and the United States begins to value the latter more dearly. Despite the reality of the differential weighting of the two dimensions by each partner in the past, relations have gone smoothly. The United States made concessions on the political-strategic dimension; Canada made concessions on the trade-commercial dimension. Now concessions may be even more possible as weighting becomes more similar for the two polities. Will this strengthen the basis of partnership?

For the United States, the most important dimension in the Canadian-American relationship remains the political-strategic dimension. This chapter has outlined the assumptions that underlie this dimension and the limits concerning what can be achieved in terms of foreign policy via this dimension. The triple problems involving the centralization of authority, the preservation of political and cultural autonomy, and the provision of security all lie at the heart of this dimension and give it substance. Although the political-strategic dimension is uncorrelated with (that is, theoretically independent of) the other two principal dimensions of the bilateral relationship, the political-strategic factor is likely to grow in importance for Canada as it wrestles with the problems that are contained therein. Conversely, the United States may discover that maintaining good relations with Canada in a political sense also means giving increasing attention to the trade-commercial and the psychological-cultural dimensions. This does not mean a reduction in importance for political-strategic matters; it means that the other dimensions no longer will "take care of themselves." It also means that to preserve the tone of the relationship. Canadian-American policy must be treated in a more holistic fashion. Strategic gains in terms of the Western alliance system, for example, cannot be obtained by thinking exclusively in terms of the political-strategic dimension. Relations between the two countries become more complicated and more difficult to manage even as they become more important and more rewarding to the respective governments.

SIX

Law of the Sea, The Environment, & Fisheries

Two large and important issue areas that, perhaps more than any others, have preoccupied statesmen on both sides of the border are the jurisdictional questions involving the law of the sea, the environment, and fisheries, on the one hand, and (as discussed in Chapter 7) national energy policy and its foreign implications on the other. These two sets of policy issues are more than case studies, because they have come to characterize much of the sensitivity and complexity in North American affairs outlined in Chapter 2. Canada and the United States do not rank these sets of issues with equivalent priority. Canada tends to stress the former issue area, whereas the United States tends to accentuate the latter. In each instance it is the spillover of domestic policy into the international realm which creates problems for the other neighbor. One cannot understand either of these issue areas from the Canadian perspective without looking at them as an outgrowth of the new Canadian foreign policy style discussed at the end of the last chapter. According to the salient policy statement, *Foreign Policy for Canadians,* given at the beginning of the 1970s, the jurisdictional issue area epitomized the new foreign policy style and the mandate that foreign policy is to address the needs and concerns internal to the Canadian body-politic.

CENTRICITY OF JURISDICTION

What unites analytically the apparently disparate set of legal and natural resource-related issues contained in this chapter? They seem divergent in terms of content, place in the Canadian foreign policy arena, and purposes. Nor, over time, has the United States or Canada assigned the same foreign policy significance to each of the issues. As of the spring of 1980, the then Canadian Secretary of State for External Relations Mark MacGuigan ranked the East Coast Fisheries Treaty as Canada's number one foreign policy problem. Thereafter, the problem of acid rain was generally regarded in some Ottawa circles as the issue that had most rapidly moved up the Canadian bilateral foreign affairs agenda.

But regardless of how urgent these matters may have seemed at any one time, they retain a disjointed, ad hoc character and have never been easily treated as a single package.[1]

Nonetheless, these issues do possess some common characteristics. They all involve problems that are incremental in nature, rather than crisis oriented. This makes them more difficult to solve, not less so, because the various attentive publics may not respond as firmly or as permanently to matters that cannot claim an abruptly focused response. These issues also all have a technical underpinning in that either technology affects the rate at which change in each area is occurring and therefore the rate at which problems are worsening or technology is critical to a solution. All of the issues involve complex matters of international law, which is itself, in most cases, also evolving, with all the ambiguities this implies for international agreement. Finally, and most important, in my view, all of these matters involve a quest for increased political and legal jurisdiction.[2] Without adequate jurisdiction, no government is able to exercise the economic and technical capacity at its disposal to satisfactorily address these problems.

Jurisdiction is essentially an international legal concept. It determines where the obligation to regulate resides. A well-known axiom of international law concerning jurisdiction is that no state has jurisdiction over any other state: all states are equal before the law.[3] But over time the sphere of national jurisdiction may change. At the least, when the boundaries between national and international jurisdiction are in flux, as is the case concerning certain types of state behavior today in areas beyond the territorial sea, the definitional problem regarding jurisdiction becomes paramount. Jurisdiction is also a relevant quesiton in environmental matters where the air space of one country is penetrated by the airborne emissions of a second. Jurisdiction thus has both a horizontal, territorial component and vertical, spatial component.

Jurisdiction is divisible as well. A state may exercise jurisdiction over certain activities but not over others. Complete jurisdiction in overall activities amounts to absolute sovereignty. But where jurisdictions overlap, sovereignty is only partial. Interdependence implies jurisdictional overlap regarding such considerations as, for example, extraterritoriality. Jurisdiction may likewise be divided along sectoral lines or in terms of categories of authority. By so subdividing jurisdiction according to legally recognized designation, a state is able to defend certain paramount interests without demanding absolute sovereignty. The divisibility of jurisdiction actually protects the international legal system against unwarranted demands made on behalf of absolute sovereignty. By allowing for degrees of authority and responsibility, the flexibility of the jurisdictional concept also acts as a device to resolve conflicts. Governments, in effect, are urged to share jurisdictional claims in complex ways rather than to press for absolute and total sovereignty.

If enhanced jurisdictional control is the centerpiece of this analysis, however, it generates a series of further questions regarding Canadian foreign policy conduct. Has the quest for enhanced jurisdictional control abetted Canadian nationalism? Has this nationalism in turn somewhat undermined the traditional Canadian regard for international solutions to problems abroad? Has Canada become openly and permanently revisionist in its attitude toward international law, thus breaking with its conventional allies Britain and the United States?

These are questions that can only be answered by placing them in the historical context of changes occurring within the contemporary international system. The standard used to judge such matters is itself undergoing transformation. But the answers will determine to some extent how traditional allies view Canada and how they will react to future Canadian diplomatic and legal initiatives. In this respect the answers are neither trivial in importance nor easily discernible through mere casual examination of Canadian foreign policy or of the international politics of the period.

The impact of the new Canadian foreign policy style on negotiations concerning law of the sea, environmental issues, and fisheries questions is best revealed in terms of a discussion of (1) interests, (2) priorities, and (3) strategies. If one contrasts and compares Canadian and American foreign policy interests in these issue areas, for example, the full significance of the new Canadian foreign policy style for contemporary international politics may become clear.

Contrasting Interests

Canada possesses the second-largest territory and the longest set of coast lines in the world. As expounded at the various conferences on law of the sea convened between 1958 and 1980, particularly at those conferences convened after 1970, this geopolitical reality anchored the Canadian state interest. But this fact alone did not determine either the style or the orientation of Canadian foreign policy. Canada could have joined either the coastal or the maritime coalition, each of which was composed of states with long coast lines. Canada ultimately joined the coastal coalition because Canada did not possess other attributes that would have made the maritime coalition attractive. Canada has a small navy, a growing but still not very visible maritime and carrying trade, and a coastal rather than "blue-water" fishing fleet. In addition, Canada has a large interest in protecting the fragile Arctic region from environmental damage and the Northwest Passage from designation as an international waterway. Because of the combination of all these realities,

Canada, out of national self-interest, would tend to favor the more expansive jurisdictional claims of the coastal coalition, as opposed to the more conservative claims of Britain, the United States, and the Soviet Union, which were in the maritime coalition.

In general, the members of the maritime coalition stressed the interest of maximum mobility, unrestricted resource access, and freedom of scientific inquiry defined in broadest terms.[4] The maritime orientation tended to favor those states with some combination of the following: large navies; an important maritime trade; global fishing fleets; major scientific establishments; temperate or tropical coastal areas where chemical breakdown of pollutants is rapid; and the absence of straits or other boundary regions where expansive claims might facilitate political control of the regions. Clearly Canada had less in common with states possessing these attributes than with the members of the coastal coalition.

Although many members of the maritime coalition had long coast lines themselves, their interest in mobility, access, and a global presence overrode their interest in expansive claims to protect their own coastal areas. But for Canada and the other members of the coastal coalition, the primary interest was to protect coastal areas through a maximal interpretation of jurisdiction, even at the cost of advantages of access or mobility elsewhere.[5] To some extent, a temporal trade-off was involved here as well. Canada may at some future time have a global fishing fleet or a larger navy (as it did in 1945). But in the short term, Canada was desirous of foreclosing her own coastal areas to hostile naval patrols or heavy foreign fishing, even if this meant that Canada would have foregone certain opportunities of access or mobility when these became technically feasible in the future. Conversely, Canada wanted to preserve as much of her own resource-related and political autonomy from foreign competition as was possible at the time. This meant pressing for maximum claims in jurisdictional terms even though the global effect of this policy was to narrow the sphere of the oceans held in common for all mankind. (Creation of an international institution to redistribute to Third World countries proceeds from areas beyond the 200-mile limit reduced the moral recrimination associated with extensive national claims.)

Canada had an additional reason for seeking maximum definition of an economic zone. As a major nickel producer, Canada had no interest in seeing governments with deep-sea capability, like the United States and Japan, harvesting the manganese and other mineral nodules from the sea bed on a global scale. Postponement of this eventuality meant that Canadian mineral exports would not have to face increased competition from the minerals obtainable on or beneath the ocean floor. Canada would probably have adopted this position on state interest grounds in any case, even though firms in Canada had the technical capacity to harvest minerals from the ocean floor. The Canadian interest was best served by postponing harvesting of mineral nodules anywhere for as long as possible; restricted access would help achieve this effect.

Canada and the United States did have one major interest in common: the mutual exclusion of foreign fishing fleets from North American waters.[6] Although this position was much more complicated for the United States, because of pressures from departments and interest groups which tended to diffuse the American definition of its interests, in general neither the United States nor Canada has much of a "blue-water" fishing fleet. Income calculations, at least, indicated that both Canada and the United States gained more in terms of net economic receipts by excluding foreign fishing fleets from their local waters than they lost by having to give up access to corresponding foreign fishing areas. Not surprisingly, the United States was first to extend its fishing waters out to 200 miles; Canada followed suit shortly thereafter. Each country reinforced the policies of the other on fishing matters because the state interests of each were virtually identical.

Similarly, the divergence of perspectives on other matters regarding the law of the sea is not unexpected. On grounds of state interest, the United States was a logical member of the maritime coalition, which favored more conservative extension of national claims of various types; Canada was likewise a plausible member of the coastal coalition, which attempted to expand jurisdictions more rapidly. Differing state interests explain virtually all of the divergencies in Canadian and American viewpoints on the law of the sea.

Interests of the two countries clashed in other issue areas as well. Environmental protection is one such area. From Canada's perspective, the incommensurability of economic benefits, on the one hand, and the environmental costs of clean-up, on the other, go far toward explaining why the two countries have found agreement difficult in the environmental area. In terms of interest alone, the reason Canada is more vigorous in pressing for clean-up of the Great Lakes system than is the United States is that although Canada suffers as much from mutually created environmental damage to Lake Erie and Lake Huron as does the United States, Canada does not benefit as much from the economic output that is the source of the pollution. On simple grounds of proportionality, assuming pollution laws and administration to be equivalent, the United States, with approximately ten times the population and GNP of Canada, is likely to be responsible for ten times the level of Canadian emissions on the North American continent. Within the national borders, the ratio is more appropriately estimated at about three to one. But if these emissions occur in waters or air space that is held in common, a disproportionality emerges which operates against Canada. Canada must contend with the same level of emissions as the United States, but the United States enjoys several times the economic output Canada enjoys from the activities associated with these emissions. Content of output, of course, is also important. If the dirty semi-processing industries, such as pulp, ore, and refining, are involved, this tends to weight pollution output seriously. Under these circumstances of incommensurate costs and benefits, the greater Canadian interest in environmental clean-up is self-evident.[7]

Naturally, if one adds to this scenario a situation, such as that of acid rain, wherein air flows actually dump a larger relative amount of U.S. pollution on Canada than Canada dumps on the United States, the incentives for greater Canadian environmental initiative are even more obvious. In this situation the larger absolute sizes of the pollution volume are combined with unfavorable physical distribution of the pollution. Neither of the above examples justifies indifference to the consequences of waterborne or airborne pollution on either side of the border. But the examples do indicate that because of current national interest, Canada is likely to push harder for clean-up than the United States. Canadian foreign policy has been sensitive to concerns related to national interest in the 1970s, and environmental issues have precipitated precisely the type of foreign policy initiative predicted for Canada because of its national interest.

A final area in which differing national interests hold significance for this group of foreign policy issues lies in the contrast between the political outlooks of the superpower and the near-great power. Canada, of course, emphasizes the economic and commercial dimension of foreign policy more than the political-strategic dimension, and the United States emphasizes the opposite. But this group of issues involving the environment, law of the sea, and offshore fisheries is a mixture of influences from both dimensions. Yet the United States tends to classify these issues as matters of "low politics" whereas Canada tends to place them in the category of "high politics." Part of the reason for these differences of designation stems from the difference between the systemic outlooks of the superpower and the near-great power. Not directly involved at present in crisis diplomacy or major policy-making concerning security, Canada focuses on the bilateral issues that will affect the Canadian power base; jurisdiction is at the heart of such power-oriented concerns.

Ironically, Pearsonian diplomacy was more deeply involved in East-West security-related concerns and in crisis decision-making through peace-keeping activity.[8] Prime Minister Pearson also gave less attention to negotiations concerning the law of the sea than has the Trudeau government. Emphasis of state interest has encouraged the Trudeau government to focus more precisely on bilateral issues with the United States than have previous Canadian governments (with the possible exception of the Diefenbaker government, which approached these issues rather defensively) and to stress jurisdictional and resource-related matters as being of great societal concern, despite, in some cases, little evidence of national popular agitation in support of these issues. But the systemic roles of the two countries enable them to interpret state interest in quite opposite terms.

Canada thinks of itself as a rising middle power more in sympathy with international legal change and with the aims of Third World countries than is the United States. For these reasons, Canada was quite comfortable, during the negotiations on law of the sea, in forging coalitions with Latin American and African coastal states on behalf of jurisdictional expansion. Canada considered itself to be on the forefront of meaningful international political and legal change in the system, confronting the conservative hierarchy of the "older" and more powerful states that had lined up together regardless of ideological perspective (witness the coalition including Britain, the United States, and the Soviet Union, for example). Canadian self-interest seemed to be on the vanguard of change, and the skillful coordination of that change found Canada in the role of coalition builder and mediator.

Conversely, the United States, as a superpower, viewed its self-interest in terms of maintaining continuity of tradition and practice. It overlooked ideological difference, for example, so as to strengthen the continuity and stability of the notion of world order which has prevailed since 1945. It played down the significance of the negotiations on law of the sea questions as a foreign policy priority while at the same time devoting considerable attention and effort to monitoring and shaping the legal outcomes. As a superpower and a leader of the Western alliance system, this perspective on legal change and jurisdictional claims suited the U.S. interest. But to some extent, concerns about the environment and law of the sea are not easily managed at the top of the systemic hierarchy. Analogously, in the context of the U.N., the Security Council is less relevant to matters of "low politics" than is the General Assembly. Aware of this impediment to oligopolistic coordination at the top of the systems hierarchy, Canada was quite effective at coordinating the interests of other middle powers with similar coastal concerns. More than other arenas, this was a setting in which "interdependence," or the forces of the international political marketplace, operated relatively free of considerations of power, leverage, and hierarchy. Unfettered by the rigidities introduced through disparities of power, bargaining could occur freely. Canada was able to operate within this international legal and political setting at the various conferences on law of the sea after 1970 effectively and with finesse.

One issue area in which the difference between the political outlooks of a superpower and a near-great power counted less was the bilateral setting of environmental protection. For one thing, Canada had more difficulty here because Third World countries, because of their greater emphasis on growth and development, were less willing to form a coalition around environmental matters. Conversely, the United States had difficulty in treating environmental issues as matters of "low politics" because the environmental movement was so strong in the United States in the late sixties and early seventies and because the United States was more responsible than most other societies for having initially raised ecological concerns to a place of foreign policy visibility (some observers would say this was because the post-industrial economy of the United States first dictated such concerns). The result was that, at the international level, Canada and the United States shared similar environmental outlooks; their perceptions regarding global environmental progress were also similar. The differences between their outlooks involved strategy and the importance of environmental protection in the bilateral context. Because of its role as a near-great power, Canada could rationalize unilateral extension of environmental jurisdiction 100 miles out from the Arctic coast much more easily than could the United States, which was more legally conservative as a result of its position at the top of the international power hierarchy. What, because of its role, looked radical to the United States, looked to Canada, from its international systemic role, practical and expeditious.

Conflicting Priorities

If national interest increasingly explains Canadian initiatives in the areas of fisheries, sea bed resources, and the environment, and if contrasting national interests account for the differences here in terms of Canadian and American foreign policy, conflicting ideological priorities and values exacerbated these differences for the Reagan administration and the second Trudeau government.[9] Although, ironically, the United States pushed Canada to take a stronger environmental stand in the late 1960s, by the late 1970s the situation was completely reversed, with Canada taking the bolder position vis-à-vis environmental protection. Despite a lingering agreement of viewpoint regarding the feasibility of collective international progress, part of the explanation for opposing views results from differences in state interest. But additional differences also emerged because of conflicting domestic priorities. The Reagan administration emphasized energy self-sufficiency and economic recovery even at the cost of less progress regarding environmental protection. As the National Energy Program revealed, Canadian energy self-sufficiency took a second seat to other objectives, including perhaps environmental protection, especially insofar as acid rain was concerned. Thus the more conservative ideological orientation of the Reagan administration tended to remove constraints on energy development and on rules that restricted efficiency. The more liberal Trudeau government encouraged a larger role for the state in the economy and greater protection of the physical environment, which federally administered programs could provide. Because the larger volume of acid rain was imported from abroad, the more activist government in Ottawa was likely to oppose even more strongly the set of priorities favored by President Reagan. If both governments had given the same relative domestic priority to environmental protection or to other domestic programs at the cost of environmental protection, the difference between their perspectives on jurisdictional matters would have been smaller.

The trade-off between development and preservation is an important example of the further impact of conflicting priorities on the jurisdictional outlook of Canada and the United States. Nova Scotia fishermen have lived off the sea for generations. They look forward to retaining fishing as a livelihood through careful management of fish stocks. For both the Nova Scotia fishermen and the federal government in Ottawa, preservation of fish stocks is equally as valuable as economic exploitation.

For American fishermen from Massachusetts or Rhode Island, the priorities seem to be different. Pessimism is omnipresent regarding man's ability to devise effective preservation schemes. Fear of the impact of pollution on fish stocks and of the consequences of overfishing adds to this negativism. Awareness of the pattern of the decline of whole animal populations, the decline of the more valuable fish stocks, and the extinction of species elsewhere seems to reinforce the urge to exploit fishing in the short term, because the long-term prospect for ocean fishing appears so depressing. The tendency for many New England fishermen to hold part-time jobs and to look at fishing as less than an exclusive occupation adds to the temporary quality of the expectations. The result is that Yankee fishermen often value exploitation over preservation because their individualism and experience makes them question the preservationist philosophy.

Negotiations between Canada and the United States on questions about fisheries are thus made more difficult, because each country's fishermen place different priorities on exploitation and preservation of fishing as a resource. These conflicting priorities are then reflected in the negotiation positions of the two governments, regardless of the attempt of each to adopt a more realistic bargaining posture toward the other.

Trade-offs between economic development and environmental protection abound elsewhere as well, especially in matters involving transboundary air and water pollution. Here local and regional priorities often conflict with the priorities of the respective federal governments. For example, Ontario's siting and operation of the Antikokan coal-fired electric utility above the Quetico-Boundary Waters Canoe Wilderness is scarcely consonant with Ottawa's objective of reduced sulfur emissions through proper application of the latest scrubber technology. Similarly, the objective of local farmers and businessmen in North Dakota to irrigate large areas of land through the Garrison Diversion Project is not consonant with Washington's objective of maximizing economic return for dollar invested while preventing possible irreversible environmental damage, in this case, the mixing of biota from eastern and western watersheds. For this reason — conflicting local and national priorities — Ottawa has been reluctant to step in on behalf of British Columbia in the controversy about the Skagit-Ross High Dam.

The existence of local disputes that may draw lines of tension in directions that contrast with those at the federal level does not conceal the reality that at the federal level, Canada and the United States currently appear to stress differing domestic priorities about development and preservation. The United States is more concerned about energy development than Canada, because the United States faces a more severe problem of energy import substitution; Canada is more concerned than the United States about transboundary air and water pollution, because in both absolute and relative terms Canada imports more pollution from the United States than the United States does from Canada. Domestic political and ideological priorities reinforce this governmental split in policy emphasis.

The divergence of domestic political priorities, even when interests are essentially the same, means that Canada will tend to seek greater jurisdiction in the environmental area in order to strengthen its policy-making hand. The provinces, for example, continually stimulate Ottawa to expand its jurisdiction. If priorities were exactly the same in both countries, commitments to environmental protection and economic development would be the same and Canada would have less incentive to push harder to claim national jurisdiction when, for example, the preservation of fish stocks or the reduction of pollution hazards in the Arctic were at stake. Priorities change more quickly than national interests. A new government in Ottawa or Washington, or both, is likely to assess differently the relative weight given to particular interests. But the interests themselves change, if at all, only very slowly; the rule regarding state interests is that continuity shapes their emergence and interpretation.

Alternate Strategies

Contrasting state interests and conflicting domestic priorities attached to those interests provide the foundation for the new Canadian foreign policy style. But the new foreign policy style, especially as it relates to the Canadian quest for expanded jurisdiction, is evident also in experimentation with alternate foreign policy strategies. One such "experiment" concerns functionalism versus sovereignty.

Functionalism has been the hallmark of Canadian foreign policy in the twentieth century.[10] For reasons examined elsewhere in this book, functionalism has appealed to many Canadian statesmen: it is constructive rather than power oriented in terms of method; it emphasizes role and responsibility within the international system rather than conflict; it is technical and task oriented; it fits the needs of a middle power that is adept at working within the framework of international organizations, such as the special agencies affiliated with the U.N. In short, functionalism expresses the kind of international system Canada would like to see evolve. It is a strategy of systemic involvement that is at once enlightened, constructive, and suited to the wealth and technical sophistication of modern Canada.

Functionalism also has specific application in the context of law of the sea and in fisheries negotiations. These meanings are narrower and indeed somewhat distortive of the larger concept. But they are also relevant to the new foreign policy style and reveal the tension between foreign policy strategies. Canada has been careful to argue, for example, that the Arctic Waters Pollution Prevention Act, which regulates all shipping zones up to 100 miles off Canada's Arctic coastline, is a functional—that is, technical and task oriented—initiative.[11] Its purpose is to prevent oil spills in the fragile Arctic region. Its provisions are carefully focused on regulations concerning ship construction, safety and navigational aids, pilotage, and matters of liability. It deliberately avoids confronting problems involving the rights of innocent passage or matters attendant upon adjacent kinds of jurisdiction beyond Canada's territorial waters. In this respect, the act is an expression of functionalism, because it is limited in jurisdictional scope and responds to technical problems arising both from the unique character of the Arctic environment and from the potentially damaging consequences of oil shipment in these largely ice-impacted waters.

Similarly, in the case of fisheries, the proposals favored by the United States in the late 1960s and supported at that time by Canada attempted to limit more absolute extensions of national jurisdiction. These proposals stressed a "species-specific" type of national control. Such a functional approach to regulation created the possibility of overlapping jurisdictions for pelagic fish that are subject to migration during some point in their life cycle. Once again, the functional character of the strategic approach to regulation was clear, dependent as the approach was upon careful definition of species type, migratory habits, and territorial responsibility. With the collapse of significant support for this technical definition of the management of fish stock, Canada moved toward the simpler and more encompassing type of regulation permitted by the concept of the 200-mile exclusive economic zone.

By shifting to the latter concept as it applied to fisheries and by insisting on a unilateral extension of environmental jurisdiction in the

Arctic, Canada gave the impression to some observers that a sovereignty oriented approach to foreign policy was being substituted for functionalism. Control over all aspects of economic jurisdiction was partially a result of anxiety regarding fishing rights. Following the *Manhattan* voyage, assertions of national sovereignty with respect to the Northwest Passage accompanied the more specific assertions of environmental jurisdiction that was designed to offset the possibility of oil spills.

Regulation is often multifaceted. Regulation to achieve one set of purposes may achieve a second set as well. By selecting a sufficiently narrow set of antipollution regulations, for example, Canada could discourage the use of the Northwest Passage for petroleum transport and could, if it chose, in effect close the area to certain types of shipping. A sovereignty oriented approach to Canadian foreign policy might tend to expand jurisdictional claims in this fashion. Similarly, a sovereignty oriented approach might use the international enthusiasm for expanded fisheries jurisdictions to claim larger jurisdictions in other economic areas as well, ultimately perhaps claiming virtually total sovereignty beyond present territorial waters. Inasmuch as most of the major international straits already fall within the twelve-mile delineation for territorial waters, the task is likely to be easier, not more difficult, regarding claims concerning increasing territorial waters beyond twelve miles.

The fundamental difference between the two foreign policy strategies is that functionalism requires extensions of jurisdiction in limited technical areas to perform certain technical tasks. But such extensions of jurisdiction are not viewed as stepping stones to more encompassing and more absolute territorial claims. Sovereignty oriented strategies, on the other hand, are innately expansionist. They use narrowly defined extensions of jurisdiction as a kind of leading edge for larger and deeper subsequent jurisdictional claims. Initial extensions of jurisdiction become precedents for larger encroachments on offshore areas previously held in common.

Thus the difference in foreign policy style stemming from the two strategies involves a difference of motivation and approach. But the difference in style also conveys a difference in impact. The sovereignty oriented approach favors more rapid and more total extensions of jurisdiction beyond areas now regarded as falling under the control of the federal government or the provinces. Indeed, the competition with the provinces for jurisdiction in some cases and the need to demonstrate that the federal government is adequately protecting the interests of Canada, is a partial explanation for the possible shift from the functional to the sovereignty oriented approach.

A second set of alternate strategies involves collective versus unilateral initiative in foreign policy matters. Historically, Canada has always favored multilateral or collective initiatives as opposed to bilateral or unilateral initiatives, whose result could be diplomatic isolation. A number of examples document this preference. Given the growing bipolarity of the late forties, with its Eurocentric orientation, Canada favored a multilateral approach to meeting the Soviet threat in Europe, an approach that would bring the United States formally into a European defensive alliance while simultaneously reducing pressure on Canada to enter into a strictly bilateral treaty arrangement for the defense of North America. In addition to providing Western Europe with the essential American strategic guarantee, thus promoting a deterrent definitely in Canada's best interests, NATO was viewed in Ottawa as allowing Canada to employ Britain, France, and the smaller powers as counterweights to the United States in negotiations over burden sharing and the best strategic posture. Similarly, in tariff and trade negotiations, Canada has tended to favor participation in collective negotiations, such as the Kennedy and Tokyo rounds, rather than participation in the bilateral context. Although two major sectoral agreements with the United States have been consummated in defense production and automobile assembly, Canada has shown little interest, for example, in a North American Free Trade area. Historically, Canada has chosen to use third parties to balance and mute initiatives coming from Washington, while at the same time Canada has sought to avoid becoming isolated on the basis of unilateral diplomatic initiatives that, having failed, might damage Canadian foreign policy.

In the recent period, some of this preference for collective initiative has diminished. One need only consider the vigorous and highly successful Canadian campaign during the negotiations on law of the sea to claim a 200-mile economic zone. Similarly, the Arctic Waters Pollution Prevention Act was a unilateral measure. Canada has become more self-confident about initiating unilateral policies and about disagreeing openly with the United States over broad foreign policy orientations. This does not mean that Canada was reluctant to express differences of opinion regarding foreign policy in the past; Canada did express differences of opinion, sometimes before a National Press Club audience, for example, but these differences normally involved bilateral issues or were intended to influence specific policies. At a time when the Reagan administration was espousing a greater effort regarding security and greater attention to East-West matters, the Trudeau government was proposing a major new set of initiatives in North-South matters, beginning with the Ottawa summit and followed by the Cancun meetings in October of 1981. Canada was thus attempting to lead a global effort not only to raise consciousness regarding North-South matters but to reorient attention away from precisely the type of defense-related concerns within NATO and the Middle East which were preoccupying Washington. The shift from collective to unilateral foreign policy initiatives is another aspect of the changing style of Canadian foreign policy. This style places a premium on autonomy and flexibility. It attempts to differentiate the Canadian foreign policy outlook from the American outlook, even when there are no fundamental differences in state interests or domestic political priorities. It attempts to use timing and action as the main instruments of differentiation. It attempts to distinguish Canadian foreign policy not so much through substance as through tone and mode of implementation. Unavoidably this means that Canada must adopt a somewhat vulnerable leadership position on multilateral foreign policy matters more often than in the past, giving up the comfortable ambience of collective, organizational initiative for the more visible but riskier activity of unilateral diplomacy.

A final change in Canadian foreign policy style which is seen most clearly in matters of the law of the sea, fisheries, and the environment is a shift away from idealism to a new foreign policy realism. Canada is spending less time on those foreign policy matters it can do less about and more on those matters that relate directly to its own domestic interest. Increased territorial juridsiction, cleaner local air and water, preservation of fish stocks for Canadian fishermen, and the exclusion of foreign fishing fleets all are subjects of practical and pragmatic foreign policy implementation. Gone is much of the lofty idealism of the St. Laurent or Pearson eras. Arms control and disarmament receive less attention, and the benefits of Third World coalition politics are explored. Less interest in peace-keeping arrangements and U.N. institutional initiatives has characterized recent Canadian foreign policy. More concern is expressed regarding how each initiative will affect the Canadian state interest. Idealism and realism, of course, exist side by side in Canadian foreign policy, but the balance has shifted toward increasing realism.

Canadian foreign aid policy stands out as a large residual of the appeal to foreign policy idealism. Canada has increased its foreign aid steadily as a percentage of GNP for the last five years. Although this aid is still not equal to the goal of .7 percent of GNP, set by the United Nations Conference on Trade and Development, Canada spends, relative to GNP, nearly twice what the United States spends on aid. Equally important, Canada tends to distribute its aid in such a fashion that the poorest countries receive the larger allocations. This is a very liberal policy not emulated by many aid donors.

Realism in foreign policy has replaced some aspects of idealism in areas of Canadian foreign policy other than foreign aid. Cynics might argue that Canada's aid program is its conscience and serves to erase a sense of guilt for its more self-interested policies in other areas. But such observations have been made regarding all aid programs at one time or another. The more important observation is that Canadian foreign policy implementation has matured to the point where the Canadian self-interest is seen very clearly and is pursued effectively even at the cost of alienating traditional allies, like Britain and the United States. This alienation, however, is never allowed to threaten valuable alliance association or joint security. Thus, Canada is willing to press its own self-interest very hard in areas of low politics; in areas of high politics, partly because it is not prepared to adopt a more costly and autonomous defense policy, Canada has been careful to coordinate its security effort with allies. In some ways, this differentiation of foreign policy style in areas of low and high politics is the epitomy of realism in foreign policy. Canada has taken the steps necessary to clearly define the outlines of its foreign policy and to pursue its own state interest, but it has been careful not to overstep the bounds established by prudence and realism.

CONTENTION AND CONFRONTATION

Canada has adopted a new diplomatic style. Although the tough, clear-eyed politics of Prime Minister Trudeau may epitomize this new style, this style probably transcends changes of government in Ottawa. But the adoption of a new diplomatic style is not the equivalent of fostering a policy of nationalism for its own sake. Nor has the Canadian attitude toward international law become openly or permanently revisionist.

Yet Canada has sought increased jurisdiction in a number of areas. This desire for increased jurisdiction has normally been expressed in functional terms, but the issues have involved limited new extensions of sovereignty. Canada's desire for enlarged jurisdiction has been bred of frustration with international solutions that are either too slow in coalescing or too weakly administered to achieve certain specific aims in foreign policy. Thus, an attempt to gain greater control over economic resources and the management of fish stocks or a larger capacity to protect fragile environmental regions is really an attempt to obtain greater efficiency of administration and immediacy of effect.

Although the need for efficacy and immediacy is well understood in Washington and other capitals, the possibility that extensions of jurisdiction will have secondary consequences of a negative sort is of some concern. In particular, the impact of extensions of jurisdiction on the traditional freedom of the seas is emerging as a major priority.

The 200-Mile Exclusive Economic Zone, the Arctic Waters Pollution Prevention Act, and Rights of Innocent Passage

Underlying the jurisdictional approach that Canada has favored in the 1970s is a strategy described elsewhere as multiple jurisdiction.[12] Multiple jurisdiction recognizes the divisibility of sovereignty for many international purposes. Multiple jurisdiction enables a government to exert the kind of authority it deems necessary at varying distances from the coastline, depending on the type of functional area involved. No more jurisdiction is demanded than is essential to complete a particular set of functional tasks. The amount of jurisdiction varies with the task and is determined by the nature of the task. Assertions of multiple jurisdiction outside the twelve-mile limit do not, therefore, add up to the kind of total sovereignty exerted inside the territorial sea. Because jurisdiction is divisible, the high seas do not have to bear the full weight of excessive national claims. Individual governments, in turn, are likely to find compromise over the varying size of national claims easier to reach because zones of partial authority will emerge over time which have some logic in terms of technical and administrative reality.

In January and March of 1977, for example, both Canada and the United States accepted the new 200-mile limit associated with fisheries and in so doing helped to legitimize the concept of the 200-mile exclusive economic zone. Although some important fishing areas lie outside this zone, both countries recognized that foreign fishing fleets were taking the bulk of the catch inside the zone and that the survival of the fish stocks was endangered. Because this limit went far toward meeting the needs of each country in fishing matters and because international legal opinion was beginning to coalesce around the 200-mile notion, this particular limit was found acceptable. The exclusive economic zone notion, of course, involved much more than fishing considerations, because mineral resources on the continental shelf as well as in the subsoil were included and were potentially far more valuable. Yet the essential character of the multiple jurisdiction idea was preserved, distinguishing extensions of authority according to functional and technical categories.

Similarly, the 100-mile Arctic Waters Pollution Prevention Act represented an extension of jurisdiction which was pragmatic and utilitarian. The argument here was that environmental protection could not be adequately dealt with through international supervision. U.N. environmental efforts, no matter how determined, were not likely to achieve sufficient institutional authority soon enough to be of much use in the Canadian north. Stimulated by the historic crossing in 1969 of the oil tanker the SS *Manhattan* through the Northwest Passage, Canadian fears of possible oil spills in the fragile Arctic region were very real. The combination of urgency and doubt concerning the capacity of international institutions to supervise tough environmental norms that were backed up by financial sanctions encouraged Parliament to act unilaterally. Of course, the passage of the SS *Manhattan* drew attention to the possibility that the true north, Diefenbaker's northern vision, might become an international transportation route, more particularly, an American transportation route. The Canadian action was partially meant to reaffirm that this territory belonged to Canada.

A possible alternative to unilateral initiative or supernational authority was multilateral agreement via international treaty. But who were the possible partners to such an agreement? Although the Scandinavian countries might have joined Canada in such an effort to codify international environmental law, neither the Soviet Union nor the United States was likely to be accommodating, despite some sympathy for stronger norms of environmental protection. Each would have perceived greater national jurisdiction as a threat to rights and privileges of other nations in the Arctic. Without inclusion of the United States and the Soviet Union — the two large nations with Arctic jurisdictions of their own — the international character of the agreement would have been seriously compromised. Thus, the 100-mile limit was sufficient to meet the technical needs of Canada to establish firm rules concerning oil spills and the dumping of wastes from tankers. Facing the alternative of either no international environmental agreement or an agreement with the lowest possible denominator of consent, Canada chose the unilateral route, which imposed tougher constraints, rather than the more internationally legitimate multilateral route, which held the prospect of much weaker environmental constraints.

For the United States, the concept of multiple jurisdiction and its specific application to the Canadian Arctic need not create any foreign policy complications. Indeed, the concept of multiple jurisdiction is a way of foreclosing contradictions. On the other hand, the issue of the right of innocent passage through the Northwest Passage is potentially problematic. Because the route chosen traverses areas that fall within twelve miles of the Canadian coastline, the issue is not easily debatable, even though the United States and a handful of other states still defend a territorial sea of three miles and refuse to recognize the assertions of the twelve-mile territorial sea. The twelve-mile limit may not be universally supported, but the legal trend in favor of that limit is empirically quite evident. Acceptance is less a matter of uncertainty than of time.

On the other hand, if other routes are chosen, such as from the Beaufort Sea through Prince Melville Sound, and experience suggests that the technical capacity to deal with ice flows and pack ice is already at hand, then the question of whether innocent passage is guaranteed becomes much more contentious.[13] International straits guarantee such movement of naval and maritime fleets. But is the Northwest Passage an international strait?

According to the *Corfu Channel* case, two factors determine whether a strait is an international strait: (1) the number of ships using the strait for purposes of trade and naval activity, and (2) the capacity of the strait for such transit regardless of actual use.[14] In the period examined for the Corfu Channel study, over 2,000 transits had occurred. In the history of surface transport through the Northwest Passage, only seventeen such transits have been recorded. Thus, according to the first criterion, the Northwest Passage is likely to be considered as falling under the legal jurisdiction of Canada.

According to the second criterion, however, the situation could be far different. Inasmuch as the Northwest Passage has only recently become important as a trade route, with the advent of oil discoveries in the Beaufort Sea and the high Arctic, and inasmuch as technology has only recently evolved to the point where size ten icebreakers and heavily reinforced tankers are capable of navigating the Northwest Passage, the existence of the passage was heretofore moot. Nonetheless, the physical existence of the Northwest Passage is not in doubt and its capacity for transit is becoming more and more evident. Over time the annual number of oil tankers passing through these narrows could become substantial. In addition, the unrecorded number of submarines passing through the Northwest Passage beneath the water surface may be sizeable. Such transit would reinforce the effect of surface travel on the character of the Northwest Passage as an international strait.

Canada has, on a number of occasions, however, indicated formally that it considers the Northwest Passage to fall into the category of the national strait.[15] Unless further differentiated in legal terms, such a strait would possess the characteristics of territorial waters wherein the coastal state could exclude certain kinds of ships (for example, hostile naval fleets) from transit and could prevent anchorage or naval exercises.

Thus, the question of whether the Northwest Passage is an international strait or a national strait is a matter of some significance, both for Canada and for other countries. Should Canada extend jurisdiction of a type associated with the right to physical transit over the Northwest Passage, the concept of multiple jurisdiction would be undermined. If, in addition to exclusive economic rights, one adds the authority over environmental protection and scientific exploration plus the right to foreclose innocent passage, such jurisdiction becomes virtually total and amounts to an assertion of complete national sovereignty in the region.

Whether Canada is pursuing a policy of multiple jurisdiction or whether it actually seeks absolute sovereignty is not yet evident. In such matters, events and the behavior of other governments in the international system may determine international legal outcomes as much as the unilateral behavior of a single state. Certainly resistance to classification of the Northwest Passage as Canadian territorial waters is likely to be substantial if this waterway becomes an important transit route. To some extent, Canada can control the nature and frequency of transit through its application of environmental norms. But this is an awkward way to assert national sovereignty; under the concept of multiple jurisdiction, the assertion of neither economic nor environmental prerogatives is the equivalent of a precedent, or "stepping stone," to full sovereignty. Indeed, the concept of multiple jurisdiction creates just the opposite prospect, namely, limited functional assertions of jurisdiction of varying dimensions. But the concept of multiple jurisdiction is itself not well-established or self-consciously articulated in international law. Hence, interpretations regarding whether Canada has or has not the authority to abridge the right of innocent passage in these waters of the Arctic will continue to be a source of some contention in the bilateral relations of Canada and the United States.

East Coast Fisheries (Non)Agreement: What Went Wrong?

Following the extension of national control over fish stocks to 200 miles from the coastline and following the collapse of several Interim Fisheries Agreements between 1977 and 1979, Canada and the United States finally initialed a set of agreements on west and east coast fisheries on March 29, 1979.[16] The failure of the U.S. Senate to ratify the East Coast Fisheries Agreement or even to get it out of committee led incoming President Reagan to withdraw the treaty and to divide it into two segments, one dealing with the maritime boundary (this segment was sent to a chamber of the World Court for adjudication), the other involving fishing rights.

The East Coast Fisheries Agreement was a complicated document that sought to provide reciprocal access to fish stocks for Canadian and American fishermen in perpetuity.[17] Proper management of the fish stocks was an aim of the agreement. An East Coast Fisheries Commission would manage harvesting and conservation. Different management guidelines governed three general categories of fish. Each country's fishermen would receive entitlements to harvest a certain fraction of the annual catch. Sophisticated machinery for the settlement of disputes was included. What went wrong with this carefully detailed and negotiated fisheries agreement?

Problems with the agreement fell into two categories, tactical and strategic. The tactical problems were largely contextual and political. Some of these resulted from historical accidents; others could perhaps have been avoided.

One tactical problem was the apparent failure of both sides to consult sufficiently within delegations, thus reducing the amount of information available upon which to base the agreement and increasing the risk of rejection at some point during the negotiation process. Canada did a far better job than the United States in consulting with its own fishermen and interest group representatives. But the Canadian delegation seemed to discount advice provided by the Canadian embassy in Washington regarding the attitude of the U.S. Senate toward the terms of the treaty, partly because the head of the Canadian delegation, a former ambassador to the United States himself, perhaps assumed he already had sufficient knowledge. Conversely, the U.S. delegation failed to consult consistently enough with the members of the fishermen's groups it represented, thus on occasion infuriating them with bargaining positions that were at odds with their expressed interests and even with situations of fact.

Consultation is laborious. Negotiations between delegations were lengthy and difficult. Hence, the natural temptation to reduce the load regarding communications within delegations was to be expected. But the cost of the lack of communication was high with respect to the nature of the treaty terms and its likelihood of ratification by the Senate.

A second tactical problem was the unfortunate scheduling of the treaty for debate in the U.S. Senate. The East Coast Fisheries Treaty was over-shadowed in importance by the SALT II Treaty in the minds of many senators. By getting caught in the log jam behind SALT II, the fisheries treaty was delayed. The longer it remained in the Senate, the more firmly the opposition against it coalesced. Its only hope was quick ratification, but scheduling delays eliminated such a possibility.

A final tactical issue, that of the duration of the treaty, sometimes arises as a supposed principal difference in viewpoint. Although the governments raised opposite concerns about duration, concerns that were legitimate, compromise was nonetheless possible. Canada did not want to have to negotiate the arduous agreement again soon; hence its claim in favor of perpetuity. The United States, on the other hand, held the equally plausible position that conditions would change over time and that the treaty should therefore be signed for a finite period, after which whatever antinomies may have emerged could be resolved through renegotiation. Neither position was implausible, and a compromise regarding temporal duration was surely feasible.

At the strategic level, the first problem concerned the data base on fish ecology in the Georges Bank area. In order to design a sophisticated management scheme, the governments needed comparatively reliable information on the size of fish stocks, mortality and birth rates, and time series on catch size. What was troubling was the enormous variance in the data concerning trends in fish stocks, etc. and the amount of error in predictions introduced by factors other than pressure from fishermen. The fishermen themselves were conscious of some of these effects of variation and were able to speculate about the sources. But the lack of reliable data and the tenuous assumptions the treaty negotiators were forced to make regarding the ecology of the various fish species reduced the credibility of the resulting agreement in the eyes of the fishermen.

A second broad, strategic problem was the comprehensiveness of the regulatory mechanisms. In general, other things being equal, the more simple the regulatory mechanism and the more the mechanism rewards honesty and is self-enforcing, the more likely the mechanism will work in practice. The regulatory mechanism envisioned for the East Coast Fisheries Treaty had none of these attributes. It was extremely complex and dependent on an administrative structure that had few analogues in domestic regulatory experience, let alone in the international setting. The agreement was far from self-enforcing and required careful monitoring and continuous updating as to the criteria to be applied by decision makers. Moreover, the agreement relied to a great extent upon the willingness of fishermen to report with accuracy the size of their own catches. By underreporting, however, they would have an opportunity to increase the actual size of their own catch. This temptation was likely to become overwhelming.

Although the agreement was a landmark of innovativeness and put exactly the proper emphases upon conservation and the management of fisheries, the very ambitiousness of its design created for it problems of credibility and administrative effectiveness. Criticisms of the New England fishermen—that they tended to be more individualistic and philosophically opposed to government regulation than the Nova Scotian fishermen—may have been correct, but the design of the control machinery contributed to some of this Yankee skepticism.

A third and final strategic problem cut to the very base of thinking about the agreement. The East Coast Fisheries Treaty, unlike the West Coast Fisheries Treaty, was designed to create reciprocal access to stocks on both sides of the border for both groups of fishermen.[18] Reciprocal access creates the most difficult jurisdictional problem imaginable. An international regulatory body such as the proposed commission becomes mandatory, and each government in effect delegates jurisdictional authority to that institution. Each government must thus determine whether the problems associated with joint management are worth the benefits of mutual and reciprocal access. But experience with fisheries management in other settings is not encouraging. Fishermen using the Chesapeake Bay, for example, have been unable to devise a better formula than to restrict access along the Maryland and Virginia state line even though migratory fish are involved as part of the total catch. Reciprocal access is difficult to implement fairly and efficiently. Unless such implementation is perceived on both sides to be equitable and unless the costs of implementation are acceptable, any management scheme will fail, no matter how ingenious it is.

The matter of jurisdiction once again looms large in contemplating future resolution of the problem of the east coast fisheries. Separate jurisdictions are probably inevitable, because they are relatively simple to manage and are intuitively clear. Separate and exclusive access may be conterminous with the physical boundaries of the two countries. Or, if access is not conterminous with state boundaries, equal and offsetting accesses across boundaries can be arranged, or access in return for financial compensation may be appropriate. In any case, reciprocal access to the same fishing grounds is only feasible if the management scheme is sufficiently intuitive to avoid bickering and accusations of unfair treatment.

Success for an east coast agreement means proper attention to the conservation of fish stock. In this, the original agreement was laudable. But the mechanism to achieve proper management of fisheries must be workable and cost efficient. Self-reporting is not likely to meet this requirement. More feasible regulatory measures are, however, within reach. One such measure is the area limit. By restricting fishing to certain physical areas determined by the proper use of map and compass or electronic locational gear, managers can reduce fishing-related pressure considerably. These areas can be increased or decreased in size as needed and changed from year to year. Enforcement is simple through periodic inspection from the air. Trespass is absolutely unambiguous.

A collateral management technique is the use of the seasonal limit. Although improvements in fishing technology can offset the effects of reduced fishing time, the use of seasonal limits continues to have value, especially when spawning grounds are endangered by indiscriminate fishing. Seasonal limits can be adjusted by species so as to create needed management flexibility. Again, violation of the rules is easily proved, and the cost of enforcement is minimal.

The final collateral technique is the control of fishing technology. When secondary species may be effected negatively, for example, prohibitions on particularly destructive technology may become necessary. Designation of appropriate net size and mesh size may be essential in protecting the younger and smaller fish. Although such technological limitations may, from the fisherman's point of view, conflict with efficiency, such trade-offs may become unavoidable if fish stocks are to be preserved. Technological restrictions are not so easily enforceable as are other management techniques but the use of random, unscheduled checks on equipment can help. When equipment is costly and highly visible, illegal substitutions are likely to be at a minimum.

On the Georges Bank and elsewhere, where Canadian and American fishermen make their livelihoods, the real obstacle to preservation and use of proper fish management techniques is, not technique, but the will to select and enforce technique. To some extent, the most ideal system possible will collapse if the interest groups to be regulated are allowed, because of their short-term interest, to undermine the controls that are in their long-term interest.

In a sense, the East Coast Fisheries Treaty failed because, in terms of strategic conception, it ran counter to other developments in the Canadian-American realm of foreign policy. For example, it ran counter to the environmental pattern set by Canada in the Arctic on a unilateral, national basis. It ran counter to the trend of more expansive Canadian national claims on behalf of the territorial sea and continental shelf. It even ran counter to the trend in Canadian claims regarding fisheries, which themselves were designed to be national and exclusive of penetration by foreign fleets. The East Coast Fisheries Treaty, its ambitious proposals for joint management, and the very conception of reciprocal access itself were all perhaps residuals of an earlier, less sovereignty conscious era. Ultimately, the architects of the East Coast Fisheries Treaty discovered that the momentum created by the jurisdictional trend elsewhere in the relationship was too great for them to overcome.

Acid Rain: Where are the Common Interests?

From the perspective of international relations theory, the real obstacle to resolving the problem of acid rain is that reciprocal jurisdictional access for control purposes is impossible; yet, because of the mobility of airborne pollutants, national jurisdictional control is insufficient. I shall return to this jurisdictional dilemma in a moment, but first I must assess the nature of the acid rain problem more clearly.

Acid rain, or long range transport of pollutants, as it is described in some parts of the American bureaucratic community, or "unbuffered precipitation," as its minimizers have dubbed it, is a complex and inexact phenomenon. Eliminating acid rain would be much simpler if we knew three things with greater precision: its content, consequences, and cause.[19] Because speculation must often substitute for scientific evidence in these three areas, opponents of tougher environmental legislation have not surprisingly been able to characterize acid rain as a bit of a phantom. Unfortunately, such characterization does nothing to cope with the problem, and in the absence of action, the problem is likely to worsen.

In content, acid rain seems to be composed of some mixture of SO_x and NO_x, with the former predominating but the latter gaining as a fraction of the total. Precipitated in either the dry or the wet form, the mixture of oxides in contact with water creates a highly corrosive porridge of sulfuric and nitric acid. The inexact and changing composition of acid rain increases the cost of clean-up substantially.

In terms of consequence, acid rain has been publicized as a principal source of sterility in woodland lakes and streams in Quebec, the Maritime provinces, and New England, which is located downwind of major sources of pollution.[20] A much larger cost, measured in strictly commercial terms, may be the impact on reduced forest production and rates of growth. In areas, such as the Canadian shield, where soil is thin and not well buffered, the impact on soil acidification is expected to be rapid.

Other costs, yet unmeasured, are likely in terms of the effect on exterior building surfaces, clothing, and human health. In environmental matters, the irony that in the absence of sufficient scientific research, clean-up dollars may be spent on the wrong problem and thus wasted is offset by the corresponding irony that when all the research necessary to unmistakeably pinpoint costs has been completed, the costs may be so high as to amount to virtually irreversible damage.

Acid rain is a product of both moving and industrial sources of pollution. Industrial processing plants, refineries, and coal-fired electric utilities are among the principal sources of sulfur oxide emissions; the automobile generates large amounts of nitric oxides, but so does combustion of other sorts. Major debate surrounds how far pollutants travel and how quickly they precipitate. The prospect of a switch to coal-fired electric power in Ohio, where high-sulfur coal is burned and where stack cleaners are not required in older plants, was sufficient to trigger an orchestrated reaction from Ottawa. New England and upstate New York probably suffer no less from such a decision to produce electricity at lower cost. The political atmosphere in 1970 in the United States would have been much less tolerant of such a decision, irrespective of Canadian opposition, than the electoral attitude was in 1980. But the reason for the contrasting responses in Canada and the United States is interesting to examine.

As discussed earlier in this chapter, the apparently converse attitudes toward acid rain, despite local aberrations (Vermont is supportive of the Canadian position, while, if clean-up is expensive, British Columbia might sympathize with the U.S. response), are not hard to decipher. Along its northern border, the United States generates at least five times as much sulfur dioxide as Canada and enjoys the economic benefits that stem from such production. Winds tend to blow from west to east, carrying more air pollution from the American industrial heartland into Canada than vice-versa. Canada's domestic priorities have seemingly downgraded rapid energy development (perhaps because Canada is a net energy exporter already) and upgraded environmental protection, whereas the United States, for the present, seems to have done the opposite. Thus, in adding up these factors, the political behavior of the two governments seems quite explicable. The United States generates a larger pollution load than Canada, more of this air pollution travels north than south, and Canada emphasizes clean-up while the United States is trying to emphasize energy self-sufficiency and economic growth. But the observation that clinches the argument is that the United States currently enjoys more of the economic benefits flowing out of the production that was the source of the pollution, and Canada suffers more of the pollution consequences. This is cost without benefit as far as Canada is concerned, and a neutral analyst can see reason for Canada's alarm.

Canada, of course, is not without fault concerning the operation of its

Poplar River facility, on the one hand, and the Antikokan coal-fired utility, which is sited directly above the Quetico Boundary Waters Canoe Wilderness, on the other. And until recently Ontario was not as progressive in some of its antipollution legislation as was the United States. It tended to hide behind the argument that it was producing so much less pollution than the United States that its pollution standards could be more lax. To some extent, the notion that carrying capacity varies and that where population and industrial density is lower pollution standards can be weaker is an argument that has some scientific merit. But in the case of acid rain the argument is much less persuasive, because by its very nature acid rain travels long distances and may therefore concentrate far from the initial source of the emissions.

With the advent of (1) the famous bill C-51, passed in December of 1980, which enables the Canadian federal government to intervene in provincial matters on behalf of tougher environmental restrictions, (2) Ontario's harsher emission rulings, and (3) greater expenditures on SO_2 reduction by Ontario Hydro, Canada no longer lags behind the United States in either the legislative potential on behalf of or the practice of environmental protection.[21] This means that the lead the United States has enjoyed in environmental matters has narrowed. Although the United States has devoted 2.5 percent of its GNP to environmental clean-up in recent years, this is not excessive relative to the load of emissions, the potential environmental damage caused by those emissions, and the increased Canadian effort to safeguard the environment in border areas.

To some extent, a trade-off does exist between environmental betterment and energy self-sufficiency in the short term. Greater use of coal hurts the environment; a cleaner environment costs something in terms of higher costs for energy. The disparity in current American and Canadian viewpoints on this trade-off is therefore real and not contrived. But from the policy-making perspective, both of these objectives are, of course, desirable. The key is not to yield too much ground on either objective, environmental protection or energy development.

Although the concerns regarding energy in the post-1973 period superseded concerns about environmental improvement for many governments, including perhaps the United States, the apparent glut of petroleum on world markets in the 1981-82 interval indicates that the world economy has once again entered a new phase. Energy conservation and substitution are beginning to have an effect, in spite of the likelihood that as the world economy climbs out of the present recession world energy demand will once again escalate, driving energy prices, in real terms, even higher. Policy makers must, however, take advantage of economic opportunity. In periods when the pressure from energy prices is reduced, the opportunity to make gains on the environmental side emerges. In the present interval, the United States needs to worry less about quick gains obtained through energy substitution than about possible major backsliding in terms of environmental damage caused by such problems as increased emissions of the sulfur oxides.

If this awareness increases, the disparity in Canadian and American outlooks is likely to narrow. Conversion of the sixty or so electric utilities in Ohio to the burning of locally produced high sulfur coal is scarcely attractive given the moderating level of world energy prices unless proper safeguards are provided in terms of air quality. If the utilities prefer to burn petroleum or natural gas instead of locally produced coal, thus worsening the U.S. trade deficit and creating fewer jobs in the hard-pressed Appalachian area, this market preference may indeed be wiser than spending large sums on stack cleaners for essentially obsolete plants. On the other hand, if this market signal is disregarded, the U.S. government could provide subsidies for the installment of the proper environmental technology. In any case, the pressure to obtain increased energy self-sufficiency is not so great at the moment as to allow further deterioration of North American air quality.

At the same time, however, Canada ought to be encouraged to make proportional expenditures at such plants as the Antikokan facility. Rather than attempt to devise some complicated cross-border treaty to deal with the highly diverse sources of transborder air pollution, the two governments ought to recognize that the global energy system has given them a temporary reprieve in which to make the necessary environmental adjustments once again. A kind of rough equilibrium exists between energy and the environment, with progress occurring only slowly on either track. Reversals of progress are likely to be costly at this stage of industrial development, both because firms and local governments will become confused and will begin to misread signals coming from the respective federal governments and because the North American economy now weighs so heavily on the common environment and is yet so demanding of dwindling global petroleum supplies; wild vacillations of policy can no longer be afforded. Moderate, deliberate policies that take into account the medium term interest will enable both the United States and Canada to surmount the acid rain problem at acceptable financial cost.

Behind the specific policy trade-offs here, however, lie the more abstract jurisdictional questions. The reason Canada cannot resolve the acid rain problem more rapidly is that reciprocal jurisdictional access (extraterritoriality) is not feasible; yet, air pollution not only crosses borders but does so in such a way that an asymmetry emerges in terms of the economic costs of clean-up and the economic benefits of production. National jurisdictional control in isolation thus fails also. What is necessary is an awareness in bilateral terms that in areas of mutual access and mutual usage serious environmental degradation is not to be tolerated. The United States cannot use the Canadian airshed as a dump any more than Canada can use portions of the American airshed as a cost-free external area. The strategy employing increased national jurisdiction can only work if both countries recognize that increased jurisdiction involves obligations as well as rights. Extension of the fisheries zone to 200 miles, despite temporary problems of delimitation, was easy because it involved increasing rights and economic benefits. Resolution of the acid rain dilemma using the same jurisdictional logic is much tougher because increased obligations are the chief currency. Whether the approach emphasizing larger national jurisdictional claims will be sufficient to deal with the acid rain problem remains to be seen. Success depends upon the degree to which each government recognizes that, in the absence of some overriding international agreement that tends to fuse and merge sovereignties on environmental issues (clearly not the preference in the current bilateral political climate), domestic political trade-offs favor a reduction of damaging emissions.

Hence, in the acid rain question one sees the two governments groping toward national jurisdictional solutions to this slowly worsening policy-making problem. The great question is whether the prevailing jurisdictional approach is equal to the demands being placed upon it.

GRAB FOR POWER OR ASSUMPTION
OF NEW RESPONSIBILITIES?

How is one to characterize the expansion of Canadian claims during the last decade in the areas of the law of the sea, fisheries, and the environment? Is the motive the expansion of Canadian sovereignty at the expense of other governments, especially the United States, or is the motive essentially functional and designed to resolve specialized problems that are new and pressing? Surely the style of Canadian foreign policy has changed, but has the substance?

One of the reasons that so many of these problems have become visible in the bilateral U.S.-Canada relationship rather than in the larger global multilateral context is that the only near neighbor Canada has is the United States. Environmental or territorial matters automatically become bilateral U.S.-Canada issues. This is a point that is often forgotten, both in Canada and in the United States. This accounts for much of the feeling expressed by Canadians about the "oppressiveness" of their relations with the United States and for much of the American feeling that their Canadian counterparts have become more "pushy."

Still, Canada seems to retain a certain idealism in its multilateral relations, idealism that is manifested in the attitude it has expressed toward North-South relations and that is missing in the bilateral context. The new realism of Canadian foreign policy is an effort to define Canadian interests more sharply in the bilateral, not the global, context of foreign policy. In part, this new willingness to assert a growing sense of power stems from a Canadian belief that during the middle decades of the twentieth century Canada drifted too far under the wing of American dominance and that the historical forces of equilibrium are now beginning to shift that balance back again.

On the other hand, the question of functionalism versus sovereignty is confused by the changing international standard in matters of the law of the sea, for example. In the twenty years between 1950 and 1970, notions of coastal jurisdiction underwent more change than in the previous 150 years.[22] U.S. initiatives, such as the Truman Doctrine, which, regarding the Continental shelf, favored national control in economic matters out to a depth of 200 meters, and the eventual decision to claim a 200-mile fisheries zone, were decisions that recognized the trend of jurisdictional thinking and that even gave impetus to that thinking. Canadian actions may, then, have looked assertive and even radical by some historical standards; but by the standards of the era in international terms, Canada was merely, for the most part, swimming with the legal tide. The problem for the United States was that this tide, more than others, washed American beaches.

In general, Canada seems to have accepted the implications of the multiple jurisdictional notion in these areas more easily than has the United States, in part because the United States feels conflicting internal pressures from the maritime interest in maximum freedom of navigation and the environmentalist's interest in greater jurisdiction to control pollution off coastlines. Multiple jurisdiction will meet its real test in the context of the rights associated with international straits and in the designation of what an international strait is. Here, the United States and Canada may find grounds for significant disagreement, because at present their interests diverge.

Certainly Canada seems to have moved away from a position displaying great confidence in international organization and complex international institutional agreement. The failure of the initial East Coast Fisheries Treaty may have furthered this distrust. But the Parliamentary passage of the Arctic Waters Pollution Prevention Act, in the absence of significant international negotiation, signifies that Canada has lost confidence in some international routes to the redress of grievances. However justified in functional terms, it symbolizes a preference in certain areas for national rather than international solutions. The decision to qualify the mandatory submission of environmental disputes to the World Court will be looked upon as slippage by the older, more internationalist, school of Canadian foreign policy thought. Yet, when contrasted to the American refusal to subject itself at all to this World Court provision, the Canadian outlook remains more liberal.

If one attempts to answer the question at the outset of this book regarding whether the new atmosphere in U.S.-Canada relations results from actions by the United States or actions by Canada, the evidence in this chapter is not especially helpful. It is perhaps too facile to point out that, historically, the United States has taken the lead in pushing for reforms in a number of areas examined in this chapter, areas that only recently have come into conflict with the aims of Canada, and then only after the United States had reversed its course. Efforts to get national economic jurisdiction beyond the territorial sea and to push harder for environmental reform at the international level are only two of the examples. Failure to ratify the East Coast Fisheries Treaty in the U.S. Senate could be regarded as the same type of reversal of prior policy commitment which has brought the two governments into somewhat greater conflict. That the United States had good and sufficient reasons to reverse its policy course in each of these areas is not the issue. Upon reversal, the perspectives of the two countries diverged further. Some of the U.S. reversal in orientation resulted from reasons of state interest and domestic political priority. Some of the reversal resulted from changing world circumstances and the outlook of the United States toward its new, more conservative role in international, economic, and legal matters.

At the same time, once Canada embarked on a somewhat tougher perspective that was oriented more toward state interest, this tended to accelerate change in the foreign policy outlooks of the two governments, as more issues collected on the respective agendas and something of a backlog in resolution began to develop. Yet, as elsewhere in the Canadian-American association, a legacy of the special relationship remained, thus smoothing the rough edges of potential confrontation on both sides.

One should also not forget that boundary issues have long dominated bilateral relations between neighbors. In the case of the United States and Canada, negotiations were handled through the U.K. embassy in Washington during the first years of the dominion. This served to buffer squabbles. Postwar boundary problems, including the Columbia River and the St. Lawrence River projects and the Great Lakes Water Quality agreement, were often overshadowed as issues by the high politics of the Cold War and the belief in the special relationship which tended to make border disputes appear abnormal.

If the special relationship is allowed to dissipate further, as a concept and as a diplomatic reality, one of the casualties may be the low politicization of jurisdictional and environmental matters. Some of these may find resolution in increased reliance on such mechanisms as the International Joint Commission. Other matters may be treated as submissions to the World Court or as valid subjects for international tribunals involving third-party mediation. A decline in the tone of the relationship is not an inevitable consequence of the deterioration of partnership. On the other hand, in the absence of a strong commitment to partnership on both sides of the border, the politicization of disputes and the escalation of regional problems into matters of national pride may complicate future efforts to resolve conflicts.

SEVEN

Canadian Energy Policy
& U.S.-Canada Relations

In a review of the recent history of Canadian energy policy with regard
to its importance in understanding contemporary developments, several
observations come to the fore.

First, more than other events, the climactic Octobers of 1973 and 1980
have shaped recent Canadian energy policy. One event, the October War
and the ensuing oil embargo, was externally imposed and precipitous.
The other event, the announcement of the National Energy Program,
was internal, self-generated, and carefully orchestrated. The events had
in common, however, a capacity to transform both the substance of Canadian energy policy and the way Canadians and others perceived that
policy.[1]

Prior to 1973, Canada and the United States espoused policies on
energy that were exact opposites of the policies they advocated thereafter.
Each eventually adopted the other's bargaining position. For most of the
early post-1945 period, the United States attempted to "protect" its independent oil industry through the imposition of quotas on "cheap imported
oil."[2] Arguing that such oil importation would undermine the price and
the strength of the smaller independent American firms, the U.S. government strove to erect barriers to the free flow of oil. Ironically, instead of
relying on the world oil market for a significant portion of U.S. needs,
the United States through such a policy accelerated the depletion of domestic oil reserves. Canada, on the other hand, sought entry into the U.S.
market and continually challenged Washington's international energy
strategy, which Canada regarded as discriminatory and restrictive of
international trade. Canada wanted to maximize sales of oil and natural
gas to the United States; the United States wanted to minimize these
imports, in part because of pressures from Venezuela to receive the same
terms and treatment accorded Canada. In the latter months of 1972, U.S.
imports from Canada reached a peak level in excess of one million
barrels of light crude per day.

After the price shocks of late 1973, each country reversed its energy
policies. Washington virtually begged Ottawa to expand its sales of oil
and gas to the United States, whereas Canada, in turn, began a new

211

policy that would within a few years phase out all sales of light crude to the United States and would also eventually reduce the export of natural gas (largely through the instrument of price increases). Explanation for why the two countries found themselves in the situation of exchanged bargaining positions is found in the altered nature of the world oil market after 1973 and in the perception of what the price increases meant. As U.S. production declined, the United States sought to fill the gap through reliance on external sources. As the world price increased, Canada, like other exporting countries, began to interpret energy as a "nonrenewable" resource that had to be conserved. Also, Canada's export capacity was declining. Suddenly the bargaining roles of the two countries reversed, in part because their situations with respect to physical production had changed and in part because they now interpreted price as an indication of security rather than of abundance. Whether the 1973 price revolution was really as critical as policy makers at the time thought is still open to interpretation. To some extent, Canadian energy policy prior to 1973 was based on the view that the oil barrel was half full; after 1973, it was based on the view that the barrel was half empty. Reality changed less than perceptions, but perceptions in the end determined policy.

The other turning point in recent Canadian policy making regarding energy was the 1980 National Energy Program.[3] Because the bulk of this chapter is devoted to analysis of the contents and impact of this program, I will simply note here the significance of the development for overall energy relations. With the advent of the NEP, Canada signalled a shift from a strategy of attempting to achieve petroleum self-sufficiency, as a first priority, to a strategy of attempting to wrest control of Canadian energy development from the international oil and gas industry. Although this strategy was often phrased in terms of a challenge to the U.S. presence, and this presence was, after all, very large in energy-related matters, the strategy was really directed at the international oil industry per se. Or more accurately, the international oil industry found itself squeezed between two sets of contending governments—the provincial government of Alberta and the Canadian federal government, on the one hand, and the U.S. government and the Canadian federal government, on the other hand.

From the more global perspective, the NEP was the last in a series of blows struck by the major oil-producing governments in an effort to increase their sovereignty at the expense of the transnational firm.[4] This trend began in the interval following the formation of OPEC, beginning with the Libyan takeovers of 1969 and the Teheran pricing agreement of 1971. Not just OPEC members but also other governments, including the advanced-industrial governments, would respond to the opportunities created by the shift of price leadership from the Texas Gulf coast to the

Persian-Arab Gulf. The key to the shift of control was the disappearance of excess production capacity in the United States and its emergence in Saudi Arabia. The key to the expansion of national sovereignty at the expense of the international firm was the rapid increase in the price of petroleum which enabled governments to use the revenue generated through taxes to buy out the interests of the petroleum firms. This purchase effort was normally also facilitated by the use of various techniques of "creeping nationalization." Considering this background, it would have been rather strange if Canada had not attempted what other governments in similar circumstances, including virtually all of the members of OPEC, had tried successfully — that is, forced indigenization of industrial assets. Canada was not the first to apply this strategy; it was among the last. But by applying this strategy, Canada indicated to the United States that a new era in the commercial relationship between the two countries had begun.

A second set of considerations involves historically determined fact. Canada was and is a net exporter of energy, chiefly because of its enormous reserves of hydroelectric power and uranium. But Canada is also now a net importer of petroleum. More than 20 percent of its total consumption of crude oil is imported from Venezuela, the Middle East, and Mexico. Canada is thus in the somewhat unusual position of selling more energy abroad than it uses at home but of having too little energy in the proper form for its current needs. Because Canada must import high-grade petroleum on the east coast to meet the domestic demand, Canada is, not surprisingly, unable to export a net volume of such crude oil. A small amount of heavy oil from Saskatchewan is presently exported to Minneapolis and Chicago, but this amount will itself be phased out as Canadian oil upgrading facilities come on line nearer the source of production. Thus, Canada will continue to export a net volume of energy while importing a net amount of petroleum.

A third historical reality in the Canadian energy situation is that the Canadian ratio of reserve quantities to production capacity was in serious decline between 1965 and 1975, and this ratio has not significantly improved since then. As a measure of a country's level of annual production in relation to the size of its proven reserves, this ratio indexes the number of years of production available at current rates. In 1965, Canada enjoyed a respectable reserve-to-production ratio of 20 to 1.[5] Ten years later this figure had plunged to less than 10 to 1, a threshold below which the production horizon looked dangerously close. Indeed, this was one of the lowest reserve-to-production ratios experienced by any of the petroleum-producing countries. Awareness of this declining ratio in 1973, more than any other single factor, convinced Canada that it could no longer continue to export petroleum to the United States or elsewhere. Neither anti-Americanism nor a host of other pseudoexplanations, such as the sudden release of data by the oil industry, was responsible for this change of philosophy regarding exports. A key question remains, however, as to why Canada waited so long to readjust its patterns in exporting and domestic consumption.

Answers to this question are found in the perceptions of decision makers and in domestic politics. Regarding domestic politics, Alberta made a strong case for continuing petroleum exports as long as possible. Likewise, the federal government needed the revenue from Albertan exports of petroleum and natural gas to cover the costs of importing oil on the east coast. Because Canada subsidized consumers (as in effect the United States did prior to decontrol) by charging them less than the world price for petroleum, a growing budgetary deficit resulted. The necessity of importing oil at the world price while distributing it at the lower domestic price created the deficit. Thus, in order to cover these costs and also to cover a balance-of-payments deficit that would occur if imports were not offset by a corresponding value of exports in the West, Ottawa continued to export petroleum beyond the time when the declining reserve-to-production ratio dictated a change of policy. A strong set of regional and consumer constituencies encouraged Ottawa, for domestic political reasons, to continue its petroleum export policy longer, perhaps, than was wise.

Perceptions of the future production situation also encouraged Canadian decision makers to misread the trend of declining reserves. Virtually everyone studying the Canadian petroleum situation in the mid-1960s was optimistic. Geologically, formations in the high Arctic, in the Beaufort Sea, and off the coasts of Labrador and Nova Scotia looked very attractive. Given the proportion of territory that had not experienced any drilling and given the huge territorial size of Canada, the discovery of large fields of the sort found in east Texas or in the North Sea was thought to be merely a matter of time. In reality, these discoveries have been much harder to make than was anticipated. Because of the high cost of exploration and development in northern Canada and offshore, finds that would have been regarded as significant elsewhere are still not classed as commercial. Because of the threat posed by icebergs in some offshore areas, for example, much exploration awaits the innovation of new submersible-rig technology. Because of the jurisdictional uncertainties involved in federal-provincial disputes or in Canada-U.S. litigation concerning the Georges Bank, exploration has been delayed. Because of the legitimate need to protect the environment in the fragile areas of permafrost, measures to protect the environment have either prohibited development, as in the MacKenzie Valley, or have delayed exploration and development, thus raising costs and postponing returns. The upshot is that decision makers in Ottawa have been consistently more optimistic about petroleum discovery than the whole complex of investment conditions justified. Combined with the domestic political pressures to continue petroleum export policies, this tendency to fantasize about the probability of major discoveries encouraged policy makers to discount the messages conveyed by the declining reserve-to-production ratio.

Ironically, decision makers may now have overcompensated for earlier judgments that were too optimistic. Very little was wrong with the prior analysis other than that the judgments about the level of activity and the length of time required to make significant discoveries were inaccurate. None of the more recent information indicates that, in contrast to the known presence of its large natural gas reserves, Canada lacks enormous reservoirs of petroleum. Recent information merely indicates that petroleum discovery is likely to cost more and to require greater effort than was at first expected. But faith in the high probability of occurrence of these discoveries remains unshaken.

This brief assessment of the history of Canadian energy policy draws attention to sets of conclusions that have importance for how U.S.-Canada relations with respect to energy are to be interpreted. Turning points occurred in 1973, when Canada reoriented its oil export policy, and in 1980, when it adopted a new industrial control strategy. Analysts, of course, may argue, as I shall to some extent, that these developments were long foreshadowed by trends such as the declining reserve-to-production ratio, on the one hand, and the increasing frustration with high levels of foreign ownership, on the other. But in these years, critical alterations of energy policy nonetheless occurred.

Similarly, the historical reality that Canada is both a net energy exporter and a net petroleum importer is significant. Analysts outside Canada frequently confuse these facts. The facts are indeed confusing, because most observers agree that Canada could become, under favorable technical and investment-related circumstances, a leading petroleum producer. But currently Canada is far from reaching this position. Hence, observers who lament Canada's apparent "uncooperativeness" in matters relating to energy ought to recognize the technical limitations that undergird its present policy stance.

The reality of a declining reserve-to-production ratio suggests that Canada was perhaps tardy in altering its petroleum export policies. The explanations for this tardiness go a long way toward enabling the contemporary analyst to understand why Canada may have overreacted recently in espousing policies that are too pessimistic and restrictive regarding the prospect for accelerated development. But the combination of these circumstances in the post-World War II interval explains the evolution of the present Canadian outlook on energy. A single event dominates current policy formulation—the National Energy Program —and it is to this program and its implications for U.S.-Canada relations on matters related to energy that I now turn.

NATIONAL ENERGY PROGRAM:
REAL AND ANNOUNCED AGENDAS

The objectives of the NEP are multiple, as they must be for so large and complex a program. Of the nonfinancial industries in Canada, excluding petroleum, the energy industry generates about 30 percent of the national income (including the petroleum-based industries, this figure jumps to 42 percent).[6] Because of the centrality of energy to the Canadian economy and industrial structure, the NEP has a potential impact that is enormous. Determining the objectives of the program and the priorities among the objectives is critical to an assessment of the direction of the program and of the likelihood of its potential actually being achieved.

Like most other complex policy initiatives, the NEP has a double agenda. It has an announced, or formal, set of objectives and an implicit set of objectives. Priorities among the announced objectives may also differ from the real priorities of the program. The explanation for this is, of course, that the real objectives, although calculated to be in the national interest, may not correspond to the short-term preferences of voters or to the vagaries of the international political climate. That the Liberal government had reason to distinguish between announced and real energy agendas was made evident by the fate of the prior energy package of the Conservative government. The admirable candor of the Tories regarding the need to accelerate the movement of the domestic petroleum price toward the world price (albeit qualified by subsidies, for example, subsidies for farmers and fishermen) was widely perceived as a major reason for the fall of the government. The real policies of the Liberals concerning energy pricing were not much different from those of the Conservatives; but the Liberal government justified the policies in different ways, de-emphasized them in the overall budget, and clothed them in the comforting language of a "made-in-Canada" price, a price that nonetheless would inevitably move closer to that established by the world market.[7] Similarly, the external response to the NEP was likely to be more muted in those instances where the real priorities were unpalatable if the more welcome official agenda were out front.

According to the official version of the NEP, a principal objective was greater energy self-sufficiency for Canada. This objective was in keeping with the stated goals of the International Energy Agency (IEA), of which Canada was a founding member, and with the objectives that the advanced-industrial democracies stated at the prior summit meeting. Greater energy self-sufficiency was, moreover, an extension of the policies embodied in the earlier Liberal program entitled "An Energy Strategy for Canada: Policies for Self-Reliance" and an extension of the energy policies of the prior Conservative government. Thus, in terms of this objective, the NEP enjoyed the virtues of continuity with prior Canadian energy initiatives. Finally, the NEP objective of greater Canadian energy self-sufficiency corresponded to the goals of all U.S. administrations since that of Richard Nixon regarding American energy policy. Therefore, on these grounds no conflict could occur between Canadian and American policy.

A second official goal of the NEP was conservation. Inasmuch as a number of studies indicate that large savings are possible through the introduction of less energy-intensive equipment and new, more energy-conscious techniques and processes, conservation ought to constitute an important part of any energy program.[8] Conservation also tends to be a politically neutral initiative. It is hard to oppose conservation; only spendthrifts would. Moreover, subsidies that consumers and industry alike seek and that politicians are fond of delivering are the normal instruments to accelerate conservation. But even in the absence of subsidies, conservation is likely to become popular, because price increases will induce firms and individual consumers to cut energy usage. True conservation ought perhaps to be defined in terms of the energy savings achieved by means that go beyond what the market mechanism already provides. But even without this qualification, an emphasis on conservation means that a government will not stand in the way of market processes and in particular will take steps to allow the rapidly increasing world price of energy to have its effect on the economy, thus reducing domestic energy demand and the need for imported energy. Again, conservation, like greater energy self-sufficiency, was an IEA goal and a goal shared by most other advanced-industrial nations. Thus, for non-Canadians, conservation was a welcome plank in the NEP platform.

A third objective of the NEP was more peculiarly Canadian but was still well understood abroad. *Nation building* was the somewhat lofty term given to this desire to sustain federalism.[9] No energy policy alone could achieve a greater sense of nation-state unity while preserving the legitimate regional and cultural differences that give Canada its richness and authenticity. But the wrong energy policy could undermine the fabric of Canadian unity. The word "undermine" in the context of nation building has, however, dual facets. On the one hand, an energy policy that generated too much strife could become the focal point for lasting and perhaps irrevocable hostility toward the federal government. On the other hand, an energy policy that was too meek and at the same time too generous (by the standards of most other federal polities) could strengthen regional autonomy at the eventual cost of unity. Thus, the NEP, by stressing the importance of nation building, had to straddle these opposite but equally damaging strategies, first by adopting a "tough federal line," subsequently by modifying the NEP position sufficiently to obtain an agreement with Alberta that did not sacrifice unity or further alienate the western provinces politically.

Fourth, the NEP officially made increased national control of the energy industry a subsidiary, but nonetheless important, aim. I will not explore either the full rationale or the nature of the proposed strategy here, but the objective itself was clear enough. The objective was to achieve at least 50 percent domestic ownership of the Canadian oil and gas industry by 1990. In addition, the NEP sought to achieve control of the industry. This meant that the 50 percent Canadian ownership was not to be spread broadly throughout the industry, comprising perhaps 100 percent ownership of some of the smaller firms and less than 50 per cent ownership of most of the largest firms. Control meant majority ownership of at least one and preferably more of the largest foreign-owned energy interests. In essence, the objective was to transfer management of petroleum and gas development in Canada into Canadian hands.

An aspect of this policy which was sometimes poorly understood concerned government intervention. Ottawa intended to employ Petro-Canada, the government-owned energy corporation, to make direct purchases of foreign assets and thus to achieve the rank of the largest energy firm operating in Canada. But the objective of Canadianization was neither completely to socialize the Canadian-owned part of the energy industry nor to drive out the foreign-owned industry. Indeed, the policy was just the opposite of this, and Ottawa took considerable pains to stress the true policy at some social and political cost.

Control and majority ownership did not require either total socialization of the Canadian industry or ostracization of the foreign-owned component. Ottawa sought to strengthen the Canadian private sector through encouragement of private energy exploration and development on Canada lands. Even though this encouragement may, to some extent, have run counter to some Liberal norms concerning avoidance of a deterioration of income and wealth equality, the overriding federal objective was to build a strong Canadian energy industry in both the private and the public sectors. Likewise, Ottawa needed foreign technology and continued supplies of foreign capital. Driving out the foreign-owned firms would scarcely accomplish this. Control and majority ownership meant exactly what the NEP stated, not more and not less. The firmness with which Ottawa proceeded was indicated in the New York speech of Marc Lalonde, minister of energy, mines, and resources.[10] As Mr. Lalonde asserted, the Cabinet was relatively united on this issue and Ottawa "meant business." This far-reaching provision of the NEP was not likely to be altered significantly through internal opposition or external entreaty or challenge.

If one reviews each of these objectives in terms of priorities—with the advantage of some hindsight—the real and the announced agendas look quite different. The first two objectives are essentially economic in character whereas the latter two are predominantly political. The real NEP agenda inverted the official priorities. Political objectives took precedence over the largely economic goals. Economic self-sufficiency may have been the top objective of Conservative party energy policy; it was not the principal objective of the NEP. Conservation may have been the overriding concern of a number of other advanced-industrial countries, including the United States, but Ottawa did not share these preferences. Interrelated and closely coordinated, nation building and Canadianization provided the major thrust of the National Energy Program.

Prime Minister Trudeau has presided over four parliaments (1968 to the present) interrupted only by the May-December 1979 reign of the Clark Conservative government. Throughout his long tenure in office, Prime Minister Trudeau has subordinated foreign policy to domestic Canadian interests. Domestic Canadian interests, in turn, have been shaped by their significance for a sense of Canadian unity and nation-state identity. The evolution of the NEP followed exactly this formula. Energy development had to further national unity. Underlying the ethos of the program was the concern about federal-provincial relations and the power of Alberta versus the power of the federal government.

Canadianization placed relations with the United States in a subordinate position to the long-term interest of the Canadian polity as defined in Ottawa. Loss of control over energy matters through increased foreign ownership was interpreted to threaten Ottawa's leadership just as Alberta's allegedly growing power challenged that leadership. Indeed, the two developments were intertwined from Ottawa's viewpoint. Foreign domination of the economy facilitated economic fragmentation. Economic fragmentation reinforced regional autonomy.

Increasingly, the foreign-owned energy industry had seen Premier Lougheed, not Prime Minister Trudeau, as the arbiter of Canadian energy policy; NEP was designed to correct that misperception. The NEP was designed to restore Ottawa's leadership by transferring ownership and control to Canadian individuals and firms, who it was hoped would, in turn, be more directly accountable to Ottawa's authority. Nation building implied greater authority at the center. In the Liberal view, nation building necessitated a shift of power from the west to Ottawa and a shift of power away from the international energy industry toward Canadian economic and political decision makers. In this view, the NEP was essential to a restoration of authority and to a sense of national direction within the Canadian policy. Other more economic concerns, such as energy self-sufficiency and enhanced conservation, would take a back seat to the Liberal vision of a united and autonomous Canada.

As I stated above, real and announced agendas of priority differed within the NEP. So did implicit and explicit goals. I have already identified the explicit goals of the energy program. Two further implicit goals involved the need to increase federal revenues, on the one hand, and the need to strengthen the Liberal party coalition, on the other.

The federal government was perturbed about the revenue situation on at least two grounds.[11] For one thing, it faced a growing balance-of-payments problem. The energy-related part of the balance-of-payments deficit resulted from the geological necessity of phasing out most exports of petroleum and (given the controlled price of natural gas in the United States) the felt political need to constrain natural gas exports through the price mechanism. Because Canada was exporting less natural gas and petroleum but was continuing to meet the petroleum needs of the east coast by importing from world sources, a rapidly growing deficit was created. In addition, there were budgetary problems because consumers east of Sarnia, Ontario (across the Detroit River) were, like other Canadian consumers, not expected to pay the world price for petroleum. Thus, Ottawa was subsidizing these eastern consumers directly from the federal budget.

The second financial problem, which was more diffuse, was even more troublesome because of its dimensions. Unless the distribution of revenue between Alberta and the federal government were altered, in Ottawa's view, Canada faced an increasingly serious problem of inequities between regional incomes. These inequities were not satisfactorily dealt with through the medium of the equalization payments. The creation of the Heritage Fund, which was composed of Alberta's excess revenues, was only the most visible aspect of the problem, from Ottawa's viewpoint. Alberta could always justify the Heritage Fund as essential to the welfare of Albertans at a time when petroleum production was in significant decline. (Of course Alberta could still rely on its natural gas revenues, revenues from oil sands production, and revenue from its expanding industrial base as well.) The more serious problem was the effect, in other parts of Canada, not just the Maritime provinces, of the boom generated in Alberta. Should these areas not receive some recompense? If Canada, like most other democracies, was to be considered a true federation, then despite provincial ownership of resources, a greater amount of the revenue generated from those resources would have to be shared with other poorer but more populous provinces. According to Ottawa's viewpoint, this was the legitimate function of the federal government. To postulate otherwise would be to derogate federal responsibilities and to increase the likelihood that Alberta would eventually think in terms of enhanced autonomy, not just for political or even ideological reasons, but for reasons of protecting its disproportionate wealth. Thus, implied in the NEP was the objective of correcting Ottawa's budgetary and balance-of-payments deficits and of gradually transferring an increased amount of the wealth from petroleum and natural gas production in Alberta to the rest of Canada via the federal government.

Related to the former implicit objective was the other objective of the

NEP, also unspoken—strengthening the Liberal party base. Without describing this motivation in detail here or describing how the NEP was designed to further this aim, I shall note the probabilistic character of the energy program in this regard. As Minister of Energy, Mines, and Resources Marc Lalonde had revealed, the NEP involved political risks for the Liberal party. If the program proved unpopular or if it failed obviously and embarrassingly, it could have brought down the Liberal government. Conversely, if it succeeded in large part or was seen to have been a success by the press and by opinion makers, the NEP could become a very useful electoral instrument. Prudent Liberal party strategists were quite sure that they had correctly read the Canadian electoral pulse.

To remain in power, the Liberal party had to retain the loyalty of central Canada, that is, Ontario and Quebec.[12] More specifically, this meant retaining the electoral balance of power in Ontario and the overwhelming loyalty of the Liberal party at the federal level in Quebec. In order to achieve this, the federal government had to deliver in energy-related matters. Political delivery meant pursuit of a consumer-oriented rather than a producer-oriented strategy, a transfer of some additional petroleum wealth to central Canada (without endangering the principle of provincial ownership of resources, which Quebec defended as jealously as Alberta), and an attack on the problem of foreign ownership and capital repatriation. In other words, the Liberal party had to be seen by central Canadians as a defender of central Canada. A defense of central Canada meant a highly visible defense of the interests of the nation-state. In general, the NEP could be oriented toward this objective even if it meant some alienation of western Canada and of the United States government in the short term. Central Canada would not argue with either of these strategies so long as they worked and were not costly in economic terms. The Liberal party felt it would enjoy enough flexibility over the next five-year term that it could heal any wounds it created in the west via these strategies. Because Liberal strategists anticipated, as most analysts at the time did, that President Carter would be reelected, they discounted U.S. opposition. Under these circumstances, the NEP looked like a policy that would only strengthen the Liberal party coalition. The interests of the Liberal party and of Canada seemed to coincide.

Ambitious and encompassing, the National Energy Program was one of the most complex energy initiatives undertaken by any of the advanced-industrial democracies. Its stated objectives were not always its real objectives; its priorities were more political than economic. It emerged out of the cauldron of events stemming from the OPEC (largely Saudi Arabian) takeover of control in global energy matters. But it also addressed the specific national interests of Canada as defined by the Liberal party in Ottawa. A more extensive evaluation of the success of the NEP objectives is necessary here.

Greater Energy Self-sufficiency

The NEP objective of self-sufficiency in petroleum production was based on a twofold strategy. The supply-oriented strategy sought to direct exploration and development activity in petroleum toward the Canada lands, in which the federal government owned the resources. Because less drilling had been done on these lands than in the vicinity of the older Albertan oil fields, the hope was that major new discoveries would result. Such discovery of large fields in the Beaufort Sea, the high Arctic, or off the coast of Labrador, would of course reverse the decline in the reserve-to-production ratio by expanding reserves dramatically. The other strategy was demand oriented. If one shifted the usage patterns within the Canadian economy from petrolum to natural gas, petroleum consumption could be reduced, again improving the reserve-to-production ratio. How could such a transformation of the energy economy on the demand side be achieved?

The NEP employed several tactics in the attempt to further this plan. Extension of the natural gas pipeline east, beyond Montreal, to the Maritime provinces was essential if eastern users were to begin to substitute natural gas for imported petroleum. Incentives to get utilities and homeowners to burn natural gas instead of petroleum would also speed the shift. Pricing of natural gas for the home market was also critical if natural gas was to remain competitive with Albertan petroleum. Over the longer term, development of the lower leg of the Alaskan Highway (Foothills) Natural Gas Pipeline was also critical. The pipeline could funnel gas from Northern Alberta and perhaps the Beaufort Sea into the east-west pipelines supplying the eastern Canadian cities. Finally, a strong commitment on the part of the federal government was necessary to convince homeowners, utilities, and industry to make the costly conversions to natural gas and to assure them that sufficient natural gas would be available when needed at a competitive price.

In order for this two-fold strategy to work, however, a number of assumptions had to be met. Regarding the supply-oriented strategy, Ottawa was playing a high-stakes game in the medium term. Because approximately seven years, on average, is needed to bring wells in full production, no one would really know for some time how successful this aspect of the strategy was likely to be. What the government was, in effect, telling oil firms was that it knew better than they where the oil was to be found. In addition to a possible lack of information on the part of government decision makers, the danger here was that the other objectives, such as nation building, might get in the way of sound judgments about the technical feasibility of actually finding oil in certain areas. This does not mean that the federal government was providing exploration monies in the form of tax write-offs to drill dry holes. It does suggest that when different objectives would send different signals to decision makers concerning where the most likely discoveries were to be made, the government might favor a decision on political grounds whereas the firm might stress the technical feasibility. Hence the NEP might inadvertently penalize exploration and development and the effort to gain greater petroleum self-sufficiency.

Another problem with the NEP's supply-oriented dimension is that if one removes incentives from a number of firms, especially the foreign-owned firms, the average level of drilling activity may be hurt. This loss of incentives, especially when combined with an increasingly attractive set of incentives south of the border, may cause, and in fact has caused, many firms to move their drilling rigs to the United States. This does not mean that such behavior is irreversible. Drilling rigs are highly mobile. It does indicate that the NEP may have cost Canada a number of years of exploration and development in the petroleum sector because the issue of relative incentives to the industry was sacrificed to other objectives. Hence, the pessimism of some defenders of the NEP regarding the medium-term decline in Canadian petroleum output was, to some extent, self-fulfilling, based on the NEP's own set of priorities.

The demand side of the NEP's plan for greater energy self-sufficiency has its strengths and weaknesses. Its strengths are that abundant natural gas has already been discovered and exists in capped wells in fields in the Albertan foothills, for example, awaiting a more favorable price for distribution. A policy of building an adequate infrastructure to get the natural gas to eastern markets and of assuring consumers that adequate supplies will be available at a competitive price makes sense.

Weaknesses associated with the strategy, however, involve timing and price. How quickly can these conversions take place? Given the cost of the conversions, are not utilities and industry likely to resist rapid change, especially given the stated objective of greater Canadian petroleum self-sufficiency? Major oil strikes could make the whole conversion process to natural gas usage look foolish, with the consumer bearing the bulk of the costs. Precedents for such governmental mistakes of judgment are found in the United States, where in the late 1960s the government urged utilities to shift away from coal, because of the environmental hazard, only to urge them via tax legislation to shift back five years later, because of the energy crisis.

Similarly, the demand-oriented route to greater petroleum self-sufficiency may be frustrated by price. By reason of its other political objectives, Ottawa may not want to raise the price of natural gas very much. Indeed, to keep natural gas competitive and attractive to new consumers, price will remain a large factor. Yet, in order to build up substantial supplies of natural gas, Ottawa must allow price increases. Although Ottawa can set interprovincial price levels in trade of resources, it cannot force reluctant producers to sell against their will. Thus, determining a price that will clear markets in a satisfactory long-term sense is no simple task, especially when that market remains highly regulated.

In short, there is reason to believe that petroleum self-sufficiency is not likely to be achieved soon. Of course, the outcome will not be known for some years. The NEP benefits from this ambiguity. But present evidence suggests that, just as the goal of petroleum self-sufficiency took a back seat to other, more political, NEP goals, so the degree of success in achieving petroleum self-sufficiency is likely to be less than the success of other NEP goals.

A possibility not entirely to be discounted is that Ottawa never really was much interested in petroleum self-sufficiency. First, Canada could always remind the international community that, after all, Canada is a net energy exporter. Second, a strategy of leaving Canadian petroleum in the ground while using crude oil from abroad—crude oil that may eventually look cheap even at today's prices—is not such a bad idea from the viewpoint of Canadian self-interest. Of course, the strategy may infuriate allies, because Canada is drawing down scarce foreign supplies of petroleum instead of relying on its own supplies, while adding to the short-term price. But from a hard-eyed realist perspective Canada might well benefit from the narrow viewpoint of state-interest, even though the benefit comes to some extent at the expense of the international community. The only possible flaw in this argument is the assumption about the world price of energy. If the real price of energy increases only at the rate of world inflation, or more slowly, Canada would do better to use its own resources and invest the savings in foreign exchange in infrastructure, education, technological innovation, or other areas in which the rate of economic and social return is far greater than the rate of inflation. Price downturns such as that occurring in 1982 will make this latter strategy appear far more plausible.

But whatever the true strategy Canada has pursued regarding petroleum self-sufficiency, the NEP does not seem to stress the expansion of petroleum reserves, and consequently the likelihood that Canada will achieve this goal soon is not great. This may be a reasonable trade-off vis-à-vis other NEP priorities, but analysts must at least recognize the trade-off for what it is.

Conservation

Per capita, Canada is an energy-rich country; Canada is also one of the highest energy-consuming nations in the world, perhaps the highest. There are a number of reasons for this: distances traveled, climate, character of industrial output, and life-styles. But the level of energy consumption is no longer taken to equal the level and sophistication of a nation's economic development. Europe has shown North America how to maintain a high standard of living and a sophisticated industrial base at a much lower level of per-capita energy consumption. Hence, conservation is a factor in the formation of any energy plan. The NEP is no exception. A dollar saved through conservation is just as valuable as a dollar gained through the discovery of new reserves.

Conservation, or, more accurately, the reduction in energy consumption per capita and per dollar of GNP, is primarily a function of price. But for various reasons the need to raise the domestic price of energy, or to close the gap between the Canadian domestic price and the world price, has created problems for the architects of the NEP.

Neither the prior Conservative government nor the present Liberal government has been able to sell to the Canadian people the notion of the need to sacrifice in terms of energy consumption. The problem is perhaps not so much the way the message has been expressed or the willingness of Canadians to sacrifice for what they deem to be worthwhile social objectives. The explanation probably lies in the awareness that Canada is rich in energy sources; therefore, to the average Canadian, the need to conserve energy simply is not very compelling.[13] Canadians are not unique in this regard. Virtually every other society that is, or has been, energy rich has behaved in the same way. Look at relative gasoline prices in Iran or Kuwait today or in the United States of the 1950s for analogous behavior. Thus, the real issue for the average Canadian is whether he or she wishes to forego spending and investment elsewhere for the privilege of energy extravagance. So far Canadians have been willing to accept this opportunity cost.

Acknowledging this voter preference, the Liberal government has resisted the pressures from producers in Alberta to raise the domestic price of energy dramatically. A further reason why the "made-in-Canada" price has been considered attractive is that, together with the exchange rate differential, the low domestic price for energy has given Canadian industry an export edge. Whether this edge is a "subsidy" in a technical sense is beside the point. Cheap energy, particularly for the producers of energy-intensive products (and even agricultural output falls into this category today), enables Canadian enterprise to compete effectively in world markets, especially close to home, in the U.S. market. Therefore most Canadians outside Alberta are reluctant to give up these trade advantages. Ottawa, moreover, can rationalize the policies in terms of the balance of payments. A strong trade balance enables the government to cover petroleum imports and other carrying costs associated with Canada's overall development program. The lack of much conservation (apart from a few subsidies to homeowners to increase the use of insulation and the like) does not seem to be much of a disadvantage in the Canadian context.

As with all policies that attempt to oppose market forces, however, the current NEP strategy of downplaying conservation does have a longer-term penalty. That penalty is the future noncompetitiveness of Canadian industry. Accustomed to the benefits of cheap energy, Canadian farmers and industrial firms are not investing in new, energy saving, and more efficient equipment in the same way that counterparts elsewhere in the advanced-industrial world are doing. The consequence is that Canada has postponed the adjustment to a more energy-expensive world; it has traded future competitiveness for present competitiveness, a future standard of living for a higher present standard of living. Although the political psychology of these trade-offs is fully understandable, the reality remains that the NEP has to some extent mortgaged Canada's future in terms of energy efficiency and high industrial performance. Following the Ottawa-Alberta energy agreement of 1981, the posited, now somewhat accelerated, domestic energy price will still only be 75 percent of the world price by 1986. Conservation is not among the highest priorities of the NEP and a great deal should not be expected of its provisions in this regard.

Nation Building

Canada is presently undergoing two major struggles in terms of economic development: whether development and growth is to follow a regional focus or some larger nation-state conception; and whether the growth and development process is to be led by the private or the public sector. To some extent these struggles have been going on since the outset of confederation, and in a mixed economy with a strong provincial base no final outcome in favor of one or other position is likely. But shifts in orientation can and do occur. Hence the significance of the NEP's extension beyond the narrow parameters of energy into what is sometimes described as a new industrial strategy for Canada.

Regarding each of these developmental struggles within the Canadian polity, the NEP has come down firmly on one side while leaving room for subsequent modifications through bargaining. Through the NEP, Ottawa has attempted to restore some of its economic leadership. It has tried to achieve this through reorienting exploration and development patterns onto lands controlled by the Canadian federal government. This both blunts directly some of Alberta's economic clout and holds out the prospect that major new finds would come largely under the jurisdiction of the federal government.

Secondly, the NEP leaves no doubt as to who calls the economic signals. From the standpoint of both the regionalism-federalism question and the issue of the private sector versus the public sector, Ottawa will take the lead. This is the message that private firms, especially foreign-owned firms, are to draw from the formulation and implementation of the NEP.

The Liberal government intends to create a new business coalition based in Ottawa as a counterweight to the one it believes is in existence in Edmonton and Calgary. Such an effort to reorient political ties and affiliations is not likely to be lost on business elites in Toronto and Montreal, either. The purpose of such coalition building is to undermine some of the political and economic muscle that Premier Lougheed has displayed over the years. At the same time, the objective is to create new all-Canadian firms with loyalties attached to Ottawa. That this strategy was not without some success was indicated by the announcement of the branch of one of the major oil companies in the spring of 1981 that it was shifting the bulk of its exploration budget out of Alberta and into the federal lands designated by the new NEP legislation. A new Canadian business elite displaying loyalties to Ottawa rather than to Alberta, plus a foreign managerial elite with a new respect for the economic leadership of the federal government, could hold some importance for the direction and composition of Canadian economic development. Ottawa would like to bring the new elite of the energy business into line with the older, manufacturing-finance elite that, coming from central Canada, has tended to identify with the federal government for protection, for example, through the Bank Act.

Yet the nation-building strategy embodied in the NEP could face several difficulties, which are already somewhat evident. First, the generation of a loyal coalition of business support is scarcely the equivalent of building a political coalition within a parliament, for example, or a consensus within a political party. A business elite is composed of autonomous actors with objectives which differ necessarily from those of a government. Any coalition formed out of such a corporate-sector elite, whether domestic or foreign-affiliated, is likely to be highly tentative and prone to strategies of maintaining balance and continual reassessment.

Second, the federal government may inadvertently stumble on two problems that could subsequently become highly politicized and serious. A new business elite with a stronger Ottawa affiliation could become dependent upon Ottawa for financial assistance and special preferences.

Local monopolies and other market imperfections could emerge because of the need to provide support to this new elite.[14] Insofar as decisions by managers who have more of an Ottawa orientation have been made on the basis of political rationales formed by Ottawa rather than on the basis of market realities, Ottawa may find it difficult to back away from the demands of coalition members. Rather than providing support, the new coalition may provide Ottawa with an oversupply of dependence.

Similarly, because Ottawa is desirous of offsetting the criticism that its strategy of economic leadership is merely back-door socialism, a criticism that was heard as far back as George Grant's *Lament for a Nation* (1965), Ottawa may lean too far in the direction of support for concentration of economic power in a few hands in the private sector. Consequently, nation building could become a metaphor for rapidly increased economic inequality in Canada, albeit inequality that has something of a focus on the public sector and is led by Ottawa.

Despite these qualifications regarding the possible success of the nation-building objective, this political direction for the NEP is strongly apparent in the architecture of the energy plan. Commitment to this goal and early evidence of some support for it suggest that it will figure significantly in overall Canadian economic growth and development. The NEP is not so much antiregional in character as it is profederal and designed to capture the dynamism and loyalties thought essential to bind the Canadian polity more closely together in the next decades.

Continued Liberal Party Political Hegemony

Allied to the goal of nation building (more closely allied, obviously, for those Grits (Liberals) who are more rather than less ideologically faithful) is the objective of strengthening and expanding the party base; or, at the least, of formulating far-reaching federal programs that do not erode that base.

The long-term strategy designed to centralize economic power in Ottawa also may possess a spin-off, namely, the aggregation of support for the federal Liberal party. Although the identity of federal and provincial parties is often quite separate in Canada, and voters tend to cross over easily, much in the same way that Texas Democrats, for example, often vote for a Republican presidential candidate, the predominance of western support for parties such as the Conservative party (Alberta), the Conservative and New Democratic parties (Saskatchewan, British Columbia, Manitoba), and the Social Credit party (British Columbia) has virtually locked the federal Liberal party out of federal representation beyond Winnipeg. But the Liberal party has learned that it can govern Canada without representation in the west. This is far from an ideal situation, but it has been a manageable situation. By creating a new coalition of commercial support in Ottawa, the Liberal party hopes eventually to transform the base of support for other parties in the west, especially, of course, the Conservative party. A cost may be that the Liberal coalition is spread even more thinly across issues and ideology; indeed the pull of such a coalition could eventually strengthen the right wing of the Liberal party itself. But given the genesis of these spin-offs within the federally led nation-building notion, the overall direction of Liberal leadership is not likely to be much affected.

Perhaps the principal element of the Liberal party objective is to sustain the political balance of power in the electoral heartland of Canada, that is, Ontario and Quebec. Here the NEP could be helpful in a much more immediate sense. First, the strong consumer orientation of the NEP indicated to industry and citizens in Ontario and Quebec that the federal government would deliver on its promise to oppose Albertan price and revenue demands. That Ottawa eventually backed off on some of its 1980 preelection promises was far less important than that it fought long and hard in defense of the central Canadian perspective.

Second, the NEP was useful in attempting to stave off the NDP challenge in ridings where the NDP holds the balance between Liberal and Conservative party victory.[15] In many ways the NEP was a brainchild of the New Democratic Party; indeed, NDP member and energy and finance critic Bob Rae had a difficult time distinguishing the NDP energy agenda from the Liberal agenda, because the Liberals had, for the most part, stolen the NDP agenda. In the history of North American reform parties, such a pattern of the transmigration of issues to the dominant coalition party is not unusual. In any case, the whole Canadianization package in the NEP is as much a NDP idea as it is a Liberal idea. The NEP thus smoothed relations with the NDP and, more importantly, served to undermine to some extent electoral support for the NDP in critical ridings at home. Thus the major short-term impact of the Liberal energy program was to help neutralize hostility to the government from left-wing groups, especially at a critical time when other activities, such as patriation of the Canadian constitution, required broad multipartisan support.

Maintenance of the Liberal party hegemony was undoubtedly on the minds of the backers of the NEP, but the strategy involved risks. For one thing, the New Democratic Party is not a single-issue party. Regardless of how much NDP voters may have sympathized with the objectives of the Liberal energy policy, they were not likely to have been willing to shift their support to the Liberals on the basis of this issue alone. Those voters who voted for the NDP out of protest, rather than out of affinity, however, might have been influenced by the interventionist stance of the Liberal energy policy. But the longer-term strategy to create a new base of business support in Ottawa could also backfire on the Liberal party. If that coalition is not fully committed to growth that is federally led and dominated by the public sector, the strategy could become a Trojan horse for the Tories, linking the west with a rebellious right wing of the Liberal party in Ontario and, if combined with other factors, in Quebec as well. Hence, the capacity of the Liberal party to make nation building work for it electorally, through the creation of a possible new indigenous energy-industry elite, is not without certain perils. Yet the prospect that such a new coalition would eventually "bite the hand that fed it" by deserting to the Tories is conceivable but not entirely compelling. This political success for the NEP may indeed contribute to the continued hegemony of the federal Liberal party in Canada.

Canadianization

At the very core of the NEP is the plan for the transformation of industrial ownership and control within Canada. A number of factors prompted the decision to acquire at least 50 percent ownership in the oil and gas industry by 1990 and the control of the Canadian interests of one or more of the largest foreign firms.

First, the structure of the industry was itself viewed as problematic. As of 1980, 74 percent of the Canadian oil and gas industry was foreign-owned, using petroleum revenues as the measurement base; nearly 82 percent was foreign controlled. Nearly 80 percent of the foreign ownership was American.[16] With the exception of Petro-Canada most of the big individual oil and gas firms were largely foreign owned and therefore were foreign controlled. Decision making about oil and gas matters, according to Ottawa, was not in Canadian hands.

Second, unlike the situation a decade earlier, the Canadian oil and gas industry had become a net capital exporter. Net capital outflows in 1978-79 amounted to 2.1 billion Canadian dollars, or 3.7 billion Canadian dollars including dividends and interest.[17] This is not the equivalent of saying that the industry was self-financing nor that it was reducing its commitments to oil and gas exploration. Indeed, in 1980, 87 percent of petroleum-related (both upstream and downstream) cash flow went into capital expenditures, up some 5 percent over the previous year.[18] The largest component of Canadian capital expenditures was in exploration, and this component had increased by 30 percent over the prior year. The problem for the government was that as the bonanza resulting from the movement of the Canadian domestic price to the world price occurred, the government anticipated a sharp increase in net capital outflow.

Third, the government was concerned that the larger foreign firms, under prior schemes of taxation and incentive and relying on their more massive cash flows, would benefit disproportionately from new development, thus pushing the Canadian firms aside. Indeed, the sense in Ottawa was that the large foreign-owned firms had already obtained access to the most geologically attractive leases, thus prohibiting Canadian entrepreneurs from participating fully in such exploration and production.

Under these circumstances, Ottawa was faced with three options: (1) it could do nothing, (2) it could halt capital repatriation and insist that all revenues generated in Canada be reinvested in Canada, or (3) it could take advantage of a unique historical opportunity to transform the nature of the Canadian oil and gas industry. If Ottawa chose the first option, foreign ownership and control would increase while a hemorrhage of profits and rents outside the country would occur. If it chose the second option, the foreign oil and gas industry would buy up much of the Canadian industrial base, thus aggravating the ownership problem. But if Ottawa chose the third possibility, it had an opportunity to use the large influx of new revenues resulting from the rapid increase in world petroleum prices to buy out sections of the foreign-owned industry. The revenue was there. The entrepreneurial leadership existed in both the public and private sectors. The only thing that was missing was the willingness of the foreign firms to sell their Canadian assets. Herein lay the special contribution of the NEP.

If the foreign firms were unwilling to sell their Canadian oil and gas interests, in part because of the expected revenue bonanza resulting from the acceleration of the domestic Canadian price toward the world price, a modest amount of investment discrimination would cause them to rethink this hesitance. Most foreign investors fear the use of national treatment, that is, the creation of tax incentives and prohibitions favoring local firms. The NEP was therefore constructed around the objective of Canadianization through the application of forceable but comparatively gentle measures to encourage the sale of foreign-held assets, not at bargain basement prices, but at plausible prices.

Mechanisms to carry out the technique of investment discrimination were initially threefold:

> 1. The 25 percent "back-in" or "Crown interest" provision, wherein the government of Canada acquires an automatic share in the revenue generated from any oil or gas discovery.
>
> 2. A gradation of tax incentives to firms which is inversely correlated with the degree of their foreign ownership.
>
> 3. A buy-Canada provision concerning oil field services and equipment whereby firms would be requested to buy locally even if the price was not competitive.

Subsequently, the first and third of these initiatives were modified somewhat. Because the 25 percent back-in provision operated retroactively on discoveries already made, when foreign-owned firms had already made considerable expenditures of their own, some compensation was provided to these firms for the expenditures.

The government offered ex gratia payments out of the crown share of production, payments of 25 percent of expenditures incurred up to the end of 1980 for significant discoveries coming on line before the end of 1982.[19]

Concerning the buy-Canada trade provision, the government removed the premium provision associated with the requirement to buy locally, only insisting that local purchase was required if the Canadian product carried the same price as a foreign-produced product. Rules regarding scrutiny of purchases by a purchasing agency were nonetheless retained.

Canada hoped, by this legislation, to induce foreign-owned firms to sell their oil and gas properties either to Canadian private firms, which now had a competitive advantage over foreign firms (although the 25 percent back-in provision would apply equally to them), or to Petro-Canada. The record of success in this effort during the first ten months of the application of the NEP was quite remarkable, so much so that Marc Lalonde could argue in Calgary that Canadianization might proceed to the 25 percent foreign ownership level by 1990.

In these first months, foreign-ownership declined from 74 percent to approximately 66 percent. Table 1 lists the major acquisitions by Canadian companies of foreign-owned oil and gas properties in Canada in the first year after the NEP was announced (October 28, 1980). Clearly, Canadianization was moving toward its goal in terms of ownership. Control had still not been achieved regarding one or more of the larger foreign-held firms, principally because the borrowing cost was high at a time when monetary policy was being used to fight inflation. At the same time, the prior purchases had heated up the Canadian economy considerably. Similarly, some of the larger potential Canadian buyers, such as Dome Petroleum, were in the process of digesting their initial acquisitions and of covering the debt payments and were therefore not in the best possible position to expand their current purchases. On the other hand, there could be little doubt that investment discrimination worked as a tool to obtain the attention of the management of foreign-held firms and to induce sales. Some of these purchases, such as the Petro-Fina purchase, were at high multiples, suggesting to some analysts that the price paid was above the market level. But this assertion was neither demonstrated by subsequent market and industrial performance nor really demonstrated by comparisons with similar Canadian energy stocks, examined over the period of several years. From the Canadian governmental perspective, the important thing was that the NEP was able to accomplish a major reorganization of the Canadian energy industry.

TABLE 1

Major Canadian Acquisitions of Foreign-Owned Oil and Gas
Properties Since Enactment of National Energy Program

Canadian Purchaser	Foreign Seller	Property Sold	Price ($U.S.)
Dome Petroleum	Conoco, Inc.	52 percent of Hudson Bay Oil and Gas	1.6 billion
Canada Development Corporation	Aquitaine-France	Aquitaine-Canada	1.3 billion
Petro-Canada	Petrofina-Belgium	Petrofina Canada	1.2 billion
Ontario Energy Corporation	Sun Company	25 percent of Suncor	539 million
Sulpetro Ltd.	St. Joe Minerals	Candel Oil	453 million
Husky Oil	Allied Chemical	Uno-Tex Petroleum	307 million
Fairweather Gas	AMAX	Alamo Petroleum and Amax Petroleum	176 million
United Canso Oil and Gas	—*	Great Basins Petroleum	137 million
Turbo Resources	—*	Merland Explorations	123 million
Drummon Petroleum	—*	Union Texas of Canada	84 million
Oakwood Petroleum	American Quasar Petroleum	Quasar Petroleum	40 million

Source: Petroleum Monitoring Agency (Ottawa); New York Times.
*No single-party seller.

From the U.S. perspective, however, this aspect of the NEP provided
serious bilateral and multilateral problems. First, although the United
States reiterated the right of any government to determine how it treats
the private sector (provided payment is prompt, fair, and effective), this
treatment must be comparable for both domestic and foreign-owned
firms. In other words, Canada had a legitimate right to embark on a
program of Canadianization; the goal was not at issue, but the means
were. According to the U.S. view, the discriminatory tax incentive plan
and the procedures associated with the purchase of oil field services and
equipment were in violation of GATT provisions on trade and investment. Moreover, the OECD resolutions that Canada and other members
signed in 1976 and 1979 (with reservation, in Ottawa's case) forbade the
use of national treatment among the member states. Behind this U.S.
criticism, however, lay the concern that these actions in the trade and

investment area would become precedents that other governments might follow. The liberal trade order, so painfully constructed after the events of the first half of the twentieth century, would therefore potentially experience erosion.

In response Canada pointed out that the rules concerning investment are far less clear than the rules governing international trade. Moreover, the Canadian legislation was specifically patterned after procedures developed by Britain and Norway regarding their North Sea operations.[20] The Canadian provisions regarding foreign investment and oil field equipment purchases are less severe than some of these European standards. Yet Britain, admittedly now under Conservative party leadership, was among the OECD countries calling the Canadian investment decisions into question. Ottawa emphasized that the structure of its own energy industry was unique among the advanced-industrial countries, and this uniquely high level of foreign investment and control ought to be taken into account by the other trading partners.

The American counterresponse was that Canada was now "on the varsity," meaning Canada now had full economic summit membership, and it therefore had to abide by the rules that the majority of the OECD countries observed in investment and trade matters. What Canada chose to do or not to do was no longer regarded as insignificant by the world trading community. The old argument of the "significance of insignificance" was no longer valid, especially taken in bilateral terms. Moreover, Canada had other options available to it to prevent an unseemly repatriation of rents abroad. It could have employed an "excess profits tax," much as the United States and a number of countries have done.

Canada continued to maintain, however, that national treatment in investment matters was by no means universally avoided and that the United States itself observed national treatment in the areas of minerals investment, ship transport in American territorial waters, broadcasting, and foreign banking. Hence, the debate over the legitimacy of the means employed by the NEP to promote Canadianization in the energy industry continued.

A second American concern, perhaps of greater long-term significance, was whether Canadianization involved only this single industry or was merely the first of possible extensions. There were reasons for this sense of ambiguity. The Canadian Cabinet continued to debate whether the Foreign Investment Review Agency ought to apply new tougher standards of social value to new investment or to investment seeking a change of ownership status. Although this proposed legislation was shelved in the fall of 1981, the concern about extensions of restrictiveness remained.[21]

If the principal justification for the actions in the oil and gas industry was the high level of foreign ownership in the upstream operations, then certainly there was little reason to believe that on these grounds a distinction existed between petroleum and other types of investment—a distinction that would halt discriminatory policies from spreading. Downstream operations in the Canadian oil and gas industry also involved high levels of ownership. High levels of ownership also prevailed in the nonfuel minerals sector and a number of other areas of Canadian industry. On what grounds was the oil and gas industry to be considered unique if the reasoning for national treatment involved high levels of foreign ownership and control?

This prospect of extension of discrimination to other areas of trade and commerce was what prompted the phrase "change of the rules of the game." Certainly a broader application of restrictive legislation would have changed the Canadian trade and commercial situation decisively.

In a number of ways, however, the oil and gas industry could be considered unique: its high rents and prospect of dramatically increased capital repatriation, its size and centrality to the Canadian industrial base, and its political sensitivity all were perhaps in a dimension of their own when viewed by citizens or government decision makers. In any case, former Ambassador to Washington Peter Towe, Deputy Prime Minister Alan MacEachen, and Secretary of State for External Affairs Mark MacGuigan each emphasized the uniqueness of the Canadianization measures in the context of this single industry.

Some reflection will indicate why these assertions were not merely feints or diplomatic diversions. The reason why Canadianization could occur in the upstream operations of the oil and gas industry was that the disparity between the domestic Canadian price and the world price created a unique opportunity to pay for the purchases, either via public sector taxation or via eventual Canadian private sector earnings. The historical timing of the decision was therefore critical to its success. Even this effort to reverse direct private investment in Canada strained Canadian bank and financial resources, in part because the effort, perhaps for political reasons, was focused within such a short interval.

This does not mean, however, that the proposed changes in the FIRA rules or the proposed buy-Canada legislation could not re-emerge elsewhere. Nor would such examples of discriminatory conduct meet with a favorable response from foreign trading partners, such as West Germany or the United States. In some of the FIRA proposals, on the other hand, a clear difference exists between application of these rules with respect to new investment and application either retroactively or extraterritorially. The latter applications are more problematic for a liberal trade and investment order.

Perhaps the greatest brake on a long-term pattern of Canadian investment and trade discrimination is twofold. First, Canadian investors are rapidly increasing their holdings abroad, especially in the United States.[22] Canadian investments in real estate, manufacturing, and the oil and gas industry are growing appreciably. Depending upon how the statistics are collected and analyzed, Canada is probably the second largest foreign investor in the United States. This trend is not likely to diminish. Canadian banks, for example, are poised to enter the American market in a significant way. Canadian entrepreneurs have demonstrated that they can compete effectively with large American firms in terms of both financing capacity and managerial expertise. Given all of this interest in investment abroad by its own firms and entrepreneurs, Canada can scarcely afford to mount a damaging campaign against foreign investment inside Canada.

The objection often raised to this point about reciprocity, however, is that the absolute and relative levels of foreign investment in the two countries are so different that there is no basis for thinking in terms of reciprocity. Although Canadian investors now own a total value of investment in the United States that equals about one-quarter of the U.S. investment in Canada, the U.S. investment is, of course, far more visible, because the Canadian GNP is so much smaller than that of the United States. But there is another way of thinking about the comparative investment situation in the two countries. This way of thinking makes more sense in the long run because it is more dynamic.

Relative to the total book value of all investment, U.S. foreign investment in Canada is falling off substantially. Between 1961 and 1977, total foreign investment fell from one-third to 23 percent of net Canadian capital stock.[23] Relative to the total book value of U.S. investments, Canadian foreign investment in the United States is increasing rapidly. The two foreign investment paths are moving in opposite directions. Given the direction of these trends, why jeopardize them with precipitous interventionary legislation?

A counterargument sometimes heard is that because of the different relative levels of investment, Canada has much more freedom of maneuver vis-à-vis discriminatory action than does the United States. Because so high a percentage of total foreign investment in Canada is American, any action that limits foreign investment in general impinges most heavily on the United States; conversely, because Canadian investment is still a relatively small fraction of total foreign investment in the United States, Canada is insulated against retaliation. The United States, according to this logic, cannot affect Canadian investment without adopting policies that would also threaten the much larger fraction of foreign investment associated with other countries; conversely, the United States does not want to set a precedent by identifying a single country's investment for retaliatory action, because this would go beyond the actions that Canada itself has taken and would amount to an escalation of the dispute. Technically, Canada's legislation does not target the investment of individual foreign countries.

The difficulty with this counterargument is that it ignores the effect that politicization can have on normally prudent actions of government. In an ugly retaliatory mood, the United States might ignore the significance of precedents and overtly target Canada in other areas. But more than this, the counterargument ignores other opportunities and benefits important to the Canadian interest that are bound up in the relationship. One such interest is that the highly visible volume of Canadian investment in the United States not be obstructed in any fashion, including by subtle or indirect means.

The second reason why Canada is not likely to pursue expanded discriminatory policies in trade and investment is that Canada continues to need foreign capital. Even in the oil and gas industry, for example, the oil sands and Cold Lake heavy oil plants, will require heavy additional financing; the Hibernia field will require substantial outside funding to bring production on line, as will Beaufort Sea discoveries. All of this capital will bear an interest premium if the Canadian investment climate becomes known as capricious. Hence, for various reasons, the use of national treatment is not likely to move beyond its present confines.

On the other hand, Canadianization will probably be viewed as one of the major victories of the NEP. It has achieved a reduction in foreign ownership. It is popular with the Canadian public. So far it has not alienated the bulk of foreign investors in Canada. It has provided reasonable remuneration to the stockholders of the companies whose Canadian interests were purchased. And to date it has not proven excessively expensive to the Canadian polity, given the stakes that Ottawa believes are involved. Hence, from such a perspective, Canadianization will be regarded by many in Canada as a justifiable and highly successful use of government intervention on behalf of the larger Canadian interest in political and economic autonomy.

Before considering the overall impact of the NEP on the Canadian energy situation, I must examine two other energy developments because they intersect in various ways with the energy plan. The first is the Ottawa-Alberta energy agreement of September 1, 1981. The second is the Alaska Highway Pipeline Agreement. Each of these developments impinges upon the other. Although conceived separately they together, in some sense, form a unit that characterizes Canadian energy policy and Canadian-American energy relations in the last quarter of the twentieth century. Although the NEP contained a strong federalist and nationalist slant, the NEP was incomplete without an agreement between Ottawa and Alberta on price and between Ottawa and Washington on natural gas transmission. Each agreement extended an aspect of the NEP but also countered elements of the NEP.

THE OTTAWA-ALBERTA
ENERGY AGREEMENT

After twenty-two months of stalemate and attempted negotiation, Ottawa and Alberta representatives closeted themselves and drafted and signed a price and revenue agreement in one week.[24] Without this agreement, investment and revenue decisions by the private sector and the respective ministries of finance were impossible. Further delay was too costly for everyone. Although Alberta had used a series of production cutbacks to pressure Ottawa into decision, the federal government had passed the cost of the additional petroleum imports along to the Canadian consumer in the form of an energy tax. The timing of the ultimate decision to negotiate was essentially Ottawa's, although the outcome of the bargaining did not necessarily favor Ottawa disproportionately.

At issue were the separate matters of the appropriate level for the domestic price of energy, on the one hand, and the appropriate split in revenues among the three principal actors, on the other. Presumably, some trade-offs were possible on these issues. Other things being equal, Ottawa would accept either a larger slice of future revenue and a higher increase in the price of petroleum or a lower increase in price and a lower fraction of future revenue. Both Ottawa and Alberta needed greater revenue. But Ottawa was constrained politically in a way that Alberta was not. For electoral reasons, Ottawa needed to defend the interests of central Canadian consumers and industrial users, a defense Ottawa pursued under the guise of "equity." Hence, the best bargaining position for Ottawa was a larger revenue fraction at the cost of Alberta (and perhaps at the cost of the private sector, if this did not diminish the pace of exploration and development) and a lower price. This arrangement would meet Ottawa's revenue needs while reducing the political pressure from consumers. Alberta, of course, preferred just the opposite formula.

Built into the bargaining, however, was an upward bias both in the revenue shares that the two governments would attempt to obtain and in the price itself. For Ottawa, the tension between politics and economics was far worse than for Alberta, because the incentives both moved in the same direction for Alberta, namely, toward a larger revenue share for itself *and* toward a much higher price. Therefore, one of the options acceptable to Ottawa—a lower increase in price in exchange for a lower federal share of the revenue—was really not likely. By putting up with some political criticism in Ontario, therefore, the federal government found itself drifting toward the solution that saw a larger revenue share for itself in exchange for an agreement to raise the domestic energy price more than it originally had intended. Not coincidentally, this was the option that, whatever the political costs (and these had pretty much been dissipated by the twenty-two months of negotiation and by the reelection in Ontario of Premier Davis, who had campaigned on the platform of lower energy costs and who, as a quid pro quo from the federal government, had supported Trudeau on the constitutional issue), would leave Ottawa in by far the best overall revenue situation. Through this option, Ottawa obtained both a larger than expected share of revenue and the extra revenue produced by the higher than anticipated domestic price.

In brief, the arguments that the bargainers put on the table were as follows:

Alberta.

    1. Ownership rights to natural resources are vested by the BNA Act in the provinces.

    2. The OPEC price for petroleum represents the international market price, and Alberta should not have to subsidize the rest of Canada at a lower price.

    3. Soon the bulk of the petroleum in Alberta will have been exhausted, and Alberta needs all the revenue it can get, including that placed in the Heritage Fund, to establish an industrial base to replace declining petroleum production.

    4. Revenue shares among the three actors should not change, and if the industry obtains excessive rents, these should be taxed by the federal government and redistributed. Alberta will provide loans from the Heritage Fund at going rates of interest to the federal government or to other provinces, much as Alberta did with Hydro-Quebec.

    5. Natural gas prices should be "realistically" priced, without an export tax, so that significant revenue is generated from both the domestic and export markets.

Ottawa.

    1. Although the provinces own natural resources, they do not control interprovincial pricing; price involves matters of interprovincial equity, which are necessarily the responsbility of the central government in a federation.

    2. The OPEC price is set by a "cartel" and is artificial. Ottawa, therefore, has the right to establish a "made-in-Canada price" reflective of the reality that Canada is a resource-rich country. Price should rise only enough to cover the "replacement cost" of finding new energy, plus a reasonable profit.

    3. Rapid movement of the world price for energy would hamper industrial production and the export of goods, which is not in the interest of Alberta or central Canada.

4. The federal government needs more petroleum and natural gas revenue, and this cannot be obtained by raising price alone. An export tax on natural gas and a larger share of total energy revenue must follow. Large-scale borrowing from provincial governments by the federal government carries unacceptable political implications.

In actuality, the outcome of the dispute was much as theory might have predicted. Set against the background of a substantially increased world price between 1979 and 1981, the ratio of the domestic Canadian to the world price was slated to increase from a ratio of about one to two to a ratio of about three to four by 1986. This meant that by the end of the period, the "made-in-Canada" price would approximate 75 percent of the world price. Because of the changed international reference price, it is difficult to judge exactly how much more rapid the price increase was than was originally intended, but there was some acceleration of the schedule.

In addition, Alberta obtained a withdrawal of the proposed federal tax on natural gas and a higher price on old suppliers of natural gas, offset somewhat by lower prices on new natural gas.[25] Alberta was no longer expected to assume the transportation costs of natural gas (the so-called Toronto gate price). Alberta would also retain the politically significant right to pay and to administer the Canadianization grants within Alberta. In general, Alberta estimated, although all such estimates at this time are highly conjectural, that it increased its revenues by about 25 percent over the previously determined NEP levels.

Conversely, Ottawa obtained an end to the economically troublesome dispute, acceptance of the bulk of the NEP provisions with relatively few changes, a new domestic energy price that it could sell to central Canada, and a larger share of the after-Alberta royalty portion of increased oil and natural gas revenues. The old formula as of 1980 had allocated approximately 45 percent of the revenue to the industry to cover costs of exploration and production, 43 percent to Alberta and 12 per cent to the federal government. Industry had increased its share by approximately four percentage points over the prior years. The new energy agreement changed all of this, transferring a larger share of the increased revenue to the federal government. It is too early to estimate what effect the agreement will have in a precise sense. In general, however, the federal government's share has increased at the cost of industry, whereas Alberta's share has remained about constant.

From Ottawa's perspective, the agreement was satisfying because it was accepted. Canada was tired of the turbulent dispute; inflation and the increasing uneasiness of the public regarding the impact of the NEP counseled a resolution of the confrontation. No theory constructed on normative or empirical grounds could determine what the "optimal" price and split in revenues ought to have been. The barometer of success was twofold: public opinion and the long-term impact on further energy development. Regarding the former criterion, the Ottawa-Alberta agreement was something of a masterpiece, especially given the timing; the agreement was reached just prior to the settlement of the constitutional question.

Regarding the latter criterion, the impact was more problematic. Reaction from the industry as a whole was predictably negative. But more significantly, the small Canadian independent companies complained more loudly than the major companies. Part of the reason was that the foreign-owned interests were attempting to adopt something of a low political profile; part of the reason was that the larger firms may in fact have escaped with less damage than they had anticipated and less than the Canadian independents experienced (Alberta's administration of the Canadianization provision favored "smaller" firms, however). But what was clear was that the joint governmental demand for greater revenue had to come from somewhere, and the industrial share was easiest to squeeze. Although this action was not likely to affect petroleum and natural gas output in the short term, over the decade the effect would probably be evident unless additional modifications in the NEP offset these negative consequences.

In short, the reason the Ottawa-Alberta energy agreement could emerge so abruptly once the disputants seriously began bargaining was that, unlike in a number of other federal-provincial confrontations, very few matters of principle were at stake. What was at stake was money and power, and each is infinitely divisible when tough opponents recognize that further acrimony is more costly to themselves in political and financial terms than is rational settlement. Neither party was totally satisfied with the agreement, but with revenue distributions and price determined, the NEP was well on the way to enactment. One other large piece of the energy puzzle remained out of place, however—the Alaska Highway Natural Gas Pipe Line. What made this matter more problematic was that American domestic politics and, perhaps, the American perception of the NEP would play a part in the decision making.

PIPE-LINE PROGRESS, U.S. NATURAL GAS DECONTROL, AND THE NEP

According to Bob Blair, one of the fathers of the Alaska Natural Gas Pipe Line and chairman of NOVA Corporation,

> We finally have a cooperative venture, instead of a branch office operation, in which one country, and normally the United States, is

the dominant financing and operating partner, either through its
domestic companies or through its Canadian branches.

The proposed Alaska Natural Gas Transportation System (ANGTS) is
the largest project ever undertaken jointly by the two governments
through financial guarantees to private investors. It involves 4,800 miles
of construction, from Alaska to Calgary to San Francisco on one leg and
from Calgary to Chicago on the other, and an estimated cost of 40 billion
U.S. dollars.[26] Following the Alaska Highway through most of Canada,
the pipe line would increase current U.S. natural gas supplies by 4
percent. Alaskan fields are estimated to contain about 20 percent of
America's total gas reserves. At 1981 U.S. petroleum import levels, this is
enough supply to offset petroleum imports for twenty years. Large as the
cost of pipe-line construction is, it is equivalent to substantially less than
the U.S. petroleum import bill for a single year.

As Blair's statement underlines, Canada is a full partner in the construction of the pipe line. In fact, over 2,000 miles of construction are on
Canadian territory. More easily laid sections of the pipe line in southern
Alberta have been "prebuilt" by Canada. These sections were constructed
in advance of other sections, and in advance of all sections built by the
United States, based on a series of executive-level understandings and
commitments between the two countries that have spanned several governments and administrations respectively. On December 15, 1981, President Reagan signed into law a waivers package. This package removed a
1977 statutory prohibition and thus enabled the three major Alaskan gas
producers, Exxon, Atlantic Richfield, and Standard Oil of Ohio to become
equity partners in the project.[27] This, combined with a commitment from
the American government to pay for the construction of prebuilt segments
of the pipe line if the whole pipe line was for some reason not completed
or went bankrupt, was a sufficient guarantee to speed financing from the
private sector for the whole project. In effect, these two waivers eliminated
most of the risk in the project to private sources of capital, thus enabling
construction of a project of this magnitude to proceed.

Such is the strength of the attraction that this megaproject has held for
all who have become closely associated with it. Yet, opposition to the
pipe line in each country has at times been similarly strong. It is interesting to compare and contrast the interests that the two countries have regarding the pipe line, and the nature of the opposition to it.

For the United States, the benefits of the Alaska pipe line seem obvious.
Natural gas is needed in the lower forty-eight states, especially in the
Midwest and on the east coast. Currently, oil field pressures and usage
patterns are such that Alaskan gas does not have to be flared; however,
soon production pressures will be such that unless the gas is brought to
market it will be wasted. At higher cost, natural gas could be liquified

and either used for petrochemical production in Alaska, where construction of a petrochemical complex at a cost of about 1.7 times that of the Gulf coast has been proposed, or shipped via specially built tankers down the west coast. According to one alternate project, the Northern-Tier Pipe Line favored by the El Paso Corporation, a pipe line would then transmit the gas eastward across the United States. But whether the natural gas is used locally, liquified and transported at higher cost via some other route, or shipped southward via the Alaska Pipe Line, the lower forty-eight states have an interest in obtaining the natural gas.

Theoretically (this is determined by price, Canada's willingness to sell, physical availability, and absence of alternate U.S. supplies), the United States is also interested in imports of natural gas from Canada. Construction of a large pipe line, such as the Alaska Pipe Line, has the advantage of allowing Canada to export virtually whatever volume of gas it wants—as long as the U.S. market will absorb it—through the prebuilt sections of the line, thus depreciating the cost of the Canadian-built sections of the line soon after construction. A large pipe line also holds out the potential of "piggybacking" Canadian gas with Alaskan gas at a later date. Eventually, as Alaskan supplies decline, the line might transport virtually only Canadian gas. From the American point of view, then, the existence of the Alaska Pipe Line is an invitation to Canada to export natural gas to the United States. This is an additional benefit beyond acquiring Alaskan gas. However, a complex series of factors, including availability and marketability, will determine whether Canada actually decides to export natural gas to the United States in significant volume.

From Canada's point of view the Alaska Pipe Line also contains a number of advantages. A large advantage of early construction was stimulation of the Canadian economy through the spin-offs associated with engineering and design, pipe-line fabrication, and construction. Foothills Corporation, Bob Blair's Canadian firm, which handled construction of much of the Canadian section, has a well-articulated buy-Canada procurement policy calculated to capture the bulk of these spin-offs for Canadian firms. In a period when the economy is in need of resuscitation and when other large megaprojects either are "on hold" or have not yet begun, the timing of the construction of the Alaska Pipe Line is critical.

A related Canadian interest is the creation of jobs in Canada. As of the winter of 1981-82, the Canada Council foresaw substantial unemployment in Canada, as elsewhere, in the 1982-85 period, with unemployment rates exceeding those of the high growth years in the prior decade. Although pipe-line construction is capital intensive, geographically focused, and temporary, jobs created by the pipe line are not insignificant.

A further Canadian objective is nation building, and the Alaska Pipe Line facilitates this through coordination of effort with the Albertan government and through the highly visible capacity of Ottawa to do something for the people of Alberta through this project. But the emergence of large Canadian-owned firms with strong ties to Ottawa in a variety of related construction and engineering fields also contributes to the notion of nation building familiar elsewhere in the National Energy Program.

Finally, from the Canadian viewpoint, the Alaska Pipe Line provides the opportunity to tap into the main trunk at various points where undeveloped natural gas fields may be located, including the MacKenzie Delta and Beaufort Sea areas. The Dempster spur and other possible spur lines are among suggested routes. Such natural gas that might otherwise be considered uncommercial, for lack of infrastructure, now can contribute to Canadian income and can offset Canadian balance-of-payment deficits. Some of this gas may also be used domestically, although Albertan supplies are probably sufficient to meet Canadian needs for many years.[28] Access to natural gas from northern areas means that Canada is not dependent solely upon Albertan gas, however, a fact that carries political implications not ignored in central Canada.

Why, then, has the Alaska Pipe Line system been criticized in both Canada and the United States? Some of the reasons are similar for the two countries; others are the exact reverse. Reflective persons in both Canada and the United States worry about the matter of timing. In politics, as in commercial development, to be right at the wrong time is the equivalent of being irrevocably wrong. In the context of pipe-line development, this norm is especially apparent, (1) because of the huge cost of the project, meaning that opportunity costs of foregone investment elsewhere in the society are potentially enormous, and (2) because interest rates are currently so high. The effect of this latter consideration is to give the present value of future earnings virtually no value at all. With very high interest rates, anything providing returns that go beyond ten years makes no sense as an investment. Not surprisingly, private firms expect to get a very high early return from pipe-line projects, or they do not invest. Societies, in some ways, must follow similar rules if they are to maximize social return from a series of major investments.

The problem for Canada is that it may not need the pipe line for the transport of its own natural gas for its own internal use until perhaps the end of the century. Then why should it invest anything in a pipe line today? Is this not carrying good neighborliness too far?

The problem for the United States is that it may not need the natural gas, either Alaskan gas or Canadian gas, for some time after the pipe line is constructed.[29] If the real price for petroleum reaches a plateau and substantial new gas finds occur in the lower forty-eight states, as seems likely, the natural gas transported by the pipe line may not be competitive for at least a decade. Once again, opponents ask, why build the pipe line now?

The only response that the proponent of pipe-line construction can give is as follows. To the Canadian critic, one can point out that there may be internal political reasons, as well as good external economic reasons, why the access to northern gas is desirable. Exports of natural gas are critical to the Canadian balance of payments; to hypothesize in the abstract as though an infinite range of choices were available to Canada regarding alternative uses for natural gas is not to focus firmly on reality. If exports continue to be necessary and possible, the Alaska Pipe Line—paid for in large part by consumers in the United States —makes a great deal of sense, especially where there are spillovers of jobs and technological development involved.

To the American critics (and also to the Canadian critics, because this response is relevant to the assumptions of the prior argument), the questions of what will happen to the world price of energy and how much American natural gas will quickly come on line are questions involving a large degree of risk. The Alaska Pipe Line is an insurance policy against risk. Societies must invest in insurance policies, and such policies are normally expensive. Suppose, for example, that another supply interruption drives the real world price of petroleum upwards again, in a period of significant economic growth, by as much as 25 percent. Suddenly the pipe line will look like both a bargain and a marvelous safety net. In addition, inflation, and hence interest rates, are likely to fall some from the peak levels in 1980-81. This will give all projects, including mega-projects such as this, a longer revenue horizon, making them look much better in investment terms. Moreover, to flare natural gas in Alaska because of a temporary glut of gas in the lower forty-eight states would seem so counter to intuition in the latter 20th century as to be unacceptable in the larger social sense, if not in the short-term market sense. In consequence, both for Canada and for the United States, the matter of timing is probably a far less serious problem than critics have imagined.

Other criticisms have emerged as well. In Canada, for example, hostility to the notion of natural gas exports is heard. Such exports involve relying too much on the supposedly antiquated laws of comparative advantage and will tend to draw down Canada's scarce and nonrenewable resources, notwithstanding the National Energy Board's attempt to carefully define the notion of surplus.[30] But what this criticism neglects is the matter of price and the matter of the substitutability of revenue. If the price of natural gas is relatively high now, sale of this gas, combined with a reinvestment of the income at a rate of return that is higher than the rate of return (inflation rate) on natural gas if left in the ground and used in the future, makes a great deal of economic and social sense. Moreover, if the price is right, revenue generated from the sale of raw gas is no different from revenue generated from products manufactured domestically with or from natural gas and then sold abroad. Provided that the original price accurately reflects the opportunity costs of foregone value-added in the manufacturing process, appropriately discounted, the seller is indifferent to whether natural gas is exported directly or indirectly. Indeed, if environmental damage is involved in manufacturing, perhaps the importer ought to be encouraged to do the manufacturing in any case. This is essentially the developmental philosophy followed by the United States in the early twentieth century, when it supplied Canada with virtually all of Canada's energy needs, a supply strategy based not so much upon altruism and faith in the liberal international economy as upon a sound awareness of opportunity costs and the rates of return on alternate investments.

Americans, too, have other criticisms of the Alaska Pipe Line project, however. One such criticism involves the waivers package. Allowing the companies that operate on the North Slope to buy into the pipe line looks to many like a serious conflict of interest. Similarly, forcing consumers to assume the risks of pipe-line failure, bankruptcy, or noncompletion appears to some observers to be unfair and perhaps unwise. If penalties did not exist for cost overruns and for postponement, if rates were not regulated by the governments involved, and if the companies were willing to do what was evidently not in their interest, namely, to assume risks without obtaining equity, then the private owners of natural gas rights in Alaska could have been excluded as pipe-line sponsors. Unfortunately for these critics, none of these conditions is valid. Moreover, because none of these conditions holds, conflicts of interest are in reality likely to be kept to a minimum.

Concerning the problem of consumers assuming the risks of the project (through governmental sponsorship of the guarantees), this is very much an American rather than a Canadian anxiety. Canadians anticipate in most cases that government will assume risks on public projects.[31] Americans would prefer that the private sector assume all risks; but at the same time many Americans would be unwilling to allow participating firms the rate of return that would encourage bankers to provide the necessary risk capital on this basis. Thus, in the absence of willingness to grant such highly attractive rates of return, the U.S. government found that the Alaska Pipe Line would fail for lack of government guarantees, a point the Canadian government as well as the pipe-line spokesmen made clear. Despite the fact that some inequity results, because not all taxpayers are natural gas users, the necessity of acting pragmatically and rapidly encouraged President Reagan to make a large social decision that to some may have appeared to compromise his "free market" economic philosophy.

What really challenged some critics of the pipe-line project, however, both in Canada and the United States, were the apparent paradoxes associated with the ANGTS. The primary purpose of the pipe line was to transport American natural gas, yet Ottawa and, on occasion, Alberta, took the lead in lobbying for the project. Until very late in the ethos of the project, the three major oil companies owning the Prudhoe Bay natural gas were among the least enthusiastic supporters of the project, and the various governments were among the most enthusiastic sponsors. Opponents of the pipe line included Canadian nationalists, on one side, fearing tighter commercial interaction with the United States, and American consumers, on the other side, fearing the obligations they were expected to assume. In both cases, anxiety over the possibility of domination was instinctively associated with the criticism. Canadian nationalists feared domination by the United States because they did not fully comprehend the dynamics of the project; American consumers feared domination by big government or big business because they did not fully comprehend the nature of the stakes and the risks. Perhaps ANGTS should have been renamed ANGST.

Keys to the successful adoption of the Alaska Natural Gas Transport System after nearly a decade of negotiation are manifold. First, as a principal proponent of the project on the Canadian side, Bob Blair was a key figure. His image as an outspoken nationalist was helpful in quieting some Canadian anxieties about the project, especially because he demonstrated that through the proper procurement strategy very sizeable economic benefits could accrue to Canada. Second, the reality that the major oil companies took a back seat on this issue was very helpful. In fact, President Carter accused them at one point of "dragging their feet," but such reticence stalled public criticism. Third, the reality that the waiver package came up for Congressional passage after American hostility to the NEP had peaked was important even if coincidental. Had the package arrived five months earlier, it might well have been defeated because of Congressional irritation over Canadianization. Fourth, ANGTS made progress because of the faith in energy scarcity in both countries, faith bred of experience with a decade of rising energy prices and threats of supply interruption.[32] Interestingly, apart from Foothills and Northwest, the private corporations directly responsible for pipe-line development and management, the private sectors in both countries were remarkably cool to the project. Explanations include not only the foregoing observations about the size, risk, and exposure associated with the pipe line; part of the hesitance involved doubts about the trend of future prices and market forces. The private sector was much less confident than the governments that the pipe line would actually be needed as soon as it was scheduled for completion. What is fascinating about this decision is that events in the next decade will determine whose judgment was the more sound, although to some extent each set of actors has the capacity, through intervention, to shape the economic and social reality by which the pipe line will ultimately be judged.

What lessons for Canadian-American energy relations are embodied in the long campaign to build the Alaska Pipe Line? The first lesson is that apart from the rhetoric heard on each side of the border concerning the relative superiority of private-sector or public-sector leadership in investment matters, the reality is that both are necessarily involved. In mixed economies and on megaprojects, a symbiosis between government and industry becomes essential, but this is a relationship based on competition as well as cooperation. For example, the Carter administration, with the encouragement of the Trudeau government, indicated to large natural gas firms that the United States would only be interested in imports from companies supporting the Alaska Pipe Line, thus generating added support for the project. Similarly, the Trudeau government, by its contracting procedures, reduced the amount of competition within the gas industry.[33] Conversely, the major oil companies were ultimately able to gain participation in the pipe line despite all governmental prohibition, because the project simply could not be financed effectively without them. Thus, the jockeying for power at the government-business interface was intense and scarcely one sided.

A second lesson of ANGTS was that some projects are not efficient unless they are large; they cannot be large if they are undertaken by a single government. If Canada had to rely on its own capital market and only the natural gas reserves in the Mackenzie Valley or the Beaufort Sea to amortize the costs of transport, these deposits might never be regarded as "commercial." Similarly, if the United States were unable to coordinate this project with Canada, the costs would either have been wastefully higher for alternate routes and approaches or simply prohibitively high.

If Canada and the United States had each insisted on separate "all-country" transportation systems, the amount of redundancy would have been so great that only the most financially ardent among the speculators would have advocated their construction. The higher probability is that the systems could not have been constructed separately at an acceptable social opportunity cost. This is a stern lesson of twentieth-century technology and socioeconomic undertaking which prevails regardless of how individual governments attempt to promote and expand their separate sovereignties.

A third possible lesson from the pipe line is the lesson Blair drew in the opening statement of this section. In future Canadian-American projects, full partnership of a joint-venture variety is likely to become the norm.[34] One-sided branch-plant approaches, in which decision-making authority is relegated to a single participant, are rapidly becoming obsolescent. This does not mean that cooperation is obsolete. Americans who worried that construction of a pipe line on Canadian soil would make them hostage or Canadians who worried that the Alaska Pipe Line was the equivalent of the Panama Canal on Canadian territory, are both far off base. Such American hyperbole is wrong because at least 40 percent of all Canadian natural gas and petroleum currently crosses U.S.

territory. The United States already has a sufficient offset to imprudent action. Conversely, from the Canadian perspective, analysts could argue, if they found such deterrent psychology compelling, that Canada has now gained, via the Alaska Pipe Line, an offset previously lacking.

Canadian anxieties stemming from this mode of interdependence are likewise not credible if the assumption is that Canada is in a dependent position vis-à-vis decision making or use of the pipe line. Despite private financing, the pipe line is a joint governmental venture, benefiting both countries in a fashion that neither alone could achieve. This is the essence of partnership, and the ANGTS, despite the uncertainties that accompany all such undertakings, is an index of what valid partnership can accomplish.

AN OVERVIEW

How do the various parts of the energy policy puzzle fit together? The dispute between Alberta and Ottawa was a direct and not unanticipated consequence of the National Energy Program. Ottawa was not afraid to wage this battle, because on political grounds it could not lose. It could continue to command the loyalty of central Canada without doing permanent damage to its relationship with the west. But the NEP would never be complete until this price and revenue dispute, which at base was a dispute over power and decision authority within Canada, was resolved.

Long in the making, the Alaska Pipe Line project could have been derailed by the advent of the NEP. But the occurrence of the NEP did not have this effect. The explanation was twofold. First, the timing of the waiver package was such as to follow the outcry against the discriminatory aspects of the NEP rather than to coincide with that outcry. This saved the pipe line in the United States. Second, the NEP was, curiously, supportive of the pipe line in Canada and perhaps even made Canadian participation possible. The NEP created a convenient outlet for anti-Americanism and assertive nationalism, diverting attention from Ottawa's effort to coordinate the pipe line project in Washington. Opponents of the pipe line in Canada suddenly became worried that Canadianization might turn Washington against the pipe-line treaty; hence the pipe line itself became something of an object of sympathy in Canada instead of an object of distrust. The pipe line was also useful to Ottawa domestically because it demonstrated that on some issues Alberta and Ottawa could pursue a clear communality of interest.

In a number of ways, the pipe-line project and the NEP had a complementary purpose, at least in economic terms. Because the impact of the NEP was likely to be a decline in petroleum self-sufficiency for Canada, the pipe line would enable Canada to offset the cost of petroleum imports by continued natural gas exports. These exports could occur without threatening supplies in the Alberta foothills or undermining the National Energy Board's definition of "export surplus." Thus, the pipe line would help Canada get through the interim when petroleum production continued to decline.

Secondly, the NEP and the pipe-line idea were complementary because the purpose of the NEP was to promote a transition from a petroleum to a natural gas economy in Canada. The pipe line would enable Canada to gain access to even greater amounts of natural gas from areas that might not otherwise be regarded as commercially viable.

Third, from Ottawa's viewpoint, both the NEP and the Alaska Pipe Line promoted the nation-building idea, albeit in very different ways. The NEP saw nation building as possible through a commercial dissociation from the United States and a greater sense of Canadian natural identity. The pipe line, paradoxically, encouraged north-south trade and commercial association as well. Still, both the pipe line and the NEP were regarded by Ottawa as ways of strengthening the indigenous private sector and therefore the foundation for national unity.

In another sense, the goals of the NEP and the pipe line, however, were somewhat at odds. Each favored a different concept of economic development, raising the question of which philosophy would prevail. Underlying the NEP is the effort to dissociate from the continental economic framework, phrased as an escape from U.S. economic domination. The pipe line, on the other hand, is a major step toward continued economic interdependence between Canada and the United States and an evolution toward a new type of trade and commercial partnership.[35]

Perhaps as Canadianization proceeds and as Canada becomes more confident of its commercial identity, aspects of the discriminatory framework will be dismantled because they will no longer be needed; indeed they will become increasingly counterproductive in Canada's efforts to become more than a regional power. In the process of dismantling these discriminatory aspects, Canada is likely to restore incentives for exploration and development (vis-à-vis, for example, the 25 percent back-in provision), not just to foreign firms but, more centrally, to its own independent oil companies. Petro-Canada, regardless of the degree of financial and administrative support it receives, will not be able to further petroleum self-sufficiency alone.

Yet, the Alaska Pipe Line Treaty reminds the analysts of Canadian-American relations that no matter how much each government seeks to amplify its own sovereignty, certain complementarities of economy and geography tend to recur. Cooperation rather than competition insistently revives itself. Indeed, the joint pipe-line project indicates that commercial cooperation is possible without loss of integrity or loss of the sense of the separate political and cultural identities of two great Western democracies.

EIGHT

A Concluding Vision:
Prerequisites of Partnership

John W. Dafoe, foremost Canadian editorialist with *The Winnipeg Free Press*, once wrote, "There are two things that are not desirable for Canada, extreme economic nationalism and abject political colonialism." The problem is that most Americans understand the former lesson and not the latter, whereas many Canadians know the latter lesson but not the former. Neither governing elite has mastered all of the wisdom in the Dafoe statement. Americans, in particular, who forget the political discomfort of having to live next door to a giant and who forget and encumber the prerequisites of that neighbor's statehood are undermining the very durability of the relationship, durability that the United States has long sought to promote.

Analysis in this book so far has led to these conclusions:

1. Canada and the United States must decide what kind of relationship they want.

2. They must then determine what strategies are necessary to achieve this preferred type of bilateral relationship.

A difficulty, however, is that there is much discussion about strategies without adequate consideration of the goals. Thus, each government talks past the other. Discussion of modes of diplomatic contact are not grounded in comparable visions of what the future relationship should look like or in visions that are complementary or acceptably divergent. Indeed, much of the discussion regarding recommendations to the two governments for action ignores a fundamental point: The most important single attribute of the relationship is its psychology. There is no substitution for a correct understanding of this psychology or, in the absence of a complementarity of goals, for subtle implementation of practice.

Indisputably, both governments want a "good" relationship, that is, one in which acrimony is kept to a minimum.

It cannot be said that Canada and the United States fail to define their own interests clearly. Each government knows what it wants in "substantive terms" from the relationship.[1] The problem is in a sense the classical one of diplomacy: the two governments have not found a way to bring conflicting interests together without generating acrimony. They have failed to accomplish this task because they have no comparable vision regarding where the overall relationship is going and how the structure of that relationship ought to evolve.

Recent proposals for a new approach to negotiation with Canada are essentially procedural. They involve changes in style and approach to negotiations. Such matters are important. But in the present circumstances, such a focus is something like the wine industry focusing its efforts on how to repair leaky bottles. If the industry is to improve the quality of the wine contained in the bottle, the container is secondary. Much more critical is the background and objective of grape growing itself. By all means mend damage to containers, but to actually improve the quality of the wine we must review the cultivation and processing that the grapes have received and the overall aim of the harvest. So, with Canadian-American affairs, excellence is a function of the understanding each government has with respect to where the relationship is going.

Creation of new bilateral commissions in the areas of, for example, economic policy or fisheries negotiation, is commendable. But the creation of such joint institutions is not new. Nor in the past, with the notable exception of a few institutions such as the International Joint Commission and perhaps the Interparliamentary Group or the Permanent Joint Board on Defense, have these entities significantly assisted the governments in formulating policy or in ameliorating disturbances. The problem is that when joint agencies are easiest to set up they are not needed, and when they are needed the effort required to set them up may be diversionary and excessive. The real difficulty is not so much the establishment of such institutions or getting them to work smoothly, but obtaining from them more than a symbolic outcome. For the most part, the time to set them up is when the atmosphere is good, when they have the best possible opportunity to succeed, not during crisis.

Although the best of the joint institutions can be helpful in terms of research and advisory functions, the architects must always bear in mind that the two governments may hold quite different expectations.[2] The United States expects from the joint agencies better management of the relationship and closer policy coordination. Canada often expects from these agencies a buffer from too intense contacts and demands. In general, the United States conceives of these institutions as a bridge; Canada conceives of them as a moat. Not surprisingly, institutional performance is complicated by these contradictory expectations.

Reinforcing the bias toward procedural discussion is the tendency to assume that Canada and the United States always think alike in terms of priorities in foreign policy. As I said in Chapter 2, the United States tends, in theoretical terms, to accentuate the strategic-military dimension while de-emphasizing trade and economic policy. Conversely, Canada tends to underscore trade and economic policy while de-emphasizing strategic-military considerations. These differences of priority have no small consequences for joint policy formulation. The United States always asks first how a particular initiative will affect alliance cohesion and the overall military balance. Canada always asks first how a specific policy measure will affect trade and exchange rates.

The disparity between the decision of what kind of relationship the two countries want and the tactics for getting there is made more apparent if one reflects on the historical analogies outlined in Chapter 1. In the mid-nineteenth century, Britain left Canada; Canada did not flee Britain. A focus upon the legalities of association, for example, between British North America and Great Britain would have done little to alter historical change. Collapse of the imperial tie was not sought in Montreal, it was precipitated in London. British decisions to adopt free trade in the aftermath of the repeal of the Corn Laws carried an auxiliary consequence of destroying the preferential trade links between Canada and Britain. The British decision to reduce security and administrative costs in its older colonies had the collateral effect of reducing the Canadian interest in accepting some of the political obligations imposed by colonial rule. The rise of responsible government was a consequence of British withdrawal; but it was also a cause of growing distance and commercial autonomy between the Canadian dominion and Britain.

If Britain had wanted to retain the old imperial association with its colony, it would have had to pay for this linkage by making an exception to its doctrine of free trade. Conversely, if Canada had wanted to alter the forces of history, Canada would have had to negotiate a new set of terms for that association, with a new understanding about the sharing of relative administrative and security burdens. At the very least, it would have been necessary for the two governments to focus on the changing historical dynamic of their relationship and the preferred directions of change if British North America were to retain its original character and foreign ties.

Analogously, in the early 1970s, the increased pressure on the American balance of payments and the collapse of the Bretton Woods monetary system of fixed exchange rates left in their wake the elimination of exceptions to financial policies, exceptions to which Canada had become accustomed. The negative outcome of the Vietnam War and the message contained in the Nixon Doctrine that henceforward allies would have to do more to protect themselves burst the myth of invulnerability that many Canadians had previously associated with the United States. By removing special economic advantages extended to Canada, the United States seemed to undercut the special relationship, because it offered Canada less. The slowdown in overall U.S. growth further hurt the U.S. image in Canada. At least some of the substantive attractiveness of the relationship for Canada seemed to have disappeared. If America was less powerful on the global stage, American leadership seemed to provide less to Canada and to create more for Canada to question. The advent of the Third Option followed rather than preceded President Nixon's speech of April 14, 1972 to the Canadian Parliament, which warned that the special relationship was dead.

Thus, in looking at the nature of Canadian-American relations in the 1980s, it is well to recall the historical analogy between Britain and British North America. Did the special relationship unwind because Canada was unhappy with that relationship or because in its attempt to resolve its global problems the United States inadvertently killed that relationship? Did Canada begin to leave the United States thirty years after the signing of the 1940 Ogdensburg declaration, or did the United States, perhaps without fully realizing the consequences of its decision, initiate the process of devolution? If one considers the broader aspects of the changing bilateral relationship, a good case could perhaps be made for the latter argument.

Yet, ironically, the actions and the preferences of the two countries regarding the direction of historical change are still more complex. The United States would, in fact, like to preserve the remnants of the special relationship today if the costs were not too high. But Canada has apparently accepted the demise of that relationship, because the rewards, on balance, are interpreted as being insufficient. Once stimulated, the momentum of foreign policy change is difficult to reverse. Peel and many of the conservatives other than Disraeli recognized this; so did the merchants of Montreal.[3]

Thus, in the 1980s, if Canada and the United States are to decide upon the kind of evolutionary relationship they prefer, they must acknowledge the emerging differences between their values and priorities. In particular, they must acknowledge a growing disparity in what they would like to see Canadian-American relations become.

THE AMERICAN PENCHANT
FOR GREATER INTEGRATION

Seldom afraid of bigness, the United States has frequently championed schemes for international integration in which the United States was a mere outside observer. The Treaties of Rome of 1957, for example, were viewed not as a threat to U.S. trade vitality but rather as an important mechanism for strengthening the international trade order and for adding stability to the Western alliance system. In the 1980s, therefore, it was not a cause of much amazement to find prominent presidential candidates advocating a North American Accord or more limited proposals for sectoral integration. In an era when the world economy has assumed more and more of a regional character, negotiations may increasingly follow the patterns established among regional trading blocs. The nation-state may have lost some of its character as the basic unit of global economic analysis. Ironically, the transnational corporation may be less a catalyst of these changes than a target. The 1970s witnessed not so much sovereignty at bay as commerce at bay. Hence, the regional outlook may be a better way of further liberalizing the international trade order while at the same time strengthening industrial productivity, commercial competitiveness, and employment.[4]

Canadians, however, have been reluctant to share this vision of the merits of closer North American integration. Aside from the psychological aspects of association, which Canadians often resist as citizens of the smaller polity, they emphasize a number of problematic asymmetries. Ottawa is concerned about the impact of possible closer integration on federal-provincial relations and upon growing north-south continental affinities within certain regions which would tend to undermine its own authority within Canada. As the effects of the Tokyo trade round further reduce tariffs, admitting 80 percent of Canadian goods free of tariffs into American markets and admitting a lesser but still large percentage of U.S. goods free of tariffs into Canada, Ottawa worries about the impact of north-south trade patterns on its ability to direct and monitor Canadian economic growth.

Although the United States, as the larger polity, tends to dismiss matters of control as insignificant compared to the obvious benefits that closer economic integration would bring, Ottawa believes that control is at the heart of Canada's problems. In particular, Ottawa is puzzled by the wide fluctuations in policy-making preferences which are visible in Washington's conduct of its bilateral relations. Within six months, the party in power could go from advocacy of a far-reaching national accord to threatened use of retaliation concerning trade and investment issues. This vacillation of policy, combined with implied willingness to use coercive action to obtain policy reversals, suggests to Ottawa that interdependence involves more than equal exchange of goods and services. Closer integration, Ottawa fears, would involve the potential for greater political and economic subordination as well.

Finally, Canada rejects measures for closer integration which would encompass fuel and nonfuel minerals policy making or water resource policy making.[5] Correctly or not, Canada believes itself to be resource-rich, whereas the United States is construed as comparatively resource-poor. Canada believes that integration in these areas would mean that Canada would continue to exchange resources for American manufactured goods. Canada would prefer that the situation were one of greater reciprocity.

The problem for the United States is that the events of the summer of

1981 reinforced in the minds of many Canadians a probably mistaken belief that they really are subject to American domination and control in trade and investment matters. Threats of retaliation and coercion reduce Canadian interest in integrationist ideas, because Canada fears that the bargain would not, and could not, be consummated on the basis of equality. In the absence of equality, the United States would use its greater political and economic power to its own advantage inside a more integrated framework, just as it seemingly has attempted to do outside that framework.

Hence the paradox: the more the United States shows interest in integration of some sort, the less Canada wants to get involved. Although the United States can point to the breakwater between economic and political integration, based on the European and Latin American experiences, many Canadians believe that economic integration in North America would lead to political integration. According to this Canadian viewpoint, Canada would be assimilated into the great American marketplace and subordinated politically.

The integrationist mode of thought has come so to typify American actions that U.S. policy-making initiatives often precipitate suspicion in Ottawa when there is no cause. But to assert that the United States sees no merit in closer ties with its immediate neighbors is to misread the decade. Mexico and Canada are rapidly growing states, have abundant resources, and are dependent for defense upon a government that at the same time presents no security threat to them. In the midst of increasing global tension and a shifting balance of power with the Soviet Union, improved relations with America's near neighbors seem prudent, nearly mandatory. Economic cohesion among the three North American polities is an emerging reality whether it is controlled by the governments or merely driven by the market. As Canadian-Mexican trade increases and as Canadian and Mexican investment in the United States grows, the scope of this cohesion will broaden even as it becomes more balanced and symmetric.

THE CANADIAN PREOCCUPATION WITH AUTARKY

Why was the Third Option so compelling for the architects of Canadian foreign policy? The emphasis was compelling for two reasons, I believe. First, the focus corresponds to deeply held values in the liberal-idealist tradition about world affairs. Second, the focus was instrumental in that it provided a counterweight to what was perceived as American regional dominance.

Well established in North America, the liberal-idealist tradition stresses (1) the cooperative rather than the conflictual basis of international society, (2) the decline in the significance of force in world politics, (3) the normative responsibilities of statesmen to eliminate poverty and injustice, and (4) the possibility of progress in world affairs. In de-emphasizing East-West tensions, Canada followed this tradition by highlighting co-operation and the decline in the significance of force and, hence, of the probability of aggression. In stressing the urgency of the North-South dialogue, Canada again accentuated the liberal-idealist tradition by appealing to the normative values of the rich countries to renew the struggle to eliminate poverty and illiteracy in the Third World.

Canada is far less concerned about a direct Soviet attack on Western Europe or the process of "Finlandization," and far more concerned that a crisis involving the Soviet Union and the United States will precipitate a military confrontation.[6] The nuclear stalemate, in this view, has made aggression in Europe virtually obsolete. Canada is less interested in the shifting military balance between East and West and more worried that the dynamics of the nuclear arms race will get out of hand and will themselves cause war. Similarly, Ottawa believes that tensions in the Third World stemming from poverty, illiteracy, and unemployment are far more likely sources of instability than is the East-West contest in the central theatre.

The second reason why Canada favors this focus is that it enables Canada to distinguish itself and its foreign policy from the identity and foreign policy of the United States. Adopting a policy of trade diversification, or Canadianization, is a direct path to this end. Adopting a focus toward the Third World when the United States is concerned with its responsibilities in NATO is an indirect way of stressing the Third Option. Canada is preoccupied with enhanced autonomy for all of the reasons that it rejected closer North American integration. But the campaign to increase Canadian autonomy from the United States is not passive or limited to vetoes of bilateral initiatives stemming from Washington. Nor, recalling Diefenbaker's promise to divert 15 percent of Canada's trade to the Commonwealth, is the desire to diversify associations a recent preoccupation.

To some extent, the Third Option has been more conceptualization than foreign policy reality; it has been more an expression of desire than an achieved goal. Shares of relative trade and of trade composition (for example, exchange of raw materials for manufactured goods) reveal as much. Yet the political momentum toward enhanced autonomy is also a major factor in the formulation of Canadian foreign policy and cannot be dismissed merely on the basis of a few recalcitrant trade statistics.

The impact of the Canadian drive for greater foreign policy autonomy on the bilateral relationship is interesting to observe. Canadians sometimes do not understand why reiteration of the desire for a more independent foreign policy is met with such disfavor in Washington. Hostility, after all, is not implied in these Canadian initiatives. By emphasizing greater autonomy verbally or by action, however, Canada threatens the whole post-1945 structure of world order which the United States has struggled to build. This is not unlike the effect that American expressions of interest in North American integration have had on Canada. The prospect of more individualistic foreign policy conduct holds out the likelihood of greater disharmony among the other NATO allies as well. Assertions regarding increased foreign policy independence chill American speculation about what the future holds for European cooperation. In the absence of this cooperation, the United States will experience even greater difficulty in holding the alliance together in the face of a troubling conventional military imbalance that has caused NATO to rely increasingly on theater nuclear weapons. This unraveling of the doctrine of flexible response has in turn contributed to the growing neutralist sentiment among liberal Protestant groups in West Germany and the Netherlands.[7] Canadian aspirations for an independent foreign policy spring from a different origin than European neutralist sentiment. But coming at the same time as this apparent loss of confidence in alliance leadership, the effect on the U.S. policy-making outlook is similar.

From the U.S. perspective, Canada is increasingly needed within the alliance as a show of solidarity becomes essential to counter rising Soviet military strength, a show that goes beyond the largely unilateral efforts of the United States to offset this challenge. The Soviet incursion into Afghanistan would, in this view, probably not have occurred if the West and Japan had been stronger. So, for Washington, the Canadian preoccupation with autonomy and with an alternate focus toward the Third World is frustrating, because it comes at a time when U.S. military capability and the military capability of the alliance as a whole has declined relative to that of the Soviet Union and the Warsaw Pact. In the American view, Canadian support for collective defense was more real when, by circumstance, the Soviet threat was less great; when that threat became more real, the diffusion of alliance energies has predictably grown more pronounced.

A Third Option outlook also has international economic implications that some American policy makers find troubling. Such an orientation, if accompanied by protectionism or discrimination, also promises lower productivity, less economic efficiency, and a declining volume of North American trade at a time when even the large American market is regarded as too small and too autarkic. Thus, far from simply defending the trade and commercial status quo, the effort to increase Canadian economic and political autonomy seems to challenge the underlying strength of the North American market just at a time when the most significant competition is emerging from Japan and Europe. Hence, to these American decision makers, such new foreign policy and international economic initiatives look self-defeating and counterproductive for both Canada and the United States.

Does all of this mean that the United States expects Canada to march lockstep with it on foreign policy matters? A lack of capacity to tolerate a diversity of viewpoints in bilateral and multilateral diplomacy can be as eroding of structural cohesion as can be the lack of genuine leadership. Every sovereign government will formulate its own foreign policy, based upon its interests and its own assessment of world events. Certainly Washington and Ottawa expect this toleration regarding each other's views. But what Washington finds worrisome is that the desire for enhanced autonomy implies that Canadian and American interests are not only different but are diverging. It implies that the old common assumptions about global priorities may be fading and that coordination of policy may become even more problematic, because this underlying consensus (or what was interpreted in the United States as consensus) is disappearing.

This assessment of, on the one hand, the American penchant for thinking in terms of North American integration and, on the other hand, the Canadian preoccupation with autarky reveal how divergent are the two countries' aspirations for the relationship at present. This assessment also underscores the difference between a focus upon where the overall relationship is going and a focus upon specific procedural changes to improve the nature of the negotiation process. Unless one copes with the former problem, the latter correctives are not likely to be helpful.

SUMMING UP THE CONTRADICTIONS

The events of 1846 led Britain into an irreversible series of initiatives that resulted within a generation in formal dissociation between Britain and Canada. Has the United States decided where its policies are leading the two countries and where Canada and the United States will find themselves in terms of association by the end of the decade? Moreover, how can one square the 1971 decision to declare dead the special relationship between Canada and the United States, thus placing greater distance between the two countries, and the 1980 presidential campaign proposals of a number of leading candidates to launch a North American Accord involving far closer integration?

The reality is that Washington cannot have the relationship both ways. It cannot dissociate itself from the special benefits and economic advantages to Canada upon which the relationship thrived, while proposing even larger doses of formal integration, which tend to frighten Ottawa. In fact, the United States must recognize that its own actions, which were designed to rearrange and reduce its own global economic and military burdens in 1971, gave the signal to Canada to seek substantially greater basic autonomy. Nonetheless, the U.S. decision to cancel exemptionalism and the U.S. effort to sponsor closer integration are related, but in complex and perhaps not completely intuitive ways.

From the U.S. perspective, the proposals that opened and closed the decade of the 1970s may have had the same purpose, although they approached this purpose in different ways. The Nixon Doctrine sought to cut losses and minimize obligations in order to shore up declining American power and to reorder American priorities. The Reagan accord idea and similar sectoral integration proposals seek to bolster American power by strengthening the economic base of the country through greater efficiency and aggregation. One proposal sought to reinvigorate the American power base by trimming unwanted obligations; the other proposal sought to do the same thing by expanding economic growth and development.

From the Canadian perspective, however, these two sets of proposals, which occurred nearly a decade apart, looked quite different. Elimination of exemptionalism seemed like a blow to the viability and integrity of Canada. It left Canada more isolated, and it demonstrated how dependence on the United States left Canada vulnerable to decisions made in Washington which might not take the Canadian interest fully into account. The accord idea and similar proposals, on the other hand, looked to many Canadians like an effort to restore American domination politically while attempting to benefit economically from Canadian energy resources. Many Canadians failed to see the mutual advantages. If the United States now wanted closer integration with Canada in order to reduce American global vulnerability, Canada now wanted greater Canadian autonomy in order to reduce what some Canadians interpreted as Canadian vulnerability to pressures from the United States. Thus, in terms of an overall conception of where the Canadian-American relationship was going, the two countries, at the outset of the 1980s, were quite at odds.

PARTNERSHIP: A PLAUSIBLE ALTERNATIVE?

An alternative to either integration or to autarky is partnership. But what is partnership in the Canadian-American setting? Is partnership not what the two governments already experience? I would argue that, if this was a goal of the relationship at midcentury, the two actors have been drifting away from it, for reasons previously discussed.

Genuine partnership has several characteristics. (1) Partnership must convey a sense of purpose, and the individual partners must each show a degree of commitment to that purpose. (2) Partnership arises because both partners recognize that they are subject to intervulnerability, and this awareness binds them together. (3) Limits govern partnership, and each partner accepts these limits because without them the association would collapse. These are the fundamentals of partnership as they apply to the Canadian-American relationship.

Purpose is something both actors can inject into the partnership; surely the larger partner cannot escape the obligation to make such a contribution. Definition stems from leadership. A definition of purpose also makes leadership possible. It is positive, sometimes tinged with ideology, and helpful in identifying problems and facilitating solutions. A sense of purpose gives an association life and prevents it from wandering. Actors infused with a sense of purpose are able to see beyond squabbles, particular interests that conflict, and personality confrontations. Because a partnership retains a sense of purpose does not mean that the interests of the actors on all foreign policy matters are identical; on the contrary, because their interests are not identical, the purposiveness of the association enables the governments to weather turbulent periods without destroying the association.

Purpose need not be stated. Indeed, it is probably more effective if it is not constrained by a charter or an explicit treaty. Moreover, the sense of purpose is such that it does not prevent the partners from involvement, separately or mutually, in other more formal associations or alliances. Such involvement does not diminish partnership, nor does partnership compete with these other involvements. A proper sense of purpose is what sustains partnership and smooths the possible rough edges in all of the multiple activities undertaken by each government.

In the Canadian-American context, purpose involves the pursuit of good government, orderly democratic processes, prosperity, and security in North America. Mutual contribution to activities that further these goals strengthens each polity.

Intervulnerability, the second reality of partnership, especially characterizes the Canadian-American relationship. Canada is fully aware that with regard to both imports and exports, U.S. trade dominance leaves Canada in a somewhat dependent status. Conversely, the United States now recognizes that the high concentration of U.S. investment in Canada makes the United States hostage to possible indigenization or creeping expropriation. Because of geography, Canada needs the United States to expedite transportation and communication between eastern and western Canada; for the same reason, the United States needs Canada as a land bridge to Alaska. Pipe lines, communications cables, and transmission lines of all sorts crisscross territories of both countries. These transmission and communication systems do not integrate the two economies in a formal sense any more than the presence of the Oriental Express integrates Paris with Constantinople. But such systems make the two governments intervulnerable if breakdowns occur or interruptions of supply take place.

Intervulnerability is also expressed outside the North American region. If the world economy is moving toward the emergence of large regional trading areas including Japan, Europe, the OPEC Middle East, and the Soviet bloc, such trading enclaves will influence the competitiveness of industries in North America. The use of subsidies and nontariff barriers may be on the increase. Regardless of what Canada and the United States attempt to do separately, they will be driven toward partnership on many projects because of the necessity of economies of scale in the context of genuine competitive efficiency (absence of artificially created national monopoly).

Intervulnerability in the security area is even more clear. Canada has a strong interest in sustaining NATO because without NATO, Canada would be totally dependent upon continental defense; conversely, the United States needs Canadian support within NATO as evidence of alliance solidarity and commitment to European defense. A negative shift in the balance of global military capability weakens Canadian security just as much as American security.

Intervulnerability extends into the sphere of the domestic policies of each country. If Canada decided to cut off the sale of natural gas to the United States, the entire American midwest would suffer short-term discontinuities of production of a serious sort. Conversely, if the United States put constraints on short-term capital availability, Canada would be among the first casualties. But increasingly, domestic policy formulation is dependent on a coordination of policy at the federal levels. The difficulty Canada had with both the governmental medical plans and the National Energy Program was that opposite policies persisted in the United States, thus undermining aspects of the Canadian legislation. Controls on the earnings of physicians which accompanied the provincial medical plan drove many Canadian doctors to Houston and Atlanta. The 25 percent back-in provision, which affected both domestic and foreign oil companies, caused many oil rigs to migrate southward. Conversely, various types of economic legislation in the United States serve to free up workers, for example, who may in turn become a source of labor supply to the Canadian developmental effort. Similarly, the problems with acid raid examined in Chapter 6 are both interprovincial and interstate as well as international.

Intervulnerability is inescapable if each country attempts to maximize productivity, expand per-capita income, and avoid reducing its own security. Intervulnerability is indeed so pronounced that neither country can adopt policies that are unilaterally coercive without damaging itself in the process. As Chapter 7 revealed, the NEP was directed primarily at

U.S. investment, but it hurt Canada because it set petroleum exploration and production back several years. U.S. retaliation against investment discrimination was prevented by the American awareness that any steps taken would hurt the United States as much as Canada while setting a bad precedent for the relationship.

A third element of partnership is a proper sense of limits. Partnership is far easier to destroy than to sustain. If the United States demands arrangements of an economic or institutional sort which so bind the two countries to the same set of policies that sovereignty is undermined, Canada will resist, eventually challenging the assumptions of partnership as well. If the United States does not tolerate multilateral differentiation in the formulation and implementation of Canadian foreign policy, Canadian frustration will eventually spill over into bilateral issues, too.

On the other hand, if Canada exceeds the limits of partnership by embarrassing the United States in the U.N., for example, or by undermining strategic initiatives in the Middle East or Central America, American anger is likely to rebound on partnership itself. This does not mean that separate Canadian initiatives, a different assessment of issues, or discussion to alter American thinking are ill-advised. Partnership requires, however, some generalized consensus between partners about where foreign policy is and where it ought to be going.

Limits also require that when irritants emerge in the relationship they receive deliberate and appropriate attention. Diplomacy and communication should never be allowed to grind to a halt. Policy makers in each government become most aroused when they think that their counterparts are unwilling even to talk about festering problems.

Thus, either the Canadian desire for autarky or the American penchant for greater integration can undermine partnership. There are limits on the conduct of foreign policy, which reinforce partnership and recognize that certain realities of geopolitics, on the one hand, and the natural evolution of the nation-state, on the other, will shape management of the Canadian-American relationship. Either country can destroy partnership. It takes both countries to make partnership work. But workable partnership is dependent on an awareness of the clear limits of the conduct of foreign policy for both partners.

Collapse of the Implicit Quid Pro Quo?

Underlying bilateral diplomacy between Canada and the United States in the post-1945 era is a single large assumption, one that has been supportive of partnership. The assumption is that the United States would not squeeze Canada too hard to share the military burden if, in trade and commercial matters, Canada, for the most part, played by the international commercial rules for advanced-industrial countries, as defined by GATT and the OECD. Canada was, in fact, exempted from some of these rules because of unique circumstances.

Because of shifts in the global military balance in favor of the Soviet Union, especially at the level of conventional arms, and because of the inability of the United States alone to match the Soviet increase in power, other NATO members are having to eliminate some of the disparity between the sizes of their contributions and those of the United States. The alternative is a return to a massive retaliation mode wherein overwhelming conventional military threats are met with a nuclear response in lieu of an adequate NATO conventional military capability. In the eyes of the Europeans, the United States has, in the past, assumed a portion of Canada's defense expenditures as the "North American share." Now the United States is less able and, under changing circumstances of partnership, perhaps less willing to assume this larger burden.

Until 1981 and the advent of the National Energy Program and the proposed increasingly restrictive FIRA provision, the assumption of this quid pro quo went largely untested. Investment discrimination designed to promote Canadianization potentially opens a new era in the relationship, however, an era in which the assumption involving the implicit quid pro quo may come into question.

Although, as we have seen, Canada's military contributions to NATO defense look better than many countries relative to population size, relative to GNP, Canada ranks virtually at the bottom of the member countries. As already noted, Canada would have to virtually double its real expenditures to move up into the category of those countries "pulling their own weight" within the alliance (see Chapter 5). Although there are many reasons why Canada is able to act as a "free rider" within the alliance, the indivisibility of Canadian and American security is the principal reason. To defend itself the United States must also defend Canada. On the other hand, such an arrangement of intentional asymmetry means that the United States is not likely to be sensitive to specific Canadian security concerns (for example, concerns regarding the Northwest Passage or the Beaufort Sea) in formulating its own security policy unless encouraged to do so through offsetting considerations. Explicit mention of these considerations is not likely, because this would amount to linkage, which, as we have already seen, is probably not in the interest of either country. But the implicit quid pro quo between the military and the economic policies is evident to all serious students of the relationship.

How will a strategy of national treatment favoring domestic over foreign investment affect American judgments regarding continental security and military burden sharing? If Canada appears to Americans to be putting pressure on U.S. trade and investment through discriminatory policies, pressure will likewise eventually build in the U.S. Congress to urge Canada to assume greater military responsibility for its own security. The United States is aware that a policy of neutralism for Canada of the type pursued by Sweden or Switzerland would be far more costly to Canada than would be a policy of full partnership in NATO. Even reduced association would be more costly to Canada, as is evident from the history of French military expenditures relative to GNP for the period after de Gaulle's 1969 decision to leave the NATO organization but to remain in the alliance. Such a step would also entail an unacceptable degree of political isolation. Hence, there is some encouragement for Canada to erase some of the disparity between its level of military expenditures relative to that of other NATO members. Should the mood in the United States change regarding whether the implicit Canadian-American bargain was still being observed, Canada could expect increased attention given to its disproportionately low level of military spending.

Although Canada can rightly point with pride to its record in the area of foreign aid — it contributes about .42 percent of its GNP, as opposed to the American .23 percent — the disparity between the 1979 American and Canadian levels of military spending relative to GNP is far greater (1.8 percent for Canada, as opposed to 5.2 percent for the United States).[8] This means that the U.S. economy is far more burdened by defense expenditures than the Canadian economy is burdened in terms of foreign aid. U.S. arms sales reduce some of the fixed costs of armaments production, but the practice of tying foreign aid to sales of exports reduces the Canadian cost of aid distribution as well.

Partnership requires some effort to achieve understanding on such broad matters as commercial and trade policy and defense spending. Currently that understanding regarding the implicit bargain is somewhat clouded. The direction of pressures for change on both sides of the border is, however, not ambiguous, and a new policy-making equilibrium is likely to emerge. Efforts to formulate this new equilibrium are perhaps at the core of the greatest challenge the post-World War II partnership has yet faced.

Some Initiatives to Improve Coordination of U.S. Policy toward Canada

First, in its own self-interest, as well as in the interest of treating Canada responsibly, the United States must increase its pool of talented manpower on matters Canadian. The United States needs a bureaucratic manpower base for dealing with Canada which is of a size commensurate with the importance of a trading and investment partner of the first rank. This means developing a corps of analysts thoroughly knowledgeable about Canada. The United States can no longer solely rely on a tiny group of able specialists who are largely clustered around the Canada desk in the State Department, plus a few individuals scattered elsewhere who may have occasionally made a visit to Toronto or Montreal. The Departments of Commerce, Treasury, and Defense, as well as the Special Trade Representatives Office and the congressional staffs, are among the most seriously undermanned. Although most governmental divisions, relating to several areas of the world, could make a claim for their need for increased analytic and operational capability, the lack of specialists knowledgeable about Canada puts an enormous burden on top decision makers when critical policy decisions come up for consideration. When important divisions of government are reduced to using unpaid summer interns for major job assignments, an adequate supply of personnel is visibly lacking. Relative to the importance of the governmental issues involved, the thinness of the manpower base, compared to expertise on other countries and regions, is a cause for reflection.

Second, top decision makers must begin to take Canada seriously, to obtain the proper knowledge of the Canadian outlook, and to acquire the facts about Canadian-American relations. In two separate sets of summit talks an American president has not had sufficient knowledge about the state of Canadian-American negotiations to respond to the discussions of his counterpart.[9] On another occasion, another president, normally well versed on foreign policy, did not know that Canada was America's largest trading partner. Historical examination of one of the most troubling recent treaty negotiations between the United States and Canada indicates that the American delegation had far less factual information upon which to base judgments than did the Canadian delegation and because of this (not, as was reported, because of a lack of bargaining skill) made concessions that ultimately doomed Senate ratification of the treaty.

A common theme runs through all of these examples. Too often American delegations have not done their homework, either because they have placed a higher priority on political-strategic questions than on trade-commercial matters or because they assumed knowledge about Canada that was in fact lacking or inaccurate. Briefing of American presidents about Canadian perspectives and sensitivities has been among the weakest of preparations, with predictably costly consequences in a number of instances; such ineptitude would not have been tolerated in, for example, the European context.

Fine American ambassadors have been appointed to Canada; others have been less able. Some have taken a long time to acquire even a minimal knowledge of the issues. Canada and Canadian-American relations are too important to risk the consequences of inadequate representation based on the false assumption that because Ottawa is so close to Washington the American ambassador will not have many responsibilities other than ceremonial ones. Even though they may not always be so taken in the United States, ambassadors are taken earnestly in Canada; Americans are judged accordingly.

Lack of information on the part of Americans is sometimes interpreted by Canadians as a Canadian bargaining advantage. But ignorance is scarcely blissful in the bilateral relationship and in documented cases has led to overreaction or misjudgment that has been damaging to Canada and to Canadian-American relations as well as to American interests. An adequate supply of skilled personnel is a prerequisite for solid diplomacy. Proper briefings for top officials are an associated, though scarcely secondary, prerequisite.

Third, at times of Presidential succession attention to the continuity of the conduct of foreign policy is a paramount consideration in all areas. In a field where expertise is unavoidably so limited, continuity becomes mandatory. Yet it is common to see expertise eliminated at below the assistant-secretary level, cuts so deep that replacement of knowledgeable personnel takes years to accomplish. By the time new personnel are trained and have, through field work, acquired familiarity with Canadian subject matter, a new administration has come into office, once again sweeping the halls of Washington clean of "holdovers."

Rapid turnover of officials and significant horizontal mobility in and out of government bureaucracy are helpful in that new ideas and fresh energy are pumped into agencies and institutions. But when the tempo of exchange is so rapid and cuts of experienced personnel are so deep that only one or two junior-level bureaucrats with any knowledge of a major trading partner are left in an entire division, such savage implementation of the rights of patronage seriously erodes the effectiveness of government. Even if patronage to this degree is tolerated, officials with immediate competence on Canadian matters should replace those whose resignations have been accepted.

Finally, proposals periodically emerge to raise the status of Canada in the U.S. governmental bureaucracy by reorganizing the State Department. Senator Baacus, for example, introduced a bill in 1981 that would cluster Canada with Mexico and the Caribbean countries instead of with Europe, in order to create a more efficient North American focus. Although some reorganization may be helpful and is often favored by Canada so as to obtain a higher priority for Canadian interests, Canadian officials prefer the association with Europe rather than with the smaller, sometimes less visible polities of North America. Because a division above the level of the country desk (for example, the level of an assistant deputy secretary) devoted solely to Canada is apparently not feasible, for reasons of precedent and comparability, the current form of organization will probably have to suffice. What is perhaps more critical than organizational locus is that issues involving Canada receive the proper attention at the cabinet level.

This is an old and well-trodden bureaucratic territory. Yet it is of continuing significance. The difficulty in matters Canadian is that power and knowledge are frequently not brought together. Divisions with greater power over decision making may not have sufficient knowledge about Canada, and divisions that have the knowledge often find themselves politically isolated within the U.S. government.

In general, two techniques might overcome some of this discrepancy between information and action:

1. Divisions of government with new personnel or with a form of organization that does not focus on individual countries ought to consider a short apprenticeship program for new middle- and upper-level employees, circulating them through other divisions with a stronger focus on individual countries or through an explicit training program designed to familiarize them with the fundamentals of Canadian-American relations.

2. Committees of people from different divisions at various governmental levels already convene to discuss policy issues involving Canada. The problem once again is that knowledge and power often do not meet. Such committee sessions are only valuable if the participants are sufficiently senior so that decisions can actually emerge from meetings. The sessions are less valuable when they amount to merely an exchange of departmental policy positions because some or all of the participants are either too junior or too unfamiliar with the subject matter to actively contribute.

In short, when decision making begins to fragment, cross-departmental committees are essential. They can become far more efficient policy-making vehicles if committee members have adequate seniority and if all participants have been adequately briefed in advance. Without such up-grading, briefing, and interchange, policy coordination within the U.S. government regarding Canada will continue to be episodic and diffused, thus creating a less efficient decision-making process and the image abroad of confusion and uncertainty.

PARTNERSHIP: NEITHER INTEGRATION NOR AUTARKY

Have decision makers begun to forget the mid-twentieth century ideal of Canadian-American partnership, either because the United States has pressed too hard for greater integration or because Canada has sought too persistently to achieve autarky? Central as this policy question is, it is not without paradox.

Existence of the integrationist mentality has elicited Canadian assertions of independence; the presence of the autarkic mentality has tended to stimulate an American integrationist counter-response. Each initiative begets its opposite.

The U.S. response to Canadian autarky has been a vacillation between assertive integrationism and petulant retaliation. Within the twelve-month period from the peak of the presidential campaign to the summer of President Reagan's first term in office, foreign policy thought toward Canada took a 180-degree turn, abetted by the mood in Ottawa. Although formal integration between the United States and Canada has never been a conscious goal of American foreign policy, integration may nonetheless have been the unintended result of U.S. proposals and actions. Assumptions regarding integration have frequently misled policy makers.[10] The reason the United States could unilaterally cancel the special relationship, for example, was that the government thought the economies of North America were already so integrated as to prevent Canada from responding in a fashion that could eventually hurt in economic terms.

Cancellation of exemptions for Canada, urged on the United States by its balance-of-payments problems, was considered comparatively cost-free because the interdependence of the two economies would ensure cooperation in trade and commercial matters. Although Canada, as well as other trading partners, might attempt trade diversification, the United States has not viewed such efforts as a threat (unless induced by tariff or nontariff barriers), because of the confidence in the competitiveness of the U.S. economy and, in some cases, because of the awareness of natural efficiencies of size and proximity. But what the United States neglected was the possibility that a Third Option policy could turn inward; that rather than discriminating against foreign trade, Canada could pursue a commercial policy that eventually would discriminate against foreign investment.

Similarly, however, Canada tended to neglect the possibility that efforts to extract greater benefits from foreign investment and efforts to reduce the U.S. share of Canadian trade might eventually impinge on the willingness of the United States to create an implicit exception for Canada in terms of sharing the defense burden. Experience with the apparent willingness of the United States to tolerate the proposed Canadian NATO deployment reductions in 1969 and the willingness of the United States to squeeze its other NATO allies harder than Canada regarding increases of military spending may have misled Ottawa into believing that a disappearance of the special relationship and a further dissipation of partnership could allow Canada to avoid increasing the level of Canadian defense spending.

Whether Canada and the United States will be able to sustain partnership is further complicated by the outcome of tensions between Quebec and Ottawa. Although the United States has been meticulous about abstinence from involvement in federal-provincial questions, the Canadian federal government has sometimes been anxious regarding the possibility of some form of U.S. political or economic intrusion on behalf of Quebec. Conversely, the apparent enthusiasm of Quebec and Alberta, in particular, for closer trade and commercial relations with the United States has been something of an embarrassment to Washington because Washington perceives that it is occasionally being used as a pawn in Canadian federal-provincial struggles.

Partnership will also have to survive the apparently growing disparity between philosophies of economic thought in the two countries. Free-market ideas and nationalist economic thought do not necessarily have to conflict. But when these ideas and forms of organizational initiative are used in such a way that they further the objectives of autarky or integration, these approaches are bound to spill over onto the opposite partner through the impact on trade and foreign investment. Such spillovers are likely to create tensions that only far-sighted leadership will be able to overcome.

Not all of the evidence is, of course, yet available regarding the present and future fate of partnership. For one thing, the United States must exert its leadership and restore a sense of purpose to the arrangement. This can occur at the bilateral and multilateral levels. At the multilateral level, the vast alliance projects emerging at midcentury created a visible manifestation of institutional progress. The collapse of European empires and the emergence of bipolarity facilitated this institutional progress, but such innovativeness is not likely to repeat itself in the absence of the emergence of additional global actors. On the economic side, the forthcoming discussions on service industries and nontariff barriers may continue the momentum of the Kennedy and Tokyo rounds of trade talks. Such programs, especially those emerging within the framework of the OECD, set the parameters for the bilateral relationship as well. Multilateral projects involving both partners, such as the plan to provide aid to countries in the Caribbean and in Central America and the abortive idea for an energy bank to sponsor exploration and development in Third World countries, likewise serve to add coherence to Canadian and American foreign policy.

At the bilateral level, there is no substitute for attention to specific irritants. Elimination of all specific grievances between the two countries would not create a condition of perfect harmony. Differences of interest and outlook would remain. But in a partnership the presence of grievances that appear unalterable and are highly publicized tends to quickly erode the sense of purpose. When Canada and the United States build on their track record of bilateral accomplishment, such as the release of the captured American hostages in Iran, the sense of partnership is felt throughout the societies of both countries.

By seeking future opportunities for joint ventures, in which individual sovereignties are respected but in which the separate capabilities of the two countries can be used to mutual advantage, partnership can reach a state of maturity at which it is less fragile. Once a sense of purpose, an awareness of intervulnerabilities, and an acceptance of foreign and domestic policy limits has been reestablished, partnership is likely to flourish again.

Only after Canada and the United States have decided what kind of relationship they want and in which direction they wish to proceed can they give attention to strategic priorities. Among these priorities should be the following:

1. avoidance of the politicization of foreign policy issues
2. employment of bilateral institutions, but no excessive reliance on them
3. use of internal diplomacy

Politicization of issues is detrimental to partnership.[11] Careful observation suggests that the attempt to use the press to catalyze opinion in favor of or against particular agenda matters normally fails, sometimes catastrophically for individual diplomats and policy makers trying to exploit these instruments. Part of the reason is that individuals in both countries often read the same newspapers and watch the same television coverage. This makes the media a far less useful propaganda vehicle.

Another reason is that politicization tends to expand the area of conflict, bringing in other actors, namely, Congress on one side and provincial governments on the other, as well as the important private sectors with their diverse and powerful elements, which the respective federal governments find they cannot control. It is certainly in the American interest not to arouse possible latent anti-Americanism in the Canadian body politic; it is certainly in the Canadian interest not to erode the large reservoir of good feeling toward Canada on the part of the average American. Politicization of issues damages each of these objectives for the respective governments.

Creation of additional joint commissions and consultative agencies, modeled perhaps on the highly valued International Joint Commission, is not to be discouraged. But the governments must recognize that until they are in agreement regarding the general parameters of the relationship, the burden on new bilateral institutions to rescue the relationship from increased acrimony or the consequences of diverging national interests in some areas is possibly too great. When such institutions serve to protect the sovereignties of the two countries as much as they provide a bridge between cultures and political systems, and when these institutions are constructed along familiar and highly useful functional lines, they can be of great assistance to policy makers in Ottawa and Washington.

But there is a danger that these same policy makers will put too great a burden on these rather fragile bilateral instruments, demanding of them far more than is practicable, thereby diverting the attention of the governments from an understanding of the deeper historical changes that are affecting the two societies.

Finally, the somewhat increased reliance upon internal diplomacy within the decision-making apparatus of each government and the federal level is an innovative and promising technique, provided that it is used with discretion. American congressmen and senators value personal contact with members of the government of Canada to clarify and amplify the Canadian position on issues. Part of the reason that such consultation is so important, of course, is the relative dearth of expertise on Canada in the U.S. government and the limited coverage of Canadian issues and perspectives in the American press. Some of this is changing, and to the extent that better information is provided Congress and the top decision makers in the executive branch of the U.S. government, the Canadian Department of External Affairs and the Canadian embassy will have fewer responsibilities. But in the meantime, representation of this sort can be quite effective, as the passage of the Alaska Highway Natural Gas Pipeline waiver package discussed in Chapter 7 indicates.

Similarly, there may be some role for direct contact in Ottawa between American and Canadian officials at the Cabinet level and below to explain the U.S. policies from time to time, although Canada already devotes considerable time to U.S. policy. Governments must recognize, however, that there is an inverse law operative here. The greater the success of internal diplomacy for one or other government the more likely opposition groups within each country will complain and will seek to embarrass not only the participants but the method of exchange as a whole. Hence, although extraordinarily valuable as a means of conveying information and influence, internal diplomacy in Ottawa and Washington must proceed with the most scrupulous care and prudence.

Analysts of Canadian-American relations ought to acknowledge a critical difference between two types of historical processes. One set of historical processes affects the convergence or divergence of economic and political structures between the two polities. The other set of processes determines the *tone* of the relationship. Canadian-American relations can be "good" or "bad" irrespective of whether the structures of the two societies and governments are converging or diverging.

Partnership is neutral regarding the matter of societal convergence or divergence. However close or distant the structures of the two governments and economies are, partnership is dependent on a diplomatic setting that is interactive and positive. Similarly, partnership will in turn help further the positive tone of this interaction.

I have argued that the future of Canadian-American relations appears bright, but that with only a slight alteration of circumstances that future could be in jeopardy. As I write, under the cloud of economic recession in the early spring of 1982, relations are for the moment somewhat precarious. We have observed that concentration on strategy and tactics is useful in bilateral diplomacy but that first the two governments must determine what kind of relationship they want. Are they desirous of greater economic interdependence or less; more of an opportunity for the private sector or greater federal intervention; a larger role for the federal governments in diplomacy or heightened activity by the states and provinces. These are some of the principal trade-offs among the tendencies and approaches that will shape the nature of the overall Canadian-American relationship.

While meeting the material and emotional needs of their founding peoples, the two countries can make out of their interaction what they want: a relationship that is unproductive or constructive; a relationship that is indifferent or highly refined and sensitive.[12] In the 1980s, the relationship is at something of a turning point, and the two governments must choose. Rarely in history have two governments had so much control over the tone of bilateral affairs and over the opportunity to achieve complementary development. Electorates of these two great democracies have endowed their political representatives with substantial decision-making latitude and a mandate to act with responsibility and imagination.

NOTES

CHAPTER 1

1. International Monetary Fund, "Statistical Tables," Appendix B, *World Economic Outlook,* Occasional Paper No. 4 (Washington, D.C.: IMF, 1981), pp. 108-54.

2. U.S. Department of the Treasury, Office of the Secretary, *Report on Foreign Portfolio Investment in the United States* (Washington, D.C., 1980).

3. Canadian-American Committee, "Bilateral Relations in an Uncertain World Context: U.S. Canada Relations in 1978," in *Improving Bilateral Consulation on Economic Issues.* Available from sponsoring organizations: C.D. Howe Institute, Suite 2064, 1155 Metcalfe St., Montreal, Quebec H3B 2X7; or the National Planning Association, 1606 New Hampshire Ave. N.W., Washington, D.C. 20009 (Washington, D.C.: 1978).

4. Marie-Josée Drouin and Harald B. Malmgren, "Canada, the United States, and the World Economy," *Foreign Affairs* 60, No. 2 (Winter 1981-82): 393-415.

5. Maxwell Cohen's proposal is quoted in Anthony Westell, "Poison Pinpricks: Neighbors North and South," *Foreign Policy* No. 41 (Winter 1980-81):109.

6. *Ibid.,* pp. 95-110.

7. Ambassador-designate Allan Gotlieb, Address for the Association for Canadian Studies in the United States, East Lansing, Michigan, October 23, 1981.

8. William R. Willoughby, *The Joint Organizations of Canada and the United States* (Toronto: University of Toronto Press, 1979).

9. George Parkin de Tweenebroker Glazebrook, *A History of Canadian External Relations,* rev. ed., Vol. 2 (Toronto: McClelland and Stewart, 1966), pp. 211-13.

10. Ronald Reagan, Address announcing presidential campaign, given at the New York Hilton, New York City, November 13, 1979.

11. Department of Energy, Mines, and Resources, *The National Energy Program* (Ottawa: Department of Energy, Mines, and Resources, 1980).

12. See Gerald S. Graham, *Sea Power and British North America, 1783-1820, A Study in British Colonial Policy,* Harvard Historical Studies (Cambridge, Mass.: 1941); Donald C. Masters, *The Reciprocity Treaty of 1854, its History, its Relation to British Colonial and Foreign Policy and to the Development of Canadian Fiscal Autonomy* (Toronto: McClelland and Stewart, 1963).

13. Donald Creighton, *Dominion of the North: A History of Canada,* rev. ed. (Toronto: Macmillan, 1977), pp. 223-32. Gilbert N. Tucker, *The Canadian Commercial Revolution, 1845-1851* (New Haven: Yale University Press, 1936).

14. R. R. Palmer, *A History of the Modern World* (New York: Knopf, 1961), pp. 462-63; D. G. Barnes, *A History of the English Corn Laws from 1660-1846* (New York: Kelley, 1930).

15. Herbert C. F. Bell, *Lord Palmerston,* Vol. 1 (Connecticut: Shoe String Press, 1936), pp. 58-104; Palmer, *op. cit.,* p. 463.

16. Quoted in Bernard Porter, *The Lion's Share: A Short History of British Imperialism, 1850-1970* (London: Longman, 1975), p. 3; Cedric J. Lowe, *The Reluctant Imperialists: British Foreign Policy, 1878-1902* (London: Macmillan, 1967).

17.   Creighton, *Dominion of the North,* p. 254.

18.   *Ibid.,* p. 256.

19.   Robert D. Cuff and J. L. Granatstein, *Ties that Bind,* 2nd ed. (Toronto: Samuel Stevens Hakkert, 1977), pp. 151-63.

20.   Marguerite Michels, "America Has Slipped to Number Two," Interview with Richard Nixon, *Washington Post Parade Magazine* (October 5, 1980):4-9.

21.   Richard Nixon, Address to both houses of the Canadian Parliament, given in Ottawa on April 14, 1972.

22.   Mitchell Sharp, "Canada-U.S. Relations: Options for the Future," *International Perspectives,* Special Issue (Autumn, 1972).

23.   Donald Barry, "The Politics of 'Exceptionalism': Canada and the United States as a Distinctive International Relationship," *Dalhousie Review* 60, No. 1 (Spring 1980):114-37.

24.   See John W. Holmes, *The Better Part of Valour: Essays on Canadian Diplomacy* (Toronto: McClelland and Stewart, 1970), pp. 151-65.

CHAPTER 2

1.

The idea that every twenty years this country should automatically and as a matter of course take part in a war overseas for democracy or self-determination of other small nations, that a country which has all it can do to run itself should feel called upon to save, periodically, a continent that cannot run itself, and to these ends risk the lives of its people, risk bankruptcy and political disunion, seems to many a nightmare and sheer madness.

Mackenzie King, *Debates,* House of Commons, March 30, 1939, p. 2419

If we remain one people, under an efficient government, the period is not far off when we may defy material injury from external annoyance, when we may take such an attitude as will cause the neutrality we may at any time resolve upon to be scrupulously respected; when belligerent nations, under the impossibility of making acquisitions upon us, will not lightly hazard the giving us provocation; when we may choose peace or war, as our interest, guided by justice, shall counsel.

George Washington, Farewell Address, (1796), in James Daniel Richardson, *A Compilation of the Messages and Papers of the Presidents, 1789-1897,* vol. 1 (Washington, D.C.: U.S. Congress, c. 1897-1922), pp. 221-23.

2.   Kenneth McRae, "The Structure of Canadian History," in Louis Hartz, *The Founding of New Societies* (New York: Harcourt, Brace and World, 1964), pp. 219-74.

3.   J. L. Granatstein, *Canada's War: The Politics of the Mackenzie King Government, 1939-1945* (Toronto: Oxford University Press, 1975), pp. 294-307; Charles P. Stacey, *Arms, Men, and Governments: The War Policies of Canada, 1939-1945* (Ottawa: Queen's Printer, 1970).

4.   S. D. Pierce and Arthur F. W. Plumptre, "Canada's Relations with Wartime Agencies in Washington," *Canadian Journal of Economics and Political Science* 11 (1945):410-17; Robert Bothwell and William Kilbourn, *C. D. Howe: A Biography* (Toronto: McClelland and Stewart, 1980), pp. 180-243.

5.   For a sampling of more popular opinion on the subject, see Michel Brunet, "The French Canadian's Search for a Fatherland," and Kenneth McNaught, "The National Outlook of English-speaking Canadians," both in *Nationalism in Canada,* edited by Peter Russell (Toronto: McGraw-Hill Ryerson, 1966), pp. 47-60, 62-71; and Richard P. Bowles et al., eds., *Canada and the US: Continental Partners or Wary Neighbors?* (Scarborough, Ont.: Prentice-Hall, 1973).

6.   Peyton V. Lyon and Brian W. Tomlin, *Canada as an International Actor* (Toronto: Macmillan, 1979), p. 62. See Barry Farrell, *The Making of Canadian Foreign Policy,* (Scar-

borough, Ont.: Prentice-Hall, 1969). For a path-breaking discussion of comparative foreign policy in the larger context, see also Barry Farrell, *Approaches to Comparative and International Politics* (Evanston, Illinois: Northwestern University Press, 1966).

7. Consider Richard W. Rosecrance, *Action and Reaction in World Politics* (Boston: Little, Brown and Co., 1963), pp. 288-92; Klaus Knorr, *Power and Wealth: The Political Economy of International Power* (New York: Basic Books, 1973). David A. Baldwin, "Power Analysis and World Politics: New Trends versus Old Tendencies," *World Politics* 31 (1979):

8. This index is based on a similar index constructed for nine industrial nations between 1815 and 1975. The index seeks to reflect the basis of national power. It is composed of surrogates of gross national product, military spending, and technological productivity as well as population size and wealth. For the specific theory and operationalization that underlies this indicator, see Charles F. Doran and Wes Parsons, "War and the Cycle of Relative Power," *American Political Science Review* 74, No. 4 (December 1980):948; or Charles F. Doran, *Politics of Assimilation: Hegemony and Its Aftermath* (Baltimore: Johns Hopkins Press, 1971), pp. 46-51, 191-94.

9. In a relationship such as that between Canada and the United States, in which force is irrelevant, these absolute size differences have much less significance than elsewhere, either for the outcome of bilateral disputes or for the style of the conduct of foreign policy. These disparities of size do, however, partly for the same reason, make an enormous difference on the global stage. For a discussion of some of these ambiguities, see Raymond Aron, *Peace and War: A Theory of International Relations* (Garden City, N.Y.: Anchor Books, 1973), pp. 57-63.

10. This thesis is expressed with clarity in, for example, John H. Redekop, "Continentalism: The Key to Canadian Politics," in *Approaches to Canadian Politics,* edited by John H. Redekop (Scarborough, Ont.: Prentice-Hall, 1978), pp. 28-55; and Robert M. Laxer, ed., *Canada, Ltd.: The Political Economy of Dependency* (Toronto: McClelland and Stewart, 1973).

11. This was the essence of the Canadian interest in NATO and the genesis of the fight for the "Canadian Article," Article two of the chapter, which broadens in economic and social terms, the military character of the alliance. Without the multilateral character of NATO, Canada would be left without Europe to balance its political and security interests with respect to the United States. See Escott Reid, *Time of Fear and Hope: The Making of the North Atlantic Treaty, 1947-1949* (Toronto: McClelland and Stewart, 1977).

12. John W. Holmes, *The Shaping of Peace,* vol. 1 (Toronto: University of Toronto Press, 1979), pp. 72-73.

13. John S. Dickey, *Canada and the American Presence* (New York: New York University Press, 1975), pp. 7, 42-58.

14. A pioneering discussion of the political agenda is found in Matthew A. Crenson, *The Un-Politics of Air Pollution* (Baltimore: Johns Hopkins Press, 1971), pp. 159-76.

15. Don Munton and Dean Swanson, "Rise and Fall of the Third Option: Forecasting Canadian-American Relations into the 1980s," in *Canada's Foreign Policy: Analysis and Trends,* edited by Brian Tomlin (Toronto: Methuen, 1978), pp. 175-211; "Canada and the United States: The Framework and the Agenda," *U.S. Department of State Bulletin* 74, No. 1921 (April 19, 1976):508-13.

16. Charles F. Doran, "A Theory of Bounded Deterrence," *Journal of Conflict Resolution* 17, No. 2 (June 1973):246, 267.

17. Robert O. Keohane and Joseph S. Nye, *Power and Interdependence* (Boston: Little, Brown and Co., 1973), p. 183.

18. Richard Cooper, *The Economics of Interdependence,* published for the Council on Foreign Relations (New York: McGraw-Hill, 1968), pp. 5-30.

19. Charles F. Doran, "Modes, Mechanisms, and Turning Points: Perspectives on the Transformation of the International System," *International Political Science Review* 1, No. 1 (1980):35-61.

20. Joseph S. Nye, "Transnational Relations and Interstate Conflicts: An Empirical Analysis," in *Canada and the United States: Transnational and Transgovernmental Relations,*

edited by Annette B. Fox, Alfred O. Hero, Jr., and Joseph S. Nye, Jr. (New York: Columbia University Press, 1976), pp. 367-404; David Leyton-Brown, "Canada and Multinational Enterprise," in *Foremost Nation: Canadian Foreign Policy and a Changing World*, edited by Normal Hillmer and Garth Stevenson (Toronto: McClelland and Stewart, 1977), pp. 63-84.

21. Donald K. Alper and Robert L. Monahan, "Bill C-58 and the American Congress: The Politics of Retaliation," *Canadian Public Policy* 4, No. 2 (Spring 1978):184-92.

22. Arnold D. P. Heeney and Livingston T. Merchant, *Canada and the United States: Principles for Partnership* (Ottawa: Queen's Printer, 1965).

23. Donald Creighton, "Economic Nationalism and Confederation," *Towards the Discovery of Canada* (Toronto: Macmillan, 1972), pp. 122-36.

24. In John Saywell, ed., *Canadian Annual Review of Politics and Public Affairs, 1974* (Toronto: University of Toronto Press, 1975), pp. 293-94.

25. Kal J. Holsti and Thomas Allen Levy, "Bilateral Institutions and Transgovernmental Relations between Canada and the United States," in Fox, Hero, and Nye, *Canada and the United States*, pp. 283-309.

26. Brian Cuthbertson, *Canadian Military Independence in the Age of the Superpowers* (Toronto: Fitzhenry and Whiteside, 1977), pp. 72-101; for a quite different interpretation, see Lewis Hertzman et al., eds., *Alliances and Illusions: Canada and the NATO-NORAD Question* (Edmonton, Alberta: M. G. Hurtig, 1969).

27. Richard M. Nixon, Address to both houses of the Canadian Parliament, given in Ottawa on April 14, 1972.

CHAPTER 3

1. Conventional assessment holds that the closer the identity of two polities and the more tightly interdependent their economies and governing structures, the easier is the task of coordinating policy, because the perceptions of foreign policy elites are so similar; conversely, opposite conditions lead to opposite conclusions. See, for example, Ralph K. White, "Images in the Context of International Conflict: Soviet Perceptions of the US and the USSR," in *International Behavior: A Social-Psychological Analysis*, edited by Herbert C. Kelman (New York: Holt, Rinehart and Winston, 1965), pp. 238-76; Robert Jervis, *Perception and Misperception in International Politics* (Princeton, N.J.: Princeton University Press, 1976); Dallas Cullen, J. D. Hobson, and Rodney Schneck, "Towards the Development of a Canadian-American Scale: A Research Note," *Canadian Journal of Political Science* 11, No. 2 (June, 1978):409-18.

2. "The essential weakness of the Canadian political culture," according to Abraham Rotstein, "lies in its derivative liberalism. This is the heritage of an intellectual colonialism, concepts and symbols of which are inadequate to our dilemma and bypass the major problems surrounding Canadian independence." *The Precarious Homestead* (Toronto: New Press, 1973), p. 191.

3. Gad Horowitz, "Conservatism, Liberalism, and Socialism in Canada," *Canadian Journal of Economics and Political Science* 32 (1966):141-71; Gad Horowitz, "Notes on 'Conservatism, Liberalism, and Socialism in Canada,'" *Canadian Journal of Political Science* 11, No. 2 (June 1978):383-99. For a contrasting explanation, see Louis Hartz, *The Liberal Tradition in America* (New York: Harcourt, Brace and World, 1955), pp. 189-97; Seymour M. Lipset, "Revolution and Counter-revolution: The United States and Canada," in his *Revolution and Counter-revolution*, rev. ed. (Garden City, New York: Anchor Books, 1970), pp. 37-75.

4. For the American reader, some general sources on the structure of Canadian government include: Donald V. Smiley, *Canada in Question: Federation in the 80s*, 3rd ed.

(Toronto: McGraw-Hill Ryerson, 1980); Peter J. T. O'Hearn, *Peace, Order, and Good Government* (Toronto: Macmillan, 1964); R. MacGregor Dawson, *The Government of Canada* (Toronto: University of Toronto Press, 1975); Richard T. VanLoon and Michael S. Whittington, *The Canadian Political System* (Toronto: McGraw-Hill Ryerson, 1981); and Richard Schultz, Orest M. Kruhlak, and John C. Terr, *The Canadian Political Process,* 3rd ed. (Toronto: Holt, Rinehart and Winston, 1979).

5. Gordon Watkins and Michael A. Walker, *Reaction: The National Energy Program* (Vancouver: The Frazer Institute, 1981).

6. John Richards and Larry Pratt, *Prairie Capitalism: Power and Influence in New West* (Toronto: McClelland and Stewart, 1979); David Smith, *Prairie Liberalism: The Liberal Party in Saskatchewan* (Toronto: University of Toronto Press, 1975); and P. Smith, *The Prairie Provinces* (Toronto: University of Toronto Press, 1972).

7. John Porter, *The Vertical Mosaic: An Analysis of Social Class and Power in Canada* (Toronto: University of Toronto Press, 1965), pp. 201-31. Although more recent analysis has attacked the validity of some of the assumptions of this brilliant work, the essential outlines of the thesis are surely valid, especially when considered in a comparative perspective. Contrast, for example, the idea of "pluralistic power" and "interest-group liberalism" attributed to the United States with the manner of interest aggregation and power management in Canada. See Theodore J. Lowi, *The End of Liberalism: The Second Republic of the United States,* 2nd ed. (New York: W. W. Norton, 1979), pp. 82-91.

8. Alexis de Tocqueville, "L'ancien regime," in *Democracy in America,* edited by Richard D. Heffner (New York: Mentor, 1956); and Tom B. Bottomore, *Elites and Society* (Middlesex: Penguin Books, 1964), pp. 129-49.

9. Walter Lippmann viewed this as the malady of democratic states. "Successful democratic politicians are insecure and intimidated men," according to Lippmann. "The decisive consideration is not whether the proposition is good but whether it is popular—not whether it will work well and prove itself but whether the active talking constituents like it immediately." Lippmann, *The Public Philosophy* (Boston: Little, Brown and Co., Mentor Book, 1955), p. 28. But George F. Kennan, writing at almost the same time, credits some of these deficiencies to the American "legalistic approach" to foreign policy. *American Diplomacy, 1900-1950* (Chicago: University of Chicago Press, Mentor Book, 1951), pp. 86-87.

10. Michael D. Wallace, "Power, Status and International War," *Journal of Peace Research* 1 (1971): 23-35; Charles F. Doran, Kim Quaile Hill, and Kenneth Mladenka, "Threat, Status Disequilibrium, and National Power," *British Journal of International Studies* 5 (1979): 37-50.

11. In the view of George Ball, Canada, in opposing integration, is fighting a "rearguard action against the inevitable." *The Discipline of Power* (Boston: Little, Brown and Co., 1968), pp. 113, 90-117.

12. Reinhold Niebuhr, *Moral Man and Immoral Society: A Study in Ethics and Politics* (New York: Scribner, 1969); and Karl Deutsch, *Nationalism and Its Alternatives* (New York: Knopf, 1969).

13. Garth Stevenson, "Continental Integration and Canadian Unity," in *Continental Community,* edited by Andrew Axline et al. (Toronto: McClelland and Stewart, 1974), pp. 194-217; Jacques-Yvan Morin, "The Treaty-making Power of Quebec," *Contemporary Issues in Canadian Politics,* edited by Frederick Vaughan et al. (Scarborough, Ont.: Prentice-Hall, 1970), pp. 128-38; Jean-Louis Roy, "Les relations du Québec et des Etats-Unis," *Le Canada et le Québec sur la scène internationale,* edited by Paul Painchaud (Montreal: Presses de l'université du Québec, 1977), pp. 497-514.

14. C. P. Stacey, *Canada and the Age of Conflict* (Toronto: Macmillan, 1977), pp. 145-49; L. Ethan Ellis, *Reciprocity, 1911: A Study in Canadian-American Relations* (New Haven, Yale University Press, 1939).

CHAPTER 4

1. For a general discussion, see John Fayerweather, *Foreign Investment in Canada* (New York: International Arts and Sciences Press, 1973); Alan Rugman, *Multinationals in Canada: Theory, Performance, and Economic Impacts* (Boston: M. Nighoff, 1980); and Judith Maxwell, *Challenges to Complacency* (Montreal: C. D. Howe Research Institute, 1976).

2. Statistics used in this section are drawn from *Statistics Canada* (Ottawa, Ont., 1979); and U.S. Embassy, Ottawa, *US-Canada Relations: Economic and Environmental Dimensions* (Ottawa: U.S. Embassy, 1980).

3. Frank W. Taussig, *The Tariff History of the United States*, 7th ed. (New York: Putnam, 1931); Edward Stanwood, *American Tariff Controversies in the Nineteenth Century*, 2 vols. (New York: Russell and Russell, 1903).

4. William Diebold, "Canada in the World Economy Over Ten Years," *International Journal* 33, No. 2 (Spring, 1978):432-56; John J. Deutsch, "Recent American Influence in Canada," in *The American Economic Impact on Canada*, edited by Hugh G. J. Aitken et al. (Durham, N.C.: Duke University Press, 1959), pp. 36-50; W. A. MacIntosh, "Economic Factors in Canadian History," reprinted in William Easterbrook, *Approaches to Canadian Economic History* (Toronto: McClelland and Stewart, 1967), pp. 37-76.

5. Charles C. Tansill, *Canadian-American Relations, 1875-1911* (New Haven: Yale University Press, 1943), Ch. 11; Robert C. Brown, *Canada's National Policy, 1883-1900: A Study in Canadian-American Relations* (Princeton: Princeton University Press, 1964).

6. Science Council of Canada, *Foreign Investment in Canada* (Gray Report) (Ottawa: Science Council of Canada, 1978), Chs. 3-4; James M. Gilmour, *The Weakest Link: A Technological Perspective on Canadian Industrial Development* (Ottawa: Science Council of Canada, 1978).

7. Richard D. French, *How Ottawa Decides: Planning and Industrial Policy-making, 1968-1980* (Ottawa: The Canadian Institute for Economic Policy, 1981); Roger Hatch, chairman of the Export Promotion Review Committee, *Strengthening Canada Abroad* (Ottawa: Department of Industry, Trade and Commerce, 1979).

8. Ronald Reagan, Address announcing presidential campaign, given at the New York Hilton, New York City, November 13, 1979; Herbert E. Meyer, "Why a North American Common Market Won't Work Yet," *Fortune* (September 10, 1979):118-24; Economic Policy Council of the United Nations Association of the United States of America, *Relationships in the North American Economic Area*, New York, 1981.

9. Jeremy Kinsman and Allan Gotlieb, "Reviving the Third Option," *International Perspectives* (January-February 1981):2-18.

10. Major industrial countries more prone than Canada to use various techniques of national export assistance include France, Germany, the United Kingdom, Japan, and Italy. Only the United States is less prone. Barry Beale, *Energy and Industry: The Potential of Energy Development Projects for Canadian Industry in the Eighties* (Ottawa: James Lorimer, The Canadian Institute for Economic Policy, 1980), p. 82; H. Peter Guttman, *The International Consultant* (New York: McGraw-Hill, 1976).

11. Jack A. Finlayson and Mark W. Zacher, "International Trade Institutions and the North/South Dialogue," *International Journal: Money and Markets* 36 No. 4 (Autumn, 1981): 732-65. Consider also Bela A. Balassa, *Newly Industrializing Countries After the Oil Crisis* (Washington: The World Bank, 1981). An Export Trade Development Board and three billion dollars of insurance and guarantees for export loans and foreign investment are designed to spearhead Canada's trade diversification effort. Government of Canada, *Economic Development for the 1980s* (Ottawa: Department of Finance, 1981), pp. 19-20.

12. Peter M. Towe, former Canadian ambassador to the United States, "Canada's National Energy Program," Address given at the American Gas Association, Washington, D.C., July 7, 1981; Mark MacGuigan, Minister of External Affairs, Address delivered at the Center for Inter-American Relations, New York City, October 1, 1981.

13. Canada, Petroleum Monitoring Agency, *Canadian Petroleum Monitoring Report* (Ottawa: Petroleum Monitoring Agency, 1981).

14. An announced "shelving" of the new FIRA proposals to further constrain foreign investment accompanied the 1982 budget projections. Inflationary pressures and high interest rates were at least as large an explanation for not accelerating Canadianization as was the "shelving" of the FIRA proposals. Allan J. MacEachen, Budget speech, November 2, 1981, Ottawa.

15. Edith Penrose, *The Large International Firm and Developing Countries: The Case of the International Petroleum Industry* (London: G. Allen and Unwin, 1968); Cedric Grant, "Political Sequence to Alcan Nationalization in Guyana—The International Aspects," *Social and Economic Studies* 22, No. 2 (June, 1973):301-22; Norman Girvan, *Corporate Imperialism: Conflict and Expropriation: Transnational Corporations and Economic Nationalism in the Third World* (New York: Sharpe, 1976).

16. What is often not understood in Canada is that if the U.S. government succumbs to pressures from certain areas of organized labor, the steel industry, and the auto industry to introduce nontariff barriers of the kind apparently broadly favored in Canada, Canada will be the first to feel the bite of this new protectionism, because Canada exports more than two-thirds of its goods to the United States. Such initiatives will end up hurting both countries. The only thing worse than trade dependence, perhaps, is a decisive decline in export markets, especially for a trade-dependent nation. Note the debate over neomercantilism and liberal trade ideas in Charles Kindleberger's review of Thibault de Saint Phalle, *The Import of Exports: Trade, Inflation, and the Dollar* in the book review section of *The Washington Post*, January 31, 1982; see also Robert J. Gordon and Jacques Pelkmans, *Challenges to Interdependent Economies; The Industrial West in the Coming Decade* (New York: McGraw-Hill, 1979).

17. Perhaps the greatest irony would stem from the following transaction. Firm X, wholly owned by a U.S. parent firm, sells its assets in the Canadian oil and gas industry to Petro-Canada at above-market prices after lamenting tax discrimination. In order to enjoy preferential tax treatment once again, firm X then invests the proceeds in a joint venture arrangement that is 75 percent owned by a prominent Canadian-American family.

CHAPTER 5

1. A good brief statement of the present alliance situation is found in Karl Kaiser, Winston Lord, Thierry de Montbrial, and David Watt, *Western Security: What has Changed? What Should be Done?* (New York: Council of Foreign Relations and Royal Institute of International Affairs, 1981), pp. 3-11. The classic statement on the Canadian defense outlook is still Robert J. Sutherland, "Canada's Long-Term Strategic Situation," *International Journal* 7, No. 3 (Summer 1962):75-86. For a good historical account, see Jon P. McLin, *Canada's Changing Defense Policy, 1957-1963* (Baltimore: Johns Hopkins Press, 1967) pp. 5-50. On more specialized aspects of Canadian defense policy and alliance participation consider Colin Gray, "Canada and NORAD: A Study in Strategy," *Behind the Headlines* 31, No. 3-4 (June 1972):3-13. Joel J. Sokolsky, "Canada in NATO: The Perceptions of a Middle Power in Alliance," *Fletcher Forum* 4, No. 2 (Summer 1980):203-26; and Nils Orvik, "The Basic Issue in Canadian National Security," *Canadian Defense Quarterly* 11, No. 1 (Summer 1981):8-15.

2. W A. Matheson, *The Prime Minister and the Cabinet* (Toronto: Methuen, 1976); Richard Simeon, *Federal-Provincial Diplomacy: The Making of Recent Policy in Canada* (Toronto: University of Toronto Press, 1972); Robert Presthus, *Elite Acommodation in Canadian Politics* (Toronto: Macmillan, 1973).

3. John Meisel, *Working Papers on Canadian Politics*, enlarged edition (Montreal: McGill-Queen's University Press, 1973).

4. David Mitrany, "The Prospect of Integration: Federal or Functional?," re-

printed in *International Regionalism,* edited by Joseph S. Nye, Jr. (Boston: Little, Brown and Co., 1968), pp. 43-72.

5. Ernst B. Haas, *The Obsolescence of Regional Integration Theory,* Research Series, No. 25, Institute of International Studies (Berkeley: University of California, 1975); Stanley Hoffmann, "Obstinate or Obsolete? The Fate of the Nation-State and the Case of Western Europe," *Daedalus* 95 (Summer, 1966):882-916; for a "non-zero-sum conclusion," see John G. Ruggie, "International Responses to Technology: Concepts and Trends," *International Organization* 29, No. 3 (Summer 1975):569.

6. Charles F. Doran, *Commercial Interdependence, Autonomy and Canadian-American Relations* (Ottawa: Institute for Research and Public Policy, in press), Ch. 5.

7. Peyton Lyon, *Canada-United States Free Trade and Canadian Independence* (Ottawa: Information Canada, for the Economic Council of Canada, 1975); Ramsey Cook, "Cultural Nationalism in Canada: An Historical Perspective," in *Canadian Cultural Nationalism,* edited by Janice L. Murray (New York: New York University Press, 1977), pp. 15-44; see also the sensitive study by Dickey, *Canada and the American Presence,* pp. 180-96.

8. The importance of the terms *independence* and *separation* is expressed in Maurice Pinard, "La dualité des loyautés et les options constitutionelles des Québécois francophones," in Université Laval, *Le Nationalisme québécois à la croisée des chemins* (Quebec: Centre québécois des relations internationales, La Collection Choix, 1975), pp. 81-87; see also Vincent Lemieux, "Quebec: Heaven is Blue and Hell is Red," in *Canadian Provincial Politics: The Party Systems of the Ten Provinces,* edited by Martin Robin, 2nd ed. (Scarborough, Ont.: Prentice-Hall, 1978), pp. 248-82. An interesting explanation for the violence of the early 1970s is found in Daniel Latouche, "Violence, politique, et crise dans la société québécoise," in *Essays on the Left,* edited by Laurier Lapierre et al. (Toronto: McClelland and Stewart, 1971), pp. 177-99; see also Carl J. Cuneo and James E. Curtis, "Quebec Separatism: An Analysis of Determinants within Social-Class Levels," *Canadian Review of Sociology and Anthropology* 2, No. 1 (1974):1-29; Dale Posgate and Kenneth McRoberts, *Quebec: Social Change and Political Crisis* (Toronto: McClelland and Stewart, 1976); and the path-breaking set of early essays first available to the American, predominantly English-speaking, audience, Dale C. Thomson, ed., *Quebec Society and Politics: Views from the Inside* (Toronto: McClelland and Stewart, 1973).

9. André Bernard, *What Does Quebec Want?* (Toronto: James Lorimer, 1978; Léon Dion, *Nationalismes et politique au Québec* (Montreal: Hurtubise HMH, 1975); John Saywell, *The Rise of the Parti Québécois: 1967-1976* (Toronto: University of Toronto Press, 1977).

10. Gabriel G. Almond and G. Bingham Powell, Jr., *Comparative Politics: System, Process and Policy,* 2nd ed. (Boston: Little, Brown and Co., 1978), pp. 348-51; for an alternate operationalization of dependence, see Raymond Duval et al., "A Formal Model of 'Dependencia' Theory: Structure and Measurement," revised paper presented at the World Congress of the International Political Science Association, Edinburgh, Scotland, August, 1976; Bernard Landry, Minister of State for Economic Development (Quebec), "Quebec's Economic Prospects within a North American Context," address given in Boston, November 17, 1979.

In order to further elucidate the significance of these indexes of dependence for the question of trade-offs between political-cultural autonomy and economic commercial costs, one operationalizes these indexes in the following fashion. For purposes of the present analysis, we define the relationships among the three components of external dependence specifically:

$$\text{External Dependence} = \left(\frac{\text{Foreign Trade}}{\text{GNP}} \diagup 100 \right) \left(\begin{array}{cc} \text{Concentration} & \text{Concentration} \\ \text{of Export} & + \text{ among Trading} \\ \text{Commodities} & \text{Partners} \end{array} \right)$$

The two concentration indexes are additively related. A very low concentration on either index would *not* negate the impact of the other index. Canada, for example, experiences a high concentration among trading partners but low concentration of export commodities. Neither effect excludes the other, and together the two effects create an indicator of how the breadth of exports and the diversity of export partners combine to shape trading flexibility.

In contrast, the relationship between the concentration indexes and relative trade importance is multiplicative, not additive. This means that if trade as a percent of GNP were zero or if the sum of the concentration indexes were zero, the entire impact of external trade dependence would disappear. In other words, some degree of partner or export concentration and some amount of foreign trade is necessary for the concept of external economic and commercial dependence to make sense. But because of the multiplicative relationship, as the level of concentration increases, the impact on relative trade importance and, hence, on overall external dependence increases very rapidly. The total effect of trade dependence on a country's foreign policy is thus more than the sum of the parts.

Based on a sample of 27 randomly selected nations in 1965, an inverse correlation of .67 resulted between the above index of external dependence and population size. Population size was transformed logarithmically to eliminate outliers. Countries included in the sample were Kuwait, Cuba, Bulgaria, Dominican Republic, Canada, Egypt, Kenya, Tanzania, Czechoslovakia, Peru, Israel, Sweden, Yugoslavia, Spain, Mexico, Britain, Italy, France, Nigeria, Austria, West Germany, Brazil, Japan, the United States, the USSR, India, and China.

11.   Allan J. MacEachen, Notes for an address to the *Financial Post* Offshore Canada Conference, held in Halifax on June 23, 1981.

12.   A pattern of preferential procurement policy seems to be emerging, but although Hydro Quebec, Ontario Hydro, and B.C. Hydro all allow a 10 percent premium over costs for purchases within the provinces, the utilities in the poorest provinces, ironically, allow none. This raises questions as to whether the purpose of the premium is merely to subsidize local producers, not to stimulate industrial growth in the less industrialized areas, as is imagined. In any case, the effect is to stimulate an unseemly competition within Canada, competition that feeds inefficiency and economic balkanization. (Beale, *Energy and Industry*, p. 91.) The effect of preferential procurement is rebounding in the United States, where, although preferential legislation is less universally applied across other industrial areas, some forty-three states, for example, now have such legislation on the books regarding steel imports.

13.   Pierre Elliott Trudeau, Prime Minister's address to the House of Commons on Canadian Foreign Policy, given in Ottawa on June 15, 1981.

14.   Escott Reid, "The Birth of the North Atlantic Alliance," *International Journal* 22, No. 3 (Summer 1967), pp. 426-40.

15.   Robert Bothwell, Ian Drummond, and John English, *Canada Since 1945: Power Politics, and Provincialism* (Toronto: University of Toronto Press, 1981), pp. 437-54.

16.   Some distance has been traveled from the days of Wrong and Pearson. See "The Possibility of War with the Soviet Union," Vol. 4, File 20, Hume Wrong Papers, statement written June 28, 1946; *Mike; The Memoirs of the Rt. Hon. Lester B. Pearson*, Vol. 1 (New York: Quadrangle Books, 1972), pp. 295-302.

17.   See David Cox, "Canadian Defense Policy? The Dilemmas of a Middle Power," *Behind the Headlines* 27, No. 5 (November 1968); James Earys, *In Defence of Canada: Growing Up Allied* (Toronto: University of Toronto Press, 1980); C.S. Gray, *Canadian Defense Priorities: A Question of Relevance* (Toronto: Clarke-Irwin, 1972). For the classic theoretical discussion of the "free-rider" situation, consider Olson and Zeckhouser, "A Theory of Alliances," *Review of Economics and Statistics* 48, No. 3 (August 1966):266-79.

18.   See John Holmes, *The Shaping of Peace* Vol. 1, pp. 235-38 for a discussion of the impact of the functional ideal.

19.   The deep insight found in Denis Stairs' *The Diplomacy of Constraint: Canada, The Korean War, and the United States* (Toronto: University of Toronto Press, 1974) involves essentially this quest for a proper Canadian defense role; for related aspects of this problem see Stephen Clarkson, ed., *An Independent Foreign Policy for Canada?* (Toronto: McClelland and Stewart, 1968); John Gellner, "A Defense Policy at Last—But Where's the Money?" *Commentator* 15, No. 9 (September 1971):16-17.

20. Proposals for certain types of specialization include Joseph T. Jockel and Joel J. Sokolsky, "Emphasizing the Assets: A Proposal for the Restructuring of Canada's Military Contribution to NATO," *Canadian Defence Quarterly* 9, No. 2 (Autumn 1979):17-20. Nils Orvik, "Canada and the North Atlantic Security," in Christoph Bertram and Johan J. Holst, *New Strategic Factors in the North Atlantic* (Oslo: Universitetsforlaget, 1977): pp. 82-85; John J. Kirton, "The Consequences of Integration? The Case of the Defense Production Sharing Agreements," paper prepared for the Inter-University Seminar in International Relations, Ottawa, April 8, 1972.

21. J. L. Granatstein, *A Man of Influence: Norman A. Robertson and Canadian Statecraft, 1929-68* (Toronto: Deneau, 1981), pp. 38-40.

22. Jeremy Kinsman and Allan Gotlieb, "Reviving the Third Option," *International Perspectives* (January-February 1981):2-18.

23. Quoted in Barbara Johnson and Mark Zacher, eds., *Canadian Foreign Policy and the Law of the Sea* (Vancouver: University of British Columbia, 1977), p. 362.

CHAPTER 6

1. At issue for the global system, not just for the U.S.-Canada dyad, is the degree to which—more than a third of a century after the founding of many international institutions and following the postwar upsurgence of transnational relations—the balance will shift back toward the nation-state, as occurred in earlier periods of European history, instead of toward further international solutions and initiatives. Two thought provoking but pessimistic accounts are Robert L. Heilbroner, *An Inquiry into the Human Prospect* (New York: W. W. Norton, 1974) and Garrett Hardin, "The Tragedy of the Commons," reprinted in *Pollution, Resources, and the Environment*, edited by Alain C. Enthoven and A. Myrick Freeman III (New York: W. W. Norton, 1973), pp. 1-13.

2. William W. Bishop, Jr., *International Law: Cases and Materials* (Boston: Little, Brown and Co., 1962), pp. 443-76; Lassa F. Lawrence Oppenheim, *International Law*, edited by Sir Hersh Lauterpacht, 8th ed., Vol. 1, 1955.

3. The equality of all states before international law—and hence the exclusivity of jurisdiction of each—is broadly accepted, despite certain applications of extraterritoriality. Hans Kelson, *Principles of International Law*, 2nd ed., revised and edited by Robert W. Tucker (New York: Holt Rinehart, and Winston, 1966), pp. 357-61; *A. M. Luther Company v. Sagor and Company*, (1921) 3 K.B., pp. 532-59; *Bernstein v. Van Heyghen Frères S.A.*, 163 Federal Reports 2nd, p. 249.

4. One of the best succinct expressions of the maritime outlook is Wolfgang Friedman's *The Future of the Oceans* (New York: Braziller, 1971); see also J. Andrassy, *International Law and the Resources of the Sea* (New York: Columbia University Press), 1970.

5. J. A. Beesley, "Rights and Responsibilities of Arctic Coastal States: The Canadian View," *Journal of Maritime Law and Commerce* 3 (October 1971); Mitchell Sharp, Secretary of State for External Affairs, "Canada Extends Its Territorial Sea," Statement to the House of Commons, April 17, 1970; U.N. General Assembly, *Draft Articles on Fisheries by Canada, India, Kenya and Sri Lanka*, A/AC 138/SC II L. 38, July 16, 1973.

6. Ann L. Hollick, "Canadian-American Relations: Law of the Sea," in *Canada and the United States*, edited by Fox, Hero, and Nye, p. 187.

7. Ronald Coase, "The Problem of Social Cost," and Ralph Turvey, "On Divergencies Between Social Cost and Private Cost," reprinted in Robert Dorfman and Nancy S. Dorfman, *Economics of the Environment* (New York: W. W. Norton, 1972), pp. 100-134.

8. Alistair Buchan, "Concepts of Peacekeeping," in Michael G. Fry, "Freedom and Change," *Essays in Honour of Lester B. Pearson*, edited by Michael G. Fry (Toronto: McClelland and Stewart, 1975), pp. 16-25.

9. Charles F. Doran, "Left Hand Right Hand," *International Journal* 36, No. 1 (Winter 1980-81):236-41.

10. Holmes, *The Shaping of Peace*, vol. 1, p. 72; Bothwell et al., *Canada Since 1945*, p. 104.

11. Canada, 28th Parliament, 2nd session, Ottawa, Bill C-202, reprinted in *9 International Legal Materials 543* (Ottawa, Government of Canada, 1970); Richard B. Bilder, "The Canadian Arctic Waters Pollution Prevention Act: New Stresses on the Law of the Sea," *Michigan Law Review* 69, No. 1 (November 1970):1-54; Ivan Head, "Canadian Claims to Territorial Sovereignty in the Arctic Regions," *McGill Law Journal* 9, No. 3 (1963), pp. 200-226.

12. Charles F. Doran, "Multiple Jurisdiction—Will it Save or Destroy the Oceans?" *Vanderbilt Journal of International Law* 7, No. 3 (Summer 1974):631-85.

13. Donat Pharand, "The Northwest Passage in International Law," *The Canadian Yearbook of International Law* 17 (1979):99-133; Richard R. Baxter, *The Law of International Waterways*, vol. 3 (Cambridge: Harvard University Press, 1964).

14. "It is . . . generally recognized and in accordance with international custom that states in time of peace have a right to send their warships through straits used for international navigation between two parts of the high seas without the previous authorization of a coastal state, provided that the passage is *innocent*. Unless otherwise prescribed in an international convention, there is no right for a coastal state to prohibit such passage through straits in time of peace." International Court of Justice, *Corfu Channel* case, Report 4 of the International Court of Justice, 1949, p. 85.

15. Prime Minister Trudeau, *Statements and Speeches*, No. 70/3 at 4, 1970. See also Louis Henkin, "Arctic Anti-pollution: Does Canada Make or Break International Law?" *American Journal of International Law* 65 (January 1971):131-36.

16. Canada, Department of External Affairs, "Reciprocal Fisheries Agreement between the Government of Canada and the Government of the United States of America," *Treaty Series*, No. 23 Article II, February 24, 1977; United States, Department of State, "Maritime Boundaries Between the United States and Canada," Public Notice 506, November 1, 1976, reproduced in *International Legal Materials* 15 (November 1976):1435-36.

17. See Erik B. Wong, "Canada-United States Fisheries and Maritime Boundary Negotiations: Diplomacy in Deep Water," *Behind the Headlines* 38, No. 6, Canadian Institute of International Affairs, 1981.

18. The source for the original 1937 West Coast fisheries convention is: United States, Senate, Committee on Commerce, Treaties and Other International Agreements on Fisheries, Oceanographic Resources, and Wildlife to Which the United States is Party, *West Coast Fisheries Treaty* (Washington, D.C.: Legislative Reference Service, Library of Congress, 1974), pp. 654-75; James A. Crutchfield and Guilio Pontecarvo, *The Pacific Salmon Fishery: A Study in Jurisdictional Conservation* (Washington, D.C.: Resources for the Future, 1969); Parzwal Copes, "Fisheries on Canada's Pacific Coast: The Impact of Extended Jurisdiction on Exploitation Patterns," *Ocean Management* 6, No. 4 (May 1981):279-97.

19. B. Hileman, "Acid Precipitation," *Environmental Science and Technology* 15 (October 1981):1119-24; L. R. Ember, "Acid Pollutants: Hitchhikers Ride the Wind," *Chemical and Engineering News* 59, No. 37 (September 14, 1981):20-31; A. Babich, D. L. Davis and G. Stotzky, "Acid Precipitation: Causes and Consequences," *Environment* 22, No. 4 (May 1980): 613.

20. Don L. Gibbons, "Acidic Confusion Reigns," *Sciquest* 10 (January 1982):10-15.

21. Don Munton, "Dependence and Interdependence in Transboundary Environmental Relations," *International Journal* 36, No. 1, Special issue on the Canada-United States relationship (Winter 1980-81):139-84; Kim Nossal, "The Unmaking of Garrison: United States Politics and the Management of Canadian-American Boundary Waters," *Behind the Headlines* 37 (December 1978):1-30; O. P. Dividedi and John E. Carroll, "Issues in Canadian-American Environmental Relations," in *Resources and the Environment*, edited by Dividedi (Toronto: McClelland & Stewart, 1980), pp. 306-34.

22. Michael D. Blecher, "Equitable Delimitation of Continental Shelf," *American Journal of International Law* 73 (January 1979):60-88; Richard Padua, "Submarine Boundaries," *International and Comparative Law Quarterly* 9 (1960):625-38.

CHAPTER 7

1. John F. Helliwell, "Canadian Energy Policy," *Annual Review of Energy* 4 (1979): 175-229; older official views of Canada's energy situation are found in: Canada, National Energy Board, *Canada, Energy, Mines and Resources, An Energy Strategy for Canada: Policies for Self-Reliance* (Ottawa: National Energy Board, Canada, National Energy Board, *Canada Oil Supply and Requirements* (Ottawa: National Energy Board, 1977); Science Council of Canada, *Roads to Energy Self-Reliance: The Necessary National Demonstrations,* Report 30 (Ottawa: Science Council of Canada, 1979).

2. Larry R. Kohler, "Canadian/American Oil Diplomacy: 1955-1973," Ph.D. Diss., Johns Hopkins School of Advanced International Studies, 1982.

3. Canada, Ministry of Energy, Mines, and Resources, *National Energy Program* (Ottawa: Ministry of Energy, Mines, and Resources, 1981); For quite different interpretations see Watkins and Walker, *Reaction: The National Energy Program;* Bruce F. Wilson, *The Energy Squeeze: Canadian Policies for Survival* (Toronto: Canadian Institute for Economic Policy, 1980).

4. Charles F. Doran, *Myth, Oil, and Politics* (New York: The Free Press, 1977); Kenneth W. Dam, *Oil Resources: Who Gets What How?* Chicago: University of Chicago Press, 1976), pp. 12-20.

5. Kenneth North, "Canadian Oil and Gas—Surplus or Shortage?" in *Energy Policy: The Global Challenge,* edited by Peter Nemetz (Ottawa: Institute for Research on Public Policy, 1980), pp. 49-68.

6. Canada, Petroleum Monitoring Agency, *Canadian Petroleum Monitoring Report* (Ottawa: Petroleum Monitoring Agency, August 31, 1981), p. 2.

7. John Stein, "The Implementation of the National Energy Policy: An Explanation of Existing Legislation, The Canadian Ownership Rate (COR), and Bill C-57," and Jerald D. Palmer, "The Canada Oil and Gas Act—Bill C-48," both in *Energy Development in Canada,* edited by Earl H. Fry (Provo, Utah: Brigham Young University, 1981), pp. 97-108, 109-18.

8. Sam H. Schur et al., *Energy in America's Future: The Choices Before Us* (Baltimore: The Johns Hopkins University Press, 1979), pp. 69-117.

9. Richard D. French, *How Ottawa Decides,* pp. 31-93. Mildred A. Schwartz, *The Environment for Policy-making in Canada and the United States* (Canada: C. D. Howe Institute, 1981).

10. Minister of External Affairs Mark MacGuigan reiterated this firm message in a speech at the Center for Inter-American Relations, New York City, October 1, 1981.

11. Deputy Prime Minister and Minister of Finance Allan J. MacEachen, Budget speech, November 2, 1981, Ottawa; Canada, Office of Minister of Finance, *Myths and Realities: The 1981 Budget* (Ottawa: Office of Minister of Finance, 1981).

12. Thomas A. Hockin, "Canada's 'Mass Legitimate' Parties and Their Implications for Party Leaders," 2nd ed., in Thomas A. Hockin, *Apex of Power* (Scarborough, Ont.: Prentice-Hall, 1977), pp. 70-85; Norman Penner, "Ontario: The Dominant Province," in *Canadian Provincial Politics,* edited by Martin Robin, pp. 205-21.

13. Canada, Ministry of Energy, Mines, and Resources, *Energy Futures for Canadians* (Ottawa: Ministry of Energy, Mines, and Resources, 1978), pp. 91-95; Douglas Evans, *Western Energy Policy* (New York: St. Martin's Press, 1979), pp. 29-46.

14. For a discussion of the problem of local monopoly, see L. A. Skeoch, ed., *Restrictive Trade Practices in Canada* (Toronto: McClelland and Stewart, 1966).

15. Desmond Morton, *NDP: The Dream of Power* (Toronto: A. M. Hakkert, 1974); John Wilson and David Hoffman, "Ontario—A Three Party System in Transition," in *Canadian Provincial Politics*, edited by Martin Robin (Toronto: Prentice-Hall, 1972).

16. Canada, Petroleum Monitoring Agency, *Canadian Petroleum Industry: Monitoring Survey, 1981, First Six Months* (Ottawa: Petroleum Monitoring Agency, 1981), pp. 30-31.

17. Peter M. Towe, former Canadian ambassador to Washington, "Canada's National Energy Program," notes for a speech to the American Gas Association, New York City, October 1, 1981.

18. Petroleum Monitoring Agency, *Canadian Petroleum Industry*.

19. Towe, Speech to the American Gas Association.

20. Beale, *Energy and Industry*, p. 60.

21. Canada, Department of Finance, *The Current Economic Situation and Prospects for the Canadian Economy in the Short and Medium Term* (Ottawa: Department of Finance, 1981), pp. 12-13; Jane Seaberry, "Administration Eyes Sanctions Against Canada," (Washington D.C.: *The Washington Post*, September 10, 1981); Jack A. Finlayson and David G. Haglund, "Oil and 'Canadianization': The Gathering Storm," unpublished paper, University of British Columbia, October, 1981.

22. John Carson-Parker, "Stop Worrying About the Canadian Invasion," *Fortune* (October 19, 1981):192-200.

23. Rowland Frazee, "Foreign Ownership in Canada: The Need for a Balanced View," remarks prepared for delivery to the Canadian Club of Winnipeg, October 19, 1981, as cited in Malmgren and Drouin, "Canada, the United States, and the World Economy," p. 398.

24. Canada, Ministry of Energy, Mines, and Resources, "Memorandum of Agreement between the Government of Canada and the Government of Alberta relating to Energy Pricing and Taxation," (Ottawa: Ministry of Energy, Mines, and Resources, September 1, 1981).

25. Peter Lougheed, Premier of Alberta, Press Conference, given at the Canadian embassy, Washington, D.C., October 29, 1981; Peter Lougheed, "Review of the Economy," Final Communiqué, given at the Twenty-second Annual Premiers' Conference, Victoria, British Columbia, August 11-15, 1981.

26. François Bregha, *Bob Blair's Pipeline: The Business and Politics of Northern Energy Development Projects* (Toronto: James Lorimer, 1979), pp. 50-52.

27. George W. Lawrence, President, American Gas Association, Letter to the Editor, *The Washington Post*, January 2, 1982.

28. John Helliwell, "The National Energy Board's 1974-75 Natural Gas Supply Hearings," *Canadian Public Policy* 1, No. 3 (Summer 1975):415-25.

29. Alexander Stuart, "The Blazing Battle to Free Natural Gas," *Fortune* (October 19, 1981):152-180.

30. Thomas L. Burton, *Natural Resource Policy in Canada* (Toronto: McClelland and Stewart, 1972), pp. 75-76; John N. McDougall, "Prebuild Phase or Latest Phase? The United States Fuel Market and Canadian Energy Policy," *International Journal* 36, No. 1 (Winter 1980-81):117-38.

31. Bothwell and Kilbourn, *C. D. Howe: A Biography*, pp. 283-98.

32. Much of the faith in continuing energy scarcity was supported conceptually by the innovative early work of Jay Forrester, later popularized by the Meadows, set forth especially in the fortuitously timed publication of Forrester, *World Dynamics* (New York: John Wiley and Sons, 1973).

33. Bregha, *Bob Blair's Pipeline*, pp. 70-89.

34. Jane S. Hughes, "Good Fences Make Good Neighbors," *Euromoney Magazine* (November 1981):127-32; see also Raymond F. Mikesell et al., eds., *Foreign Investment in the Petroleum and Mineral Industries* (Baltimore: Johns Hopkins University Press, 1971); Louis T. Wells, Jr., *The Evolution of Concession Agreements*, Economic Development Report No. 117 (Cambridge: Development Advisory Service, Harvard University, 1968).

35. A. E. Safarian, *Foreign Ownership of Canadian Industry* (Toronto: University of Toronto Press, 1973), pp. 299-312.

CHAPTER 8

1. See, for example, the report of the Atlantic Council's Working Group on the United States and Canada, *US Policy Towards Canada: The Neighbor We Cannot Take for Granted* (Washington, D.C.: Atlantic Council's Working Group on the United States and Canada, 1981).

2. Annette B. Fox, "On Living Together in North America," *International Journal* 36, No. 1 (Winter 1980-81):1-16. Note in particular the insightful suggestions contained in this article for ameliorating some of the tension between Congress and the federal government in Ottawa.

3. J. M. S. Careless, *The Union of the Canadas: 1841-1857* (Toronto: McClelland and Stewart, 1967), pp. 96-112; Donald G. Creighton, *The Commercial Empire of the St. Lawrence* (Toronto: University of Toronto Press, 1937).

4. Lawrence S. Eagleburger, U.S. Assistant Secretary for European Affairs, "U.S. Policy Toward West Europe and Canada," Statement before the Subcommittee on Europe and the Middle East of the House Foreign Affairs Committee, June 2, 1981; Lawrence S. Eagleburger, "US-Canada Relations," Address before the Center for Inter-American Relations in New York, October 1, 1981; a durable expression of the regional view is found in Nye, *International Regionalism*, pp. v-xvi.

5. Harold D. Foster and W. R. Derrick Sewell, *Water: The Emerging Crisis in Canada*, The Canadian Institute for Economic Policy Series (Toronto: James Lorimer, 1981); Burton, *Natural Resource Policy in Canada*, pp. 126-27.

6. Trudeau, Prime Minister's address to the House of Commons on Canadian Foreign Policy, given in Ottawa on June 15, 1981; consider also, however, the statement made by Pierre Lamontagne, Canadian Minister of National Defence, before the U.S. Senate Committee on Foreign Affairs. See Canada, Department of External Affairs, *Proceedings of the Subcommittee on National Defence*, 32nd Parliament, 1st session, Nos. 4-6, 2, 9, and 16 December, 1980.

7. On the need for new consultative approaches, see Karl Kaiser et al., *Western Security*, pp. 42-48.

8. International Institute of Strategic Studies, *Military Balance* (London: International Institute of Strategic Studies, 1980), pp. 2-20.

9. See Hedrick Smith, "White House Hit a Last-Minute Snag on Canada Trip," *The New York Times*, March 11, 1981.

10. Misunderstandings about integration have occurred in spite of informed analysis that has long been publicly available. Dale C. Thomson, "Option Three: What Price Tag?" *International Perspectives* (January-February 1973):4-5.

11. Heeney and Merchant, *Canada and the United States: Principles for Partnership* (Ottawa: Queen's Printer, 1965).

12. Written with grace, humor and a sensitivity to nuance, John Holmes's *Life With Uncle* (Toronto: University of Toronto Press, 1981) is indispensible reading.

INDEX

45,109

E
183.8
.C2
D67
1984

Doran, Charles F.

Forgotten
   partnership